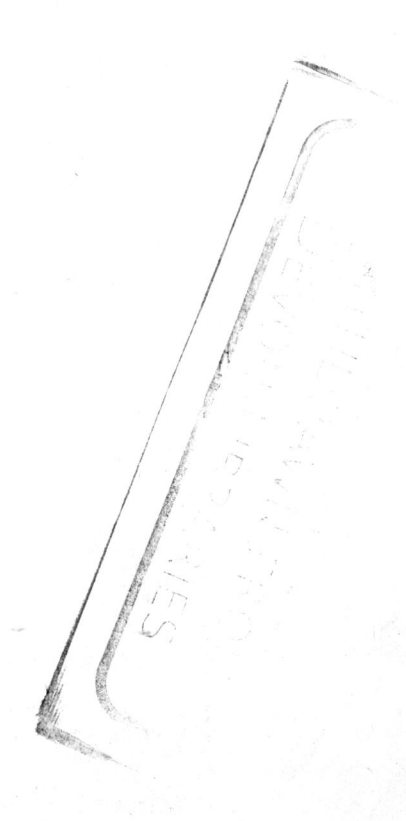

TORRE ABBEY
TORQUAY, DEVON

ISBN 0 9505949 0 3

TORRE ABBEY

by

DERYCK SEYMOUR

An Account of its History, Buildings, Cartularies and Lands

The Common Seal of Torre Abbey

Printed in England by James Townsend & Sons Ltd., Exeter, Devon
1977

For Ida Larmor

Acknowledgements

During my researches in connection with this book I have come into contact with a great number of people in all walks of life. I think I would first like to acknowledge my great debt to the farming community, for without their friendly co-operation and understanding I could not have undertaken such detailed work on the subject of the former lands of Torre Abbey. In particular I must mention Mr. R. E. Andrews at Oldstone, Mrs. Bamsey and her mother, the late Mrs. J. Rendell, at Court Barton, Mr. F. J. Carter of Stowford House, Mr. Jayne at Monksmoor, Mr. A. J. Michael at Skidbrook, Miss E. M. Parsons at Winkleigh, Mr. & Mrs. Paul at Shillingford Barton, Mr. & Mrs. Pearce at Underhaye, Mr. Soper at Ashclyst, Mr. E. J. Taverner of Woodbury Salterton and Mr. Tope of Stone. I am afraid there must be some whose names I have forgotten; nevertheless, I thank them all for their help.

I would like to record my appreciation to the Abbot of Buckfast for allowing me access to the Abbey Library, and to the late Dom John Stephan who helped and encouraged me in a number of ways at the outset of my task.

I am grateful to many others for help and advice, including the Rev. D. Lambert, Dr. C. A. Ralegh Radford, Mr. C. T. Collacott, Mr. A. M. Dowdell, Mrs. U. Brighouse, the late Miss Hilda Walker, B.A., Mr. & Mrs. H. G. White, Mr. H. Goodson of Waddeton Court, the late Commander W. R. Gilbert of Compton Castle, Mr. Mantle, and Mrs. Grant of Nutcombe Manor who assisted me in establishing the whereabouts of the lost village of Dunnyngestone.

The Rev. J. G. M. Scott, vicar of Newton St. Cyres, deserves special thanks for placing at my disposal his great knowledge of mediaeval church bells. Through him I was able to locate many in the towers of churches formerly belonging to Torre Abbey. Mr. A. P. Lee, the Custodian of the Abbey, has also been most helpful in assisting me in my researches there.

The Devon Record Office must be thanked for their co-operation in many ways; at Lincoln I was equally well supplied with the information I sought.

On the photographic side I had the help of Mr. G. Court Jones and Mr. M. Leach who seemed always ready to travel far and wide with me to take pictures for the excellent photographic section of this book. Brigadier W. Hine-Haycock, Mr. and Mrs. H. G. White and others also contributed old photos. Exeter Cathedral Library, the Air Ministry and the Public Record Office have given permission for the reproduction of photos.

Beryl Newman, the well known Devon artist, has taken great trouble over the excellent drawing for the dust-cover, and the lively result is a delight.

I must not forget to thank John Daniels for his welcome advice on many matters connected with the production of the book, and also Elizabeth Beveridge and John Parry who so kindly read the proofs.

Finally I must thank my wife for the sustained help and constant encouragement which she has given me in the long task of preparation.

Arlesey Dene, Torquay.   June, 1977.

Contents

		Page
	Acknowledgements	v
	Index of Plates	ix
	Index of Drawings, Plans, etc.	xii
	List of Abbreviations	xvi
1	An Introduction	1
2	The Foundation of Torre Abbey	7
3	The Abbey Buildings	13
4	The Succession of Abbots	25
5	A Consideration of the Abbots	29
6	Lord William Brewer, Founder of Torre Abbey	47
7	William the Younger	51
8	The Strange Story of Prior Richard de Cotelforde	53
9	The Torre Abbey Chantries	57
10	The Cartularies	59
11	The Acquisition of the Manor of Tormohun	63
12	Collected Records of the Premonstratensians in England	65
13	A Document of A.D. 1300	73
14	The Suppression	75
15	The East Ogwell Grave Coverstones	77
16	The Foundation Charter and King John's Charters	81
17	Torre	85
18	Torre Sanctuary Lands	93
19	Ilsham and Shiphay Collaton	95
20	Wolborough	101
21	Hennock	115
22	Buckland-in-the-Moor	127

CONTENTS

23	Greendale	133
24	Dunningstone	147
25	Haggelegh	151
26	Ashclyst	153
27	Bampton	161
28	Skidbrook	163
29	Bradworthy and Pancrasweek	171
30	Shebbear and Sheepwash	187
31	Buckland Brewer	193
32	Townstall, Dartmouth	201
33	Kingswear	213
34	Waddeton	217
35	Blackawton	219
36	Monksmoor, Ugborough	231
37	Glascombe	235
38	North Shillingford	239
39	Cockington	247
40	Daccombe and Coffinswell	257
41	Holrigge	269
	Addenda	279
	Bibliography	281
	Index I, Places and People	283
	Index II, Subjects	299

Index of Plates

Plates appear after the page numbers shown

AIR PHOTOS
    Stowford   168
    Waddeton   216

ALFARESWORTHY
    The Chapel   184
    ,,   ,,   mediaeval door   184
    ,,   ,,   outline of east window   184
    ,,   ,,   roof   184

BRADWORTHY
    Boundary banks of Hidesburga   184
    Parish Church   184

BUCKLAND BREWER
    Parish Church   200
    ,,   ,,   mediaeval Guild Chapel adjoining   200
    ,,   ,,   Romanesque doorway   200

COCKINGTON
    Parish Church   264

COFFIN OF WILLIAM BREWER THE YOUNGER
    See Torre Abbey

COFFINSWELL
    Court Barton c. 1950   264
    ,,   ,,   Courthouse wing   264

DARTMOUTH
    St. Saviour's Church   216
    ,,   ,,   ,,   screen and pulpit   216
    ,,   ,,   ,,   south door   216
    Townstall, St. Clement's Church   200

DUNNINGSTONE (CLAYHANGER)
    Denscombe Mill   168

GLASCOMBE
    Remains of farmhouse   264
    View of Abbey land   264

INDEX OF PLATES

GREENDALE (WOODBURY SALTERTON)
    Greendale Barton, ancient foundations of Courthouse   168
    Huntisbere (Aylesbeare)   168
    Stowford House (Colaton Raleigh)   168

HENNOCK
    Charter of gift of Church to Torre Abbey   120
    Monastic boundary between Fluda and Huxbear   120
    Parish Church   120
        „   „   ceilure   120
        „   „   mediaeval font   120
        „   „   panel of rood screen   120
    Tithe Barn and remains of Rectory gatehouse   120

HIDESBURGA
    See Bradworthy

HUNTISBERE
    See Greendale

IDEFORD
    Charter from William de Holrigge   264

KEYBERRY MILL
    See Wolborough

KINGSWEAR
    Kittery Court, old houses   216
        „   „   the old approach   216

MONKSMOOR
    Ruins of ancient enclosures   216
    Torr's Barn   216

NEWTON ABBOT
    See Wolborough

PUTFORD, EAST
    Font in Chapel   200

SHEBBEAR
    St. Michael's Church, south doorway   184

SHEEPWASH
    Upcott Barton, mediaeval building   200

SHIPHAY COLLATON
    Monastic Barn at Shiphay Manor   88

INDEX OF PLATES

SKIDBROOK (LINCS.)
    Approach to Church 168
    Details of tower 168
    St. Botolph's Church interior 168

TORR'S BARN
    See Monksmoor

TORRE
    Parish Church of St. Saviour 88
    ,, ,, ,, ,, ,, north Chancel window 88
    Upton village, Penney's Cottage 88

TORRE ABBEY
    Abbot's Tower 16
    Beneath the Crossing 16
    Chapterhouse doorway 16
    Cloisters, east wall 16
    Coffin of William Brewer the Younger 16
    Engraving of 1662 16
    Exchequer Charter 16
    Gatehouse 16
    South Transept 16
    South Transept Chapel, Miss H. H. Walker in 16
    Presbytery, south-east corner of 16
    Tithe Barn from south-west 16
    Undercroft, central passage of 16
    Undercroft, looking across passage 16
    Undercroft in Western Range (north) 16
    Undercroft in Western Range (south) 16
    Western Range from site of Cloisters 16
    Western Range of Monastic Buildings 16
    Window 16

TOWNSTALL
    See Dartmouth

UPTON
    See Torre

WADDETON
    Air photo of "Torr's" 216
    Pier 216

WOLBOROUGH
    Keyberry Mill 88
    St. Mary's Church 88
    Tower of former St. Leonard's Chapel 88

Index of Drawings, Maps and Plans

ASHCLYST
    Farmhouse   155
        ,,   plan of   156

BLACKAWTON
    Bowe   228
    Cliston, Lower   229
    Oldstone   224
        ,,   plan of   225
    Wadstray, Middle, old kitchen fireplace   227
    Yanston, barn   222

BLACKBERRY
    Map of Abbey land in manor of   143

BOW
    See Blackawton

BOWHAY
    See Northshillingford

BRADWORTHY
    Map of Hidesburga   178
    Parish Church, piscina   177
        ,,   ,,   south-east corner   176

BREWER
    Coffin of Lord William   50

BUCKLAND BREWER
    Old Vicarage, plan of   197
    Parish Church, doorway in south aisle   195
    St. Michael's Chapel, Bulkworthy   196
    Sanctuary land, map of   198

BUCKLAND-IN-THE-MOOR
    Abbey holdings, map of   128
    Ruddycleave   129

INDEX OF DRAWINGS, MAPS AND PLANS

CLISTON, LOWER
    See Blackawton

CLAYPARKS
    See Hennock

COCKINGTON
    Church Tower   254
    Fulleford Mill   89
    Monastic water supply, map of   252

COFFINSWELL
    Court Barton, plan of   265

DARTMOUTH
    Higher Norton   202
    St. Clement's Church Tower   208

DUNKESWELL ABBEY
    Coffin of Lord William Brewer   50

EXETER CASTLE CHAPEL
    Norden's drawing of   158
    Swete's sketch of   158

GLASCOMBE
    Abbey land, map of   236

GREENDALE
    Greendale Barton   135
    Greendale Barton, map of   134
    Greendale, plan of   136
    Higher Greendale   137
        ,,   ,,   upstairs   138

HAGGELEGH
    Tithe Map, extract from   151

HENNOCK
    Abbey holdings, map of   115
    Clayparks, the shippen   124
    Rectory, plan of   117

HIDESBURGA
    See Bradworthy

HOLRIGGE (IDEFORD)
    Underhaye   270
        ,,   plan of   271

INDEX OF DRAWINGS, MAPS AND PLANS

ILSHAM
 Chapel from north   97
 „   from south   96

MAPS
 Blackberry (Abbey land) 143, Buckland Brewer (Sanctuary land) 198, Buckland-in-the-Moor (Abbey land) 128, Disposition of Abbey Properties 277, Glascombe (Abbey land) 236, Greendale Barton 134, Haggelegh (Extract from Tithe Map) 151, Hidesburga 178, Monksmoor 231, Waddeton (Abbey land) 218, Wolborough (Old Holdings) 103, Upton (Mediaeval village) 88, Monastic water supply 252.

NEWTON ABBOT
 See Wolborough

NORTON, HIGHER
 See Dartmouth

NORTHSHILLINGFORD
 Bowhay, old chimney   241
 Shillingford Barton   239
 „   „   plan of   244

OLDSTONE
 See Blackawton

PANCRASWEEK
 Glebe Cottage   184
 St. Pancras' Church   183

PLANS
 Ashclyst 156, Buckland Brewer (Old Vicarage) 197, Coffinswell (Court Barton) 265, Greendale Barton 136, Hennock Vicarage 117, Northshillingford (Barton) 244, Oldstone 225, Torre Abbey 8, Underhaye 271.

RUDDYCLEAVE
 See Buckland-in-the-Moor

SHEBBEAR
 St. Michael's Church   190

SHILLINGFORD BARTON
 See Northshillingford

SKIDBROOK
 St. Botolph's Church from north   167

INDEX OF DRAWINGS, MAPS AND PLANS

TORRE
    Map of Upton village   88

TORRE ABBEY
    Common Seal   Title page
    Disposition of Properties, map   276
    Plan of   8
    South Frontage   13
    Torre Abbey c. 1539   17

UNDERHAYE
    See Holrigge

UPTON
    See Torre

WADDETON
    Map of Abbey land   218

WADSTRAY, MIDDLE
    See Blackawton

WOLBOROUGH
    Elizabethan House   108
    Map of old holdings   103
    Wolborough Street at rear of Manor House   106
    Woodbine Cottage   107

YANSTON
    See Blackawton

Abbreviations

A.O., Augmentation Office.

C.P.R., Calendar of Patent Rolls.

Dartmouth, "Dartmouth Mediaeval Town" (Watkin).

D.C.N.Q., Devon and Cornwall Notes and Queries.

D.C., Dublin Cartulary.

F., Folio.

L.P., Letters and Papers of Henry VIII.

MS, Manuscript from Exchequer Cartulary.

T.D.A., Transactions of the Devonshire Association.

T.N.H.S., Torquay Natural History Society.

Tot., "Totnes Priory and Mediaeval Town" (Watkin).

All figures of one, two and three digits usually refer to charter numbers in the Exchequer Cartulary.

I

An Introduction

This book is written for young and old alike. It tells a tale of long-forgotten things, and is the story of what was once a splendid Abbey. Its monks were Canons of Prémontré and so were known as Premonstratensians. Its Church is now a ruin, and after the dissolution the domestic buildings were soon absorbed into a country house and forgotten. At the present time most people are quite unaware that, behind the facade of the house we see today, a great deal of the monastic buildings remain undisturbed. When in the 1930's the Torquay Corporation bought Torre Abbey it became a very attractive Art Gallery and from time to time it is used for Civic functions. So there has been a tendency to forget the splendour of mediaeval days when the Abbot of Torre was the most important personage for many a long mile, and when the buildings of the monastery, presided over by the massive tower of its church, dominated the foreshore of Torbay. The object of this book is to try to recapture something of the vitality of the Abbey's past and to put it on paper for you to read. Fitting together the mass of evidence which I unearthed when I began my task some ten years ago has been just like assembling the pieces of a huge jig-saw puzzle. The picture that eventually emerges is most exciting, for it will show us what an important Abbey this once was. The study of its former possessions, too, is most fascinating, for it will take us along many a winding Devon lane to remote spots far from 20th century motorways. These lovely places I should never have seen but for a fixed determination to visit all the lands which the Canons of Torre owned all those centuries ago.

If the reader will but stay the course I shall take him all over Devon, into Somerset and even on a trip to Lincolnshire. I shall show him ancient farm buildings, old churches and ruined chapels, deserted mills and the leats which supplied them with water. I shall show him the houses of many an old local family which had dealings with the Abbots of Torre, and best of all I shall introduce him to people from all walks of life who lived and toiled where we do today. Over the years which we are to consider our charters will tell us of kings and princes, tradesmen and humble serfs. We shall realise that to each in his generation the Abbey was a place of consequence. And so it was with all monasteries of the middle ages; their buildings were beautiful and their churches often magnificent. They were centres of learning and culture of every kind. Such communities ministered to the sick, looked after the needy, fed the wayfarer, sang the praises of God and were beacons of civilised living in that particular locality where they happened to be.

The task of writing any kind of history of this particular Abbey would have been impossible but for the existence of two very fine Cartularies. Now a cartulary is a book into which the wording of important charters and deeds was copied. These documents deal with gifts of lands, churches and other rights and privileges given by benefactors to the monks of a particular community. The precious charters themselves would be safely locked away in the Abbey's muniments room and could not be got at easily; but a cartulary was always to hand for quick reference.

The two Cartularies of Torre Abbey are pearls of great price, and from the salient facts contained in them I have been able to draw conclusions which give a very fair picture of the Abbey's growth from humble beginnings to decided opulence in the 16th century.

On the debit side of our researches is the almost complete lack of any other kind of written evidence. The precious account rolls are missing and so are the reports made by the annual Visitations, except for a few short years in the 15th century. In the case of some Abbeys such things have survived, and then a much more comprehensive history may be written.

The great monastic churches of the Middle Ages may be divided into two categories. Firstly the more fortunate which, upon the dissolution of their monasteries, survived intact because they already enjoyed the status of a cathedral as well as being Abbey churches. Secondly those which had no diocesan standing and were not necessary even as parish churches. These were pillaged by the ministers of King Henry VIII, stripped of their lead roofing and allowed to fall into ruin. This was the fate of Torre Abbey in February, 1539. The secular buildings which surrounded the churches were sometimes adapted and made into dwellings, but often they, too, were demolished and a grand new house might later rise on the site, sometimes retaining the title of "Abbey". Torre was fortunate here because much was preserved as part of a new house. The whole of the old western range of monastic buildings still stands, and so does the attractive gatehouse and barn. The latter was the store-house of the Canons where they kept their hay, grain and general provisions. Quite a lot of the buildings which make up the Torre Abbey of the present day therefore do go back to mediaeval times, and there are more walls and foundations which cannot be seen unless the undercrofts are explored.

Some of our ruined Abbeys are still remote and far from the rush and bustle of modern life, lying in deep country; but others stand on sites which have changed so dramatically that every vestige of their former solitude has vanished. Westminster Abbey is perhaps the most obvious example of this sort of change. Torre Abbey is another, for at the outset it was situated on a lonely stretch of coast, continually threatened from the sea, and could only be reached by insignificant and meandering roads. Now its windows look out upon the sea front of one of the country's best known resorts, where a continuous stream of traffic is constantly on the move. The surrounding hills are covered with hotels which in the 19th century were the luxurious homes of an opulent society. All around are signs of a flourishing civilisation. But the Abbey, for all that its meadows, gardens and galleries are wide open to the public yet retains an air of aloofness. It blends magnificently with the animated activity around it, and yet never seems a part of it. The spirit of past ages clings to its old buildings; its lawns and gardens are still a sanctuary.

A word must now be said of the post-dissolution story of the Abbey. After the Canons had departed its buildings and vast territorial possessions were all seized by the King. The various manors and estates he sold separately over the next few years. Torre Abbey and its demesne were granted to one of his favourites, John St. Leger. He quickly disposed of it to Sir Hugh Pollard in the very same year that he received it. The Pollards held it until Sir Hugh's grandson sold it to Sir Edward Seymour of Berry Pomeroy in 1580. His son disposed of it in 1598 to John Ridgeway who was at that time lord of the manor of Tormohun. The Ridgeways held the Abbey until 1649 when it and the demesne were sold to Sir John Stowell of Bovey Tracey. In 1662 he sold it to Sir George Cary, and with that family it remained until the 1930's. It was the Carys who built the south-facing part of the present house. To do so they adapted the southern range of monastic buildings. Under this family the Abbey enjoyed the quiet dignity of a country house.

By the mid nineteenth century Torre Abbey was no longer a country house, for the growing town of Torquay had been gradually creeping up to its gates. As the Carys owned quite half the land on which the new town was built, they developed from country gentry into influential members of the well-to-do society which flourished in Torquay at that time. The Abbey became a social centre for the new town and much entertaining went on there. Finally the Carys in their turn sold out to Torquay Corporation.

It must not be forgotten that during the Napoleonic Wars Torre Abbey sprang into importance for a short time when Nelson visited it more than once for meetings with other admirals. It is beyond the scope of this book, however, to deal with the post-monastic story of Torre Abbey, however interesting it may be. That I shall leave to others to write.

My researches have brought to light certain things which may be of interest to the student of mediaeval times. One concerns the style of building adopted for the courthouses of the manors which the Canons of Torre owned. I have found that in several cases they were halls built onto the barton farmhouses of these manors, and generally at right-angles to the main buildings. They were about 45 ft. in length and consisted of a dignified chamber similar to a small greathall of those days. They were of one storey only and had open timber roofs. There was usually a large hearth centrally placed in the wall. A point which they all have in common is that they had no connection with the house of which they formed a wing. They were in fact separated from it by a wall of considerable thickness which continued right up under the roof. It was as if to emphasise the fact that the farmer and his family had nothing whatever to do with the business of the courthouse. These facts have been stumbled upon by accident, as it were; research into the courthouses of other monastic manors might be rewarding, if only to discover whether the style of building mentioned was peculiar to the Premonstratensians. Certainly that Order had its own way of doing things. Many such buildings may exist up and down the country, although it is too much to hope that any will be found in their original condition. In Devon I discovered six examples of ecclesiastical courthouses belonging to the Canons of Torre. Most were wings built at right-angles to the farmhouses, but in two cases the house was continued in a straight line. They are at Court Barton (Coffinswell), Greendale Barton (Woodbury), Oldstone (Blackawton), Shillingford Barton (Shillingford Abbot), Ashclyst (Broad Clyst) and Underhaye (Ideford).

The gradual disappearance of the mediaeval farmhouses of Devon is a twentieth century phenomenon, and there is little that can be done to stem the tide. During the preparation of this book many such houses which I have described have been demolished or allowed to fall into decay. It is therefore fortunate that I have been able to record things which the next generation will not see.

The assessment of the extent of the mediaeval measure of the ferling is always a matter of difficulty. Throughout the charters the gift of a ferling or so of land crops up again and again. In some cases the ancient boundaries of the farms concerned can still be traced with some certainty, and then the extent of the ferling can often be calculated. I found that it varies considerably in different types of country—the average measure being 25/26 acres; but it was considerably less on the inhospitable slopes of Dartmoor where at Monksmoor, above Ugborough, it was only 16/17 acres. The biggest measure was at Waddeton where it was 36 acres. It would seem that the harder your land was to plough the smaller the ferling became. Yet the reverse does not hold good, because the Waddeton acres are not necessarily the most tractable soil in the county. I think, therefore, that there is scope for research into the extent of the ferling in Devon. I feel I have merely scratched the surface of an interesting subject in the case of a few monastic farms.

Absorbing as these considerations may be, yet in the end we must return to the simple title of this book—"Torre Abbey". What do we know about Torre Abbey itself? The answer is extremely little–for no one has done any considerable research on the subject apart from Hugh Watkin. He must now be introduced to the reader, because he is the only person ever to have devoted a great deal of time and study to the subject. He was a keen local historian whose books on the subject of mediaeval Dartmouth and Totnes are of much value. In the first decade of the present century he carried out an excavation of the site of the Abbey church, and later procured photographs of each folio of the Dublin Cartulary. From these he transcribed the whole of that Cartulary in its original Latin. Some of his writings are among the Transactions of the Torquay Natural History Society and the publications of the Devonshire Association. All this devoted work was undeniably a great achievement, and it is small wonder that Watkin's opinions on Torre Abbey have been much quoted for the past fifty years.

Another keen local historian was Arthur Ellis whose book "An Historical Survey of Torquay" is still quite unrivalled. In it he wrote a very comprehensive chapter on Torre Abbey which set down in scholarly style all the information then available on the subject.

In the 19th century White, Blewett and others mentioned Torre Abbey in their local histories. In this century Percy Russell's "History of Torquay" appeared, and in it he devoted space to our subject. Nevertheless their mention of it takes up but a small proportion of their works. The latest publication is an excellent pamphlet by Hilda Walker which was produced to mark the 770th anniversary of the foundation of the Abbey.

These pages record my own researches into the territorial possessions of the Canons. They were made possible by a study of the Cartularies and a determination to visit every place mentioned in them. I have made a transcription of the Exchequer Cartulary of Torre Abbey from the original Latin; a very reduced version is included in these pages so that at long last the student of the period may know something of what it contains. I have also recorded as far as possible everything still existing today which the Canons themselves saw and handled, and it is surprising how much there is. In this way I hope to have produced a book written from a fresh angle, and one which will, I hope, stimulate others more able than I to follow up my researches. The field is certainly a wide one.

There is much to be done, too, at the Abbey itself. Nothing has been attempted there since Watkin's excavation nearly 70 years ago. We have no up-to-date plan to produce for this book. The lawn in front of the west frontage has (so far as is known) never been explored. Yet if Torre followed the plan of other houses of the same Order then there ought to have been a whole range of buildings there. At the north-east corner of the ruins Watkin mentions remains of buildings earlier than the date of the Abbey's foundation. What they were we simply do not know. The time is surely ripe for a first-rate excavation, carried out by experts, to settle these points, and also to discover whether the Church had a western tower.

Then again the buildings ought to be presented to the public for what they still are—the splendid remains of the most affluent of the Premonstratensian Abbeys in the country. It is not enough to maintain just the exterior of the fabric when most of the interior is not on show at all. The Abbot's Great Hall and the guard-room in the gatehouse could all be made of great interest to visitors, and filled with information about the Abbey's past. The monastic kitchen could also be brought back to something of its former appearance. As there is so much to show surely the best should be made of it.

2

The Foundation of Torre Abbey

Torre Abbey was founded in 1196 by Lord William Brewer. One of the most influential men of his time and the favourite of four successive Kings, he was in his generation a pillar of the state. Amongst the many important offices which he held there was one humble one—he was lord of the manor of Torre, and you will read later on how he was probably born there. He founded Torre Abbey so that monks should pray for the souls of King Richard Coeur de Lion and his father, King Henry 2nd, and possibly also in thanksgiving for the safe return of his son William. He had been sent abroad as a hostage in connection with the ransoming of King Richard I who was captured and imprisoned on his return from the Crusade of 1189. The monks who came to Lord William's foundation at Torre were of the Premonstratensian Order, and there is said to have been a connection between them, the paying over of the King's ransom and the eventual freeing of the hostages. Whether this had anything to do with Lord William's choice of the Order of monks for his new foundation we cannot be sure, but it is a possibility.

The Order itself was a most interesting one and well worth our consideration here. The main peculiarity of the Order was the fact that its monks were always priests, being referred to as Canons Regular of Prémontré. In honour of the Virgin Mary they wore white cassocks instead of black and their head-dress was a kind of loose skull cap. At St. Saviour's, Torre, this is clearly to be seen in a well-represented head which is a part of the north chancel window. It seems that in the Middle Ages this Order with its distinctive dress and dignified Canons Regular was respected more than most. It has been said that its members were Canons who were also monks, and this seems an apt description of their position.

The Order was founded in the first half of the 11th century by St. Norbert after a dream in which he saw white-clad figures carrying lights and crosses and singing as they walked in procession. He was much helped in his work by Bishop Bartholomew of Laon, who made him grants of land in his Diocese in Northern France which made the new Foundation possible. The origin of the name Prémontré from which the Order took its name is uncertain, but if we think of it as meaning the "chosen place" or the place "pre-ordained" in St. Norbert's dream we shall probably not be far out. The Order spread rapidly, but in England there were never more than 32 houses, and in Scotland only six. Newhouse Abbey in Lincolnshire was the first foundation in this country. It dates from about 1143. Of the rest the bulk were established before the beginning of the 13th century. The Order was an austere one, somewhat akin to the Cistercian rule. Its peculiarity was that the discipline and running of the monasteries was dependent entirely upon the Order itself. The later houses were looked after by the long-established ones; the parent house of Torre, for instance, was Welbeck Abbey, and the Abbot there was responsible for its discipline, appointment of Abbots etc. Newhouse Abbey was

← TO GATEHOUSE
← TO GATEHOUSE / TO GUESTS' LODGING

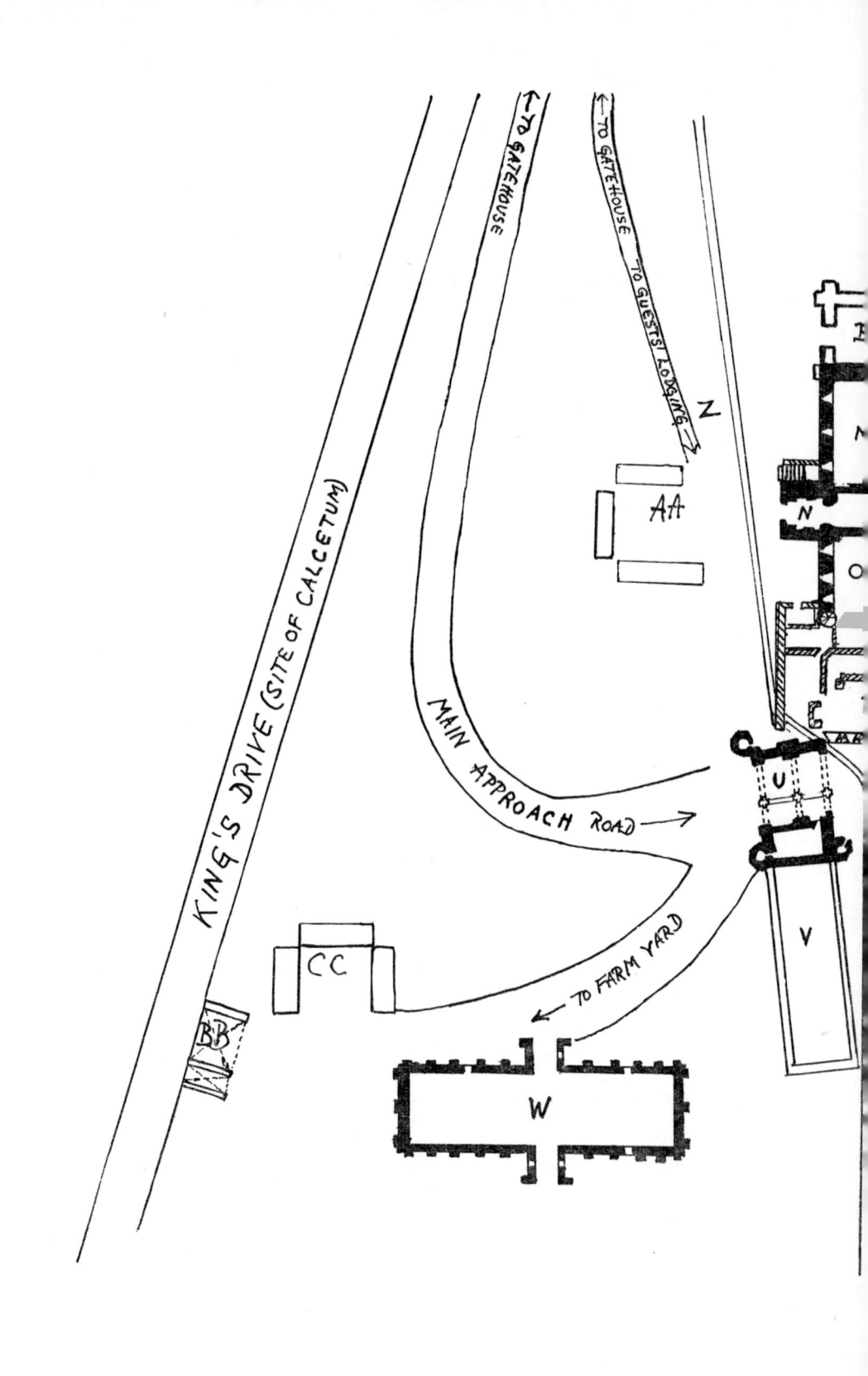

N

AA

KING'S DRIVE (SITE OF CALCETUM)

MAIN APPROACH ROAD →

CC

BB

→ TO FARM YARD

U

V

W

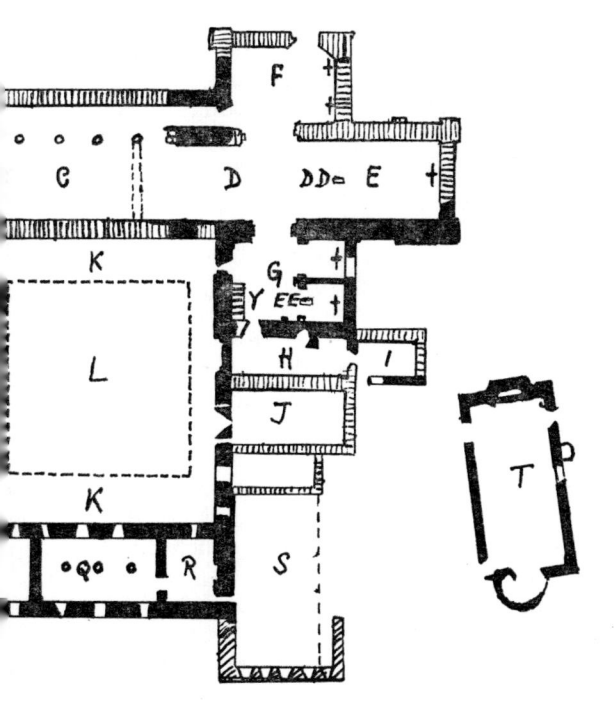

A	Canons' Burial Ground
B	Probable site of west end tower
C	Nave
D	Canons' Quire
E	Presbytery
F	North Transept
G	South Transept
H	Sacristy
I	Muniments Room
J	Chapter House
K	Cloisters
L	Garth
M	Vault with Abbot's Hall over
N	Tower
O	Vault with Abbot's Dining Hall over
P	Kitchen
Q	Vault with Frater over
R	Vault with Calefactory over
S	Canons' Dorter over
T	Probably the Infirmary
U	Gatehouse
V	Fawden
W	Tithe Barn
X	Site of former buildings
Y	Night Staircase
Z	Leat
AA	Probable site of Guests' Lodging
BB	,, ,, ,, Gatehouse
CC	,, ,, ,, Farm buildings
DD	Tomb of William Brewer the Younger
EE	Tomb of unknown Benefactor

TORRE ABBEY

THE MONASTIC BUILDINGS

(FROM PLANS BY H. WATKIN
AND W. M. ST. JOHN HOPE)

■ MONASTIC BUILDING STILL EXTANT ▨ LATER ADDITIONS
▥ FORMER POSITION OF ROBBED WALLS
▭ CONJECTURAL SITES AS YET UNEXCAVATED

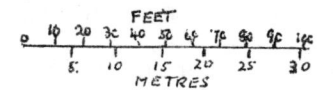

responsible for Welbeck and so on through the French Abbeys of Licques and Laon back to Prémontré. For a short while Torre came under the paternity of Durford, but was returned to Welbeck in 1232/33 (Welbeck Cart. f. 129).

No Bishop had any kind of authority over the Premonstratensian Abbeys in his diocese, neither could he so much as enter their precincts. Once a year, beginning on October 9th, St. Dionysius's Day, all the Abbots assembled at Prémontré for a meeting of the General Chapter of the Order, and there all problems were discussed and settled. Nothing was to prevent each Abbot from attending this Chapter, except sickness or extreme old age. As the 14th century wore on, however, English Abbots went less and less to Prémontré, assembling in England instead. Unlike other Orders the Canons were allowed to leave their monasteries to undertake parochial duties in the churches with which they had been endowed. This must have entailed long spells of absence, but we have proof that the Canons of Torre did duty as vicars at Townstall and Bradworthy churches, whilst they were continually responsible for going to take the services at Wolborough, Torre and Cockington. When one of the Canons left the Abbey for pastoral duty at a distant church for a long period, he was bound by Canon Law to take with him a canon-vicar of his own Order for companionship. If such a priest could undertake the duties of a chantry priest at the same church, so much the better from a financial point of view. The Canons were also ordered to retire from the world at times, or as we should say, go into retreat at one of their granges where an Oratory would be provided. At Ilsham the tiny chapel which still stands shows exactly the conditions under which they lived at such times.

For some centuries there was a custom in Premonstratensian Abbeys of admitting lay brothers to wait upon the Canons, who, being priests as well as monks, were fully occupied by their special duties. These lay brothers were known as "conversi". They wore grey robes and were bearded; but they were not allowed to receive the tonsure. In the words of Anselm of Havelberg, writing in the 12th century they were "illiterate men who turn to us from secular life, having left all to bear the yoke of Christ. They do not desire nor are they able, to be raised to the clerical status, but they live laudably in every monastic perfection, labouring with their hands, and in penitential habit crucifying their flesh with its vices and fleshly desires". They were not permitted books and seem to have been regarded very much in the light of servants. They seem to have done all the daily chores and worked on the Canons' farms and granges. Other Orders admitted them, and from time to time there are records of discontent among them. The references to them become fewer as time goes on, and among the Premonstratensians in England they had died out by the end of the 14th century. There is no indication in the ground plans of abbeys of this Order that they ever lived in the precincts. If there were any at Torre then they must have been specially housed in their own dwelling outside the main buildings.

The Order was not one to produce learned men or great scholars; the only one to achieve a bishopric of standing in this country was the Abbot of Shap, Richard Redman or Redmayne. He was successively Bishop of St. Asaph's, Exeter and Ely. He died in 1505 and is buried in a sumptuous tomb in Ely Cathedral. He came to Torre Abbey more than once to make a Visitation. At about this time other Abbots were appointed as suffragan bishops.

Hospitality played a large part in the curriculum of any Abbey. According to "Statutes of the Realm" (i, p. 150) the Statute of Carlisle had permitted monasteries to be founded so that the sick might be tended, hospitality dispensed, alms given to the needy and prayers said for the souls of the founders and their successors. In "Les Statuts de Prémontré" Pope Gregory IX directed that in all churches of the Order hospitality and alms should be dispensed; a guest-house was to be built for the poor and a special person was to be appointed to superintend this department of the Abbey. On pp. 61/2 we read that the Canon who held the office of porter was to open the Abbey gate to visitors after he had taken their names. They were then to be conducted to the Church to pray, after which they were placed in the hands of the brother hospitaller, who showed them to the guest-house, offering them refreshment and ministering to their immediate needs.

The porter also dispensed alms daily at the Abbey gate and brought the "broken meats" left over after meals. Abbeys near ports or on important highways must have had, too, a constant stream of upper class travellers claiming a night's lodging, or what we would call today "bed and breakfast". Titchfield Abbey, which was so near to Southampton, often had Royalty as guests, and there in 1445, Margaret of Anjou, after her arrival in England, was married to King Henry VI. According to Titchfield Register (f. 87) 189 people could be seated for meals, 47 of which were accommodated in the vault. This may at times have been the use to which the spacious vaults at Torre Abbey beneath the Great Hall were put. Whilst Torre was not on any main road, yet it no doubt had its share of visitors and needy people. Their sleeping quarters must have been in buildings to the west of what we now see and have long since vanished.

When all these aspects of the Premonstratensian Order have been considered we must return to our starting point—the reason for Lord William's act of the foundation of Torre Abbey. We have already stated that it was so that monks should pray for the souls of King Richard and his father King Henry, but there was much more to it than that. The Premonstratensians were committed to prayers for the souls of all their benefactors. Obits were kept annually for them as well as for their own community. These obits were sent round from one Abbey to another. One which has survived is the Beauchief Obituary which was begun in the first quarter of the 13th century. At first the obits were even sent to the Continental houses as well as the English ones, but after a while this became unworkable. Even here as the years went by the number to be commemorated became impractical and the older names were erased.

The founder of an abbey in particular was remembered on his first anniversary by a prebend, that is to say his ration of food for the day would be set aside and given to the needy. The Canons also received corporal punishment on his behalf, but the lay brethren were excused this if they so desired.

Generous benefactors could become confraters, and the prayers and masses offered for them would be made just as though they were Canons of the Order. Chantries, which are dealt with elsewhere, were granted to even more liberal patrons. Then in extreme old age such persons could assume the habit of a monk and die among the Community. Lord William Brewer himself did this at Dunkeswell Abbey, his other foundation, for it was the special privilege of a founder.

The Order seems to have chosen remote and barren sites for its monasteries. Torre in those far-off times was situated on a sparsely populated coast, far from a town of any size and was only reached by devious and dangerous roads. There would be no defences between the Abbey and the sea which in times of storm must have been a real threat to its safety.

One would have liked to ask Lord William Brewer why out of all the many fertile manors in his possession he had to choose this spot on which to build an Abbey. I think the answer must be that the Canons themselves favoured the site because it was at once remote from the world and a challenge to their initiative. It was on March 25th, 1196, that Adam, the first Abbot, arrived there with six monks from Welbeck Abbey, the parent house, in Nottinghamshire. It would not be long before the walls of the building, which was to influence the lives of countless people, began to rise behind the golden sands of the bay.

When Lord William Brewer founded his Abbey he was decidedly generous with regard to its endowments. First came the gift of the churches of Torre, Wolborough and Bradworthy, with its chapel of Week St. Pancras. On the secular side there were grazing rights in the manor of Torre, a part of the manor of Coletone, the vill of Wolborough, the fertile farm of Greendale at Woodbury, the whole of North Shillingford near Alphington, land at Ugborough with grazing on Dartmoor, the mill of Bradworthy and a ferling of land there; and finally the fields around the Abbey which composed Rowedone, possibly the name of a former holding there; in the bay were fishing rights. Sundry privileges such as making leats to conduct water to the Abbey were also granted. As the years went by Lord William was influential in obtaining for the Canons the church of Shebbear through King John in 1207, and his last gift so far as we know was the church of Buckland Brewer c. 1224.

It was not long before other benefactors, possibly at the instigation of the founder, began to shower gifts upon the newly-founded Abbey. At Townstall William FitzStephen gave the church to the Canons and Philip de Salmonavilla gave them Hennock church. Far away on the east coast of Lincolnshire Richard de Parco gave Skidbrook church. Other gifts included a considerable amount of land at Kingswear from William de Vascy, farms at Hennock and Buckland-in-the-Moor. In north-east Devon the manor of Dunnyngestone, and just in Somerset a farm called Haggelegh were given. Nearer home Daccombe manor with further land in Coffinswell came to Torre through Jordan de Daccombe, and later the large manor of Blackawton. The manor of Ashclyst which supported a prebendal stall in Exeter Castle Chapel was given by the Courtenays. As time went on the Canons acquired the manor of Torre. All this was an amazing endowment for a Premonstratensian Abbey to hold, for such affluence was more akin to a Benedictine house. It all seems quite out of keeping with the traditional poverty of the Order. Torre Abbey was eventually the richest Premonstratensian house in the country. In 1535 its income was £396.11.0., according to "Valor Ecclesiasticus"—a truly great sum for that time.

3

The Abbey Buildings

The Church

Any description of the buildings at Torre Abbey must begin with the Church, however ruinous it may be, for in monastic days it was the centre around which the life of the Community revolved. We shall notice later in the charters of the Cartulary how it was to the Church of St. Saviour and the Holy Trinity that all gifts and endowments were made; the Canons and the monastery always came second. The twofold dedication of the Church is quite clear by evidence of the charters, although both dedications were not always used in the same document. A third dedication to St. Mary has been asserted by some writers, but I have found no mention of this anywhere. Some gifts were made "for God and St. Mary", but that is not the same thing at all. The Premonstratensians as an Order were, however, specially dedicated to the Virgin Mary, and the white cassocks which they wore were a reminder of this.

It is no easy matter to describe a building of which so little is left, and one must admit

Torre Abbey South Frontage, 1977. *D. Seymour.*

that the scanty remains of the Church are at first sight disappointing. But there is just enough left for a comparison to be made with the ruins of other Churches of the Order, and in this way one may gain an insight into the probable appearance of the Church in the days of its splendour.

After the suppression of the Abbey in 1539, it fell gradually into ruin. Stripped by the King's Officers of its lead roof and undermined by stone quarrying, it became a prey to the despoiler. It is known that in the cases of some Abbeys glass, fittings, lead from the windows and all marketable appurtenances were sold to the first comer. So it is not at all surprising to find that a birds-eye view of Torre Abbey, drawn in 1662, shows but scanty remains of the Church apart from its massive tower. In plan it followed the design of other Premonstratensian churches in England, and was at first a simple, cruciform building. Its overall exterior length was about 170 ft. and that of the transepts 105 ft. Probably somewhere between 1350 and 1400 a north aisle was added. This marked the beginning of the Abbey's most prosperous period, and the aisle would be needed to house the chantry chapels and tombs of generous benefactors. In the early years of the present century Hugh Watkin carried out an excavation of the Church; he found that most of the walls, particularly on the north and west sides, had been robbed of their stone to the very foundations. The levels of the Nave and Aisle were about four feet lower than at present. Fragments of the columns supporting the arcade were laid bare and there were burials in two of the five bays. Watkin considered that the north aisle was contemporaneous with the building of the church, but there have always been those who strongly disagreed with this interpretation.

The plans of other Premonstratensian churches show that most of them were aisleless. When in the first place the south wall was built right up against the north side of the Cloisters, then, of course, a south aisle could never be built. Shap and Torre both had north aisles, and at the former only the easternmost part of the aisle dates from the foundation. Torre was the offspring of Welbeck Abbey, and it is most probable that it greatly resembled the parent house with regard to its church. But at Welbeck the church has unfortunately quite vanished. Bayham and Dryburgh both had north and south aisles, but this seems to have been exceptional. The churches of the Order were less ambitious at the outset than those of the Cistercians. The simple cruciform plan with a low tower at the crossing was the main characteristic of the churches in this country. They were nearly all built in the latter part of the 12th century, but after a hundred years or so, when the Order had become in many cases more affluent, ambitious additions took place both in the churches and the claustral buildings. There is no doubt that the buildings of this later period provide much that is still a splendid contribution to the ecclesiastical architecture of this country. Particularly outstanding are the remains of the noble church at Bayham, the great east window at Egglestone (considered by some to be unique for its period), and the remains of the Frater at Easby. Dryburgh in Scotland also has notable remains to show, whilst at Shap a very fine west tower was added as late as 1500; it is in the same tradition as the tower at Fountains, though less spectacular.

The style of the Church of St. Saviour would doubtless inherit many of the features of these other churches of the Order. It had a west tower which in 1662 was still standing according to the drawing already mentioned.

Amongst writers on the subject of Torre Abbey there have always been those who consider that an even older church of St. Saviour stood on the site long before the Abbey was contemplated. Perhaps this is the moment to consider this possibility. The claim for this older church is due to a sentence in the Foundation Charter which describes the Abbey as built where St. Saviour's was founded ("fundata est" in the Latin original). Whilst admittedly there may be some ambiguity here with regard to the precise meaning of the phrase "fundata est" yet I would point out that the Foundation Charter of Welbeck Abbey (c. 1154) contains similar wording, i.e. "the place where the church of St. James was founded". A footnote in A. Hamilton Thompson's book "The Premonstratensian Abbey of Welbeck" (p. 13) is much to the point. The writer comments that "fundata est" implies that the church was in existence by this time whether complete or not. Further discussion on the subject of an older church on the site therefore seems unnecessary in the light of the Welbeck charter.

The next step is to consider the Church at Torre in detail as far as this is possible.

Nave

The Nave in churches of this Order was robbed of one or two bays by the intrusion of the stalls of the Canons' Quire at the eastern end. The termination of the Quire was usually marked by a screen and sometimes a step or two down into the Nave proper. This shortening of the Nave shows how congregations were looked upon as coincidences rather than necessities. This treatment was carried to an extreme at Egglestone which had an extremely short Nave, only two bays of which were left for congregational use. At Torre there were five bays, and the plan shows about 60 ft. of the Nave west of the Quire steps. All that is to be seen of the Nave today is the beginning of its walls which stand to a height of two or three feet at the former crossing. The remnant of a single carved capital is the solitary reminder of former grandeur .The line of the south wall is still discernible because it is some feet above the level of the Cloisters, the position of which is still an undisturbed open square. In common with other churches the west wall came as far as the east wall of the western range of buildings, but no further. It is curious that Watkin does not seem by his plan to have carried his excavation further west in order to ascertain once and for all whether there really was a western tower. W. St. John Hope, however, in his plan, produced in the "Archaeological Journal" of 1913, shows that he believed in the drawing of 1662 for he shows a west end tower, indicating its probable extent and position.

The Nave was 25 ft. in width and the aisle 10 ft. It has been calculated that the vaulting of the roof reached a maximum height of about 38 ft. The general effect of the interior of the church must have been long and narrow, giving a feeling of considerable length.

Presbytery

The east end of the Church is sufficiently well preserved on the south and east side for one to be certain that the original simple east end had never been extended. At Easby and Shap, for instance, there was a later extension eastwards, whilst at Dryburgh a spacious chapel was added east of the Presbytery. In the later 13th century a three-sided apse was built at Bayham. There was nothing of this sort at Torre, and we may be sure that the Presbytery remained to the end just as it had been built. Fortunately the lower courses of the east wall still stand to a height of three or four feet, so it is still possible to determine where the high altar stood. The south-east corner is the best preserved, and the line of the southernmost window can be distinguished. It is close to the south-east corner, suggesting that there were triple windows at the east end. The first window in the south wall also remains in part.

Just east of the crossing lies the coffin of William Brewer the Younger; it is of Purbeck stone and is the only burial which can be safely identified. This interment is fully described later.

Canons' Quire

It has already been mentioned that the Canons' stalls would be west of the crossing, and this was the usual arrangement in all monastic churches. At Torre the length from the west end of the Canons' Quire to the east end of the Church was 96 ft.

The Crossing and Tower

The only Premonstratensian church to have preserved a fragment of its crossing and central tower is Talley Abbey. Here the arches on two sides still stand and support above them a part of the tower to a height of 95 ft. At Torre no strong shafts are showing which might have supported a tower, but at Talley there is exactly the same arrangement whereby the tower can be seen to have been built upon strong walls and nothing more. At Shap there was trouble with the central tower, and owing to structural failure much reinforcement and rebuilding took place in the 14th century.

Lying across the Canons' Quire and extending under the crossing are large blocks of masonry which are considered to be all that remains of the central tower. What is to be seen here seems perfectly consistent with the tradition that it was finally blown up by gunpowder as it was considered unsafe.

The Transepts

The overall length of the transepts was 105 ft. and the width 45 ft. The two chapels in the south transept are still clearly to be seen and were separated by a wall: but whether this was originally a low wall surmounted by a screen, or whether it continued to the height of the roof we cannot tell. In the south wall of the south chapel is a piscina which is in a remarkably good state of preservation. The central space is occupied by a crude coffin of sandstone raised on masonry above the level of the floor. It is believed to be in situ.

The north chapel on excavation produced a few bones and part of a skull. At a lower level was much rubble. This Watkin removed and found a cavity which he considered by its shape once to have held a coffin. In size he said it was exactly the same as a large granite trough to be seen nearby in what was once the brewhouse of the Cary family. If they had been brewing their cider over the years in a coffin one can only hope the flavour was good! In actual fact this huge trough is most unlike a coffin of the Canons' day, although of course it needed no adaptation if it ever was used for a burial.

The two chapels of the north transept have entirely disappeared, but their former existence is hardly in doubt for in the transepts of other churches of the Order two or even three chapels in each transept were usual. The body of a large man 6 ft. 4 inches in height was found in the north transept. There has been much speculation as to who the people were whose interments have been discovered, but it is quite useless to speculate, for we simply do not know. All that can be safely said is that they were benefactors of the Abbey who were given burial there. I am told by Brother Gilbert (of the Premonstratensian Priory at Storrington, Sussex) that it was usual to bury Abbots in the Nave.

In the south-west corner of the south transept the remains of the night staircase may be seen. It was by this stair that the Canons reached the Church for the night Offices from their Dorter on the first floor.

Torre Abbey: Western range of monastic buildings.

Photo by G. Court Jones.

Torre Abbey: Abbot's Tower.　　　　　　　　　　　　　　　　　Photo by G. Court Jones.

Torre Abbey: Western Range from site of Cloisters.   *Photo by G. Court Jones.*

Torre Abbey: Beneath the Crossing, fallen masonry of central tower.   *Photo by G. Court Jones.*

Torre Abbey: South-east corner of Presbytery. *Photo by G. Court Jones.*

Torre Abbey: Doorway of Chapterhouse. *Photo by G. Court Jones.*

Torre Abbey: East wall of former Cloisters. Door into South Transept of Church on left. Chapter House entrance on right. *Photo by G. Court Jones.*

Torre Abbey: Coffin of William Brewer the Younger. *Photo by G. Court Jones.*

TORRENS
in Com Devo
p

Vt prisca Majorum pieta
memoretur   posuit
IOHANNES STOWELL
de Bovytracy in Com:
  Devon: Armiger

O

M

Torre Bay

I

K

A

W.J.W.97
DIRECTORY CO., LITH.

TORRE

Drawn on Stone by W m. J. Wyatt, from

ABBATIÆ
nc in Ruinis

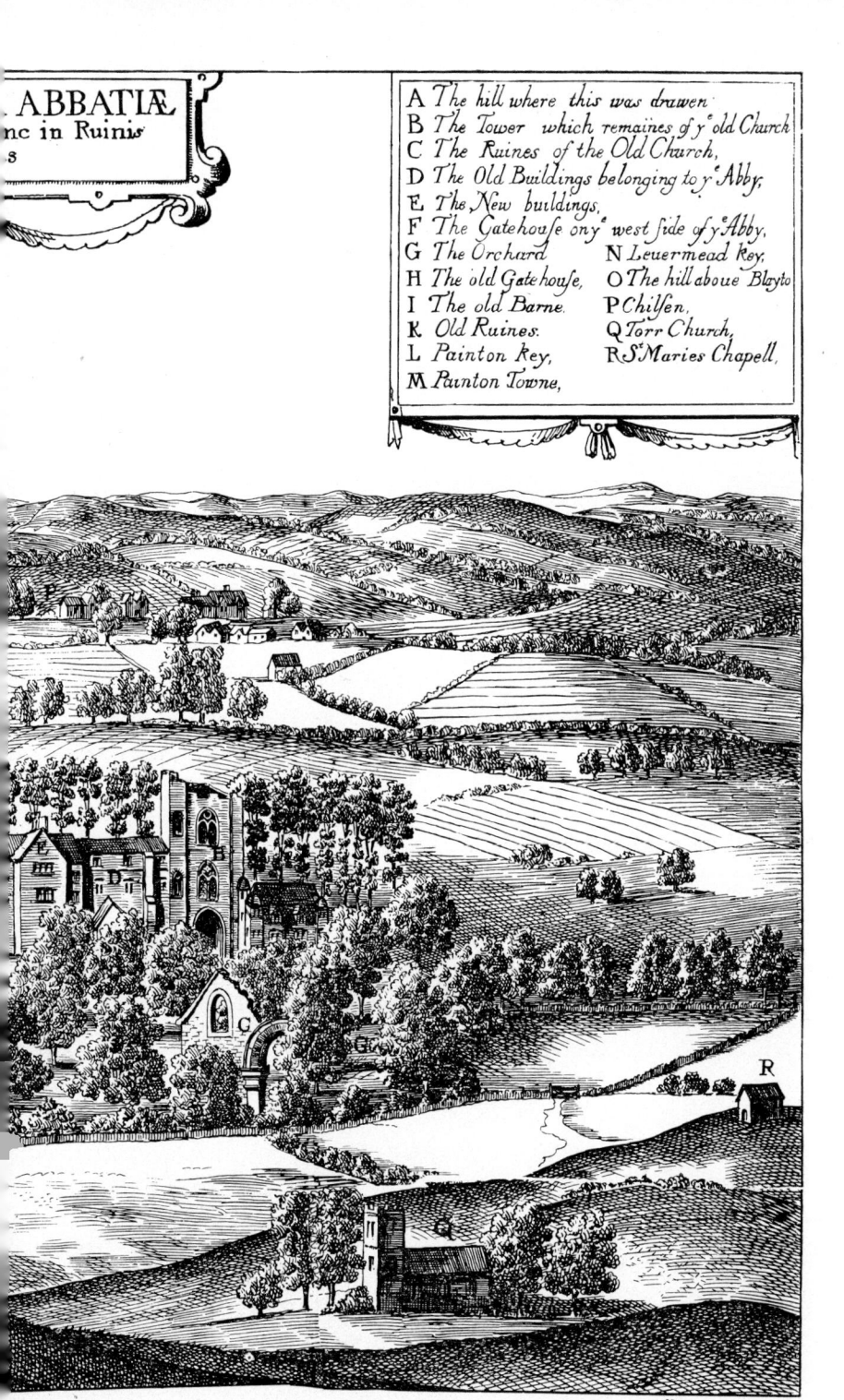

A The hill where this was drawen
B The Tower which remaines of yᵉ old Church
C The Ruines of the Old Church,
D The Old Buildings belonging to yᵉ Abby,
E The New buildings,
F The Gatehouse on yᵉ west side of yᵉ Abby,
G The Orchard   N Leuermead key,
H The old Gatehouse, O The hill aboue Playto
I The old Barne.   P Chilsen,
K Old Ruines.   Q Torr Church,
L Painton key,   R Sᵗ Maries Chapell,
M Painton Towne,

HISTORY OF TORQUAY

EY, 1662.

in the possession of Mr. R. Dymond, F.S.A.

Torre Abbey: Gatehouse. *Photo by G. Court Jones.*

Torre Abbey: Miss H. H. Walker in the south transept chapel.

Torre Abbey: Undercroft in Western Range (South). *Photo by G. Court Jones.*

Torre Abbey: Undercroft in Western Range (North). *Photo by G. Court Jones.*

Torre Abbey: Undercroft, looking across the passage. *Photo by G. Court Jones.*

Torre Abbey: Undercroft window. *Photo by G. Court Jones.*

Torre Abbey: Central passage of Undercroft. *Photo by G. Court Jones.*

Torre Abbey: Tithe Barn from south-west.　　　　　　　　　　　　　　　*Photo by G. Court Jones.*

Torre Abbey: Looking down on Chapels in South Transept.　　　　　　*Photo by G. Court Jones.*

Carta Radulphi Crispin.

Tunstalle

Universis sancte matris ecclesie filiis hanc cartam presentibus et futuris Radulphus Crispin salutem in domino. Noverit universitas vestra me dedisse et concessisse et hac presenti carta mea confirmasse Deo et ecclesie sancte Trinitatis de Dunstaple et canonicis ibidem Deo servientibus villanos illos meos cum tota sequela sua et catallis suis videlicet Rogerum filium Villani et Willelmum fratrem eius et Walterum et Thomam et Robertum filios Godrici et Rogerum fratrem eorundem et Thomam Mulewart et Willelmum Ace et Edwardum fratrem eius. Ego vero et heredes mei predictos villanos cum sequela et catallis suis predicte ecclesie de Dunstaple et canonicis ibidem Deo servientibus contra omnes homines warantizabimus. Hiis testibus...

Torre Abbey as it might have been, c. 1539.

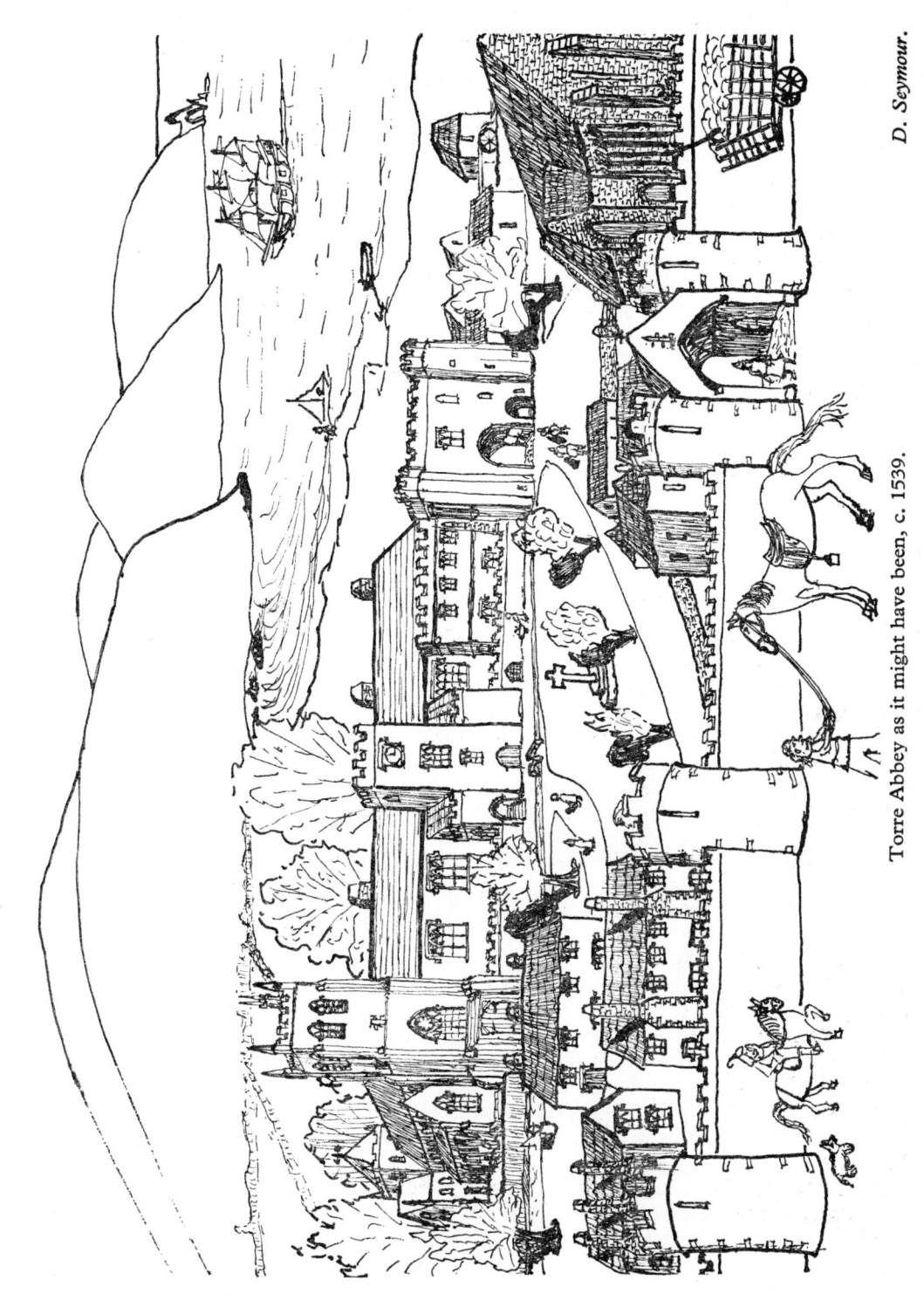

D. Seymour.

The Monastic Buildings

Sacristy and Muniments Room

Immediately beyond the wall of the south transept stood the Sacristy which opened into what is thought to have been the Muniments Room. In some Abbeys the Library is considered to have occupied this position. The plans of other monastic buildings of the same Order show a great similarity of design, and at Torre everything conforms to the usual pattern. In the north wall of the Sacristy is the beginnings of a circular stair which evidently led up to the tower. Remains of a fireplace are also to be seen in this wall. The excavation proved that the original floor level was 18 inches lower than at present.

Chapter House

The most important of the monastic buildings, apart from the church, was the Chapter House. It was entered from the Cloisters by a fine roundheaded Norman doorway which is flanked on either side by windows in a similar style. This entrance is one of the Abbey's most treasured remains, but apart from the west wall nothing further remains to be seen today. Here all the important business of the Canons was conducted and the meetings of the Chapter held. Many of the charters in the Cartulary conclude with the words "Given at Torre", and it was in this Chapter House that they would be signed. The very document of the surrender of the Abbey to the King in 1539 was doubtless signed here, and that may have been the very last occasion on which the Canons met.

This quadrangular chamber measured about 38 ft. by 17 ft. and apart from the Chapter House at Egglestone is the smallest of which we have records. Some were much more elaborate with two or even three aisles, with vaulting resting on columns. In some cases a vestibule was also included, but these examples to be seen at Titchfield and Bayham were probably later rebuildings. The simple quadrangular chamber seems to have been the most usual, and in style the Chapter House at Torre may have much resembled that at Bristol Cathedral, although it is a little later in date and, of course, on a smaller scale.

The floor was four feet below the present level and here fragments of tiles were found. These are to be seen at Torquay Museum. Coats of arms of other Abbeys of the Order are displayed on some of them, amongst which are Tongerloo in Belgium (Or 3 chevrons Gules) and Beeleigh in Essex (Azure 6 fleur de lys Gules 3, 2, 1).

The Cloisters

The Norman doorway of the Chapter House opened onto the east side of the Cloisters. The level square which they occupied is all that is to be seen now. This is bounded by the Nave of the Church on the north side, by the western range of buildings on the west and by the Frater on the south. The enclosure was 88 ft. square and the Garth 60 ft. square. At the north-east corner a door led into the South Transept of the Church, and this would be the way by which the Canons always entered it by day.

At Shap, Easby and Dryburgh the main entry to the claustral buildings was by way of a door and passage at the south-east corner of the Cloisters. It may well have been so at Torre, for some way of entrance from the main courtyard south of the buildings must have existed.

A circular stair in the south-west corner of the Cloisters formerly connected with the Abbot's quarters on the floor above. Here two windows dating from the 15th century are still to be seen. One is of four lights, but the other, at a slightly higher level, is a single light window.

Lavatorium

In the south-west corner of the Cloisters are remnants of the Lavatorium. Here the Canons washed before entering the Frater to eat. A modern wall unfortunately cuts right across these remains, but even so traces of the "dog-tooth" ornamentation of the period can still be distinguished.

Frater

Those who visit Torre Abbey for the first time find it hard to realise that the present house is by no means large. The central portion, for instance, is only about 25 ft. in depth. This is because it is built upon the lower courses of the Frater and Calefactory walls which still exist beneath their coating of stucco. The Frater was reached by stairs leading up from the south-west corner of the Cloisters. It appears to have measured about 42 ft. by 22 ft. It was the usual thing for the Premonstratensians to construct undercrofts beneath their Fraters and western range of buildings; this is the case at Torre where the undercroft still remains in perfect condition, though now not lit by any windows beneath the Frater.

It is strange how the Canons of Torre seem to have had little ambition to extend their house in the days of their affluence. Apart from the probable addition of the north aisle to the Church and a western tower all seems to have remained as it was at the outset. There may be many reasons for this, but the most obvious was that the Community can be seen from the Visitations never to have been a large one; and then again some Canons were permanently absent as vicars of outlying churches. The Abbey, too, was remotely situated and not often called upon to provide hospitality for large retinues. Its original accommodation must have been considered adequate.

So the Frater at Torre remained to the last a simple, unadorned building, and did not compare with the later magnificent remains which are to be seen, for instance, at Easby.

Calefactory

East of the Frater was the Calefactory. Apart from the Abbot's Hall this was the only room where a fire was kept burning. Here the Canons could relax and warm themselves in winter after long spells in the cold Church. In modern terms it was the parlour of their house.

Kitchen

The kitchen usually occupied the south-west corner of monastic buildings, but the site really depended upon the position of the water supply. At Torre the water reached it from the leat on the west side of the Abbey. Kitchens, too, were placed as far from the Church as possible so that the noise and bustle of preparing meals could not disturb the Canons at their prayers. The level of the floor is well below that of the Frater, so all food had to be carried upstairs before it could be served. The monastic kitchen was in use right up to the time when the property was sold to the Corporation of Torquay.

Infirmary

The Infirmary in most monasteries was a detached building, usually at the south-east corner. Watkin on his plan marks it in this position, but adjoining the main buildings. Russell, however, in his "A History of Torquay" places it in the very building which Watkin regarded as the remains of the former manorhouse of Torre. Much uncertainty therefore prevails over the true position of the Infirmary.

Dorter

As in other houses of the Order the Canons' Dorter was situated on the first floor at the south-east corner of the building. Stairs connected it with the Cloisters and Church.

The Western Range

The western range, which stands on a slight downward slope to the south, is still very complete, and it is doubtful if its walls have been disturbed in post-monastic times. It occupies about 145 ft. in length. Because of the sloping ground it was decided to construct an undercroft, so the main apartments are reached by stairs in the Abbot's Tower. On the left is the former Great Hall which may in monastic times have had the width of the present entrance hall added to its length to form a screens passage. It now measures about 40 ft. by 22 ft. and seems to have been a dignified, if simple, hall. It retains its old, moulded roof timbers and four bosses are still preserved. The fireplace on the east side has been filled in. The large north window of three lights is probably 17th century in date, but the other windows are early 19th century replacements. The Cary family made this hall into their Chapel, but prior to 1779 it had been used as the family laundry. The Carys were Catholics and previously had to worship in secret in a small room constructed under the spacious roof. When the laws against Catholic worship were relaxed the hall was used as a chapel by the Catholics of the neighbourhood until 1854 when the Church of the Assumption was built in Abbey Road. A reredos and altar stand at the north end, and pews fill the rest of the hall. There are memorials to various members of the Cary family upon the walls. Now that the old Great Hall is no longer used as a Chapel it would perhaps be a happy thing if the pews and reredos were removed and the hall restored to something of its former appearance.

On the other side of the entrance hall is another large room which was the dining room of the house. Its walls and ceilings are heavily disguised with plaster work of a post-monastic period; but it is still a charming apartment of pleasing proportions and is considered to have been the Abbot's dining room. The Abbot's guests and those who lived permanently at the Abbey, through the granting to them of a corrody, would use the Great Hall and Dining Room, entering them by the staircase in the Abbot's Tower.

In the entrance hall at the top of the stairs and on the right of the doorway is a recess containing a large bowl which is built into the thickness of the wall. Here the guests and others using the Dining Hall would wash their hands before eating. They would be lodged probably in a group of buildings long since vanished which may have stood before the west front of the monastery. In this way they lived apart from the Canons and only entered the precincts for the services in the Church. Their number would no doubt have amazed us, for they would include old retainers and aged tenants of the Abbey as well as guests and those with corrodies.

Beneath these two large rooms is an undercroft divided by a passage into two chambers. In one the massive vaulting is supported by two slender, circular piers of Purbeck stone, but in the other it is supported by square shafts of masonry. We can be certain that in this ancient undercroft we are seeing just what the Canons saw all those centuries ago, for here nothing has been changed. The vaults are lighted by small windows of single lights. One in particular is a delightful example of the transitional Norman style. They are just above ground level. What the original use of these chambers may have been we cannot tell, but in the northern chamber there are indications that water was once brought in at floor level. Further passages lead to vaults under the Frater and to the Kitchen.

The entrance to the undercroft was by means of a door at the foot of the tower which opens onto the passage which separates the two chambers just described. As the level outside has been raised several feet we now step down into this passage. An inner archway shows where another door was hung; the socket for the huge bolt which could be drawn across is to be noted.

The two salient features of the exterior of the western range of buildings are the Abbot's Tower and the embattled gatehouse. It is hardly possible to assess the age of the square clock face, but a print of 1879 shows a diagonal wooden face, perhaps superimposed over the old one. The bell on which the hours are struck is an "alphabet" bell of the 16th century, but the Rev. J. G. M. Scott, the authority on church bells, tells me that it is a little later than the monastic period. Whether the tower itself is of this later residential epoch is hard to determine. But it is so simple and unsophisticated in design, and so much a part of the ground plan, that it may quite well go back to the earliest period. Indeed it strongly resembles the early towers of the Canons' churches at Torre and Wolborough. Its sturdy silhouette is so much a part of Torre Abbey that it is difficult to think that Abbot Adam did not see it built.

The fact that this part of the Abbey buildings has remained quite undisturbed since monastic days has recently been substantiated by extensive work on the north end of the roof. Experts consider the timbers to be of late 15th century date.

It is interesting to compare this western range with a similar one at Welbeck. There, although very little remains of the Abbey, the western range was incorporated into the large house built on the site. As at Torre there is an extensive undercroft still in existence and an outside staircase led up to the former camera of the Abbot. This can be clearly seen in a print of 1726. Other monastic houses have mostly perished, and so the existence of the whole of the west wing of Torre Abbey is a notable survival among Premonstratensian houses in England.

The Gatehouse

The gatehouse at the southern end of the buildings is a delightful survival. It has excellent proportions, and the pleasing use of red sandstone for the arches, doorways and windows contrasts happily with its limestone walls and polygonal turrets. The central passageway is under a lofty arch which is slightly pointed, but the smaller archways are completely rounded. Such building was typical of the transitional Norman style prevailing at the time when the Abbey was built. There are two bays of vaulting, and on the keystones are carved (1) the Abbey's Arms (Gules, a chevron between 3 croziers Or) and (2) the arms of de Brewer (Gules, 2 bends undy Or). These are much worn and crudely cut. After 1232 when the de Mohuns became lords of the manor of Torre their Arms were cut on the small corbels below. First came Reginald de Mohun (Gules a maunch dexter Ermine, the hand proper holding a fleur de lys Or within a border Azure). Next came the double-headed eagle of his son John, and thirdly the engrailed cross of the third John de Mohun (Or, a cross engrailed Sable). On the keystones of the smaller arches, under which pedestrians entered, are engraved what appear to be wheels with many spokes. There has been much speculation as to what they represent.

In this passageway a door leads to a porter's room. On the first floor is a large chamber with a garde-robe and chimney. This would be the guardroom, and there is little doubt that in troublous times the Community had to maintain a guard there, when attack from the sea was a very real threat. Permission to crenelate the buildings was granted by King Edward III in 1348 (D.C. f. 93a), but earlier than this, in 1326, John de Mohun is said to have paid a large sum to the Abbey for the purpose of rebuilding this gatehouse. Certainly it is known as the Mohun gateway and his liberality may have gained it this title.

The huge irons on which the former gates were hung are still in position. It was the duty of one of the Canons, known as the Circator, to go his rounds and see that these gates were locked at night. They were also closed at certain hours of the day, probably during the hours of services in the Church.

A further point of interest is that the gatehouse is not on line with the monastic buildings. It is joined on to them clumsily by a short passage near the kitchen quarters. But it is on line with a building at the south-east corner of the ruins, which Hugh Watkin thought to ante-date the Abbey and to be the de Brewer's former manorhouse. Nevertheless some do not accept this theory, and so the strange alignment of the gatehouse has yet to be explained.

This gatehouse in the early days was obviously the main entrance to the precincts and it may have been approached exactly as it is today. The tarmac road from the present entrance gates, instead of leading straight to the gatehouse, makes a quite unnecessary sweep round the lawn. This could be because the lodgings of the guests and servants once stood there. The gatehouse would open onto a quadrangle with buildings probably on all but the east side. These show up in the engraving of 1662. According to Watkin another gatehouse stood about 20 yards inside the present entrance gates, and this would have been the entrance to an outer courtyard around which the quarters of guests and retainers were grouped.

Leland, writing in the 16th century, mentions "three fair gateways". There is a tradition that the third was close to the barn and opened into the present King's Drive. The farm buildings are thought to have stood here, and so it would have been an entrance for all farm traffic; it therefore seems reasonable to suppose that the third gateway occupied this position.

In 1662 the engraving already mentioned and attributed to Hollar was made for John Stowell, then owner of Torre Abbey. It was drawn from a spot on Waldon Hill evidently not far from St. Luke's Church. Many have pored over this engraving trying to read into it first one thing and then another. One has only to consider the obvious defects in the distances portrayed in the surrounding countryside and to the very approximate shape of Torre Church to realise that a great deal of artist's licence went into its making. The gateway, for instance, is shown with only one arch and far too many windows, whilst the house seems to have no south-facing frontage at all. The tower of the church has buttresses coming down to ground level and shows no indications that the church roof was ever attached to it. In fact it does not look as though it were ever a part of the church. I feel that little sense is to be got from this highly-stylised drawing, and that it does not help much in our study of the buildings. What it does show is that a very stalwart tower was then standing practically to its full height, and showed very little signs of decay. Also we see how there were buildings south of the house, one of which would almost certainly have been the mill.

It remains to discuss one more secular building and that is the barn. Its exterior is quite unaltered, so far as one can see, from the day it was built. It measures externally

124 ft. by 33 ft. and is supported by ten buttresses on either side. Because of its great doorways and ample transepts wagons could be drawn into it to unload. We may expect the roof originally to have been thatched. Its timbers are considered not to be original, but to have been once renewed. It is the only one of the Abbey buildings not to be plastered over with stucco and its walls of mellowed limestone and sandstone are delightful.

The title "Spanish Barn" originated after the capture by Sir Francis Drake of a galleon of the Spanish Armada of 1588. She was the flag ship of the Andalusian Squadron. Three hundred and ninety seven of the crew were imprisoned in the barn until prisons at Exeter and Dartmouth could accommodate them. A plaque let into the floor records:—

> The Spanish Barn built 1196
> Herein 397 prisoners of war from the
> Spanish Galleon
> Nuestra Senora del Rosario
> were incarcerated
> July 26th, 1588.

The space to the north of the church is considered to have been the Canons' burial ground, and here in 1825 the Rev. J. MacEnery found two stone coffins containing human bones. We may expect that the buildings were surrounded by strong walls which have long since disappeared. A moat is also said to have existed, and Watkin's plan marks part of this in front of the western range of buildings; it was finally filled in during 1876. It is quite certain that the Abbey water supply entered the grounds where now the two lodges stand. A conduit met the main drain of the house at the north-east corner of the gatehouse and flowed down to the sea in a straight line. When the Torquay Corporation redesigned the meadow a bridge was built across this conduit which I well remember. The latter has now been filled in, but the bridge still remains, and the line of the water course is still visible as a sunken ditch.

In addition to the buildings a few things of interest deserve mention. Standing before the west front of the Abbey is a fluted granite shaft. It was found among the elm trees near the King's Drive and was set up here by the Cary family. It obviously belongs to the monastic period and could have been used for many purposes.

Near the south transept a curious piece of granite is preserved which has three circles of different sizes incised upon it. There has been much speculation as to its use. Close by is the keystone of a gable and a hand quern.

Further finds during Watkin's excavation included the carved fragments of a tonsured head, hands raised in prayer, and other small pieces of very superior workmanship. On the north side of the Church was a ditch some 18 inches below ground level. In it portions of window moulding and stained glass of the 14th century were found.

Masonry and débris from the ruined Church are known to have been dumped in several places. Much was used in raising the level before the west front, whilst more was deposited into the former fishpond to fill it in. This pond was in the hollow south-east of the house. A great deal of stone is also said to have been deposited in the sea when the walls of the harbour were constructed.

4

The Succession of Abbots

Those who have tried to compile a list of Abbots of Torre have not found the task an easy one, and there has been much divergence of opinion over the sequence of the first ten; but from John Berkadone onwards all agree. As to the number of Abbots there is no doubt at all, for at East Ogwell church are to be seen inscribed stones which once covered the graves of Abbots Norton, Cade and Dyare. Norton is there described as the 14th Abbot and Cade as the 18th. There were two more to follow, Abbots Dyare and Rede, so this brings the total irrefutably to 20. The Canons' own reply as to how many Abbots they had had may be read in the chapter on the Visitations; it will be found to agree with the evidence of the gravestones.

Whilst there is no doubt at all that the first Abbot was Adam (who was translated to Newhouse in Sept., 1199), yet there has been disagreement as to the second. Colvin in "The White Canons in England" mentions an Abbot John in 1200, quoting Rot. Charters, 1837, p. 99, and also a mention in Beauchief Obituary. The latter, however, was not begun so early as this, and a retrospective entry was very liable to inaccuracy. References such as the former are also not always reliable. That is why the Cartulary, transcribed from actual charters at Torre Abbey itself by one of its Canons, gives the most accurate information of all. The Canons knew perfectly well who their Abbots had been, for they were meticulous in observing their obits. In these early days of the Abbey's history a mistake is hardly possible. Now there is no mention in the Cartulary of an Abbot John—and much business was transacted at Torre at the turn of the century. The most we can say of him is that he may have been an Abbot-elect who died or was translated elsewhere before ever coming to Torre. After Adam there were 19 more Abbots to come, all of whom can be vouched for either in the Cartulary or the Bishop's Registers; so another is inadmissible.

I consider that there is evidence enough to place Roger as the second Abbot. He is mentioned by name in 35 and 160, and as "R." in 36 and 259. These are all early charters and the latter two are too early, I feel, to refer to Abbot Robert, first mentioned in 1223 (146). Now in 260, which dated from Oct. 8th, 1203, Master Walter de Pembrok, Rector of Rattery, quitclaims his interest in the chapel of Cockington because he has seen a quitclaim of it in favour of R., Abbot of Torre, made by St. Dogmael's Abbey in 259. This latter charter can therefore be no later than Oct. 1203.

35 and 36 (also undated) concern a 9/- rent at Aller, which is confirmed to Roger (35) and then to "R." in 36. This rent is first mentioned in 16, the principal Wolborough charter, where a tenement held by one Ingelramus is mentioned. In 34 his brother, Gervase, confirms this rent to Abbot Adam, and then in 35 it is confirmed again to Abbot Roger, this time by William de Boteraus at the instance of his wife, Avelina. She was evidently a sister of Ingelramus and had inherited the Aller property. In 36, after the

death of her husband, she confirms it again to Abbot R. The point is that Ingelramus, William and Avelina all appear to be of the same generation, and so the confirmations fit comfortably into the years 1200/07 when I consider Roger to have been Abbot.

Then again Lord William Brewer's daughter Isabel, according to the de Brewer pedigree, married as her second husband Baldwin Wake or de Wike, who in 160 gave land at Week St. Pancras to Abbot Roger. As Baldwin died in 1214, the gift must have been earlier than that year.

The third Abbot was "W.", who is mentioned (174) in 1207 when he was admitted to the advowson of Shebbear Church. Now although in both Cartularies the letter "W" is perfectly clear yet this Abbot has not previously been noticed. This is the only mention of him in the Cartularies, but he spans the gap between the years 1207 and 1223 when his successor Abbot Robert is first mentioned.

From Abbot Robert to the death of Simon de Plympton there is no difficulty in placing the Abbots. In 1264 the Bishops of Exeter's Registers begin to record Benedictions of Abbots as they took office, so that we know exactly what their dates were: but even here some names are inexplicably missing.

In 1345 there begins the most difficult period of all in which to trace the correct succession of Abbots. With the help of the Bishop's Registers for the years concerned, however, the tangled evidence can be unravelled.

On the death of Simon de Plympton John Gras received Benediction from Bishop Grandisson in 1345 at Chudleigh on Dec. 21st. (fol. 27, Grandisson's Register, vol. 1). On May 21st, 1349, another Abbot John received Grandisson's Benediction (ibid. fo. 161). The next entry in the Episcopal Register concerning the Abbots of Torre is Dec. 6th 1351 (fol. 108b) when a Letter of Testimony was given to John Gras and refers back to his Benediction of Dec. 21st, 1345. Between these two entries the most dramatic events in the Abbey's history had taken place; they are related in the chapter on Prior Richard de Cotelforde. The effect on the succession of Abbots was that John Gras was withdrawn from Torre Abbey in 1349 when another Abbot John succeeded. He ruled for two years after which Abbot John Gras was reinstated. His successor, John de Berkadone, was first mentioned in 1372, after which there can be no divergence of opinion over the order in which the Abbots ruled. The succession I therefore consider to be as follows:—

1. ADAM (1196/99) men. 34. Translated to Newhouse Abbey. "Ruled three and a half years" (col. Ang. Prem).
2. ROGER (1199/c. 1207) men. 35, 36, 160, 259.
3. "W." (c. 1207/22) men. 174.
4. ROBERT (c. 1223/31) men. 146, 187, 253.
5. LAURENCE (c. 1231/46) men. 126, 284, 295.
6. SIMON (c. 1246/63) men. 13, 111, 147, 230, 293.
7. BRIAN (1264/70. Benediction by Bishop Bronescombe, June 28th, 1264) men. 205.
8. RICHARD (1270/c. 1305. Benediction by Bishop Bronescombe, May 22nd, 1270).
9. JOHN LE ROUS (c. 1305/30) men. 189, 299.

THE SUCCESSION OF ABBOTS

10. SIMON DE PLYMPTON (1330/45. Benediction by Bishop Grandisson, August 15th, 1330).
11. JOHN GRAS (1345/49. Benediction by Bishop Grandisson, Dec. 21st, 1345).
12. JOHN (1349/51. Benediction by Bishop Grandisson, May 21st, 1349). (JOHN GRAS re-instated by Letter of Testimony from Bishop Grandisson, Dec. 6th, 1351. Ruled until c. 1370).
13. JOHN DE BERKADONE (c. 1370/82) men. 194.
14. WILLIAM NORTON (1382/1412. Benediction by Bishop Brantyngham, July 27th, 1382).
15. MATTHEW YERDE (1412/14. Benediction by Bishop Stafford, July 19th, 1412).
16. WILLIAM MYCHEL (1414/42. Benediction by Bishop Stafford, March 18th, 1414).
17. JOHN LACY (1442/55. Benediction by Bishop Lacy, Jan. 30th, 1442).
18. RICHARD CADE (1455/c. 1482).
19. THOMAS DYARE (c. 1482/1523).
20. SIMON REDE (1523/39. Benediction by Bishop Thomas Chard, suffragan to Bishop Veysey, August 21st, 1523).

Lists of Abbots of Torre have been compiled by Oliver, White, Gasquet, Ellis and Colvin. Some give too many abbots and some too few.

The above list is based either on mention in the Cartularies or in the Bishops' Registers. There may still be inaccuracies and the student must form his own conclusions.

5

A Consideration of the Abbots

It is no easy task to try to reconstruct the lives and characters of twenty men who lived so long ago. Whilst some are little more than names, yet during the rule of others, through events which happened, we get more than a glimpse of the sort of person who was guiding the Abbey's destiny at that time. At one period, through the charters in the Cartulary, we find, for instance, that the Abbey had a reputation for its benevolence to the sick and poor; so we are probably not wrong in deducing that the Abbot at that time was a man of more than usual kindness and gentleness. When several charters concerning the acquisition of land follow closely on each other's heels, then it would appear that an astute business man was in charge at the time. When at the time of a Visitation the buildings and their appearance were singled out for praise, then it looks as though the Abbot of the day took a great pride in his monastery and its upkeep.

It is quite wrong to picture a mediaeval abbot as tied to his monastery. He moved freely about the country on matters of business and affairs of state. Abbot Richard, for instance, was four times summoned to attend Parliament during his abbacy. A Premonstratensian Abbot of the 13th century also travelled abroad each year to Prémontré for the Chapter meeting of his Order. Only sickness or old age excused him from attending.

1. ADAM. The first Abbot was the pioneer who supervised the building of the Abbey. He arrived at Torre on the Feast of the Annunciation (March 25th) 1196, attended by six other Canons. They all came from Welbeck Abbey, which was throughout its existence the parent house of Torre. The choice of Abbots and all matters of importance were always referred to the Abbot of Welbeck. I often wonder what sort of a day greeted the travellers after their long journey. Did they first see the site on a day when a black east wind was whipping the sea into great waves which broke over the marshes, threatening the very place on which they proposed to build? Or was it a mild spring day of brilliant sunshine which welcomed Adam and his companions? I like to think that Lord William Brewer, the Founder, was there to greet them and encourage them right away in their great task.

We in Devon have in our generation seen Buckfast Abbey rise again from the dust, all the work being carried out by a very small team of monks. Was it the same at Torre, and did Adam and his six Canons actually build their Abbey? Dunkeswell Abbey, for instance, is known to have been built by 12 monks at about the same period. On the other hand, Lord William may have procured skilled masons from Exeter Cathedral to fulfil the task. Stone would be available from the two great limestone quarries at Torre Hill and Chapel Hill, although there is no mention in the Cartularies that this was the case. At a later date Roger de Cokynton granted the Canons stone from Corvenasse,

(Corbyn Head), but this was some time after the original building had taken place. Of one thing we may be sure, however, Abbot Adam would be there from day to day supervising everything.

The actual building cannot have been the only task which he supervised, for the site had to be made habitable for a community. Channels had to be constructed to bring water to the Abbey from the springs at Northville, given by Lord William; Rowedone had to be stocked with sufficient sheep and cattle to support the newcomers, whilst the remaining land had to be developed as a productive crop-growing farm.

Perhaps the most important outside task which Adam would perform would be visiting the land and churches with which his generous patron proposed to endow the Abbey; all these estates would have to be organised under bailiffs and worked to the best advantage. At this time the Foundation Charter had not yet been given, and so Adam must have wondered all the time whether Lord William would really do all that he had promised. All these worries must have been brought to a triumphant conclusion, however, when the great charter was at last given, probably not until 1199 when the church was finally completed and consecrated and dedicated to St. Saviour and the Holy Trinity. The assembling of the witnesses at the Abbey and the impressive ceremony of the giving of the charter must have been the most thrilling moment of Adam's life. All had been most quickly completed in about three years under what must have been most able supervision on his part; and all his arduous efforts were rewarded with a generous endowment from Lord William.

Adam is only mentioned once in the Cartulary, and this is in charter 34 where he gave Gervase the son of Odo 40/- in recognition for the land of Aller which Gervase rented for 9/- per annum. Adam therefore was the pioneer Abbot who during his short rule of three and a half years must have worked with might and main.

It would be in September 1199, that he was translated to Newhouse Abbey, Lincs.—no doubt to enjoy a less arduous existence. So departed from Devon a man who by his achievements must have earned the respect of the whole countryside, and who must have known Lord William Brewer and his family intimately.

2. ROGER. The second Abbot is a much more shadowy figure than the vigorous Adam, yet he must have been very active in consolidating the Abbey's position. This was a time when the Canons were anything but well off, for the bulk of the gifts of land which were to come to them had not at that time been thought of. Roger would begin his rule late in 1199 or early in 1200. It lasted at the most 7 years, for his successor is first mentioned in 1207. But we have no means of knowing just when Roger died. The great help given by the Registers of later Bishops of Exeter for that period is not available. Roger is mentioned in four undated charters, 35, 36, 160 and 259. The latter, however, almost certainly dates from 1203.

We can picture Abbot Roger as the head of a new and enthusiastic community which was just beginning to feel its feet, but which could scarcely be described as prosperous. The days of the Abbey's affluence were as yet far off.

3. "W". Abbot "W" has been quite unnoticed by previous writers. He is mentioned in charter 174, where the initial "W" is perfectly clear. In Dublin Cartulary it is also perfectly clear, yet this Abbot has been completely overlooked. Had there been a mistake in the earlier Cartulary it is most unlikely that it would have been repeated

in the later one—the carefully undertaken fair copy. The Canons themselves must have been only too conversant with their former Abbots' names, for their obits would be most meticulously observed. A mistake is therefore unlikely. Moreover this Abbot fits perfectly into the years between 1207 and 1223 when his successor is mentioned. The charter in which he occurs concerns the gift of "Shefbere Church" to the Abbey. In it Abbot "W" is canonically instituted to this church by the Archdeacon of Totnes, acting upon the presentation of King John—the See of Exeter being vacant owing to the Interdict. Judging by the dates we have, "W" can have ruled as long as 15 years. The gift of the church at Shebbear and its appurtenances was undoubtedly made by the King at Lord William Brewer's instigation. So Abbot "W" left his house in a slightly more prosperous position than it was when he took office.

4. ROBERT. The fourth Abbot, Robert, seems to have been an astute business man, for during his abbacy several charters confirming gifts to the Canons appear in the Cartulary. It is all too easy to imagine that such gifts were poured into the laps of the waiting Canons, but in reality they were the results of patient negotiation. This might often involve months or even years of uncertainty before a piece of land finally came into the hands of the Abbey. People are not found to part with land easily at any period of history, so Robert must have known just how to handle those who were kindly disposed towards his Abbey.

The most important transaction which he brought about was undoubtedly the confirmation given by Serlo, first Dean of Exeter, of the advowsons of the churches of Torre, Bradworthy, Wolborough, Shebbear, Buckland Brewer, Hennock and Townstall. This was the first time that the advowsons of the seven churches concerned were mentioned together in one document. This charter was given in 1226 and was immediately produced in 1300 when the Abbey's right to these churches was challenged.

The first mention of Robert in the Cartulary is in 1223 when he was at Westminster procuring a Final Concord with William FitzRobert over the $\frac{1}{4}$ share of the advowson of Skidbrook church, Lincs. He is mentioned by Oliver as witnessing a covenant between the Dean and Chapter of Exeter and the Abbot of Buckfast. In 1228 Abbot Robert went to Wilton to defend his right to the church of Buckland Brewer, the Prioress of Kinkitone petitioning against him. But he wisely solaced her with the Abbey's land at Newenham, Berks., which consisted of $1\frac{1}{2}$ virgates given by Walter, son of Ives. Here Robert showed much wisdom in parting with land which was so far from Torre as to be a liability.

In the same year he was at Exeter where a Final Concord was given concerning land at North Shillingford. He also entered into negotiations with the Guril family over Abbey land at Aller. His successor is first mentioned in 1231. So it seems that Robert ruled for about 8 years. Much business seems to have been transacted during that time.

5. LAURENCE. There is an early mention of this Abbot in Dublin Cartulary (folio 155). He there acknowledges a letter from Abbot E., the father abbot of the Order at Prémontré. A fact which emerges during Laurence's abbacy is that Torre Abbey at that time was not finding it easy to make both ends meet. It was evidently not until the middle of the next century when the Canons came into possession of the manor of Torre itself that the house became well-to-do, and eventually the richest Premonstratensian house in the country. Proof of its poverty is to be found in the fact that Laurence

obtained permission to receive from any nobleman a donation sufficient for the maintenance of a Canon at Torre. Hugh Peverel, for instance, was allowed to present a suitable Canon and to provide for him. Then again in 1237 Abbot Laurence was presented with the Prebend of Ashclyst which was very much a sinecure; the reason for this is expressed in a much later document from Bishop Quivel where he confirms the manor of Ashclyst to the Canons so that they would be able to continue to provide sustenance for the poor and needy—a thing for which their house was noted.

The expense attached to the philanthropic side of a mediaeval abbey must often have been a matter of acute embarrassment to its treasurer. It had become the custom for monks to care at their abbeys for the poor, the sick and needy, the aged and those who had corrodies and so were allowed to reside there. The numbers cared for in this way must often have rivalled the number of the brethren, whilst the cost of their maintenance must have been anything but welcome. Abbot Laurence, however, seems to have made the wants of his house known in the right quarters, and so got the support which he required for carrying on his care for the needy.

During this abbacy the manor of Daccombe was given to the Abbey by Jordan de Daccumbe, and Laurence had to go to London in 1239 for a Final Concord. On this occasion he granted Jordan an annual payment of 20 marks in silver for the duration of his life. At the same time a tenement at Holeridge in Ideford was granted to the Canons.

Laurence was again in London in 1239 at the Court of Westminster where he leased the mill at Bradworthy to Richard de Langeforde (166). He is also recorded as exchanging land with Reginald de Albamara at Woodbury (95), and two ferlings of land at Cockington with Roger de Kokynton (264). Abbot Laurence is also mentioned in charter 215 where he agreed to pay the Prior of Totnes 8d. annually for an acre of land at Kingswear and a $\frac{1}{2}$ acre at Upton (Brixham).

Lastly he had dealings with William de Cantelupe, Lord of Totnes, whereby he was granted permission to buy 60 hides each year at Totnes market free of toll; this was on the understanding that the Canons provided William and his wife Eva with two pairs of boots annually at Michaelmas. Further agreements with William and Eva gave leave to land any goods on Torre Abbey land at Kingswear, in return for which they granted freedom from toll to 24 of the Abbot's men selling fish which they had caught at sea (D.C. folio 153a).

From all this evidence it seems therefore that Abbot Laurence was a good business man as well as a compassionate one who was especially concerned with the wants of the sick and poor.

6. SIMON. Abbot Simon is mentioned in D.C. (folio 153a) as early as 1241, but Watkin considered this an error and thought it should read "Abbot L". However, a grant by Ralph Breyse to Totnes Priory was witnessed by Abbot Symon and William, Abbot of Buckfast, in 1246, and this seems a reasonable date for the beginning of Abbot Simon's rule. It lasted until 1264 when his successor was blessed by Bishop Bronescombe.

Simon's seems to have been an active period for the business side of the monastery and several transactions were undertaken. An interesting occasion was the granting of permission to Reginald de Mohun, lord of the manor, for the construction of a chapel in his courthouse at Torre. The private chapel at the manorhouse was almost a status symbol of the period, and although the manorhouse might have been but a stone's throw from the parish church, as at Torre, yet still the lord and his lady insisted on having their own oratory, usually with a domestic chaplain attached. The charter of March 1st, 1252, shows Abbot Simon insisting that the rights of the parish church were by no means to be set aside. The usual stipulations were made and half the oblations came to the Abbot. The whole affair is of interest to us today because it shows that the long-vanished courthouse at Torre was in the 13th c. a house of consequence, and the home of the de Mohuns whose name has for so many centuries been attached to the parish.

In 1253 the Abbot obtained a quitclaim from William de Skitebroc for the quarter share of the living of that church (147). In 1259 he was at the King's Court at Westminster for the purpose of a Final Concord with John Fitz Matthew on the subject of suit of mill at Avetone from the men of Stoke. (230).

It was always a condition that the clergy presented to livings in the diocese of Exeter by the Abbots of Torre should meet with the approval of the Bishop. Abbot Simon had a rap over the knuckles on April 13th, 1262, when Bishop Bronescombe appointed one Syward to the living of Shebbear, because the candidate of the Abbot and Convent was unfit (inepta). One senses that the Bishops rather resented the privileges of the Premonstratensians in being exempt from diocesan authority. Here was a case where the Bishop could get the better of them for once. He did not let the opportunity slide.

In 1263 Abbot Simon acknowledged six acres of land at Kingswear to be the right of the Prior of Totnes (Tot. p. 162). This is the last recorded act of this Abbot.

7. BRIAN. The benediction of Abbot Brian is to be found in Bishop Bronescombe's Register on June 28th, 1264. As his successor was blessed in 1270 we know that Brian ruled Torre for six years all but a month.

On Sept. 30th, 1264, he made an interesting agreement with the Guild of Merchants at Totnes, whereby the Canons were permitted to buy and sell at Totnes market, but were not to hold a stall. For this he agreed to pay 2/- per annum (Tot. 163).

In the following year, on March 15th, he was at the Bishop's house at Chudleigh, together with the Prior of Bodmin and the Prior of Totnes. In the same month he undertook to provide 20/- annually for a clerk, Thomas de Boclonde, until such time as a benefice came his way. (D.C. folio 169a).

There were in his time two undated business transactions concerning Kingswear: (1) a lease of Lidewichestone to Peter de Fissacre and his wife Beatrix for 18/- annually, and suit of court at Kingswear (205), and (2) Abbot Brian granted to Michael de Lideford the hall (house) at Kingswear which formerly belonged to Osbert le Franchys (D.C. 158a).

At North Shillingford the Abbot confirmed land at Southbinheie to Walter Fitz-William (D.C. folio 158a).

It is not usually remembered that the Canons had an official house in Exeter, and as far as I can make out it was in Paul Street. The character of the street has of course completely changed over the centuries and consists now largely of warehouses, so it is quite impossible to locate the site. In addition the Abbey owned property in Smithen Street, and there are four charters in Dublin Cartulary in connection with it:—(1) Edward the fisherman grants his tenement in Smithen Street to Brother Brian (D.C. folio 80a), (2) Master Peter Quivel gives a quitclaim of the same, (3) A quitclaim from Johanna, widow of William de Alre, of a messuage in Smithen Street and (4) A quitclaim from William de Alre of a house in Smithen Street—no doubt the same as that mentioned in the third charter. So it looks as though the Canons owned two or three houses in

Smithen Street. At the moment of writing this street is awaiting development after lying derelict for some years. It is possible to make out, however, that the former houses occupied narrow strips of land which stretched back from the road; by their shape and size the old mediaeval area occupied by these houses seems to have been preserved right into the present century. Once again we have no clue as to where the Canons' houses were.

The only other records that we have of Abbot Brian are a letter which he wrote to Bishop Bronescombe asking that a clerk—one William Morland—may be admitted a subdeacon so that the Abbey might receive him as a Canon and Brother (D.C. 166b), and another letter to his faithful Robert de Esse requesting him to pay 8/- to Walter de Nimet—an annual rent which the Abbey paid. (D.C. 168a). Abbot Brian's short rule came to an end in 1270, and probably the most interesting of his recorded acts was the furthering of the Abbey interests in the towns of Totnes and Exeter.

8. RICHARD. This Abbot ruled at Torre for over thirty years, so his span of office is one of the longest. He was blessed by Bishop Bronescombe in London on May 22nd, 1270, and first mention of his successor is not until c. 1307. It is possible therefore that he ruled for 37 years, although 35 is probably nearer the mark. It was only to be expected that much business was transacted during these years. He is mentioned in no less than 12 charters in the Exchequer Cartulary.

It was during this period that the important charters were given which concerned the manor of Ashclyst (124-134). They marked the first decisive advance in the Abbey's income. The prebendal stall at the Castle chapel in Exeter was maintained by the Manor of Ashclyst; this income provided just the extra money which the Canons needed to continue providing for the sick and poor. A cleric whose name should be mentioned as one who helped on the Ashclyst transaction was William de Somerford who appears in the Dublin Cartulary in folios 167b and 104b. Again in folio 79b Abbot Richard undertakes to pay William 10/- annually from rent in Exeter on the eve of St. Mark's day. After his death the money was to go for the keeping of his obit. This was done in gratitude for many benefits received when the Canons were in urgent need. Watkin has pointed out that in the index of Dublin Cartulary this friend in need is also classified as 'de Werplisdone'. So William de Somerford was the same man who leased the manor of Ashclyst to the Abbey in 1284.

During Richard's abbacy improvements were carried out on certain of the Abbey estates. At Greendale for instance the working of the mill was improved by taking water from a pond which was the property of Michael de Wynklegh. This pond was conveyed to the Canons (113).

At North Shillingford Abbot Richard improved the water supply at his courthouse by sharing water with his neighbour, Henry Pynde, of Bowhay for six months of the year. In 1275 the Abbot effected an exchange of land with Henry, no doubt to the Abbey's advantage. (254-255).

At Blackawton much business was carried out, all of which may be read in charters 234-238. At Pancrasweek the Abbot granted Robert de Bosco permission to build an oratory, providing the rights and dues of the chapel of Pancrasweek were respected.

Lastly, at Wolborough, the farm of Teignaller was leased to William the Archer, and its interesting boundaries may be traced to this day. This transaction is discussed in the chapter on Wolborough.

In a Totnes Priory deed ciii (p. 179 Tot.) it is recorded that the Prior of Totnes remitted to Abbot Richard in 1276 his claim to the tithe of Hokesbeare in Hennock. The small seal of the Abbot is appended to this document.

Gasquet (vol. 2, p. 203) tells of a certain Canon P. who was sent to Torre Abbey for punishment between the years 1281-1287. He had brought a false charge against his abbot and two fellow Canons. That it was a fact that erring Canons were sent to other monasteries for correction is borne out by the chapter on the Visitations which took place at Torre at the end of the 15th C.

One senses that in his latter years Abbot Richard was afflicted with some kind of infirmity which prevented him from leaving the Abbey. As early as 1290 he excuses himself from attending the General Chapter of the Order at Prémontré, and Brother Gilbert, Father Abbot of the Order, writes to acknowledge his excuses (D.C. folio 164b). Indeed several letters exist in the Dublin Cartulary appointing various people to act as his proxy at meetings and convocations held at a distance.

The final event of note in this Abbot's life was the enquiry into the Abbey's title to the advowsons of the churches in Exeter diocese with which it had been endowed a century earlier. We find there that Richard showed extreme caution in parting with his precious charters even for a few hours—flatly refusing to send them to Exeter for perusal. But all was well, and Abbot Richard died knowing that the precious endowments were regarded as authentic. Between the years 1294-1303 Parliamentary Writs show that Abbot Richard was summoned as follows:—

1293, summoned to attend Council of Clergy held before the King in person at Westminster on Feast of St. Matthew the Apostle, Sept. 21st. (22 Ed. I).

1294, summoned to Parliament at Westminster on Sunday next after the Feast of St. Martin, Nov. 13th. (23 Ed. I).

1296, summoned to Parliament at Bury St. Edmund's on Morrow of All Souls, Nov. 3rd. (24 Ed. I).

1300, summoned to Parliament at London on Second Sunday in Lent, March 6th. (28 Ed. I).

1301, summoned to Parliament at Lincoln in eight days of St. Hilary, Jan. 20th. (29 Ed. I).

By his long rule and wise guiding of the Abbey's affairs Richard must be regarded as one of the outstanding Abbots of Torre, and when in about 1305 he at last died, the west country must have lost a most respected churchman.

9. JOHN LE ROUS. On account of his nickname "le rous" this Abbot must have been a red-headed man. Such a soubriquet helps to distinguish him from other Abbots named John. His rule lasted from c. 1305, until 1330. Once again Torre had an Abbot who ruled for a considerable time. Not a great deal of business of note was transacted, however, during this time, although some interesting things are recorded in the Dublin Cartulary about this period. In 1329, for instance, Townstall church was laid under an interdict because of the suicide of the vicar, Richard de Wydecombe. Bishop Grandisson repealed this on Dec. 21st of that year so that mass could be held on Christmas Eve and the following day (Register p. 550). Another suicide which concerned John le Rous very closely was in July of the same year when the Bishop asked him to reconcile the churchyard at Torre, where the body of a suicide had been interred. (Register p. 517). On account of incidents now to be related I gather the impression that

this Abbot may very well have been as fiery and impetuous a person as his red head suggested. For instance in 1316 he and a fellow Canon, Thomas de Plympton, and two layman were summoned by the vicar of Stoke Fleming, one Robert de Pentelowe, for carrying away his goods at Wike and Little Dartmouth (Cal. Pat. Rolls 9 Ed. IIp. 503). Then again in 1329 the Bishop of Exeter ordered an enquiry into the cause of a quarrel between Robert Maloysel, vicar of St. Marychurch, and the Abbot and Convent of Torre. Consider, too, Abbot John's high-handed action at Coffinswell when he attempted to possess himself of the whole manor. His case was not strong enough, however, and the Canons had to be content with half.

A dramatic episode is recorded in D.C. folio 89a which relates how a certain Miles de Lyfton who had commited a felony in the Hundred of Winkleigh was apprehended at Dunnyngestone, which was of course a part of the Abbey lands. He was duly hanged at Exeter on Feb. 2nd, 1328.

In 1326 no less than 21 people were summoned at the Assizes at Exeter for depriving the Abbot of Torre and Andrew Treverbyn of their free tenement and 26 acres at Strete. It was proved that the Abbot and Andrew and their antecessors had held the land time out of mind. They recovered possession and 60/- indemnity. (D.C. folio 144a). Besides the Coffinswell charters the only further mention in the Exchequer Cartulary of Abbot John le Rous is an agreement with William de Combe, Abbot of Dunkeswell. (189).

It seems that the last years of this Abbot were clouded by ill health, for in 1316 he granted general powers to represent the Abbey in all matters of business to T. de Plympton, cellarer, and to Master John de Hurbertone, clerk. The former had already represented the Abbot at St. Paul's Cathedral in April of the same year. Again in the following year John le Rous wrote to the Archbishop of Canterbury saying that owing to grave infirmity he could not attend at St. Paul's; we have no means of knowing whether he recovered from this illness or whether from then onwards until his death in 1330 he was an invalid.

Between the years 1305-1323 Parliamentary Writs show that Abbot John le Rous was summoned as follows:—

1305, summoned to Parliament at Westminster on Tuesday in Fifteen days of the Purification, Feb. 16th. (33 Ed. I).

1307, summoned to attend Parliament at Carlisle in eight days of St. Hilary, Jan. 20th. (35 Ed. I).

1307, his name entered on the Roll of Parliament accordingly.

1307, summoned to Parliament at Northampton in fifteen days of St. Michael, Oct. 13th. (1 Ed. II).

1309, summoned to Parliament at Westminster in the month of Easter, March 4th. (2 Ed. II).

1311, summoned to Parliament at London, on Sunday next after Feast of St. Laurence, Aug. 8th. (4 Ed. II).

1312, summoned to Parliament at Lincoln on Sunday next after Feast of St. Mary Magdalene, July 23rd. (5 Ed. II).

1312, summoned to Parliament at Westminster by Prorogation on Sunday after Assumption, Aug. 20th. (6 Ed. II).

1316, certified, pursuant to writ tested at Cliston, 5th March, as Lord of the townships of Aveton Abbots cum Engleborne Prior' and Diddisham in the County of Devon. (9 Ed. II).

1322, requested to raise as many men at arms and foot soldiers as he can to march against the rebels or adherents of the Earl of Lancaster. Muster at Coventry on first Sunday in Lent, Feb. 28th. (15 Ed. II).

1323, commanded to attend provincial Council of Clergy to be held at Lincoln before the Archbishop of Canterbury. (16 Ed. II).

1323, specially commanded to appear in the Convocation to be held at St. Paul's in Eight days of St. Hilary, Jan. 20th. (17 Ed. II).

1323, discharged from attending the above-mentioned Convocation. (17 Ed. II).

10. SIMON DE PLYMPTON. We know from Bishop Grandisson's Register that this Abbot ruled from 1330-1345. The cartularies give us no clue whatever as to the character of Simon de Plympton and he remains a much more unsubstantial figure than his predecessor. It must be remembered that by this time the various estates in the hands of the Canons had been theirs for well over a century, and so important charters recording the giving of land to the Abbey are seldom to be found. There was one very important gift of water, however, which was given by William de Cokyntone during the time of this Abbot, (see charters 268 & 270). Through this gift he granted William burial in the Abbey church and a chantry both there and in the chapel of Cokyntone.

There are certain happenings in Abbot Simon's time which are well worth recording. For instance in 1331 Bishop Grandisson granted the Abbot licence to celebrate mass in the chapel of St. Clarus at Dartmouth for the benefit of old and infirm parishioners. This was of course prior to the time of the building of the chapel which grew into the present St. Saviour's church, and was done to save the arduous climb to the parish church of Townstall; it was to become an issue a few years later, however.

In 1340 the Abbot, together with John Raleghe of Beaudeport, John de Chuddeleghe, John de Sudbury and Ambrose de Novo Burgo were commissioned to collect a tax of one ninth from sheep, lambs and fleeces. (D.C. folio 93a). In the following year the Abbot is recorded to have attended the funeral of Hugh de Courtenay, Earl of Devon, in the church of the convent at Cowick. (D.C. 93b).

The conditions of a lease of $6\frac{1}{4}$ acres of the Sanctuary land at Torre are interesting; John atte Roche, the lessee, was to pay 2/- annually, and to render one day's ploughing and the best beast as heriot. (D.C. folio 141a).

In 1338 John de Ferrers made an agreement with Simon, Abbot of Torre, to pay him £8 on May 3rd next. John evidently hoped to get this debt reduced, for the very next day it is recorded that he sent the Abbot 4 casks of wine (D.C. folio 145a).

In 1341 a tax was levied by Edward II of one twentieth. The Abbot paid a total of 60s.10d. from nine parishes;—Wodebyri 6s.2d (for Greendale), Clistoune 13s.4d (for Ashclyst), Clayhangre 6s. (for Dunnyngestone), Exmu' 4s.5d (for Shillyngeford), Heanoak 14d. (Various farms), Yuddeford 2s. (for Holrigge), Wolbeburgh 8s.5d, Seyntmarichurche 12s (for Daccombe and Coffinswell) and Blakeavetone 7s.4d. (D.C. folio 146a).

A final item of a certain whimsical interest concerns one Richard, son of Richard Carre. To him Brother Simon, Abbot of Torre, granted his subsistence which consisted of three loaves called 'free', a gallon of beer or a pottle of good cider and a dish of meat from the kitchen just as the free servants receive: and 4s. for his clothing at Michaelmas. From this we learn that there were servants at the Abbey and that they had the status of freemen. Richard may have been a gardener or farm worker who had made himself indispensable to the Abbot, so he made a solemn undertaking to grant him daily subsistence. (D.C. 165b).

In Abbot Simon's final days occurred the ridiculous episode at Dartmouth which concerned Hugh, the charlatan, self-styled bishop of Damascus. It is impossible to think that Abbot Simon did not know of his escapades at Dartmouth and it is even probable that he deceived the Abbot, and with his approval carried out a pseudo consecration of the chapel which the parishioners of Townstall had built without the Bishop of Exeter's permission.

11. JOHN GRAS. Poor John Gras had a stormy passage at the opening of his term of office. His election was unpopular because Richard de Cotelforde, the Prior, had been elected by the Canons themselves. The strange story of Prior Richard de Cotelforde is related in its own chapter and need not be told again here. It is sufficient to bear in mind the sequence of events as they affected Abbot John Gras. He received the benediction of Bishop Grandisson on Dec. 21st, 1345 (Register p. 1002), but later was withdrawn from Torre, most probably at the instigation of the Abbot of Welbeck, and was followed by:

12. JOHN. This Abbot received the benediction of Bishop Grandisson on May 21st, 1349 (Register p. 1002), and we know nothing more than this about him. He was evidently sent to Torre by command of the Order to restore peace there. No doubt the Premonstratensians, who must have known all the ins and outs of de Cotelforde's bid for the Abbacy, decided that to appoint a new Abbot was the only solution to the problem. Probably they were right, for we hear of no more trouble during the next two years. Unfortunately Abbot John either died at the end of this time or was removed to make way for a restoration of Abbot John Gras, when it appeared that all trouble was at an end. I think it quite probable that he died of the Black Death which was so virulent in Devon just at this time.

John Gras was reinstated at the end of 1351, receiving a Letter of Testimony from the diocesan on Dec. 6th of that year. This was the turbulent year when a mob broke into the Abbey, apparently at de Cotelforde's bidding. All this trouble began no doubt because of John Gras's reappearance. There then followed the imprisonment and murder of de Cotelforde, after which peace seems to have come at last to the unhappy Community. Abbot John then ruled on for some nineteen or twenty years. Unfortunately we have no record in the Bishop's Register of the Benediction of his successor.

We may now turn to consider the administrative side of Abbot John Gras's rule. During his first period there is record of letters patent to the Abbot from King Edward III. granting permission to crenellate the walls of the Abbey. (D.C. folio 93a). Such crenellation still survives today on the Mohun Gateway, whilst that on the west wing may also date from this period, though it is quite possible that this is of later date. This elementary fortification of the buildings must have been really necessary or the King would never have given permission for its construction. The Abbey was wide open to attack from marauders landing from hostile vessels. During the wars with the French the danger would be particularly acute. In November of the same year Abbot John applied to the King for the removal of the distraint under which the Abbey had lain since 1340—the levy being one ninth on all flocks. The appeal was granted owing to the position of the Abbey on the seashore and the intolerable burden borne by the Abbot and Convent for the defence of the bay in time of war. (D.C. folio 93a and b). This shows how very real the danger was and how it was thoroughly appreciated by those in authority.

During the period of calm which followed John Gras's reinstatement there was concluded a most important piece of business. This was the final stage of the transfer of the manor of Tormohun to the Canons. All that need be stated here is that on Oct. 2nd, 1363, John de Mohun, Lord of Dunster, quitclaimed to John, Abbot of Torre, all demands which he or anyone in his name could make in the manor of Tormohun. This important charter was "given at Torre Mohun" and was no doubt the last time that a de Mohun visited the manor. A chantry for John de Mohun and his wife Johanna had been granted as early as 1351, but it was not until May 6th, 1370, that King Edward's Licence in Mortmain was given. This was just about the time when John Gras is thought to have died, and one cannot but hope he lived long enough to see the final act of the transfer of the manor carried through. Whilst his rule saw the most disgraceful scenes of violence take place within the walls of the Abbey, yet there is no reason to suppose that Abbot John was in any way to blame. His can have been no easy office to hold. He was elevated to the Abbot's chair against the wishes of his brother Canons, and placed over the Prior to whom he had been subordinate. It was small wonder that trouble occurred. To be willing to return to Torre in 1351 showed great courage, and he must have risked his life to do so. But he outlived all his troubles and latterly saw his house, through the acquisition of the manor of Tormohun, become affluent to a degree undreamed of in its early days. The standing of the Abbot of course was greatly enhanced, for he now become Lord of the manor as well as Abbot, thereby wielding authority over secular affairs of the district in which his Abbey stood. It was John Gras's privilege to help bring all this about. In spite of all his early troubles I see him as one of the outstanding Abbots of Torre.

Other items which are recorded of Abbot John's period are (1) the lease of Glascombe to William atte fenne (241) and (2) a strange item which is recorded in the Cal. Pat. Rolls (37 Edward III, p. 369). A certain Guy Bryene complained to a Commission that John, Abbot of Torre, George de Grymeston, William de Norton and Geoffrey Baroun (all Canons) and several others took away a ship of his worth 500 li. at Dartmouth and carried away his goods. Nothing more is heard of this strange accusation and we do not know the result of the enquiry.

13. JOHN DE BERKADONE. John de Berkadone was the first Abbot to assume office knowing that his house was by that time the richest of the Premonstratensian monasteries in England. The new Abbot, who had long been a member of the Community, had played an important part in bringing about the transfer of the manor of Torre into the Abbey's hands. He was one of the clerics in whom it was temporarily vested. Watkin thinks that he came from Barkingdon, a farm in Staverton, known then as Berkedone. If this was the case then he was a Devonian and his family was doubtless well known and respected in this part of the county.

After his succession he appears very little in the Cartularies. The only charters in which he is particularly mentioned is 194, which dates from 1372. This was the important agreement between the Bishop of Exeter and the Abbot of Torre on the one hand, and the Vicar of Townstall and the Corporation of Dartmouth on the other, which established the present church of St. Saviour on a legal footing. In Bishop Brantyngham's Register (vol. I p. 33) Abbot John de Berkadone is mentioned as patron of Townstalle.

In 1376 an inspeximus was made once more of the Abbey's title to its churches; it was carried out by Bishop Brantyngham. This was recorded by a public notary, Robert Warthel, and entered in the Bishop's Register. The original is in the Dartmouth Municipal Collection at the City Library, Exeter.

In Bishop Brantyngham's Register (p. 156) it is recorded that Thomas Warloke, vicar of Hennock, complained that he could not live on the stipend which the Abbot of Torre allowed him. This cry from the heart has a distinctly modern flavour; there is no mention of the Abbot having given him any more, however.

On March 8th, 1382, Abbot John de Berkadone was appointed as one of a commission set up to establish quiet in the country. Apart from these few facts no more is at present known about this Abbot who lived probably until 1382, and ruled for about 12 years.

14. WILLIAM NORTON. This Abbot is known to have held office from 1382-1412 and his long rule of 30 years saw the beginning of the 15th C. There are several things which we can see or handle today which bring us very close to William Norton. In the first place at Bradworthy, where he was vicar for nine years, the priest's doorway in the chancel is still there. By this door he must have entered and left the church many times. Close beside it is a rather unusual piscina which he also used, whilst at the end of the church is the old Norman font at which he must constantly have officiated. In East Ogwell church his grave coverstone is still to be seen.

There is no mention of him in the Exchequer Cartulary, but Dublin Cartulary (folio 2b) records that on Dec. 27th, 1408, William Beare did homage and fealty to Lord W. Norton, Abbot of Torre, for the land which W. holds in the domain of Aysclyst. Also on Sept. 29th, 1409, Thomas Boway did likewise for the land and tenements which he held at Schillingforde (ibid.). It is also recorded that on Dec. 28th, 1393, at Dartington, the Earl of Huntyngdon, Chamberlain of England, acted as arbitrator between the Abbot of Torre and John Hawley, Mayor of Dartmouth, concerning payments to the chapel of Dartmouth.

Watkin records the visit of William Courtenay, Archbishop of Canterbury, to the monasteries in Cornwall in 1384. He asked to spend the night of August 2nd at Torre Abbey on his way thither "if the Abbot wishes". Did Abbot Norton stand on his dignity as a Premonstratensian on this occasion and refuse to receive the Archbishop? Certainly there is no record of any such visit.

On March 4th, 1411, at Exeter Assizes, a suit between "Wm. Norton and the burgesses of Newton Abbot" was heard. It concerned St. Leonard's chapel. It was decided that whilst the Abbey owned the free tenure of the land on which the chapel and market stood, the public was entitled to free use of the chapel. (Mon. Dioc. Exon, p. 171).

An interesting document concerning Townstall, drawn up by Bishop Stafford, states that the stipend of the vicar is to be 20 Li. per annum—20s. fine to be paid to the Bishop should it be fifteen days in arrears. The vicar is to have the house and garden which of old belonged to the vicar, also funeral offerings both at Tunstall and the chapel of Dartmouth, also tithes of cheese, geese and pigs. The Abbot and Convent to repair desks in the chancel and books for matins, because they were rectors (Powderham Records, 853) Dated July 27th, 1400.

It seems that the thirty years of Abbot Norton's rule were peaceful ones, and little happened to hinder the day to day curriculum of the Canons.

15. MATTHEW YERDE. He received the episcopal benediction on July 19th, 1412, and his rule—one of the shortest, lasted for just under two years. Nothing is recorded of him in either Cartulary. Prior to his election he had been vicar of Townstall, resigning in 1396. The only further mention of him which has so far come to light is a lease of land at Townstall on Nov. 23rd, 1412. (Dartmouth Pre-reformation p. 94).

16. WILLIAM MYCHEL. In the chapel at Clyst the Bishop of Exeter gave this Abbot his benediction on March 18th, 1414. (Register p. 214), and we know that his successor took office in Jan. 1442; Abbot Mychel must therefore have died in 1441 after ruling for 27 years. This was quite a long span, but little is recorded of the doings of this Abbot or his successor, John Lacy. One can only presume that the Abbey under them pursued its way in peace and prosperity.

It is pointed out elsewhere what a large number of the Canons who were raised to the Abbot's chair had previously been vicars of Townstall. The promising men were evidently sent to the busy seaport town of Dartmouth to gain experience. It was also close at hand, so that the Canon who was vicar could always be in close touch with the Abbey, and also keep an eye on affairs in the large manor of Avetone. Abbot Mychel was vicar there from 1406, apparently until his appointment as Abbot.

There is a mention in the Bishop's Register and also in Tot. (p. 347) that William, Abbot of Torre, and John, Prior of Tywardraith, are still in arrears to the Papal Collector.

17. JOHN LACY. This Abbot took office on Jan. 30th, 1442, and died on Nov. 24th, 1455. Like his predecessor he was vicar of Townstall up to the time of his succession.

All that is recorded of him is that he attended four Convocations of the clergy in 1442, 1444, 1449, and 1453. On account of this we may assume that he was in demand for his administrative ability. He was one of eight Abbots and eight Priors summoned to attend, and it therefore looks as though he was highly thought of and his opinions valued on church matters. It is also possible that he was a relative of Edmund Lacy, then Bishop of Exeter, and so he may have been brought forward by the Bishop himself. But of this we cannot be sure.

At the very end of his life the precious records of the Visitations of the Abbey begin. The Abbot's death, we read, was reported by special messenger to the Abbot of Welbeck on Nov. 24th, 1455. It was usually the business of the Prior to undertake this duty, but on this occasion another Canon, William Gambon, was sent because the Prior was detained by "various great and arduous matters of business concerning their church". We have no clue as to what was going on at Torre at the time, and we have no inkling as to what the great and arduous matters can have been.

So in 1455 yet another of the long line of Abbots died, and was no doubt buried beside his predecessors in the Abbey church.

18. RICHARD CADE. With the advent of Richard Cade in 1455 the final epoch of the Abbey's life is approached, for this Abbot had only two successors. Yet throughout his abbacy not a ripple of trouble appeared on the scene, and it would have been a more than astute reader of the times who could have predicted that in less than a century Abbot Cade's Abbey would be a deserted ruin.

His rule began badly, for a letter to him from the Abbot of St. Radegund's Abbey which is included in Col. Ang. Prem. folio 64, and quoted later, states that his rule lacked firmness, that strife and discord abounded, and that the Abbey was dilapidated. He was summarily ordered to set his house in order or else render up his seal and retire on 20 marks. Three days later the Abbot of St. Radegund's wrote to the Abbot of Welbeck asking for letters patent enabling him to go to Torre to settle matters himself on the spot. We have no evidence as to what happened, but things were evidently settled in a satisfactory manner for Abbot Cade ruled on until 1482. Later Visitations report much grounds for complaint against certain of the Canons, and one gets the impression that this Abbot was no disciplinarian.

Towards the end of his life, however, there seem to have been much less grounds for complaint. In 1482 Bishop Redmayne praises the excellently constructed buildings which formed the monastery, and one cannot but wonder whether an extensive programme of rebuilding had recently taken place. It would be at just the period when such things might have been expected. At this same Visitation the impression is given that Abbot Cade was a sick and ageing man, for the bretheren are exhorted to minster to him when sick with filial diligence and are not to dispute his orders.

One very important thing which was settled during Abbot Cade's time was an agreement with the Abbot of St. Dogmael's Abbey over the chapel of Cockington. It will be seen in charters 259 and 262 how Torre Abbey acquired this chapel in the 13th C. from St. Dogmael's Abbey, paying 5/- per annum for the sanctuary land which went with it. Whether this payment had been kept up for some 250 years we cannot tell, but it rather looks as though it had lapsed, because the Canons paid St. Dogmael's in 1468 what was in those days a considerable sum—£63-6-8. The Abbot of this far away monastery in Pembrokeshire seems to have been laying claim to tithes and offerings from the chapel and had despatched an attorney to Torre, John Prise by name. To settle all legal disputes, which if dragged into court might have gone on for years, Abbot Cade wisely settled the whole matter for an agreed sum. It was an expensive but no doubt diplomatic move and showed great wisdom on the Abbot's part; from that time Torre Abbey's possession of the chapel of Cockington, its tithes, oblations and lands was an unassailable fact.

Richard Cade ruled for 27 years, but there is little else worth recording of his life and times. The chapter on the Visitations of the Abbey fortunately gives us a vivid picture of the life of the Community in his day. The names of the Canons are all there for us to read, and the petty troubles and squabbles of the day to day life of a 15th C. monk are all recorded and set to rights by the Visitor. Abbot Cade's tombstone is one of the three preserved at East Ogwell church. Through the Visitations we get a picture of a man who at first was timid and lacking in authority. As time went on, however, he seems to have learnt the knack of managing his Community and emerges as a dignified and respected churchman.

19. THOMAS DYARE. Thomas Dyare was the last of the Abbots of Torre to complete his term of office and be buried with due solemnity in his abbey church. He had formerly been vicar of Bradworthy and it seems that he was recalled to Torre, where in the Visitations of 1478 and 1482 he is mentioned as Prior. He ruled from c. 1482 (final mention of Richard Cade) to 1523–a span of at least 40 years, and it was most appropriate that the last Abbot to complete his life at Torre should also have ruled the longest.

In 1488 he travelled to Durford Abbey (Hants.) where Bishop Redmayne conducted a Visitation by proxy. The sub-Prior accompanied the Abbot on this occasion as procurator for the community. A curious fact came to light at the Visitation of 1494, for a certain Canon named Colynson was there, having deserted his own Abbey of Welbeck. Bishop Redmayne had no sympathy at all for this desertion and sentenced the luckless Canon to 40 days of heavy punishment; he was then to be kept for three years in custody at his own house, unless given dispensation in the meantime.

One of the Powderham Records bears witness to a transaction between Abbot Thomas and ten of the parishioners of Torre, whereby he granted them land adjacent to the Parish Church of Torre for the use of the church. The position of this land is discussed in the chapter on the village of Torre. It measures 70 ft. x 24 ft., and the site was used for the erection of the church house. The agreement is dated May 21st, 1520.

In 1503 Abbot Dyare was among eight abbots and five priors summoned to Convocation. Nothing dramatic or indeed outstanding appears to have occurred during this long abbacy. The Abbey seemed to be enjoying a kind of Indian Summer of prosperity and tranquillity, and one supposes that when finally he died in 1523 he had no inkling that the end of his beloved Abbey was so near.

Abbot Dyare's elaborate tombstone is in East Ogwell church beneath the chancel step. It is the most ambitious in design of the three stones there, and still shows traces of colour. It has unfortunately become sadly mutilated by the passage of the feet of four centuries of villagers, however, and the inscription is well nigh illegible.

So in 1523 the last complete abbacy drew to its end.

20. SIMON REDE. We now come to the unfortunate Simon Rede, the last of the Abbots of Torre. His rule began just as that of any of the other Abbots, and he was blessed by Thomas Chard, a suffragan to Bishop Veysey, in August, 1523. We cannot tell how soon it was that the Canons realised that it would be only a matter of time before the affairs of their house were likely to fall into the King's hand; but from 1529 we can be sure that Abbot Rede was quite certain of the coming dissolution—the reason being that from then onwards, like other heads of monasteries, he began to lease the Abbey lands one after another for long terms.

Abbot Simon's leases were as follows:—

1529. Chief messuage and dwellinghouse of manor of Ashclyst and the barton lands. £4-0-12d. (Powderham Records p. 857).

1529. Right of way in a lane in Kingswear, 99 years. 14d.

1535. Tenement in Clifton Dartmouth, 99 years. 18s.

1535. Close in Barton lands at Wolborough. 3s.

1536. Closes at Newton Abbot. 20s.

1537. Parsonages of Buckland Brewer, with chapels of Bulkworthy and East Putford.

1537. Bradworthy church and chapel of Pancrasweek.

Shebbear church and chapel of Sheepwash, with all the manors etc., excepting Watercombe at Bradworthy. £46 per annum.

1538. Closes in Dartmouth. 24d.

At Townstall tithes of corn, hay, wool, calves, lambs, eggs, offerings, provisions, tithes, oblations, fishes etc. Exceptions pygs, gose, tithings and butter which went to the vicar. £11-13-4d.

Land at Wolborough. £4-17-8d.

Tenement in parish of St. Pawle of Excetter. For 63 years 6s 8d.

". . . And the said Geoffrey (the lessee) shall loge the said Abbot at such time that he comyth to the said cytie and his servants as longe as it shall plese hym in the said tenement at the cost and charge of the said Geffery . . ."

1539. Court Place and Court garden at Daccombe. 11s 8d.
Bartonland at Daccombe. 26s 8d.
Rectory, great tithes and lands at Hennock. £10.

1538. Land at Daccombe. 26s 8d.
Closes and meadows at Wolborough. £7-13-4d.

But the Abbot had done better for himself than might appear on paper, for as early as 1531 he had himself nominated vicar of Townstall. Actually the presentation was made by Nicholas Kirkham to whom the Abbot had granted the advowson of the church. All this was done apparently with the full approval of Bishop Veysey, who instituted him on July 7th, 1531. So that when on February 23rd, 1539, the sinister figure of Sir William Petre appeared at Torre, all Simon Rede had to do was to sign the order for the suppression of his Abbey, saddle his horse and ride to Dartmouth, there to spend the remainder of his life. No one knows how the suppression of an Abbey such as Torre affected the neighbourhood in which it stood. That the whole life of the manor would be thrown out of gear goes without saying. One would much like to know how the tenants regarded the Canons in their latter years. Were they looked up to with deep affection? Or were the people of the locality just longing to see the power of the Abbey brought low, and the Abbot humbled to the dust? If the latter were the case then the Canons went forth into a hostile world. No one knows whether they had to quit the shelter of their house on the very day of Petre's visit, or whether they were allowed to remain until such time as they could make their own arrangements. One wonders too, what happened to the sick and aged who were housed at the Abbey. Perhaps they had been found homes long before; but however it was it must have been a time not only of grief but of great hardship too.

Simon Rede remained at Townstall church until his death in 1555/6. He expressed a wish to be buried in the church at Stoke Fleming. This was a strange whim, and one cannot but wonder if he was on bad terms with his parishioners. His position there during those 15 or 16 years of his ministry cannot have been anything but difficult. His loss of prestige when he descended from the office of Abbot to parish priest few men could have borne with dignity. We must not blame him for his attempts to secure his own future in the way he did.

There are indications that he was a generous man, for he granted pensions and annuities to several gentlemen just before the suppression. No doubt they were particular friends of the Abbey who, he thought, deserved recognition. It is remarkable to notice, too, that these sums were guaranteed later by the Court of Westminster as "bona fide and without fraud". In this way the Abbot had granted to Sir Thos Denysse 40s. from the manor of North Shillingford; to Thomas Carewe and to John his son 40s. To Sir John Fulford and Andree his son 40s, by letters patent. To Humfrey Colles, esq., a rent of 20s and to Thos. Wolcote, gentleman, 20s. by letters patent.

From 1547-53 the Abbot, as vicar of Townstall, must have had to contend with the Protestantism of Edward VI, and one wonders how he coped with the great changes in the church. The fact that he never got any kind of preferment seems to point to the fact that he did not support the new regime. Then in Mary's reign all was reversed again, but it would be too late for Simon who was no doubt an old man by that time with only a couple years to live.

His will, dated Sept. 23rd, 1554, was proved on March, 15th, 1555/6. "In the name of God amen the xxiij day of September the yere of our Lord God a thousand fyve hundreth Liiij, Symon Rede vycar of Townstall beying perfyt of mynde and hole of remembrance renounces all formall wylls before this day by me made and do make my testament contaynyng my hole trewe and last wyll in this manner following. Ffirst I geve my sole to almighty God and my body to be buried within the church of Stokeflemyng. Item i bequeth to the before namyd church of Stokeflemyng xxd. Item to the church of Townstall iijs. iiijd. Also I do geve and bequeth to Mr John Predyaux and Sir Thomas Ffrynd, prist, the £xxxiijj vjs. iiijd the which Nicholas Adams of Dartmouth receaved for me for my pencion of Mr Mylleworth for which said some of xxxiijli. vjs. viijd. onely doo make the said John Predyaux and Thomas ffrynd mine executors and for none other cause or intent. The rest of my goods unbequeth I give and bequeth to John ffurseman my servant whome I do make my hole executor of all my goods moveable and unmoveable and he to dispose it as seemth hem best for the welth of my sole and to this berith wytnes Robert Fayer junior Vynssent Deyman and Richard Ball with others".

All who have patiently followed the fortunes of the Abbots of Torre thus far should complete the picture of them by making a pilgrimage to the church at Stoke Fleming where Simon Rede, the last of the line, was buried. The church is set high above the sea and its noble tower has for centuries been a landmark for shipping. I think Simon must have loved this spot, and I do not wonder that he requested to be buried here. The interior of the church was thoroughly restored by Victorians, and the floors are now covered with tiles of this period. Beneath the base of the tower, however, are a group of old burial stones which must once have been in the aisles. One or two of these are very similar to those at East Ogwell both in size and shape. Although the oldest dates from the 17th century, one cannot but wonder if the stones may not have been re-used. I should much like to turn them over, just to see if by a remote chance one of them may have covered the last Abbot of Torre.

6

Lord William Brewer, Founder of Torre Abbey

The birthplace of Lord William Brewer, the founder of Torre Abbey, cannot at the present time be established with any degree of certainty, for among the old writers there are varying accounts of it. The most probable places seem to be Mottisfont, Ilsham, or Torre itself. At the first he established his second great religious foundation, and some consider that this was because there were strong family connections with the district. Other authorities state that his father, Henry Brewer, had purchased Ilsham before Lord William's birth; yet there is contrary evidence that Lord William himself purchased Ilsham in 1180 for 31 Marks in silver (Dugdale, Baronage, vol. I, p. 700). So if he was born there then the family must have parted with Ilsham soon after. It might then have been a second purchase that took place in 1180. This does not seem very likely, and so we are thrown back upon Torre itself as the birthplace, remembering that this theory has the authority of Camden. There are, moreover, two indirect facts in support: (1) that the manor of Torre is nowhere mentioned among the many gifts of lands which Lord William received from the various kings he served, and (2) William the Younger, his son, is definitely shown to have lived at the Courthouse of Torre by the evidence of charter 11. When Lord William became a prominent statesman it would have been impossible to live so far away from his activities at court. It is therefore most likely that his eldest son at the time of his marriage took over the courthouse. All this points to the manor of Torre being the family patrimony, so it is not unlikely that Lord William himself was born there.

His father, Henry, does not seem to have been a man of mark, but William, who adopted the law as his profession, must have risen to high places at an early age. Indeed his rise must have been unusually rapid, for by 1179/80 we find him Sheriff of Devon (Pole, 3758) and also, by the latter part of King Henry II's reign, an Itinerant Justice. His rise was quite possibly due to services rendered to the royal family, for he was the friend and confidant of four successive kings, Henry II, Richard I, John, and Henry III. Indeed, the founding of Torre Abbey was expressly for the purpose of prayers to be offered for the repose of the souls of King Richard I and his father, King Henry. This fact the Foundation Charter clearly states. Throughout these troublous reigns Lord William kept his place at the side of the king, making himself indispensable to each successive monarch; and whichever way the wind blew he trimmed his sails accordingly. Such a policy doubtless made him many enemies.

At his worst he must have been an unscrupulous time-server, at his best a faithful servant of the crown. Matthew Paris describes him as "inexorable and cruel". His policy, however, paid rich dividends, for grateful monarchs raised him to the baronage and showered estates upon him, until he became a very rich landowner. In spite of his enemies, Lord William lived to a ripe old age. He ended his days in peace at Dunkeswell

Abbey in the year 1226. There is no record of his birth, but as his life was a long one it was probably c. 1150.

It is not easy to reconstruct the character of one who lived so long ago. We can only assess Lord William on his achievements as a statesman. I see him as a shrewd, hard-headed man of affairs; one who was well able to dictate the terms of important treaties, carry through the delicate negotiations required to ransom a captive king, or play a prominent part in maintaining a throne which was anything but stable. Indeed if he had one chink in his armour it was his almost fanatical devotion to the monarchy for its own sake; a devotion which was quite undismayed by the poor characters of some of the kings he served.

By the time that King Richard I departed upon his ill-fated Crusade in 1189, Lord William was already well established as a figure of importance in affairs of state, for he was appointed then as one of the four Justices in whose hands the King left the government of the country. His tenure of this office was no sinecure, for it was not long before one of the four, Hugh, Bishop of Durham, was displaced by the Chancellor, William Longchamp, Bishop of Ely. The latter was an insolent and unpopular man, and on account of his high-handed ways was displaced on the King's orders by the Archbishop of Rouen in 1191. Lord William must have acted strongly against Longchamp for his name was high on the list of those whom the latter threatened to excommunicate.

Brewer's next important undertaking was the arrangement for the ransom of the king who had meanwhile been taken prisoner. In 1193 he therefore left England to discuss with the Emperor, Henry VI, the ransom of the royal captive. He arrived at Worms on July 29th of that year and arranged that the King should be released on payment of 150,000 marks in silver. In the meantime 60 young men were sent as hostages, presumably until the ransom had been paid in full, and there is a tradition that Lord William's own son, William the Younger, was one of these unfortunate young men. It has been asserted, but never proved, that Lord William in gratitude to God for his son's safe return founded Torre Abbey in 1196. Certainly the dates are in accordance with the story. The Premonstratensian Order are said to have played a part in the raising of the King's ransom and in the freeing of the hostages; and this may be a clue as to why Premonstratensian Canons were established at Torre. The whole story must, I feel, be treated with caution, however, for William the Younger was definitely taken prisoner by the King of France in April, 1204, and his father had to borrow 1,000 marks from King John as a part of his ransom. As there is such a similarity between the two stories, there is a likelihood that they have become mixed over the centuries.

Lord William was later sent abroad once more to arrange peace terms with King Philip of France. On his return those who had proceeded against the Chancellor were deprived of their shrievalties; but they were soon appointed to others. Stubbs (Const. Hist. i, 503) says "it was as if the King, although he could not dispense with their service, wished to show his disapproval". Brewer's shrievalties eventually included those of Devon, Oxford, Bucks., Berks., Notts., and Derby, so he could not grumble at the eventual outcome.

During King John's reign he continued to occupy a place at the King's right hand. In an attempt to reconcile John and Archbishop Langton in 1206, he was one of those who guaranteed the Archbishop a safe-conduct out of the country. When the stormy years of the Interdict blew up he strongly upheld the king and is mentioned by Wendover (iii, 238) as one of the King's evil advisers who cared for nothing but to please him.

Extortions from clergy and monks took place at his suggestion. He was one of those, however, who signed the Charter whereby King John surrendered his crown into the hands of the Pope. But in 1215 he refused to join the Barons against the king. Nevertheless after their entry into London he was bound, with other ministers of the Crown, to sign Magna Carta. His heart was not really in the business, however, and when war broke out he became one of the leaders left by the King to watch the baronial forces, cut off their supplies and ravage their lands. Present at Henry III's Coronation, he was also at the founding of Worcester Cathedral, and in 1221 he sat as baron of the Exchequer.

A new epoch now began for the ageing statesman who became the favourite of the young king. We are told that his influence was not for good. In 1223 Archbishop Langton and the Lords of the council asked the king to assent to Magna Carta. Brewer answered for the king saying, "The liberties which you ask for ought not to be observed for they were extorted by force". The indignant Archbishop rebuked him in these words, "William, if you loved the king you would not disturb the kingdom". Seeing Langton's anger the king yielded.

Of Lord William's domestic life we know nothing. He married Beatrice de Valle and by her had seven children, two sons and five daughters. She was of Norman descent and the possibility that she had previously been married to Reginald, Earl of Cornwall, need not concern us here. She was also a cousin of Henry de Pomerio, apparently, through her mother. It is through the evidence of Charter 9 that we can be certain that she brought Lord William the manor of Coletone—as a part of her dowry, very probably. This manor her family had held from the de Nonants. It was apparently a custom of the times for a daughter to have as her dowry estates which had belonged to her mother. Reichel identifies Coletone as the Pomeroy manor of Domesday, and suggests that a daughter of the house of Pomeroy may have married a de Valle, these being the parents of Beatrix who in her turn had Coletone as her dowry. She is mentioned in the Cartulary as "Foundress" and she there (Charter 67) confirms her husband's gifts to Torre Abbey. She was thus clearly regarded by the Canons as co-founder with her husband.

Both William the Younger and his brother Richard died childless, and so Lord William's vast estates descended to his five daughters. It is small wonder that these rich heiresses all made advantageous marriages.

The acts of piety of their by no means scrupulous father were many, for in addition to Torre, he founded the abbeys of Mottisfont and Dunkeswell, and the Hospital of St. John the Baptist at Bridgewater. This latter was for the maintenance of 13 poor, sick people, besides "religious and pilgrims". (Dugdale Mon. vi 663).

In October, 1224, Lord William brought his public life to a very definite conclusion, for he renounced all his wordly possessions in favour of his one surviving son, William the Younger, who did homage for them to the King at the time. He then retired to Dunkeswell Abbey where he ended his days as a monk. He died just over two years later on Nov. 24th, 1226. His wife predeceased him in 1217. They were eventually buried before the high altar at Dunkeswell Abbey. Between their tomb and the altar a candle was to be kept burning for ever. It marked the giving of the land of Lincumb (Ilfracombe) to Dunkeswell Abbey. After the Dissolution of the Abbey the church gradually disappeared —destroyed both by time and the quarrying of its stones. The tomb seems to have been left undisturbed however, until the present church was built on the site. Two huge coffins were then uncovered and considered to be those of Lord William and his wife, no doubt on account of the position which they occupied. The coffin believed to have been

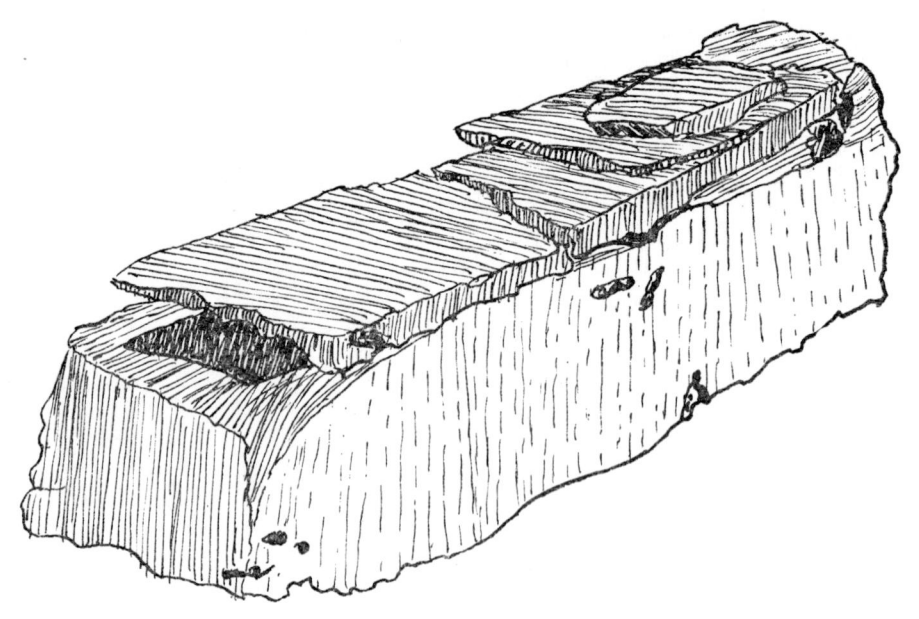

Dunkeswell Abbey. Reputed Coffin of Lord William Brewer.   *D. Seymour.*

Lord William's, together with its cover of Purbeck stone, was placed in the north-west corner of the interior of the new church, where it still is. On the wall above is a tablet which bears the following inscription: "This coffin and a similar one were found when the foundations of this church were laid. They were believed to contain the remains of the Founder of the Cistercian Abbey of Dunkeswell, Lord William de Brewer and his wife, who were buried A.D. 1226. The bones of both were reverently re-interred in the second coffin in 1842 by Mrs Simcoe, wife of Lt.-Gen. Simcoe, who was a direct descendent of Lord William de Brewer. This coffin was moved into the church and the inscription placed by Mrs Simcoe of Walford Lodge 1914".

The opinion of Watkin that the Brewers were buried in the centre of the Chapter House may be safely disregarded in the light of the facts quoted above.

So this powerful statesman—the friend and adviser of four Plantagenet kings—rests amid the peaceful hills of East Devon, in a distant and remote spot, as yet quite untouched by the clamour of the 20th century.

7

William the Younger

No history of Torre Abbey would be complete without an account of Lord William's elder son who was buried in the place of honour before the high altar in the Abbey church. He sometimes describes himself in our charters as William Brewer junior, and so the title of "William the Younger" has attached itself to him. The date of his birth is unknown, but considering that his father was certainly not born later than 1150, then it is unlikely that he was born prior to 1170, possibly a little later. His marriage to Johanna, the daughter of William Fitz-Baldwin, was childless, and on his death in 1232 the manor of Torre came to his sister Alicia, who had married Reginald (1) de Mohun. So it was through this marriage that the de Mohuns succeeded the de Brewers at Torre.

Of William's early life but little is known. By the time of King John he was evidently much in Court for he witnesses charters for the King during the years 1212-1214. In the latter year, together with his younger brother, Richard, and Alan de Bokelonde, he was in charge of the castle of Hastings. His capture by the King of France in 1204 and subsequent ransom has already been mentioned. It will be seen that there is quite sufficient evidence to show that William the Younger in early manhood was busy in the King's service just as his father was.

He is of interest to us as witness to the Foundation charter of Torre Abbey where his name appears low on the list of signatories. Of more importance are the charters which he himself gives. These are (7) which is a quitclaim and confirmation to the Canons of all the gifts of land etc., which his father and mother had made to them in the Foundation Charter, (8) a gift of the lands of Ilsham and Coletone together with the meadow of Cokyngtone, (11) a gift, together with his body, of water from the spring of St. Petroc, (182) a confirmation of his father's gift of the church of Bokelonde.

It has already been told how he came into his inheritance in 1224, for in that year his father renounced all his possessions in his favour. So at the stroke of a pen William the Younger became an exceedingly wealthy man, for Lord William had basked in the royal favour all his life, and the royal family certainly had not let him go unrewarded. His son did not live to enjoy the family fortune for long, for he died in 1232 (Dugdale, Mon. vol. 6, p. 481).

Now it must have been much to the chagrin of the Canons of Torre that Lord William, their Founder, did not elect to be buried in their Abbey, choosing rather his other Foundation of Dunkeswell. The place of honour before the high altar, no doubt reserved for him lay empty; and so after his death charter 11 shows how they were assured that William the Younger should occupy this place. In this way the slight on the part of Lord William was somewhat mitigated. Hugh Watkin reads into this giving of the place of honour to William the Younger corroboration of the story that the Abbey had originally been founded as a thankoffering for his safe return from abroad after being a hostage.

Be this as it may, the splendid coffin of Purbeck stone still lies before the site of the high altar in the ruined Abbey church. Its coverstone is unfortunately missing. Watkin believed that this was disturbed in 1770, when the whole of the debris which covered the floor of the church was removed to fill in the former fishpond.

During the removal of bushes growing in the S.E. corner of the Chancel, the skull and bones of a human skeleton were in 1915 unearthed quite near the surface. They had obviously been taken from somewhere else and buried in a heap in a shallow hole. Watkin states that the appearance of the bones showed that they had not originally been in contact with the soil, but by their condition had evidently been contained in a sarcophagus; he had no doubt that they were the bones of William the Younger. Col. Cary had them placed in a casket of cement, and they were reinterred at the head of the empty coffin.

8

The Strange Story of Prior Richard de Cotelforde

It is now time to relate the most extraordinary episode in the Abbey's long history. From one source or another the story may be pieced together to make an understandable sequence of events. Even so there are various points and motives which are buried for ever in the mists of time. The story is one of lust for power, and it ended tragically in the violent deaths of two people. By piecing together the evidence of the Patent Rolls for the period and comparing it with Bishop Grandisson's Register a story of absorbing interest emerges. On the death of Abbot Simon de Plympton in 1345 the Prior of Torre, Richard de Cotelforde, was elected by the Canons to succeed to the Abbacy. The choice, however, was not approved by the Abbot of Welbeck, the parent house to Torre. He, or perhaps even the Canons at his direction, then elected John Gras, another Canon of Torre, to the office of Abbot. This appointment seems to have caused much discontent, rival factions springing up in the Abbey itself and apparently outside its walls as well. The years between 1345 and 1351 must therefore have been very unhappy ones. In addition to this internal strife the Black Death was raging, and discipline may have been lax. By 1349, however, a new Abbot, also named John, was appointed, receiving Bishop Grandisson's Benediction that year. Reading between the lines it seems most likely that John Gras had been removed, no doubt by the parent house of Welbeck. It looks as though internal strife had been disrupting life at the Abbey and that the Abbot of Welbeck considered the appointment of a fresh Superior was the only way to bring peace to the monastery. We know nothing of this new Abbot, but he appears to have ruled for only two years. Probably he died of the Black Death. So by 1351 Torre was again in need of an Abbot. By that time the Abbot of Welbeck evidently thought that tranquillity had been restored, for he reinstated John Gras. But this was a fatal error, for the ambitious de Cotelforde immediately made a determined bid for the Abbacy. The power of his friends must have been considerable, for he gained the backing of Edward III, received the Benediction of the Bishop of Porto and obtained a papal bull appointing him Abbot. These facts are related by Colvin in "The White Canons in England". Unfortunately he does not give his source for this information. It would appear to be borne out, however, by later events related in the Patent Rolls which state under Aug. 20th, 1351, Westminster, "Whereas brother Richard de Cotelford, lately elected to be abbot of the Premonstratensian monastery of Torre in the diocese of Exeter, after the death of Simon, late abbot of the said place, appealed to the apostolic see because brother Robert, Abbot of the monastery of Welbeck of the same order, in the diocese of York, father abbot of the monastery of Torre, refused to confirm his election and appointed one called "Gras" then canon of the monastery of Torre to be Abbot, and afterwards on the death of the said John, while the appeal was pending in the court of Rome, of his own accord ceded to the pope all right which he had in respect of his election as Abbot, and has been appointed by the pope, after admitting the cession, as abbot of Torre, as by the pope's bull to the king appears, for which cause he has made petition to the king for an indemnity lest he may hereafter be impeached on account of his prosecution of his right herein, the king has taken the Abbot, and his men, things and goods, into his special protection, in going to the said monastery, staying there and prosecuting his right as shall be for the good of the house, provided that he attempt nothing to the prejudice of the king or his crown, for one year".

This statement, it will be noticed, states that John Gras was dead. As we know from the Bishop's Register of 1351 (December) that this was not so, it is evident that his name has been confused with that of the other Abbot John, (appointed in 1349) who no doubt was indeed dead by 1351. There is certainly no reason to suppose that de Cotelforde began his high-handed intrigue prior to this year.

Meanwhile public opinion in the neighbourhood must have been all on his side, for the Patent Rolls show that by November, 1351, the Abbey was in danger of an armed attack and must have been practically in a state of seige. An entry for Nov. 6th, Westminster (p. 186) reads "Protection for two years for the abbot of Torre Mohun, on his petition showing that a large confederacy of disturbers of the peace, men at arms, and others purpose to come to the Abbey and the granges, manors and other places annexed to the Abbey, and consume and waste the goods and things therein".

I think that there is little doubt that these unruly elements had been triggered off by the Abbot of Welbeck's disastrous mistake in reappointing John Gras. That he had every reason to seek royal protection is borne out by the dramatic events which took place one night that very November. The Abbey was attacked on Nov. 20th by a riotous mob as the Patent Rolls testify. "Commission of oyer and terminer to Hugh de Courtenaye, Earl of Devon, William de Shareshull, Thomas de Courteneye, John de Stouford, Richard de Birton, John Dabernoun, Richard de Braunkescoumbe and Hugh de Aston, on complaint of John, Abbot of Torre Moun, that Adam de Fenton, Henry de Brixton, Richard Geffard, John de Falewille, Robert de Falewille, chaplain, John Hereberd, Richard Attewille, Stephen Derneford, Richard Ballood, John Vayreson, Philip Simon, Walter Verlecombe, Richard Brigge, and others broke by night his close church and treasury at Torre Moun Co. Devon, carried away his goods and assaulted his men and servants, whereby he lost their service for a great time". (Nov. 20th 1351, Westminster. p.204) "The like to Hugh de Courteneye, Earl of Devon, Thomas de Courteney, John de Stouford, Richard de Birton, John Dabernoun, Richard de Brankescombe and Hugh de Aston, touching evildoers who came armed to Torre Mohun, co. Devon, and broke by night the close, church and treasury of the abbey and carried away chalices, vestments books and other ornaments of the church and other goods of the abbot" (Nov. 25th, 1351. Westminster. p. 176). Never at any time in its history can the prestige of the Abbey have sunk to so low an ebb. The scandalous feud which had simmered for six years had at last flared up in violence on a scale which must have involved the whole district. But worse was to follow: Richard de Cotelforde was later imprisoned, and he and a certain Roger de Queryngdon were killed by one Geoffrey Gras. Where and when this took place is not stated. The Patent Rolls (June 18th, 1352, Westminster. p. 292) tell us the end of the story in these words; "Pardon at the request of Guy de Bryan, to Geoffrey Gras of Teynghebruer of the king's suit for the imprisonment of Brother Richard de Cotelford, canon of the Abbey of Torre Mohun, for the death of the same Richard and and for the death of Roger de Queryngdon, also for the robbery of two horses worth 20 li.

and other goods late of the said Roger and in his keeping at Torre Mohun and the robbery of a protection of the king sealed under the great seal, also of his keeping, and tearing asunder and breaking of the protection in contempt of the king, whereof he is indicted or appealed, and of any consequent outlawries".

Now who was Geoffrey Gras? There can be of little doubt that he was a kinsman of the Abbot, John Gras; Geoffrey had taken the law into his own hands and put an end to the man who had long disturbed the peace of the Abbey. The family of Gras owned Teignbrewer which later, taking their name, became Teigngrace. The name was no doubt even then pronounced "Grace". How did Geoffrey get away with this crime? In those days the life of an obscure and troublesome Canon did not count for much, and the terrible Black Death ravaged the population of Devon most cruelly; men had worse troubles to deal with.

Roger de Queryngdon who was also killed was evidently the bearer of the king's protection. In the Patent Rolls for 1352. p. 209 there is mention of a "grant for life to the king's late confessor, Roger de Querndon, of the order of Friars preachers, now dwelling in the Convent of Friars of his order at Beverley, who is broken by age, of 100s yearly towards his sustenance out of the farm rendered at the Exchequer by the Abbot of Hayles for the manor of Pynnokshire, co. Gloucester". It may have been this unfortunate old friar who was despatched to Torre with the king's protection. There is another Roger de Queryndon mentioned (p. 161) in the Patent Rolls. He supervised the purveyance of bacon, pigs and carcases of beeves in co. Leics. in 1351. He does not seem so likely to have carried the king's protection as the friar who was formerly connected with the king as his confessor, and would be persona grata in the royal household.

It must be pointed out that John Gras on his reinstatement as Abbot could not again receive Bishop Grandisson's Benediction, so he issued a Letter of Testimony referring back to the ceremony of 1345 instead. At this juncture it will be necessary to point out Hugh Watkin's errors in his "Abbats of Thorre" wherein he states that John Gras and John Cras are two different Abbots. The difference in spelling is I feel a point not to be pressed, for a careful examination of Grandisson's Register shows us the 1345 entry with a most doubtful—"G". The scribe's "G's" and "C's" were much alike. But at any rate in those times variants in spellings of the same name were rife; and this is borne out by a host of charters in the Cartulary. So judging by the spelling alone and the probable pronunciation as "Grace", there is little to be said for the theory of two different men with such similar names.

A more serious error was the fact that Watkin did not grasp the meaning of the 1351 Letter of Testimony, for he took it to be tantamount to the usual form of Benediction of a new Abbot, together with the appearance of the senior Canons. He completely overlooked the evidence of the dating, however. Given at Chudleigh on Dec. 6th, 1351, the Letter of Testimony mentions Dec. 13th as about the date when the Benediction was sought, and Dec. 21st (St. Thomas's Day) as the date upon which it was given. Now how can these latter dates make sense if the Letter of Testimony itself was issued on Dec. 6th? The conclusion of course is that the December of a different year is being referred to; and so the Letter of Testimony is therefore looking back to John Gras's original Benediction of Dec. 21st. 1345. I am informed that a ceremony of Benediction of the same man could not be administered twice, so this Letter of Testimony given on the Abbot's reinstatement to his office is just what would be expected.

Finally if we admit of the two Abbots with the names Gras and Cras, then there would be 21 abbots. But we know indisputably that there were only 20. Watkin of course did not know of Abbot "W" (Charter 174), so the real reason for his insistence on two abbots, Gras and Cras, was that his theory needed another man to make up the right number of 20 abbots!

If the events of 1351 seem startling enough to us today, how must they have appeared to Bishop Grandisson and the contemporary clergy at Exeter? Here was a first-rate scandal in the diocese and the Bishop could take no action because Torre was a Premonstratensian house and he could not so much as enter it. It was small wonder that when John Gras was reinstated he, the Bishop, caused Richard de Cotelforde himself to appear before him at Chudleigh together with John Deghere, the sub prior, and Richard de Hamptisforde, the Cellarer. They brought with them a letter bearing the seal of the Convent which attested to the lawful election of the Abbot, referring back of course to 1345 when the election took place. With their hands on their breasts they all swore to this, and Richard de Cotelforde before them all renounced whatever pretensions he may have had to the Abbacy. Little did the Bishop suspect that the worst of the story was yet to come, for it cannot have been many weeks before de Cotelforde was murdered. Ellis in his "An Historical Survey of Torquay" places the murder at Teigngrace but gives no reason for this assertion.

It is a happy thing to be able to record that Abbot John Gras lived down all the strife and turmoil caused by de Cotelforde, and ruled on at Torre in peace for twenty years or more. His successor John de Berkadone is first mentioned in 1372 in Charter 194.

9

The Torre Abbey Chantries

The good churchman of the Middle Ages gave generous donations of lands and money to the Church so that after his death masses might be said for his soul for ever. Small chapels in parish churches, Abbeys and Cathedrals were set aside for this purpose. Some of these were adorned in a very costly fashion. Those who did not arrange a chantry for themselves prior to their death often left money enough to found one after their decease. It was then the responsibility of their heirs to see that all was carried out according to their wishes. So many were these endowments that special chantry priests were maintained simply to say masses at one chantry after another. In our parish churches a priest's door beside the altar in a side chapel often indicates the position of a former chantry; for the priest could enter the church, perform his mass and leave again without disturbing what might be going on in the body of the church.

At Torre Abbey we know of seven such chantries, all of which were guaranteed by charter and were to be maintained for ever. Probably the earliest was that founded by Sampson ffoliot (c. 1210/20), who gave 3/- per annum from his rents at Coffinswell. This sum was to be paid on the Feast of St. Peter's Chains, and its purpose was to provide wax (for candles presumably) so that masses might be said for his soul and those of his parents. The Abbey went further and promised that prayer would be made for him just as though he were a Canon of the house. By this we can assume that he was made a Confrater.

Another early chantry was founded by a charter of 1213. Jordan de Daccombe gave all his land at Daccombe to the Abbey so that a chaplain might be assigned to say masses for his soul, that of his wife, Cecilia, and for those of his ancestors and successors, for ever. This no doubt was a daily mass.

Henry de Ferendone, in about 1230, gave all his land at Dunnyngestone, in the parish of Clayhanger, so that a perpetual chantry might be founded at Torre Abbey on behalf of his own soul and those of his ancestors, successors and all the faithful departed. One of the Canons was to be assigned to perform this duty, probably a daily one.

A chantry with an interesting condition attached was that founded by Isabella de Wadetone c. 1270. She gave a ferling of land at Wadetone to the Abbey in return for which a weekly mass was to be offered in perpetuity for herself and her husband, Martin de ffisacre, at the altar of the Holy Cross. Before this altar a lamp was to be kept burning; but if the lamp was allowed to go out, then the land was to revert to herself or her heirs.

An outside chantry, which was no doubt the responsibility of the vicar of Bradworthy, was founded for Robert le Deneis, the Lord of the manor of Wike. It was in the chapel of Week St. Pancras, then a chapel dependent on Bradworthy. It was founded on behalf of the soul of Robert le Deneis, his wife, ancestors and successors. There can be little doubt that it stood in the north transept of the church. Close to this transept is the walled-up Norman doorway which no doubt gave access at one time to the chapel from the Deneis's manor house, which is thought to have stood near the church. Here there was to be a daily mass, but on the days when mass was normally held at the church the benefactors were to be remembered secretly, and in the prayers which followed the mass. Very little seems to have been given to the Abbey in return for this chantry—only a house and garden and an exchange of land whereby the Canons gained half an acre. Behind this small gift, however, there may have been a lifetime of generosity to the Abbey of which the Cartulary tells us nothing. Certainly chantries and their attendant priests cannot have been lightly granted, for they were founded for all time, and the expense of their maintenance must have been considerable.

Finally we come to the two most important chantries at Torre Abbey which were the de Mohun and de Cokynton chantries. The first was for John (5) de Mohun and his wife Johanna. Through them the important manor of Tormohun came into the hands of the Abbot of Torre. The story of how this came about may be read elsewhere in this book. The chantry was granted on Feb. 7th, 1360, the undertaking being that two Canons were appointed, each to say a daily mass. Unfortunately we do not know at which altar this took place.

William de Cokynton's chantry was also a 14th century foundation, but the exact date when it began is not known. William's great gift to the Abbey was water from Sherwell Brook which perfected the domestic water supply, for it provided enough water to drive a mill within the precincts in addition to what was required for the house and fishpond. In return for this important gift William was buried in the Abbey church before the altar of St. John the Baptist. Above this altar the charter giving the water supply was displayed "so that all who pass by may see, read and understand". Here a daily mass was said for which a special chaplain was maintained. This was in a way a double chantry for a weekly mass was also to be said for William's soul in the "ancient chapel" at Cockington. It was to be held each Wednesday, but if that day was a feast day then the mass was to be said on the preceding Tuesday or the Thursday following. The purpose of the chantry was not only for William's soul, but also for his wife, Johanna, his parents, brothers, sisters and friends. In the charter concerning this important chantry the watchful Canons inserted a clause whereby the chantry was to cease immediately should the water from the Sherwell brook ever be diverted.

It may be thought strange that some of the great donors of land and property to the Abbey had no chantry there. Lord William Brewer, the founder, is an outstanding example of an apparent omission; but it must be remembered that his chantry was at Dunkeswell Abbey—another of his foundations—and the spot where he and his wife were buried. So it may be that others, too, had chantries elsewhere. But it must never be forgotten that the Premonstratensians were most meticulous in praying for their former benefactors, lists of names being drawn up and sent from one monastery to another. For those who had been made confraters obits were as faithfully observed as those of the Abbots and Canons themselves. Indeed the business of offering masses and praying for the faithful departed was looked upon as the main occupation of the Abbeys. It was the "Opus Dei"—the work of God, and nothing was allowed to interfere with it.

10

The Cartularies

It has already been explained that a cartulary was a book into which the wording of important charters and legal documents was copied. They might concern an Abbey's title to the churches, manors or lands with which it has been endowed. It was a handy book of reference and would be transcribed with great care. Some cartularies are of great beauty with illuminated letters and colouring, and are works of art in themselves.

There are two Cartularies of Torre Abbey still in existence, and without them it would not have been possible to compile this book. The older is in the Library of Trinity College, Dublin, and is known as the "Dublin Cartulary"; the other came into the hands of the Exchequer because it was used in Court in the reign of Queen Elizabeth I. It was later handed over to the Public Record Office in London, where it still is. Oliver mentions yet a third cartulary, but its whereabouts has not been known for about 150 years. It was said to have been among the papers of the Rev. Richard Lane of Cofflete, Brixton, S. Devon; all my attempts to trace it have been in vain and it is most doubtful if it still exists or really was a cartulary.

There is a micro-film of the Dublin Cartulary in Exeter Cathedral Library, and also a transcription in Latin in the Library of Torquay Natural History Society at The Museum in Torquay. The work was carried out early in the present century by Hugh Watkin. He never lived to see his transcription published, but it has been of great use to those interested in Torre Abbey. Now this Cartulary was the first and decidedly untidy collection of the Abbey's charters. Together with them are included several bulls and letters, one might almost say the circulars of the period. There are also various memoranda. The whole, therefore, makes up an unwieldy but fascinating collection of some 500 documents.

The Exchequer Cartulary, on the other hand, is a fair copy of the other and compiled later. The unnecessary or out of date documents are excluded, and there are some fifty extra charters not in the Dublin Cartulary. They are throughout neatly grouped under their respective subjects and the handwriting is for the most part easy to read. I have transcribed this Cartulary in the original Latin and hope that one day it may be published. For the purposes of this book I have included a very brief summary of each charter in English, so the student of the period will now know something of what the Cartulary contains. There are 319 charters, all of which have been included. Two papal letters at the beginning have been omitted on account of their length, and also because they are not of general interest; otherwise nothing is left out.

The Exchequer Cartulary was written almost entirely by one hand which is considered to be of the 15th century. Charters 210, 222 and 281 are in a very different style of writing, however, whilst the final four are in yet another later hand. As these charters date from 1471 they must have been copied in that year, or a little later.

By and large the task of transcribing was an easy one, for very few pages are stained or blurred by process of time. A torn away fragment at the top of the first page is all that is missing. Our scribe was not without humour, for little faces and strange animals sometimes peer at us across the centuries from his more elaborate capitals. Swinging censers and angels are also scattered about, whilst once, drawing our attention to an important clause, is a nicely drawn gauntlet. All this elaboration adds much to the interest that we feel in our scribe's arduous task. Now and again he has lapses and spells wrongly or omits words; sometimes his quill needed sharpening and then, as though to alleviate the discomfort of writing at all, he screws up his letters and contracts his words unmercifully. But these occasions are few and far between, and the further we delve into the Cartulary the more he becomes our very good friend.

In the case of the later charters the scribe's work was never completed, for the large capital which begins each document has been left blank; all that is to be seen is a minute letter showing what the florid capital was to be. The rubric headings are decidedly curious, too, for very little trouble has been taken over them. Where one might have expected ornate lettering we find the words squeezed in, often beginning on the same line as the previous item. At the end the headings are omitted altogether, and the inference is that they did not form a part of the original scheme, but were added later by an impatient writer.

At the beginning of the volume are two flyleaves and also one at the end. There is an entry on the first in a hand dating probably from mid 16th century; it states that the book is the property of the heirs of John Gaverock and contains evidence of property formerly belonging to the Monastery of Torre. Now Gaverock was the first lay owner of Wolborough after the Dissolution, and he was the last manor steward under the rule of Torre Abbey. When this came to an end he and his wife purchased the manor from Henry VIII for £592.14.2. This was a large sum, but when one remembers that the lord of the manor, like the Abbots before him, extorted a toll on all goods sold at the thriving market at Newton Abbot, then it was not surprising that Gaverock was prepared to pay a good price. There is in existence among a collection of old Wolborough papers an impressive document of the reign of Philip and Mary confirming the sale of the manor. At the head of the sheet is a large pen and ink drawing of Philip and Mary seated on thrones. It is in excellent condition and only the large seal shows signs of crumbling away. John Gaverock and his wife are said to have lived at Forde House. The Cartulary did not remain long in his hands, for the second flyleaf tells us that it was produced in Court on Feb. 5th 1579, by one Richard Malford or Melford, and on the final page he is again mentioned in the same hand.

The two letters at the beginning have already been touched upon. The first and shortest is part of a letter sent to Bishop Simon of Apulia by Pope Innocent 3rd or his successor Pope Honorius 3rd. It must be mentioned because it contains a list of donations made to Torre Abbey, some items of which are not mentioned elsewhere. The second and longer document is from Pope Gregory IX who revised the Premonstratensian Rule. It appears to date from c. 1233.

In studying the charters and their subjects the student must understand that they are not in chronological order, and it is sometimes by no means easy to grasp the sequence of events. Dating, too, is usually omitted by the scribe, also the names of witnesses. Only 83 charters are dated, and this is most unfortunate because it makes a document much less valuable as historical evidence. Often the approximate date can be deduced if the names of witnesses are appended. But the result has been that far too many charters are only tentatively dated, and these must be treated with great reserve. That the bulk of the charters date from the 13th century there can be no doubt, but there are quite a few which antedate the founding of the Abbey.

With the names of witnesses we are even less fortunate, for in only 53 cases do they occur. A few charters are witnessed by the King alone. So this aid to dating is not as helpful as one could have wished. The Canons were very meticulous in recording previous deeds in connection with land which came to them. You will find many charters, for instance, where Torre Abbey is not mentioned. This is because they deal with previous ownership.

For the sake of convenience I have numbered the charters in the order in which they occur in the Cartulary. Throughout the book when a number only occurs, it is a charter number, unless of course it is obviously a date. Over 600 people are mentioned in the Exchequer Cartulary, and I have tried to omit none. They form an amazingly varied cross-section of the life of 13th century England, for there are kings and popes, barons and bishops and nobles of all degree. There are knights and their ladies, rich widows and humble housewives, archers and foresters, bakers and tailors, villeins and humble serfs, all of whom contributed to the rich pattern of life in 13th century England.

II

The Acquisition of the Manor of Tormohun

At the time of the foundation of Torre Abbey the manor of Torre was the property of the de Brewer family, but it was not destined to remain in their hands for long. Lord William's son, William the Younger, inherited the manor in 1224 when his father retired to Dunkeswell Abbey. But he himself died without issue only eight years later. Now his sister Alicia had married Reginald (1) de Mohun and it was their son Reginald (2) de Mohun who inherited the manor of Torre. The de Mohuns were to hold it until about 1370 and theirs was the name which was to attach itself permanently to the manor, although it was briefly known as Torre Brewer, Torre Prior and even as Torre Ridgeway in post-monastic days. By the 19th century the title had become, quite incorrectly, Tormoham. Today the correct ecclesiastical title of the parish is Tormohun.

The story of the acquisition of this manor by the Abbey is an absorbing one which took 22 years to complete. Very slowly, and by devious courses, the de Mohuns lost their hold upon the manor; and in spite of the Statute of Mortmain and all sorts of obstacles, it was drawn as though by a magnet into the hands of the Canons, who for so long had been patiently awaiting it. In the mid 14th century it belonged to Sir John de Mohun, a colourful figure who had fought with the Black Prince at Crecy and in several other campaigns. He was one of the original 25 Knights of the Garter, but was also one of those unfortunate people who seem never to be able to live within their means. Being in straitened circumstances in Jan. 1348, he granted the manor of Torre to Robert le Pil, parson of Crukurn and to Edmund le Gras, parson of Teignbruer (later Teigngrace). This, it appeared later, seems only to have been for a period of ten years. Now Edmund le Gras bore the same name as John Gras, then Abbot, and there is little doubt that he was a close relative; so it seems that as early as 1348 the Canons were well aware of the possibility of wresting the manor from the grasp of the embarrassed Sir John. Succeeding documents show how Sir John granted away several manors for short periods; but at last in June, 1351, a very important event in our story took place, for Sir John came to Torre himself, and in a charter in f. 94a of D.C. he conceded what was virtually the whole manor to nine persons, probably all clergy. They were Robert le Pyl, parson of the church of Crukurn, Thomas Bernhous, parson of the church of Dertingtone, Richard de Wodelonde, parson of the church of Stoke in Tinhide, William de Rasselegh, vicar of the church of Bradeworthi, William Davis, chaplain, William Busschyl, John de Bercadone, John de Pyn and John de Northcote. He quitclaimed to them 18 messuages and 18 ferlings of land in Uppetone in the manor of Tormoun, with rents and services, and all lands and tenements to the south of the way from Walflute towards Ilsham. There were also 1½ acres extending over Waddone within the bounds of the manor of Coletone. There is also mention of a watermill. The giving away of this huge tract of land was witnessed by Henry de la Pomeray, Walter de Wodelonde, knights, and Richard

Brankiscombe, John de Ferariis, John de Dabernoun, Ralph Tregor, Laurence de Dunigeston, John de Berkadon and others. The charter was dated at Torre Mohun on the Monday before the Feast of the Nativity of St. John Baptist, in the 25th year of King Edward III.

The theory has been advanced elsewhere that Uppetone, the modern Upton, was the principal village of the manor, and this seems to be substantiated by the mention of no less than 18 messuages there. That this important occasion was an indirect giving of the manor to the Canons must have been obvious to all who were assembled on that day, for of the names mentioned on the list it is most likely that the last four were Canons. Certainly John de Bercadone was, for he later became Abbot.

It was to be many years, however, before the necessary letters patent were obtained from the King himself. The next step was not taken until Feb. 7th, 1360, when for 40 marks paid to the King, exactly the same items mentioned in Sir John's charter of 1351 were granted to John de Bercadone and John de Pyn, so that two Canons should be maintained to celebrate mass daily for the souls of John de Mohun and his wife, Johanna, and all the faithful departed for ever. (D.C. f. 94b). On the same folio is another charter whereby John de Bercadone and John de Pyn grant all the land which came to them from John de Mohun to Torre Abbey. What had happened to the other seven men? It is more than likely that they had been carried off by the Black Death which was rampant in Devon during the middle of the century. We know that mortality among clergy was particularly high.

The next charter in the series dates from July 5th, 1362, and in it John de Bercadone alone grants the 20 messuages etc. in the manor of Tormohun to John, Abbot of Torre. Various other official sanctions were granted over the next few years, e.g. Hugh de Courtenay, as Lord of the fee, licenced the gift on Aug. 4th, 1362. On Sept. 29th, 1363, John de Mohun quitclaimed all demands which he might make in the manor to John, Abbot of Torre.

It was to be another seven years, however, before a Fine was procured from the Court of Westminster. This was in 1369, and now the manor was vested in Walter de Columpton, clerk, Roger Boghermore, clerk, and John Northcote of Nywetone. They gave John de Mohun and his wife Joanna no less than 200 marks for this fine, a very considerable sum of money. Lastly we have King Edward III's Licence in Mortmain dated May 6th, 1370, which is granted to the same three men, "so that they may convey the manor to the Abbot of Torre". 40 marks was paid to the King for this licence. So the total cost to the Abbey of procuring the manor seems to have been 240 marks.

Those who wish to read more on this subject are recommended to read Hugh Watkin's able paper entitled "The Manor of Tormohun". (T.N.H.S. vol. 4, part 2), On pp. 141 et seq, nevertheless, he assumes that Abbot John Gras was dead by 1362. The Abbot John referred to in the charters he considers to be the next Abbot, John de Berkadone. Realising, that in this case, he could not be the same person as the John de Berkadone in whom the manor was vested before it came to the Abbey, Watkin assumed that they were two men of the same name. This of course is absurd; the Abbot John referred to was John Gras who was reinstated in 1351 (see the de Cotelforde story).

The first mention in the Cartulary of John de Berkadone as Abbot is not until 1372 (Charter 194). That he played an important part in the delicate negotiations leading to the final acquisition of the Manor by the Canons is obvious to all who read the pertinent charters. So by 1370 Tormohun was irrevocably in ecclesiastical hands.

12

Collected Records of the Premonstratensians in England

The "Collectanea Anglo-Premonstratensia" (Camden Series 6, 11, 12) was edited by Gasquet and published in 1904/06. The references to Torre Abbey are to be found in Vol. 3 pp. 136-156, under eighteen different headings. These record visitations of the Abbey by Bishop Redmayne, letters concerning Torre from one Abbot to another, and perhaps most interesting of all, the actual names of the Community at the times of the visitations. The period covered is from 1455-1500, so it appears that the earlier records which would have told us so much of what we want to know are missing at present.

The records of Torre begin on folio 149 and the first entry is a list of Abbots. The editor relies very much on Oliver's list in the "Monasticon" which is decidedly faulty. Abbot Geoffrey is now known never to have existed, and Laurencius is given as living in 1293/94—Bishop Quivel's Register, p. 378 being quoted. Now the Register gives no mention at all of this Abbot in the text. In a footnote, however, the Torre Abbey Cartulary rubric headings are quoted with regard to Ashclyst; and there a fine is mentioned where Abbot Laurencius's name is certainly to be seen. But the date is indisputably 1238 and not 1293/94 as quoted. So the argument for a second Abbot Laurencius ever having existed seems therefore to have depended on this misquotation only.

The records follow numbered headings and begin:—

590. *Prior and Convent of Torre to the Abbot of Welbeck* (P. folio 63. Reg. Prem. f. 91b).

This is a letter sending news of the death of Abbot John Lacy to the Abbot of Welbeck —the parent house. It is dated Nov. 24th, 1455. The Abbot is begged to supervise the election of a successor quickly "for the brethren are as sheep among wolves until a new shepherd is appointed". Stating that it is the custom on such occasions to deliver up the seal of the former Abbot, the Prior goes on to say that it cannot now be done "as the church was in the midst of many and divers kinds of difficult negotiations concerning things both temporal and spiritual". So he sends the said father's communal seal by the hands of William Gambon. The letter concludes with the pious hope that the Abbot will have a long rule. William Gambon was a witness to 239 in 1469 and was also Incumbent of Townstall.

591. *Letter from the Abbot of St. Radegund's to the Abbot of Torre* (P. folio 64).

This letter, dated Sept. 10th, 1456, is from John, Abbot of St. Radegund's Abbey, to Richard Cade, then Abbot of Torre. The writer was head of the Order in England, and his Abbey was in the diocese of Canterbury. He states that he has been informed that William Nowell, the Prior of Torre, was a disturber of the peace and a trouble maker. He had therefore summoned him to appear before him on a certain day and place. This the Prior had done and had completely cleared himself of the charges against himself. He had therefore been allowed to depart unpunished. The Abbot went on to say that it now appeared that Abbot Richard was to blame—that his rule lacked firmness, that strife and discord abounded and that the Abbey was dilapidated and its light extinguished. Abbot Cade was abruptly ordered to set his house in order or else to render up his seal and retire on 20 marks per annum.

592. *A letter from the Abbot of St. Radegund's to the Abbot of Welbeck.* (P. folio 65. Reg. Prem. folio 101).

Three days after despatching the above letter, the Abbot of St. Radegund's seeks permission from the Abbot of Welbeck to go to Torre himself to settle the discord existing there. He therefore writes asking for authority to act, and for letters patent if necessary which will give him full powers. Evidently all was settled in a satisfactory manner, however, for Abbot Cade did not resign and ruled Torre for many more years.

593. *General answers to questions made at the Visitation, August* 1, 1478. (P. folio 66. Reg. Prem. folio 18).

The house of Torre in the county of Devon and the diocese of Exeter was founded A.D. 1196 (temp. King Richard I) by William Brewer in honour of the Holy Trinity. The Abbot of Welbeck is the father Abbot. Adam, a canon of Welbeck, came to the monastery of Torre in that year with six other canons on the Feast of the Annunciation. Adam was the first Abbot; he ruled for three and a half years and was translated to Newhouse. The monastery has six churches, of whose vicars one is a canon instituted by the bishop. There have been 18 abbots. The Earl of Devon is the patron (fundator). Several words in this account are in brackets and it is unfortunately not possible to discover the reason for this.

594. *Visitacio de Torr.* (A. folio 14b).

The visitation of August 1, 1478, was conducted by Bishop Redmayne who was at that time both bishop of St. Asaph's and Abbot of Heppa, alias Schapp. He was accompanied by Hubert who was the head Abbot of the Premonstratensian Order in the British Isles, and also by Robert Kyppyng of the monastery of Durforde. The visit of this formidable trio must have been anything but pleasing to the Canons of Torre, for on this occasion there was much amiss. In the first place brother Walter Speyer was accused of apostasy, robbery, open rebellion and several other crimes. He confessed before the full Chapter that he was guilty on all counts and was sentenced to 40 days severe punishment at Newhouse, and three years imprisonment there; and then to remain there for 10 years unless pardoned meanwhile. Next a certain brother Richard Byggode was accused of apostasy which he did not deny. He was sentenced to 40 days of severe punishment at the monastery of Welbeck and was then to remain there for three years.

At this point intercession for both men was made by their own Abbot and by the Abbot of Durford, also by the Prior, sub-Prior, Cellarer and indeed by the whole community. As a result the sentences were suspended until the next convocation.

Injunctions to the Abbot included the increase of the number of Canons and also that they were to be promoted to the livings of the churches belonging to the monastery, as was the custom of the Order.

The Prior was ordered to correct the faults of the brethren daily. Under penalty of contempt the precis, versicles and collects were to be sung in Chapter as well as in Church within 40 days of the bishop's departure. The brethren were enjoined to attend divine service both in the Choir as well as in Chapter, under penalty of three days on bread and water; they were further ordered to wear amices beneath their hoods both within and outside the monastery.

The seculars also, under penalty of three days on bread and water, were ordered not to associate with the brethren in eating, drinking or recreation in the infirmary or refectory. Boys especially detailed by the Abbot were to be excepted.

The brethren were exhorted to obey the orders of their Abbot under penalty of the greater excommunication. Brother Henry Babidon, who through his own demerits had been deprived of his rights and privileges, now had these restored to him at the intercession of the Abbot.

As a kind of postscript various memoranda are added:—
(1) Richard Coryngton to be admitted to the office of circator and cantor.
(2) John Stevyn to the office of infirmarius and refector.
(3) Under penalty of three days on bread and water the bretheren are not permitted to drink after compline, unless for special reasons, and then only by order of the Prior or his deputy if absent.
(4) Vespers not to be before four o'clock both summer & winter.
(5) All are to be in bed by eight o'clock except officials and their assistants.
(6) Under penalty of the greater excommunication accounts of receipts and expenses are to be rendered once annually in the presence of the Abbot. Returns from remote churches are to be made once every three years.

The bishop then declares all the brethren gathered in Chapter to be absolved from all sentences touching law and order. Under penalty of contempt they are ordered not to resort to places of bad reputation.

595. *Nomina Canonicorum Monasterii de Torre.* 1478. (A. folio 22).

Dominus	Richard Cade, abbot	Frater	Richard Coryndun, circator et cantor
,,	Thomas Dyer, prior	,,	Johannes Chester, vicarius de Dermothe
,,	Willelmus Collyng, supprior	,,	Johannes Stephun
,,	Willelmus Hamont	,,	Henry Babidon
,,	Johannes Dymock	,,	John Drycke, novicius
,,	Richard Bittecom, cellararius	,,	Roger Legge, novicius
,,	Richard Byggegoode		
,,	Thomas Burnell		
,,	Walter Speyer		

An account of the founding of the house of Torre then follows which is the same as in 593.

596 & 597. *Letters of Dimission of a Canon of Torre* (A. folio 23).

Bishop Redmayne writes to John Swyfte, abbot of Newhouse, sending Walter Speyer, a canon of Torre, convicted at the visitation to be reformed at Newhouse.

TORRE ABBEY

In 597 the letter is given. It is dated August 3, 1478. The Bishop states that at his visitation of Torre Abbey brother Walter Speyre, a canon of that church, "to the scandal of our religion" was accused of apostasy, incontinence, robbery and open rebellion. He was sentenced to Newhouse for punishment and to be imprisoned for three years. After this he was to remain there for a further ten years, unless pardoned in the meantime.

598. *Visitation of Torre, September 21, 1482. (A. folio 39b).*

Bishop Redmayne on this occasion praises the excellently constructed buildings which formed the Monastery, and also the devotion of the brethren both by day and by night. Certain injunctions are:—(1) that silence is to be observed in the four places, (2) the tonsure of the minor brethren is not to exceed the breadth of three fingers above the ear, (3) all the brethren are to obey the prior and subprior, (4) all those who sleep in the dormitory will rise and proceed to matins or pay the penalty of one day on bread and water, (5) the psalm "laetatus sum", with versicles and collects is to be said daily in the morning mass and sung when in the choir; but (not?) at High Mass.

A certain brother, Richard Coryndon, was accused of having keys made to the Abbot's treasury chest and of helping himself to not a little of the gold and silver therein. He cleared himself of the charge however, and was acquitted.

If the abbot is sick the brethren are enjoined to minister to him "with filial diligence" and are not to dispute his commands. The abbot is ordered to appoint canons and not secular priests to the benefices which belong to the monastery.

599. *Names of the Confraternity of our Order at the monastery of Torre.* (A. folio 46b).

Dominus Richard Cade, abbot of the same	Brother Richard Coryndon, Circator et cantor
Brother Thomas Dyer, prior	,, John Derke
Brother William Cullinge, supprior et sacrista	,, John Dymoke
,, Richard Bitcome, cellararius	,, John Cherchefford
,, Richard Biggott	,, John Trompindon
,, Robert Bentele	,, John Ostreyge
,, Henry Babydon	,, Thomas Humffray
	,, James Compyne
	,, Roger Legge

600. *Visitation of Torre, 25 July, 1448. (A. folio 79).*

Names of the Confraternity of the Monastery of Torre.

Dominus Thomas Dyare, abbot of the same	Brother Thomas Humfray
Brother John Derke, supprior	,, John Hayman
,, William Cullynge, vicar of Tunstall	,, John Ostrege
	,, John Michell
,, Richard Byggegod	,, James Complyn
,, Robert Bentley	,, Adam Coke
,, Roger Legge, vicar of Bradeworthy	,, Richard Milton
	,, William Schere

The Visitation was held at the monastery of Durford. On this occasion Bishop Redmayne was assisted by Robert Bedall, canon and prior of Schappe. The Abbot of Torre appeared in person and the convent was represented by a proctor. The affairs of the monastery and the administration of the abbot are praised. A debt of 50 marks has been paid off. The monastery owes nothing—in fact the canons are owed 100 marks. They used to possess 60 sheep, now they have 200, through the abbot's circumspection. They have sufficient grain and other necessaries in store.

601. *Visitation of the Monastery of Torre of our Order, May 24, 1491. (A. folio 91).*

The Bishop visits in the company of Robert Bedall of the monastery of Schappe. He finds a certain Thomas Umfray accused of consorting with a woman named Johanna Guly. He clears himself of the charge, however, and is restored to favour. The rest of the confraternity are ordered to avoid association with women of bad reputation and are not to drink in the Infirmary, Dormitory or suspicious places. Under penalty of apostasy they are not to leave the monastery without special leave from the abbot, neither are they to drink at or resort to the homes of the laity within a league of the abbey. They are not to play games for money, particularly the game vulgarly called "tenys". At mass the deacon and subdeacon are not to genuflect at the Elevation of the Host, but are to bow reverently "as is our custom". Those absent from the Visitation are to be dealt with at the abbot's discretion. Other matters requiring correction will not need to be reported to the General Chapter.

The Monastery is not in debt, neither is anything owing to it. Thanks to the abbot there is a good supply of grain and household necessities.

602. *Nomina Confratrum Monasterii de Torre. June 12, 1494. (A. folio 112).*

Dominus Thomas Dyer, abbas
Frater John Derke, supprior
    „   Richard Biggegood circator
    „   Robert Bentley
    „   Thomas Umfray, cantor
    „   John Haymane, succentor
    „   John Ostryge
    „   John Michelle
    „   James Cumplynge ⎫
    „   Adam Coke   ⎬ diaconi
    „   Richard Myltone ⎭

Frater William Cullynge, vicarius de Dertmothe
    „   Roger Legge, vicarius de Bradworthy
    „   Edward Tryveigy ⎫
    „   John Hoper   ⎬ novicii
    „   Phylip Mogge ⎭

603. *Visitacio Monasterii de Torre.*

Bishop Redmayne made this Visitation in the company of Robert Bedalle, canon of Schappe. A certain brother, Edward Colynsone, a canon of Welbeck, appeared before them accused of apostasy and tearfully asked for pardon. He was given 40 days of heavy punishment and was then to be kept for a further 3 years in custody at his own house, unless given dispensation by the bishop in the meantime.

604. *Names of the Brothers of the Monastery of Torre.* 1494. (A. folio 116b).

Dominus Thomas Dyer, abbas
Frater Johannes Derk, supprior
" Richard Bygode ⎫
" Robert Bentley ⎪
" Thomas Umfray ⎪
" John Haymane ⎬ Priests
" John Ostryge ⎪
" John Michelle ⎪
" James Compyne ⎪
" Adam Cok ⎭

Frater Richard Dyrler, deacon
" Edward Trevergyne ⎫
" John Hoper ⎪
" Philip Mugge ⎬ Novices
" Peter Milwarde ⎪
" John Skary ⎪
" James Suttone ⎭

605. *Names of the Bretheren of the Monastery of Torre,* 30 *November,* 1497 (A. folio 140).

Dominus Thomas Dyre, abbas
Frater Thomas Umfray, supprior
" Ricardus Bygode, circator
" William Collynge, vicar of Tunstalle
" Roger Lege, vicar of Bradworthy
" John Durk, chaplain of Townstalle
" Richard Miltone, succentor
" John Hopper
" Philip Moge, subdiaconus
" Peter Mylwarde, acolite

Frater John Haymane
" John Maychylle, cantor
" John Ostryge, cellararius
" James Cumpyne
" Adam Cok, custos infirmorum
" Edward Trevergy
" John Scary
" James Suttone
" Thomas Lorymer, acolite
" William Shyrwille

Bishop Redmayne has, since the last visitation, been translated to the See of Exeter (1496), and he insists that he visits the Abbey as a Premonstratensian Abbot and not as Diocesan. By the rules of the Order, of course, the Diocesan could not so much as enter any of the Premonstratensian Abbeys. He brings with him Robert Bedalle, canon of Schappare, and also the worthy Doctor William Sylk as his special advocate, who will attest that in future succeeding bishops of Exeter will not visit the Abbey as this would infringe the privileges of the Order. He certifies that the present visitation is at the instigation of the Father abbot.

The Bishop on this occasion found that everything at the Abbey concerning matters both great and small was in an edifying state. No debts have been incurred, and there is a sufficiency of grain, animals and other necessities.

606. *Nomina Confratrum Monasterii de Torre,* 7 *August,* 1500. (A. folio 147b).

Dompnus Thomas Dyer, abbas
Frater Thomas Umfray, prior
" Richard Byggode, supprior
" John Haymane
" John Ostrage, cellararius

Frater John Mowchelle, circator
" James Cumpyne, succentor
" Adam Cok

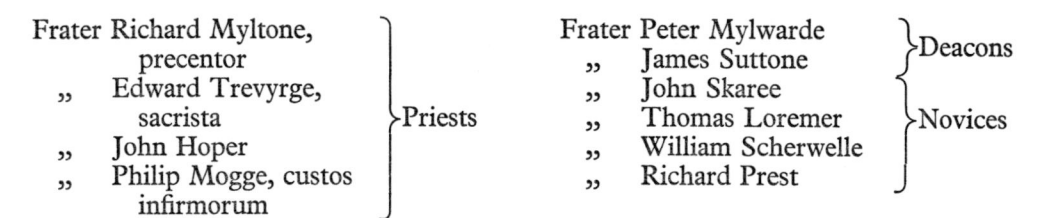

Frater Richard Myltone, precentor		
„ Edward Trevyrge, sacrista	} Priests	
„ John Hoper		
„ Philip Mogge, custos infirmorum		

Frater Peter Mylwarde	} Deacons	
„ James Suttone		
„ John Skaree		
„ Thomas Loremer	} Novices	
„ William Scherwelle		
„ Richard Prest		

Bishop Redmayne renews his protest that he visits by order of the Premonstratensian father abbot and not as Bishop of the diocese. He is accompanied by Robert Bedalle, canon of the monastery of Schappe.

Brothers Robert Myltone and James Suttone prostrated themselves before him as they had broken the rule of silence; they were recommended for discipline. All were exhorted to reform themselves in this matter, and were enjoined to honour each other mutually—particularly are the younger brethren to show reverence and patience towards the elder brethren.

Felt skull caps are to be worn within the monastery both at work and during the priestly offices. The bishop had nothing further to criticise. He praises the abbot by whose providence no debts have been incurred and pronounces that the abbey has abundance of the necessities of life.

The report concludes by stating that it was given at Torre at supper time on the morrow of the Visitation and on the seventh and concluding day of the bishop's stay at Torre Abbey.

13

A Document of A.D. 1300

In the Exeter Diocesan Registry there is a document of considerable interest wherein proof was given by the Canons of Torre of their title to certain churches in the Exeter Diocese. The reason for the drawing up of such a document was indirectly due to the Statute of Mortmain of 1279. This famous Statute was the first serious check which the monasteries had received to their acquisition of land, churches and property. All during the first half of the 13th century and before, rich donors had showered gifts upon them, hoping thereby to evade the pains of Purgatory. So by the close of the century an impressive proportion of the country was in the hands of the Church. After the Statute had been passed, King Edward I issued a mandate whereby all religious houses had to produce irrefutable proofs of their title to churches whose advowsons they claimed to hold. The document now to be discussed was one of many such, drawn up at the instigation of diocesans throughout the land. The return from Torre is believed to be one of very few to have survived.

It covers a large parchment measuring 27" by 16¾", and is in a fair state of preservation. Time is responsible for illegibility here and there, but this does not in any way detract from the value of the document whose meaning is clear throughout. The preamble states that the Abbot and Convent of Torre have been summoned to Exeter Cathedral to produce evidence of their titles to the churches of Torre, Wollberwe, Braworthi, Hanok and Tunstalle. It is to be noted that the churches of Shebbear and Buckland Brewer are omitted.

Abbot Richard Cade, who was in office at the time, seems, however, to have been an exceedingly cautious person who was quite unimpressed by the Bishop's demand. Being a Premonstratensian he was in no way under the thumb of the diocesan, and one senses that he took full advantage of his position on this occasion. Instead of sending the precious documents to Exeter he despatched as his procurator Brother Richard de Yameton. The Bishop was at that moment at his manor of "Clist juxta Exon". Here the procurator humbly begged for another time and place to be appointed for the inspection of the documents, "as it would be exceedingly perilous to send them to Exeter". It may seem that the Abbot was playing for time and could not immediately lay his hands on the required charters, but the reason given was after all quite plausible. The month was November, and a journey on horseback to Exeter in winter might have taken more than one day. If the coast road were taken, then there was the Teign to be negotiated at Shaldon. If the Canon chose the road through Chudleigh then he would have had to cross the lonely Haldon Moor where he might have been beset by robbers who could have carried off the precious charters. On the whole, the Abbot was very wise to take the course he did. The Bishop, too, obliged him by appointing a day later in the month when he expected to be at his manor at Paignton, only three miles from the Abbey.

So a date was fixed for the Wednesday after the Feast of St. Martin (Nov. 11th), and on that day the procurator duly appeared at Paignton carrying eight charters with him. They were all ecclesiastical confirmations of the Abbey's title to six of its churches. They were:—(1) Bishop Marshall's confirmation of the gift of the church of Torre (14), (2) His confirmation of the gift of Bradworthy church (153), (3) his confirmation of the gift of Wolborough church (22), (4) Bishop Simon of Apulia's confirmation of the gift of Shebbear church (171), (5) his confirmation of the gift of Townstall church (193), Bishop Brewer's confirmation of the same (195), his confirmation of the gift of Buckland Brewer church (183). Then there followed the confirmation from Dean Serlo and the Cathedral Chapter of the validity of the charters from the three bishops. The list of churches which the Dean gives is very illegible, yet the name of "Hanok" is just discernible—and this is interesting because Hennock gets no mention previously, and it looks as though the procurator did not produce the requisite charter (48). One cannot but wonder if the original had been lost meanwhile.

At any rate these ecclesiastical confirmations did not satisfy the Bishop and the next day after mass in the chapel at Paignton the procurator returned bearing the actual charters from the donors of the churches concerned. As the precious Foundation Charter of the Abbey was produced as evidence that day, it is small wonder that Abbot Richard was reluctant to part with such precious muniments, even for a few hours. The documents are stated to have borne the seals of King John, William Brewer, Philip de Salmonavilla, William FitzStephen and Gilbert FitzStephen. They concerned the churches of Shebbear, Buckland Brewer, Hennock, and Townstall, whilst in the Foundation Charter Torre, Wolborough and Bradworthy were accounted for. After this all was well, and Thomas Hemingford of the diocese of Lincoln set to work to copy the wording of the charters onto the sheet of parchment which we are considering.

The great value of this restatement of the original charters is that the names of nearly 100 witnesses are included, whereas in the Cartularies they are omitted. So students of the early 13th century will find much to interest them in this document of 1300.

In a footnote, preceded by an elaborate cross on the lefthand side, the writer tells us that he is Thomas Hemingford of the diocese of Lincoln and that the document has been drawn up at the instigation of Bishop Bytton as a "public instrument" whereby the title of Torre Abbey to its ecclesiastical possessions is there for all to see. He concludes with mention of a few corrections and interlinings which should be made in certain lines of which he gives the number. Thus ends one of the most detailed documents extant on the subject of Torre Abbey.

14

The Suppression

So much has been written on the subject of the downfall of the monasteries that it would be idle to add to it. It is sufficient to say that by the 16th century they had, in the eyes of most people, outlived their usefulness. The very gifts which pious donors had showered upon them had carried the seeds of eventual destruction. Affluence was no part of Orders sworn to poverty, and a great many monasteries were blatantly wealthy by the 15th century. As early as 1279 the Statute of Mortmain had been introduced to prevent more land falling into the hand of the Church, which by that time owned a considerable portion of the country. Yet our charters show how by the sale of a licence most kings were willing to over-ride that statute. Tales of corruption and vice surrounded the monks in their latter years, and it is strange how even today they are still credited. Mud sticks, and it is a fact that the popular image of the old monasteries is that they were places of idleness and indulgence. Yet these stories, put about by their enemies, were probably little more than the propaganda of the day. The unfortunate monks were very much the victims of circumstance—and rather defenceless ones at that. Their vast possessions presented a sure target for a rapacious king. The ease and speed with which they were suppressed one by one is quite amazing. At Torre, for instance, all the gifts of land which had been lavished upon the Abbey in its early years were seized by King Henry VIII and quickly sold to his favourites; and it was the same everywhere.

Between February 14th and March 8th, 1539, the king's ministers, Petre and Tregonwell, suppressed no less than fifteen foundations in the Exeter diocese without the slightest opposition anywhere. It would be a sad time at Torre during that February when the Canons realised that the unwelcome visitors were drawing nearer and nearer. They would hear that on February 20th St. John's Hospital at Exeter had surrendered to the king. On the 23rd their friends doubtless warned them of Petre's approach. On that day the bells would ring out across the bay for the last time and the usual Offices be sung. All was done just as it had been for almost three and a half centuries. Then the long-awaited sound of a mounted party would be heard approaching, and the king's officers would ride under the Mohun gatehouse into the courtyard. How did Petre find the community? We know that they made no resistance to his demands, and probably after putting on some pitiful show of hospitality they all signed the fatal document which brought their Abbey to its close. All valuables and church vessels were seized and escorted to London.

The Canons through their peaceful surrender to the king all received pensions, and one much wonders whether, after the first payment, they ever received any more. The payments were as follows:—

Simon Rede, Abbot	£66.13.4.
Richard Mylton, Prior	£7.9.9.
John Asteridge	£6.0.0.

Henry Bagwell	£6.0.0.
John Wyll	£5.0.0.
Thomas Lawdymere	£5.0.0.
Thomas Clement	£5.0.0.
Thomas James	£5.0.0.
John Payne	£5.0.0.
John Shapeley	£4.0.0.
John Lane	£4.0.0.
John Farmer	£2.0.0.
Thomas Brydgeman	£2.0.0.
Thomas Emett	£2.0.0.
Thomas Knoll	£2.0.0.
Richard Yonge	£2.0.0.

They also received gifts, evidently for their immediate use, of from 10/- to 35/-. Simon Rede, the Abbot, retired to his vicarage at Townstall which he had held since 1531. He, like other Abbots, had been busy leasing the Abbey lands for long terms, and in the account of him in the appropriate chapter you may read the details of these transactions. The Abbey Church at Torre was immediately stripped of its lead roofing, and the building left to moulder to ruin, a home for bats and owls, the work of centuries destroyed in a few short hours. The chantries were silent now, the tombs of the Abbots lay all uncared for, and no one seemed to mind.

15

The East Ogwell Grave Coverstones

It is a remarkable thing to be able to record that the coverstones of the graves of no less than three of the Abbots of Torre are to this day a part of the floor of East Ogwell church. Enquiries amongst Premonstratensians of the present day have proved that it was the custom in the Middle Ages to bury Abbots in the nave of their Abbey church. It seems that at some time between 1539 and 1566 (when one of the stones was re-used) these three handsome coverstones were removed from the roofless, ruined nave of Torre Abbey. The most prosaic reason is, of course, a purely utilitarian one. Perhaps the floor of East Ogwell Church was being renewed at the time and so the stones were purchased from the new lay-owner of the Abbey. Records of Dunkeswell Abbey, for instance, show that a certain person there was granted the right to sell stone, wood, lead, glass etc. from the abandoned church just as he thought fit. Such a practice would be rife all over the country, for it is one of the peculiar things in connection with the suppression of the monasteries that the people of England had no sympathy with the disinherited monks, or any respect for the magnificent churches which they left behind them. The loss to the nation when they fell slowly to ruin seems to have been quite unappreciated at the time. So the pillaging of the Abbey Church at Torre would excite little comment.

It is just possible, however, that the slabs were brought by a pious churchman to East Ogwell for safe keeping. It must not be forgotten that the Abbots owned a tenement at East Ogwell, no doubt Tor Barton, which until recently stood not far from the church. The Canons, too, were owners of the neighbouring manor of Wolborough; as landlords they may have been respected highly, and so the rescue of three of the later Abbots' gravestones from wind and weather may have been due to a warmth of feeling on the part of those who had known them.

There is a distinct possibility that more such stones may be discovered in local churches. The sides may very easily have been reversed and used again, so all 16th C. burial stones of similar size, shape and material to the Ogwell slabs should be carefully considered.

Another curious fact with regard to the East Ogwell slabs is that they had not been recorded or even noticed until J. V. Torr wrote about two of them in D.C.N.Q. (Jan. 1964). He missed the third, however, which is covered by a mat. Learned historical societies had visited the church, and historians had held forth upon its points of interest; no doubt they had planted their feet firmly upon the Abbots' gravestones but had never glanced at them; yet in all cases but one there is no difficulty in reading the inscriptions. In the same way the 6th Century celtic inscribed stone which is built into the walls of the church was not recorded until the same year, 1964.

The slabs of Abbots Norton and Cade lie side by side in the north chapel. The former is the older and the inscription (partly covered by a radiator) reads "Hic jacet frater Willelmus Norton Abbas XIIII cujus anime propicietur deus Amen Amen". The twofold "Amen" does not suggest excess of piety but was simply done to fill up the stone. The lettering is very plainly cut, but there are embellishments at the corners in the shape of simple floral medallions. The inscription follows the outside edge of the stone, which is light in colour. Norton's successor was blest by the Bishop of Exeter on July 19th, 1412. So that year no doubt saw Abbot Norton's burial. Two later inscriptions are placed one above the other in the centre of the stone and show that it was twice reused. The first commemorates one of the Holbeme family and reads "Here lieth the body of Johe Holbeme Esquier who died 17th of November a.d. MCCCCLXVI cujus anime propt. deo". The old Latin prayer with its pre-Reformation petition is a late example of such a thing, but no doubt the old ways lingered on in out of the way places for many a long year.

The Holbeam or Holbeme family held the manor of Holbeam in East Ogwell parish for 14 generations, and it is mentioned in Domesday. So this inscription records the burial of an important parishioner. It is quite possible that this north chapel was a former chantry of the family, and no doubt became the family "pew" in Protestant times. The second inscription is "Here lyeth ye body of Richard the sonne of John Gortley who died ye 10th day of July, 1658".

The second stone in the north chapel is that of Abbot Richard Cade. The lettering in this case is more elaborate, and at the corners the medallions are worked with greater care. In the centre of the slab has been a brass figure of the Abbot in eucharistic vestments with his crozier resting on his right shoulder. So much can be discerned from the impression which still remains, for the brass has long since vanished. The inscription reads "Hic jacet dns Cade istius loci Abbas XVIII qui obiit ultimo die Mesis Maii anno dni Millo CCCC(?) – – cuj aie pctr ds Amen". It is unfortunate that the final figures of the date are so illegible for the date of the benediction of Thomas Dyare, Cade's successor, is apparently not in the Bishop's Registers. Abbot Cade is mentioned in Hugh Watkin's "The Abbats of Thorre" as dying in 1482, but he gives no reason for this date, neither have I been able to find any confirmation of it. There is no secondary inscription on this stone, so we have no indication of its ever having been used again.

The third and latest of the burial stones was first noticed by the writer whose curiosity prompted him to see what was under a mat. This has been the most beautiful of the stones, for even today one can see the remains of handsome engraving of an elaborate design. It was given the place of honour beneath the Chancel step, but this proved its undoing, for the passage of many feet to and fro over the centuries has all but obliterated the inscription. Indeed had it not been for the fact that it follows the formula on the other stones its original use as an Abbot's burial stone would never have been suspected. Thomas Dyare who was commemorated here was the last Abbot but one, and so the very last to be interred at Torre. The elaborate design of the engraving is typical of the early 16th Century and shows the Abbot seated; in a good light his figure is to be seen quite plainly surrounded by florid decorations. At the head of the stone traces of colour can still be faintly seen between the letters. Much hard work in deciphering the inscription was carried out by Dr C. A. Ralegh Radford in Sept., 1968. He was satisfied in the end that the usual formula was employed and as far as he could tell the reading is "Hic jacet dns Thmas (Dyare) (Ab) bas q(ui) obiit....mille....anime propicietur deus". Fortunately the word "Thomas" is very clear, and this clinches the matter with regard to the identity of the abbot, for although the surname is obliterated, Dyare was the only one of the twenty abbots to have the Christian name of Thomas. He died in 1523 and his successor, the last of the line, received benediction on Aug. 21st of that year. According to Oliver (Mon. Dioc. Exon. p. 171) this Abbot was commemorated formerly in Bradworthy church where an inscription read " Orate pro anima Thome Dyer abbatis de Torre quondam vicarii istius loci". The burial stone seems to have been of handsome black marble, probably from Ashburton.

Since the ruin of the abbey church is so complete the discovery of these three slabs at East Ogwell is all the more valuable. Here at least we can see with our own eyes objects which must have been familiar to the Canons of the 15th and 16th centuries.

16

The Foundation Charter and King John's Charters

It is not surprising to find that the first charter in the Exchequer Cartulary is the great Foundation Charter which Lord William Brewer gave to the Canons of Torre in its final form c. 1199. It is unfortunate that both here and in the Dublin Cartulary it is undated. There are, nevertheless, several hints in other charters pointing to the fact that it was certainly not signed as early as 1196 when the Abbey was founded. Torre parish church and the manors of Bradworthy and Northshillingford, which are all mentioned in it, were not given to the Abbey as early as this. The church was confirmed to the Canons by Bishop Marshall "in the fourth year of our Consecration" (14), i.e. in 1198. Then again Lord William did not purchase Bradworthy until April 26th, 1198 ("Devon Feet of Fines" 8), neither could he have purchased Northshillingford from William de Tracey until after January, 1199, when at Wilton both Drogo de Montgiron, lord of the fee, and William de Tracey quitclaimed it in favour of the Abbot of Torre. The Abbey buildings, too, must have taken at least three years to build, so it is reasonable to assume that by early in 1199 the Church was completed and ready for consecration. This would be the most likely time for the giving of the Foundation Charter by Lord William Brewer, and its date could be any time after Jan. 13th, 1199.

The question now arises as to where the ceremony of signing took place. It surely ought to have been at the Abbey itself; I believe that this was the case, for a careful consideration of the names of the witnesses proves that most were Devon gentry. It would therefore be only the clergy who came from afar; and why should they not have done so, for the founding of an Abbey was primarily their affair?

As we do not hear of any Premonstratensian Bishops in the 12th century, it is most likely that Bishop Henry Marshall of Exeter performed the consecration ceremony. He is the first witness to the Foundation charter and this may be another reason for assuming that it was given at Torre Abbey on that occasion. Whilst the customs of the Order excluded bishops from entering the precincts of their Abbeys, yet on this occasion the Bishop must have been more than welcome.

The first gift mentioned is the place where the Abbey stands, viz, Rowedone. Now this is the hill which is nowadays traversed by Falkland, Bampfylde and Bridge Roads; the name is happily preserved in Rowdens Road, a cul-de-sac, off Bampfylde Road. The bounds of the land at Rowedone are next given and are, so far as one can tell, as follows: Mill Lane (the road from Cockington) as far as the vill of Torre, and in front of the door of Parson Richard's house (say the "Rising Sun" at the top of Mill Lane), and thence down Belgrave Road to the sea, and from there to the great calcetum. This was a causeway built across ground then marshy, and was a manorial road of much importance for it led to the small harbour near Corbyn's Head. The evidence of a map of c. 1860 shows it running along the line of the present King's Drive. In 1199 it was of such importance that it was not given to the Canons, but formed their western boundary as far as the Abbey gate. The last leg of the demesne boundary was by way of the stream below the present Avenue Road as far as Mill Lane. This stream was known then as Efrideswille and is discussed among the documents relating to Cockington. Other privileges given to the Canons in the manor of Torre were grazing rights for 100 sheep, just as the parson had, and the right to fish and trawl in the bay; the right to construct ponds at Northwille (probably the high ground near the Police Station where springs are known to have existed) and to convey the water over Lord William's ground to the Abbey by way of a leat.

The Great Foundation Charter is of such importance that a full translation from the Latin is now given:—

1. "I, William Briewera, send greetings in the eternal Lord to all the sons of holy mother church, and bring to the notice of you all that for the sake of charity and for the salvation of the souls of Richard, King of England, and the King Henry, his father, as much as for my own soul and those of my predecessors and successors, I have given, conceded and confirmed by this present charter to God and the church of St. Saviour of Torre, and to the Premonstratensian Canons serving God therein, that place for building of an Abbey where St. Saviour's was founded—to wit, the cultivated land called Rowedone in the vill of Torre, whose boundaries are given below; that is by way of the road from Kokyngtone as far as the vill of Torre, and so in front of the door of Richard, then parson of Torre, and continuing by the road down to the sea; then by way of the sea as far as the great causeway, and along this as far as the road from Kokyngtone, passing through land where there is the brook known as Efrideswille.(I have given) whatever is contained within these boundaries, and such freedom for fishing and trawling in the sea of Torre as I or my heirs may have.

"Besides this I have given them (the Canons) the church of Torre complete with all its privileges and liberties, and in the same way pasture for 100 sheep, just as the parson has and should have. I have also given and conceded to them my vill of Wolleburgh together with the advowson of the church and all its appurtenances and liberties, just as William de Brywere gave them to me for my homage and service and for 40 marks in silver.

"I have also given and conceded to them my land of Grendel, which is in the manor of Wodebiry, with all its liberties and appurtenances, which Reginald de Albamara gave to me.

"I have given them also a ferling of land at Uggeburgh with pasture and right of common on Dartmoor which belongs to this manor, and with all its liberties and appurtenances; and a ferling of land at Braworthi, with all its liberties and appurtenances, also the church of the same vill of Bradeworthi together with the chapel of Panckardeswike, with all its liberties and appurtenances.

"I have also given the aforesaid Canons Bradeworthi mill with molture from all my men of the same vill and from all others accustomed to make suit of mill there whilst it was in my hands; and with all the appurtenances, liberties and free customs belonging to the said mill. I concede also that the Canons may repair the millpond on my land freely, and with no hindrance from me or my heirs on that part which lies in my territory.

"Besides this I have given the aforementioned Canons the whole of my land of Northschillyngforde, with all its liberties and appurtenances, which I bought from William de Traci for 80 marks in silver.

"I have given and conceded to them a certain part of my land at Coletone which lies within these boundaries, viz:—by way of the road from Torre, which goes through la Wyngate towards the vill of Coletone as far as the other road from Torre; and thus ascending by that road as far as the land of Karswille and its hill of Kyngesdone, and thence returning by way of Kokyngtone wood and the boundary which divides Kokyngtone and Coletone, as far as the aforesaid road which goes through la Wyndgate and comes from the aforesaid vill of Torre.

"Besides this I have given the Canons permission to make a millpond and a fishpond of a part of Northwille at Torre, for the purpose of making a leat to convey water to the Abbey for their domestic offices; thus they may use the water just as they think fit. And they may make leats and conduits for bringing the water through my land from all springs from which water may be conveniently taken, whether on my land or that of others who have given permission (for the taking of water).

"Wherefore I wish and strongly command that the aforementioned Canons may have and hold all the abovementioned lands and tenements, with all their liberties and appurtenances and everything mentioned above, well and peacefully, freely and quit, honourably, completely and wholly, in wood and plain, in roads and footpaths and rights of egress, in meadows, pastures and commons, in churches and church benefices, in turbary, (gathering of) rushes, in fisheries, in water, aqueducts and conduits, in millponds and fishponds, in mills and their sites, and in all easements, liberties, and free customs belonging to such lands and tenements; (they are to hold it all) in free, pure and perpetual alms, free and quit of all services of work or custom, all secular exactions, suits and demands for ever.

"And if any of the liberties which I have granted to them should in the course of time and through any contingency not have been made use of, however, they (the Canons) may later on use the same liberty without any objection on my part or on that of my heirs, in spite of the fact that for some reason they may not have been used hitherto.

"However, I and my heirs guarantee to warrant, discharge and uphold the abovementioned lands and tenements, with all their appurtenances and liberties to the said Canons and their successors, against all living people for ever.

"These bear witness:—Henry, Bishop of Exeter; William, Abbot of Buckfast; Osmund, Abbot of Rupe; Richard, Abbot of Welbek; William, Abbot of Rufforde; Stephen, Prior of Wirksope; John de Toritone; Henry, son of Count Richard of Flanders; William de Briwera, William de Punchardone; Richard son of Walter, Robert de chaumpeaus, Henry de Campo Ernulpho, Ralph de Sicta Villa, John Briegwere, Reginald de Albamara, Geoffrey de Albamara, Hugh de Stoddone, Luke de Tetteburne, Walter Colum, William Saunzever, Ralph son of Richard, Geoffrey de Estre, William de Kelly, Baldwin de Bellastone, Henry de Toritone, Thomas de Rocheforde, William the cleric of Eysselegh, William Briegwere, my son; ffubert de Dover; William de Rotomago, Alan de Bokelonde, Robert Germyn, Roger Burnel, Walter, son of Ives, and many others".
MS: Folios 4/5.

2 and 3 are also versions of the Foundation Charter. Whilst 2 is exactly the same as 1 with regard to its contents, yet the names of only the first three witnesses are included. Why it was written out again is hard to understand. In the case of 3, the gifts of the church and mill at Bradworthy, the chapel of "Prankardswike" and Northschillingford

are not mentioned. This could therefore be an early draft of the Foundation Charter, dating from before 1198. No names of witnesses are given.
MS: Folios 5/6/7.

King John's Charters

4. "John, by the grace of God King of England, Lord of Ireland, Duke of Normandy and Aquitaine and Earl of Andegavie sends greetings to his Archbishops, Bishops, Abbots, Earls, Barons, Judges, Sheriffs, Bailiffs and all the faithful, and bids them know that at the petition of his well-beloved and faithful William Briwere he has confirmed to God and St. Mary and to the Church of St. Saviour of Torre and to the Premonstratensian Canons serving God therein the following gift which William has made to them." (There follows here a list of Lord William's gifts to the Abbey, just as was stated in the Foundation Charter). In addition there is mention of John de Toritone's gift of the vill of Haclega and Walter de Vasci's gift of land at Kyngeswere.

The King then confirms that the Canons are to have Soch and Sach, Thol and Theam, Infangenethef and Utgangenethef throughout their lands. They are to hold their lands free and quit from suit of Court at the Shire Court, the Hundred Court or at any Court at all. They are excused paying such demands as Gelde and Danegelde, Hideage, etc. also from Serdwite, Leirwite, Hundredpeny, Tethingpeni, de hengwita, fflemesfreth, Hamsocum, Wapeni, Blodwirta and ffighwita. They and their men are to be free from paying tolls on bridges, ferries, from Lastage and Tallage and feudal aid to Sheriffs and their Bailiffs etc. None of the King's Sheriffs or their Bailiffs are to have any right of entry to the Canons' lands or tenements. If malefactors should be arrested on the Canons' property and cannot be tried in their Courts, then they are to be handed over to the King's Sheriffs or Bailiffs without any difficulty or delay.

The Canons and their men are to be free from service on juries or at Assizes. If any of their men commit a felony for which he should forfeit his cattle then that cattle shall come to the Canons. All fines from their men are to come to them, and they may exercise distraint for non-payment. etc., etc.

Date: 1199/1200. MS: Folio 7/8. Witnesses:—H(ubert), Archbishop of Canterbury, our Chancellor, H(erbert), Bishop of Salisbury.

5. A shorter and more concise version of 4. The gift of 1½ virgates of land at Newenham, (Berks.) from Walter, the son of Ives, is included here but not in 4.
Date: 1199/1200. MS: Folio 8/9. The same witnesses.

Charter 4, given by King John, is a confirmation from the King of all Lord William Brewer's gifts to Torre Abbey; it also grants several rights and privileges in connection with the laws of the land. The capital "J" with which this charter begins is so elaborately treated and the pages so ingeniously adorned and decorated that one can see at a glance that the writer of the Cartulary considered this the outstanding charter. Altogether the Canons must have had a high opinion of King John, for by this charter he freed them from many irksome duties and services. Recent writers on the subject of this King have stressed the fact that he took an enormous interest in the laws of his land, travelling about the country and administering justice in the various courts of law in person. So this charter, drawn up at the instigation of Lord William, himself an eminent Judge, was in all probability perfectly understood by the King, who, being so conversant with the law, would thoroughly appreciate the implications of its contents.

17

Torre

The Charters

6. A confirmation from Beatrix de Valle of all the gifts which her husband William Brywere made to the Church of St. Saviour of Torre. It is given for the souls of King Richard and his father, King Henry, for her husband and all her forbears and successors. She also confirms Rowedone and its boundaries, fishing rights and grazing rights in the vill of Torre, a ferling of land at Uggeburgh and the site of fishponds at North(wille) in the vill of Torre from which leats may conduct water to the Abbey.
Date: c. 1196.   MS: Folio 9.

7. A confirmation of all his father's gifts to the Church of Torre from William Brewer the Younger. Given for his own soul and that of his wife, Johanna.
Date: c. 1224.   MS: Folio 9.

Charters 8, 9 and 10 refer to Ilsham and Shiphay Collaton and are placed in that chapter.

11. A gift from William Brewer the Younger to the Church of the Holy Trinity of Torre, consisting of his own body (for burial there) and water from St. Petroc's spring which rises near the Courthouse kitchen. It may be conducted to the Abbey for use there. Grant of access for making and cleaning the leat. Clause of Warranty.
Date: 1224/32.   MS: Folio 11.

12. A confirmation in perpetual alms from Reginald de Mohun to the Canons of Torre of all the gifts which his grandfather and uncle made to them. Given at Thorr.
Date: Tuesday next before the Feast of St. Edmund, King and Martyr, 1252.   MS: Folio 11.

13. A cirograph between Symon, Abbot of Torre, and Reginald de Mohun whereby Reginald is permitted to build a chapel at his courthouse at Thorre. It is for himself and his family, and his own chaplains will celebrate the divine office. The servants of the courthouse are to attend the parish church. No baptisms or parochial rites are to be carried out in the chapel. The claims of the parish church with regard to offerings and oblations are to be carefully observed.
Date: Tuesday before Palm Sunday, 1252/53.   MS: Folio 11.

14. A confirmation by H(enry), Bishop of Exeter, of William Briwere's gift of the church of Thorre to the Canons of Thorre.
Date: Given at Peyntone, June 17th, 1198/99.   MS: Folio 12.

15. An incomplete charter. The rubric heading states that it is a confirmation from

W(illiam Brewer), Bishop of Exeter, of the gift of the parish church of Torre to the Canons.
Date: c. 1224.   MS: Folio 12.

The Torre charters are easily understood and no special comment on them is necessary here because the more important of them are fully discussed in other chapters. So we turn next to consider the large mediaeval parish of Tormohun in which the Abbey stood, and to discuss what links with monastic times still exist.

In few towns has the destruction of all that is ancient been so complete as in Torquay. In the parish of Tormohun, for instance, only one house of any antiquity survived into the mid 20th century and that was Lavender Cottage in Avenue Road. It was a thatched house with a pleasant 18th century frontage and dormer windows. The actual shape of the building was an L, and one red sandstone chimney survived at the back which looked as if it might have been mediaeval. All this was demolished in 1968 to make room for a petrol station. Torre Cottage, the first house in Upton Road, seems to have ancient roots, because by a strange clause in its original lease, a hogshead of water was to be presented as rent to Torre Abbey. Nearby, in the vicinity of the Torbay Inn, a mediaeval well was uncovered during road widening not long ago, and near Castle Chambers a similar well was found when the bowling alley was being built.

Apart from the parish church, however, and the former existence of the Courthouse nearby, the only evidence of any mediaeval houses at Torre was provided by (1) an old house in Church Street, now gone, and (2) adjacent to it, the old Church House, which was immediately outside the church gate. Both these buildings I well remember. The latter had been divided into two or three cottages and had irregular, bulging walls covered in stucco. When demolished about 1935 it was seen to have been built of cob. The other house was of stone; I seem to remember that it was L shaped and it abutted right onto the pavement. Besides these houses there was in the 12th c. the parsonage where Richard lived. Mentioned in the Foundation Charter, it sounds as though it was at the top of Mill Lane, perhaps close to where the "Rising Sun" Inn now stands. A smithy is said to have occupied a site near the present All Saints' Church. The Church House site was granted by Abbot Dyare in 1520. A deed of that year survives among the Powderham Records the gist of which is as follows:—"1529, May 21, Abbot Thomas granted to Thomas Worsset, John Bartlett the elder, William Colcott, Roger Bartlett the Younger, Thomas Waye, Thomas Stremer and Thomas Bushuppe a parcel of land in Tormohun between Torr land on the south side, the land of John Cokeman on the west side, the Kingsway on the north side and the churchway on the east side, containing 70ft. in length and 24ft. in width. To have etc., for the use of the parish church of Torremone. Rendering annually 16d." Measurement shows that the two semi-detached modern houses at the north gate of the churchyard occupy a site which still corresponds with the area mentioned in this old document.

The site of the Courthouse is unfortunately far less certain. With the passing of the manor to the Canons in the 14th century it would cease to be occupied by the lord of the manor and no doubt degenerated into a farmhouse, though presumably the manor court would still be held there. Octavian Blewett says that in his day some ruined walls stood east of the church which were at that time (early 19th century) said to be the remains of the Courthouse. Now the Spring of St. Petroc is stated in charter 11 to rise near the Courthouse kitchen and was to the east of the church: indeed an early 19th c. print of the church shows a woman carrying two pails actually going to draw water from the well near its source. It seems that at that date it was still the established well for the locality. I think therefore that there is very little doubt of the position of the Courthouse, in spite of what Watkin and Ellis say to the contrary. Their assumption that it stood north-west of the church is directly contradicted by the document just considered; this states that the land west of the new Church House belonged to John Cokeman, so how could the Courthouse with its outbuildings and curtillage have stood there?

The site of St. Petroc's well was perpetuated by a drinking fountain placed near the church gate in St. Efride's Road in the 19th century. When houses were built in the locality the old spring dried up, and the drinking fountain was supplied with water from the main supply. Originally of much importance to the Abbey as a water supply, the former stream crossed Tor Hill Road and Lucius Street diagonally in the direction of the steps which lead to Scarborough Road. From there it probably followed the contours of the hill and would reach the Abbey by way of a leat roughly on the line of Chestnut Avenue. The late Dr. Harper who lived at "Fiveways" (now the Trades Club), told me that he had seen the bed of the stream when the roads were being repaired, and its direction was quite definite.

It seems to me that Torre in the days when the Abbey flourished was nothing more than a hamlet. If indeed there ever was a sizeable village there it has vanished without a trace—even the street plan, which often survives when all old buildings have gone, is typically early 19th century. Old roads coming towards the church are Upton Road, Barton Road, Mill Lane and Sand Lane, (now Belgrave Road). From the document just quoted, we know that there was a highway, presumably Church Street or Church Lane north of the new Church House.

I believe that the bulk of the population of the manor lived not at Torre but at Upton, three quarters of a mile to the north-east, where there is ample evidence of a considerable village in mediaeval days. Here, in a snug valley, ringed round with protecting hills, the villein farmers undoubtedly dwelt, and four of their houses survive to the present day. Evidence of the size of Upton is provided in the Dublin Cartulary where a charter discussed in the chapter on the Acquisition of the Manor of Torre, given by John de Mohun in 1351, quitclaims 18 messuages and 18 ferlings at "Uppetone". A plan of the old village fortunately survives on a large-scale map at Torquay Museum. Dating from the 1860's, it shows that Upton at that time had not been engulfed by new buildings and so was essentially still unchanged. There were in fact two villages, Higher Upton and Lower Upton which were separated by the Fleet brook. From several prints and photographs we know that all these houses were thatched, and it is reasonable to assume that they dated back a long way. In my book "Upton-the Heart of Torquay" I have mentioned that there are several place names close by which seem to be of Saxon origin. All this points to an early origin for Upton. Over 20 buildings are shown on the map, and the general idea that one gets of it is that, just as at Daccombe, it was a village where all the villeins had their farm houses close together in the main street. The isolated farmhouse surrounded by its own fields was not common in this coastal district. The same pattern is to be found at Cockington, Daccombe, Coffinswell and Combe- and Stoke- in-Teignhead. This system is amply demonstrated by evidence from the Tithe map, where it can be seen that right up to the opening of the present century the farmers at Upton went forth from the village to work in their fields which were anything up to 2 miles away. It is interesting to note that Upton preserved its title as "Upton in

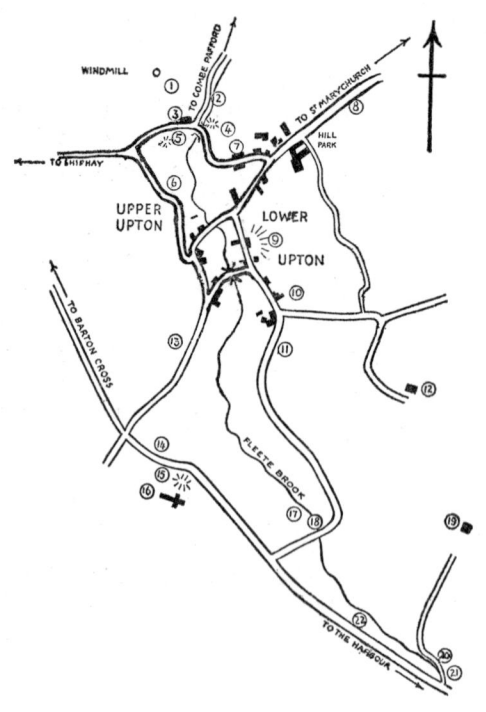

UPTON
1. Staddon (Windmill Hill)
2. Stoneycombe
3. Penney's Cottage
4. Daison Rock
5. Thurlestone
6. Stantaway Hill
7. Upton Farm
8. Chatto Road
9. Quarry and Limekiln
10. Manor Farm
11. Thurlow Hill
12. Site of Ash Hill Farm
13. Upton Road
14. East Street
15. Rock on Torre Hill
16. Torre Church
17. Upton Church
18. Town Hall
19. Ellacombe Barton Farm
20. Pimlico
21. Site of Fleete Mill
22. Abbey Road

The plan of the mediaeval village was quite undisturbed until the coming of the Turnpike Roads in the 1820's.

Tormohun" to the very end of the 19th c., when it was finally over-run by a spate of building. A census carried out early in that century shows an active community engaged in many differing pursuits. This, I consider, was where the bulk of the Abbey's tenants lived, when in the middle of the 14th c. the manor passed to the ownership of the Canons. Old houses still surviving are Penney's Cottage, Upton Farm, Upton House, nos. 17 and 19 St. James's Road, and the kitchen wing of Hill Park. Old people living now (1977) can remember fields and orchards at Upton, and it is fascinating to think that we have the plan of a village to insert in this book which through the ages had probably scarcely changed since the days when the Abbot of Torre was lord of the manor, and in his Courthouse of Torre could punish the miscreants of Upton with imprisonment or even death.

One further house in the manor of Torre must be mentioned and this is Torwood Grange. After the Dissolution the Ridgeways built their manorhouse here. In monastic times it was an important grange, and this is attested by the very considerable barn still to be seen there. It has long been converted into a dwellinghouse, but is quite a remarkable survival of mediaeval times, and it seems that this was the only old building allowed to remain when the 16th century manorhouse was erected. As the name "Torwood" suggests, there were no doubt extensive woodlands surrounding the grange, whilst further east was Wellswood which merged into the next manor of Ilsham. Forestry would therefore be an active pursuit here.

Until the harbour was built at "the bottom by Torre Prior" the manor was not at all well off with regard to a sheltered haven. The above quotation from Leland dates from

Torre: Parish Church of St. Saviour.

Torre: Parish Church of St. Saviour, north chancel window. *Photo by G. Court Jones.*

From an old photo lent by Mrs. Bolt
Penney's Cottage (c. 1870) John and Peggy Penney and their Donkey

Upton, Torquay. Part of old village.

Shiphay Collaton: Monastic barn at Shiphay Manor.   *Photo by A. W. Everett F.S.A.*

Newton Abbot: Tower of the former St. Leonard's Chapel.

Newton Abbot: Keyberry Mill. *Photo by G. Court Jones.*

Wolborough: St. Mary's Church. *Photo by M. Leach.*

the time of Henry VIII, and shows that the harbour, in later days to become so famous, already existed. But who built it? As we hear nothing of it in the early days of the Abbey I would suggest that it was done at the instigation of the Canons themselves sometime after they acquired the manor of Torre in the mid 14th c. Previously the only haven which the manor seems to have had was right in front of the Abbey on the east side of Corbyn's Head beach, where at low tide a natural inlet among the rocks may be seen. They have been much eroded by the sea since the time with which we are dealing, and the sea front itself may cover quite a lot of this little harbour. What is quite certain is that it cannot have been beyond Fulleford Brook which has its outlet just here, for this was the boundary between Torre and Cockington. We know from the Cartulary that the latter manor owned Corbyn's Head and worked a quarry at its base. So there is no doubt that Torre's harbour cannot have been there.

The little haven was connected by a causeway with firmer ground to the north. There is little doubt that it ran upon the line of the present King's Drive and was the 'magnum calcetum" mentioned as a boundary of the Abbey's property in the Foundation Charter. Since it was mentioned as a boundary it must have antedated the Abbey. It is interesting to note that it connected in a straight line with Avenue Road, St. Michael's Road and Barton Hill Road. Its continuation ran inland in a northerly direction to Great Hill, Barton, where was an old earth work. Here it met the ridgeway which came up from Milber Down. Indeed from Old Woods Hill northward it was itself a ridgeway. The inference is, therefore, that this old road and the causeway at its beginning could date from very early times.

Fulleforde Mill. (From Lithograph in "Picturesque Europe").   *D. Seymour.*

There was one more building which we know to have existed in monastic days and this was a mill, for it is mentioned in the quitclaim of 1351 which has just been discussed. It is most probable that this was Fleet Mill which stood at the bottom of Union Street. We have no evidence of a mill higher up the Fleet Brook, and everything points to this as the manorial mill. It existed until early in the 19th century, and there are romantic sketches of it done by Swete and others.

The Parish Church of St. Saviour, Torre

The old mother church of Torquay stands amid pleasant lawns and trees and flowering shrubs of all varieties. The crowded gravestones which had become broken and untidy have in recent years been removed and the best of them placed against the surrounding walls. The result is most satisfactory. There are seats, too, where the lover of history may sit and meditate upon the origin of this little building, which until a century or so ago stood amid green fields; now it is surrounded by houses and shops and ceaseless traffic—a quiet backwater in the midst of a busy town. Torquay people in my youth always referred to it as "Old Torre", and how right they were, because the church was there before Torre Abbey, and was given to the Canons by Lord William Brewer in the Foundation Charter of c. 1199.

It is quite certain, therefore, that a small Norman building stood here, and it is unfortunate that not a trace of it remains. We have more than a hint as to its size, for about three-quarters of the way up the nave there is an unaccountable step which is just at the place where overhead there is an irregular join in the nave roof. From outside this is easily seen from the north side of the churchyard. Inside the join has been overcome by a massive rib beam, resting on two corbels; these are carved into the likeness of heads. It seems clear that the east wall of the short Norman church stood here. When the building was extended eastwards, then the old east wall was demolished, but the continuation of the roof was never satisfactorily disguised.

It has been asserted that the old dedication was to St. Petroc, for St. Petroc's well had its source beside the churchyard. Then again there is a record of a 16th century burial in St. Petroc's aisle. Some, assuming the dedication to St. Petroc to have been a fact, have let their imagination wander back to Celtic times when his missionary work was active in the south-west. They have seen him baptising fresh converts at St. Petroc's well, with a small chapel beside it. There is also the evidence of the 6th century burial stone at East Ogwell, which shows that by that time Christianity had advanced very close to Torre. But a Celtic connection with St. Saviour's must be treated at present with the greatest reserve.

Bearing in mind the possible great antiquity of the site of St. Saviour's, it is more than a little disappointing to find an entirely perpendicular building. The tower, certainly, may be earlier. The rebuilding and addition of aisles was, nevertheless, well carried out; the roofs are lofty in comparison with the length of the church, and the exterior view is in many ways pleasing. The interior has been heavily furnished in the Victorian period, and the walls covered with memorials to the invalids who flocked to Torquay in the early 19th century. All that remains to see of monastic days are:—the simple arcade of Beer stone; the corbels already mentioned and another grotesque head at the west end of the north arcade; piscinas on both sides of the altar; the excellent font which is of an unusual and most graceful design.

The chancel suffered a second extension eastwards in the last century, and a window said to have had very good tracery was destroyed. Built into the east wall are three coats of arms from this window. They are those of Torre Abbey, Brewer and Mohun. More interesting still are two carved heads used as stops to the hood moulding of the north chancel window. These are also from the former east window. The westernmost and best preserved shows a Premonstratensian Canon wearing his distinctive head-dress. The other head shows a bishop or an Abbot, perhaps. His mitre is much damaged, however.

The fabric is of limestone, but much of its attractiveness lies in the occasional piece of sandstone which probably came from Corbyn's Head. A built up doorway in the north aisle possibly gave access to a chantry there. All is plastered over within and this door cannot be seen. The two rood loft doorways are also covered over. A screen is known to have existed until the refurnishing of the church.

No bells remain from monastic times, but there are details of an old treble bell in the ringing chamber. It was probably by Dawe of London (1385-1415). It bore a laver-pot shield and another with trefoils and also a cross used by Dawe on bells at Brushford and Abbotsham.

A church path, so I am told, which connected with Torre Abbey could still be seen before Lucius Street was built. The Canons were throughout entirely responsible for the services here and at Cockington. They would see very little difference in the exterior of their parish church if they could come back today; but as regards the environment it is a very different story. The courthouse, the church house and a cottage or two would be the only signs of habitation then. Fortunately the modern buildings have not encroached too much; the old mother church of Torquay still stands with nearly 800 years to its credit, amidst green lawns and protecting trees.

18

Torre Sanctuary Lands

Very little of the Sanctuary Lands belonging to the parish of Tormohun can be identified. This is not at all surprising because the church parted with its glebe lands soon after the beginning of the 17th century. In Exeter City Library there exists a letter from R. Abraham to Rev. R. Mallock, dated Sept. 18th, 1793 (48/13/5/44/1a), in which there is reference to letters patent of Oct. 4th, 1607/8 when George Bingley and William Blake were granted all glebe lands, tithes etc. of Tormohun and Cockington. This list of Sanctuary Lands in Dublin Cartulary (f. 138b) is:—

1 parcel called Lampit near the road leading to Daccumbe.

11 acres at la Wyndehat (Thought to be the hill above Torre station where Pilmuir now stands).

12 acres at Wetedene.

1½ acres by Storedenes Weye (Storedene may be an older spelling of Staddon, the original name of Windmill Hill).

3 parcel near the calcetum (The Abbey's demesne land stretched from the sea to Mill Lane, occupying all the land east of the calcetum—the present King's Drive. To the west was a field called Twynbrok and William the Younger's meadow; so perhaps these three parcels of land were beyond the latter and close to the sea).

1 acre above Blyndeswille (Blindwylle Road perpetuates the old name of this well or perhaps small tributary of the Sherwell Brook. It is below Pilmuir on the S.W. side).

2½ acres in a parcel at la Hele (at the northern end of the parish near the Cemetery).

11½ acres at la Hele.

3 acres in the northern part of the same.

1 acre in 1 parcel in higher part of la Heale.

1½ acres in another parcel in higher part of la Heale.

3 acres at la Erokelond.

½ acre at Cellenescobbe.

1 acre at Scirewill (Sherwell Lane and Brook keep this old name alive).

7 acres at Fallendeclive (Evidently close to the sea, possibly near Livermead Head or Corbyn's Head).

2 acres at Bade Weye (Walter praepositus holds another in exchange for land at la Wyndehet).

19

Ilsham and Shiphay Collaton

The Charters

8. A confirmation of a gift made by William Brewere the Younger to the Church of Torre of all his land at Ylsham and Coleton: given for his own soul and those of his wife, Johanna, and William and Beatrix his parents. Also his meadow which lies between the causeway (which runs down from the Abbey to the sea) and the meadow of Cockyngtone.
Date: 1224/32.   MS: Folio 9.

9. A quitclaim of the service of half a knight's fee at Coleton made to William Briwere by Henry de Nonant with the consent of his brother Roger. This service ancestors of Beatrix, William's wife, had made to Henry's ancestors and later William to Henry. He also gives the service of Alan, son of Guy de Bokelonde, for the land of Bokelonde, la ho and Compton for one knight's fee. For this William and his heirs hold the service of Coletone in demesne from Henry and his heirs, and the service and homage of Alan for the aforesaid tenements free and quit, for the service of one knight.
Date: pre 1196.   MS: Folio 10.

10. A gift from William Briwere to the church of St. Saviour of Torre of a certain part of his vill of Coleton. Its boundaries are: the road from Torre by way of the Wyngate to a point where it meets another road from Torre; thence ascending to Karswille land at Kyngesdon; returning thence through Kokyngton wood, and by Coleton land to the road which comes from Torre by way of the Wyndgate.
Date: c. 1196.   MS: Folio 10.

Ilsham

Ilsham was a Domesday manor which formed a part of the large parish of St. Marychurch. The Domesday picture is of a modest manor where, beside the demesne farm, there were two villeins' holdings and two bordars' small holdings. It belonged to William the King's Usher and was held by a certain Roger: it was worth 10/-. The spate of 19th century building in Ilsham undoubtedly destroyed all trace of the old holdings, and by the present century their names and positions had been lost. One farm remained beside the Grange farm, however, and this was Hope Farm which stood in the Ilsham Valley below Kent's Cavern. Ilsham Grange was a going concern until the 1920's when the making of the Ilsham Marine Drive opened up the district for building, thus putting an end to most of the farming. Its old farmhouse was demolished to make way for a large house which was built on the site. It is now the Junior School of Stoodley Knowle Convent School. The farmyard and outbuildings were not destroyed and the most important of the monastic buildings to survive was the chapel.

In Saxon days the manor was held by Berus, then after the Conquest it came to William the King's Usher. Tradition says that the Pomeroys had it next, and that it was purchased from them by Lord William Brewer's father. William the Younger gave "Ylsham" to the Canons of Torre sometime between 1224/32, because his father entered Dunkeswell Abbey in 1224, and in 1232 he himself died. It remained in the hands of the Abbey to the end, but is not mentioned in "Valor Ecclesiasticus", probably because it would be looked upon as a sub manor of Torre.

The first thing that catches the eye of the visitor to Ilsham is the chapel which is contained in an elegant little three-storeyed tower. This, with its tapering sides, and gable surmounted by a cross and bell-cote is of great charm. How it has survived the centuries is quite remarkable. This and the chapel at Alfaresworthy, so far as I can see, are the only two domestic chapels remaining which had Torre Abbey connections. They are quite dissimilar in plan, for whilst the latter is a simple quadrangular building, the Ilsham chapel is on the first floor of a three storeyed building and reached by an external flight of steps. The ground floor may have been the living room of the Canon who presided there, whilst over the chapel were his sleeping quarters. This high loft must also have served as a lookout because it contains several slit windows facing in various directions. Both Torbay and Lyme Bay are in view, so a watch could be kept for hostile shipping, and Torre Abbey could be quickly alerted if danger threatened.

Ilsham Chapel. *D. Seymour.*

Ilsham Chapel. D. Seymour.

Unlike the Alfaresworthy chapel the Ilsham chapel is so small that it is a mere oratory. It measures about 12½ ft. by 9 ft. There is little doubt that this was the cell of one Canon and it exactly fulfills the requirements laid down by Pope Gregory IX for the Premonstratensians. They were exhorted to build themselves oratories at their granges where they could retire from the distractions of the world. When necessary they were to celebrate the Divine Offices for the family of the grange only. Thus at Ilsham we have what appears to the the sole survivor of this type of Premonstratensian oratory, and it is a most precious legacy from the past. Every step should be taken to preserve it and keep it in good repair.

With regard to the other farm buildings, it is unfortunate that little of interest now remains. The large mediaeval granary collapsed in the centre and has been restored as two separate buildings. But fields still come up to the old chapel and stretch away to the sea as of old. They are fortunately all the property of Stoodley Knowle. The remains of Ilsham Grange are perhaps best viewed from the school garden. From this vantage point one can look down upon the former enclosure which is still watched over by the old chapel. From whichever side of the valley the old Grange is viewed glorious scenery meets the eye; and quite enough of the original countryside remains for us to recapture in the mind's eye the former appearance of this once secluded valley.

Further References

Taxation of Pope Nicholas, 1288
  Valued at £1.15.0.

Devon Monastic Lands
  p. 8. "Graungia de Elsham infra parochia predicta valet in: Firma graungie ibidem cum ortis pomariis gardinis terris pratis pascuis et pastoris vocatis Warbury parke, XVI acr., Stanberehill XX acr., Stowlles XII acr., Forendene parke XXX acr., Asshynden parke XVII acr., Litelberie XX acr., Calfen parke IIII acr., cum certis ad Hope C acr., et Long Acre ibidem cum omnibus et singulis suis pertinenciis per annum £6.13.6. :—£23.4.2.

Examinatur per Mathiam Coltehirste. vi die Februarii anno xxxi regis nunc Henrici VIII: Summa totalis valoris possessionum predictarum ut supra £23.4.2. Inde pro decima de premissis exita et domino regi annuatim solvenda, 46/6, et remanet clare £20.7.8., which rated after X yeres purchase amountythe to the summe of £417.13.4., to be paid in forme folowynge, that is to seye in hande £217.13.4., and at the firste daye of September nexte followinge £200.

        Johannes Ridgeweye
(signed)   Thomas Crumwell   Richard Ryche"
                                      (A.O., Particulars for Grants 933)

Coletone

The former Saxon manor of Coletone is known today as Shiphay Collaton. There are no less than four manors named Coletone in the Exeter Domesday book, and unfortunately we cannot be sure which is the subject of this chapter. In every case Coletone has become Collaton, so it is more than probable that it was always pronounced thus. The prefix "Shiphay" or "Sheephay" was added later—probably in monastic times when the Canons were using the demesne land for extensive sheep rearing. This manor, like Ilsham, lay in the parish of St. Marychurch whose western boundary extended to the lofty summit of Kingsdon.

Shiphay Collaton, now a suburb of Torquay, was still an entirely agricultural settlement until as late as the 1920's when building first began. The writer can remember when not a house was to be seen, apart from the village and the manorhouse. Shiphay Lane was then a narrow road with steep banks which in spring time were covered in primroses. It was easy to see at that time how the manorhouse site was an entirely separate entity, situated some half a mile from the village which was across the fields to the north, beside the church. Here in monastic times the villeins must have dwelt whilst the Canons farmed the demesne land—their grange having been on the site of the present 19th century manorhouse and its outbuildings. All that remains of their day is a barn which is considered to have its original roof timbers. There is an interesting account of it in T.D.A. 1965, by A. K. Everett, F.S.A.

We know that there was a parochial chapel at Coletone, but in Bishop Stapledon's Register (p. 377) it is described as "prostrata" as early as 1301. The fact that it had been allowed to fall into disrepair may have been due to the fact that the Canons had their own chapel at the grange where their tenants were allowed to worship, and so their parochial chapel was neglected and finally disappeared without a trace.

Hilda Walker has written on the subject of this manor (T.D.A., 1965). She suggests as a site for this chapel a former field named Halwell, once at the top of Dairy Hill. She has also pointed out the splendid banks which still flank part of the south side of Marldon Road. These would form the northern boundary of the Canons' demesne land and are much akin to the great banks which surrounded the Canons' property at Bradworthy, and which are considered later. It is probable when such banks surround the demesne land of a manor mentioned in Domesday that they may go back to Saxon times.

There are three charters concerning Coletone in addition to mention of it in the Foundation Charter. The oldest is 9, which ante-dates the founding of the Abbey. It tells us that ancestors of Beatrix, Lord William Brewer's wife, formerly held this manor from the de Nonants. Elsewhere it is told how Coletone was probably a part of her dowry. It naturally appeared to Lord William as a convenient manor with which to endow his new Foundation which was so close at hand. Henry de Nonant therefore quitclaimed Coleton for half a knight's fee. The homage of Guy de Bokelonde for 1 knight's fee for the lands of Bokelonde, la ho and Compton was included. These places are the estates of Egg Buckland, Hoo and Compton Giffard near Plymouth.

In the foundation charter the donor gives land at Coletone with exactly the same boundaries as those mentioned in 10. To understand them it is necessary to grasp where the hill of "la windiete" or "wyndgate" was situated. Some writers disagree over this, but I consider it is the hill on which Pilmuir stands and which continues above Torre Station to the top of Shiphay lane close to the Torquay Girls' Grammar School. Behind the station there is still to be seen the beginnings of an overgrown lane going in the required direction. The other road from Torre was Shiphay Lane, and they would meet probably near the top of Shiphay Lane. We then ascend by Marldon Road in what is nearly a straight line to the summit of the hill of Kingsdon which is now crowned by a reservoir. The return was made by Cockington Woods, which still exist below the farm of that name; then it seems that the boundaries were meant to go straight back to the starting point behind Torre Station, crossing Shiphay land all the way. All this land centered on the grange and I think that it was a part or even the whole of the demesne land that was being given to the Canons.

When Lord William died his son confirmed his father's gift in 8 and then gave the Canons the whole of the manor. As in the case of Ilsham this must have been between 1224 and 1232.

It will be noticed in the grant to John Ridgeway which follows, that many of the fields are mentioned by name. Some of these re-appear on the Tithe Map three centuries later. The eastern boundary appears today as though it must have been the main road to Newton Abbot, but we must remember that both it and the railway are entirely 19th century constructions which cut through the old enclosures of Broad Park and Little Broad Park. Even today there are three fields beyond the railway which were formerly a part of Coletone.

After its long sojourn in monastic hands the old manor of Coletone passed at the suppression to the Ridgeway family.

Further References

Taxation of Pope Nicholas, 1288
    The return for Coletone was £1.5.0.

Valor Ecclesiasticus
　The manor was valued at £9.10.3.

A.O., Particulars for Grants 933
　"To John Ridgeway of Newton Abbot, 4th March, 1540, the manor of Collaton and the granges of Ilsham and Shiphay.

pro Rudgeway
Comitatus Devonie

　Nuper monasterium de Torre
　Manerium de Colaton infra parochiis de St. Marie Churche et Torremohun valet in: Redditibus liberorum tenentium ibidem per annum 18d; redditibus customariorum tenentium ibidem per annum £8.7.2.; perquisitis curie ibidem communibus annis 6/8.:—£8.15.4. Firma grangie de Shiphay cum omnibus messuagiis ortis pomariis gardinis terris pratis pascuis et pasturis vocatis Swardon parke XIII acr., cum 1 parco prope domum ibidem XVIII acr.,; Lang parke XVIII acr., Branhay V acr., Culver parke VIII acr., Hod VI acr., Colaton parke VII acr., Weste Wetherhill XV acr., Este Wetherhill XV acr., Brode parke XVI acr., ii pratis vocatis Brodeparkemeade iiii acr., Whiden parke XVIII acr., Whiden woode VI acr., cum omnibus et singulis suis pertinenciis dicte grangie pertinentibus per annum £7.15.4.:—£16.10.8."

20

Wolborough

In the Devonshire Domesday it is stated that Vlveberie was held by Radulfus de Brueria. In 1196, when the manor was given to the Canons of Torre, it was in the hands of William de Bruera, evidently a descendant of Radulfus. In 1086 there was 1 hide, and of this 1 virgate was demesne land, and the other three were in the hands of six villeins. There were 7 bordars and 4 serfs, 12 head of cattle and 100 sheep. There was also a mill worth 5/-; this was probably Keyberry Mill, which until a few years ago proudly claimed to be the oldest working mill in the country.

The picture given by Domesday is of a manor of very little importance given over entirely to agriculture. There was as yet no sign whatever of the market town which was soon to spring up under the encouragement of successive Abbots.

From a geographical point of view Wolborough divides into two sections; the land to the south of Wolborough Hill which still retains its agricultural character, and that to the north which is taken up by the town of Newton Abbot. This grew up in the first place round the thriving market for which the Canons obtained a charter from King Henry III. So much were the Abbots to the fore in developing the town that it became known as the new town of the Abbot, and so we get the modern name of Newton Abbot. It had also an older title—Schireborne Newton, and the name of Sherborne Mills shows that the older name still held its own in the vicinity right up to the present century. It is quite likely that in "Scirburn" we have an older name for the River Lemon, so important in Saxon days because it divided the Hundred of Teignbridge from that of Haytor. The fact that the Abbot of Sherborne owned land in Abbotskerswell is pure coincidence, and there is no evidence to prove that he ever owned property at Newton Abbot or Newton Bushell. The likelihood of the town's former name deriving from Sherborne is not possible because in those early days Abbotskerswell belonged to the Abbot of Horton.

Wolborough Barton, which stands beside the ancient parish church, almost certainly marks the site of the former manorhouse. Whilst no traces of it remain, yet its site is remembered, and Mr. R. J. Rew, the present farmer, could point it out. The Canon's tithe barn still stands, however; built of limestone it has outlasted the other farm buildings. It is of generous proportions, but has unfortunately lost its old roof.

Charter 16 refers to the vill of Wolborough, and there is a strong local tradition that buildings once stood west of the church, occupying the unusually wide expanse of road to be seen there now. It was connected with the town by the Church Path which is of decided antiquity, for it is mentioned in a law suit between the Abbot of Torre and the townsfolk in 1411.

The church of St. Mary is a typical Devon church, rebuilt from humble beginnings in the spacious perpendicular style. There is about it an air of magnificence when compared with the Norman font and insignificant west tower which are all that remain of the first church. I do not believe that the Canons of Torre undertook the cost of this rebuilding as has been frequently stated; for up and down the country at that period it was the burgesses of the towns who were rebuilding their churches on stately lines. One town vied with another in this respect, and the prosperous merchants of Newton Abbot would see to it that their parish church was as worthy as its neighbours at Ashburton and Totnes. The Canons would, of course, encourage the work but I doubt if they gave much towards the cost. The wonderful rood screen with its unusual little parclose chapels would be the last thing to be added, and it is not to be disputed that apart from St. Saviour's, Dartmouth, the result was the finest of the Canons' churches.

One mediaeval bell survives on the floor of the church, and the crown and inscription band of two others. The Rev. J. G. M. Scott says there were three bells in 1552 and they remained until the 1920's, when the smallest were scrapped after the crown of one and the inscription band of the other had been removed. They and the whole of the Tenor are preserved. They were all by John Bird of London c. 1400. The inscriptions are:—
(1) Crown only: "Sum Rosa Pulsata Mundi Katerina Vocata"; (2) Celorum Xpe Placiat Tibi Rex Sonus Iste"; (3) "protege Prece Pia Quos Convoco Sancta Maria". These are certainly notable survivals.

Other things remaining from the Canons' day are a nicely worked piscina on the south side of the chancel, the splendid lectern, vestiges of stained glass in the tops of the windows and a stoup beside the tower door.

The list of rectors displayed on the south wall is correct in that it gives a list of Abbots of Torre for Monastic times. This was a church whose services were maintained by the Canons themselves.

Considering now the agricultural side of the manor, we saw that in the Domesday account there were 6 villeins and 7 bordars. This does not suggest a great number of small holdings, and I believe that in the 11th century there was a good deal of moorland and uncultivated scrubland. We have proof of this in Dublin Cartulary (folio 157b) in connection with the ancient holding of Cauebury (now Keyberry) "....and thus along the moor to the turf pits, as far as the old boundaries of Cauebury", and later " . . .turf sufficient for one soc in our land of Cauebiri". A stretch of this wild, uncultivated land is even now to be seen west of Decoy at the bottom of Gamekeeper's Lane, where tracts of bracken and heath stretch away to the top of the hill.

The Tithe Map is not much help with regard to the old smallholdings at Wolborough, for in the apportionment none of the fields are classified under farm headings. However, among the papers of the Earls of Devon, whose family owned the manor until the present century, I came across another version where the holdings are all mentioned by name. They consist, for the most part, of small farms ranging from $12\frac{1}{2}$ acres upwards. This is the old measure of the half ferling, and there is no doubt that here we have the mediaeval holdings dating from the days when the Canons held Wolborough. The patterns of the farm boundaries were quite clear, except on the steep slope above the town on the northern slopes of Wolborough Hill.

At the southern extremity of the manor came Wottons—a little farm of just under 16 acres. It consisted of the fields surrounding the present Augustinian Priory. The mediaeval name has unfortunately been forgotten, for "Wottons" is clearly a personal name. Charter 32 refers to a field called Ellacome, which Abbot Richard leases to Nicholas Clou(n)esworthi for 10/- per annum, in 1301. This field of Ellacome or Alicome is still so called, and the farmer there could immediately point it out to me. It is the actual field in which the Priory stands. When the pleasant country house which preceded the Priory was built it was called, most aptly, "Abbotsleigh", thus showing that the owner realised that he had built in the Abbot's leigh or meadow. At this time the little farm of Wottons may have lost its identity and the name is quite forgotten now.

On the opposite side of the road to Abbotskerswell stood Hennaborough. The site of its farm buildings is marked by a fine old cob barn which stands on the slope of the hill about ¼ mile below the road. This farm consisted of about 42 acres—representing 1½ ferlings. "Henneburghe" is mentioned in Dublin Cartulary (folio 154a), and Henbury Wood in 1543.

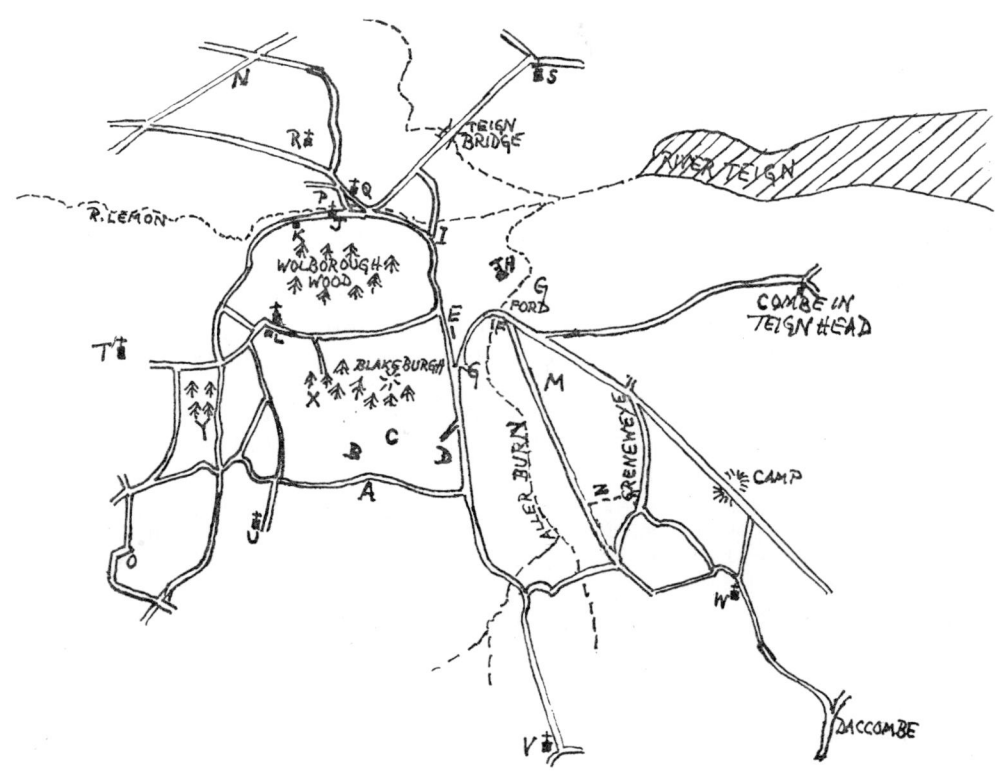

The Mediaeval Holdings at Wolborough.   D. Seymour.

A	Wottons	J	St. Leonard's	R	Highweek Church
B	Hennaborough	K	Manor House	S	Kingsteignton Church
C	Goldmoors	L	Wolborough Barton and Church	T	East Ogwell Church
D	Silverhills			U	Abbotskerswell Church
E	Cavebiri	M	Teign Aller Farm	V	Kingskerswell Church
F	Cavebiri Mill	N	Maynbogh	W	Coffinswell Church
G	Aller Burn Farm	O	Rydon	X	Hennaborough Wood
H	Forde House	P	Newton Bushell	Y	Westwood
I	Bartletts	Q	St. Mary's Church	Z	Horscombe

The next farm to the east of Hennaborough was Goldmoors, and it occupied about 25 acres or 1 ferling. Here again all that remained to see was a barn which survived until recently. Becoming unsafe it was demolished, and so well has the site been cleared that the visitor will look in vain for any trace of it. The name still exists on the old O.S. Map, however; it stood on low ground, close to a stream which comes in from the west. The lane from Decoy at the foot of Black Ball Copse led to it.

Further east was Silverhills—another small holding of half a ferling or $12\frac{1}{2}$ acres. Practically all its land was swallowed up by clay pits which, in their turn, were filled in and the land "developed". Oddly enough Silverhills had no farm buildings among its fields, and according to the map these were at the mill yard at Keyberry.

The next farm was Aller Burn (mis-spelt Aller Barn in the Courtenay document) which was a considerable property, extending on both sides of the stream; that on the east side being in the parish of Combe-in-Teignhead. It began a little south of Decoy and stretched past Forde House to a point where the stream joined the River Teign. I much wonder whether this may not have been the property at Aller owned by Ingelramus in 1196 and for which he paid a 9/- rent. It is mentioned in 16, 17, 34, 35, 36 and 37 and must have been an important holding. Its farm buildings may very well have occupied the present site of Forde House.

On the land now occupied by the railway station and its sidings was another holding under the heading of "part of Bartletts". It stretched as far as the River Lemon, but where the farmhouse stood we cannot tell. There must have been at least two holdings on the slopes of Wolborough Hill, directly behind the town. An old house in the lane behind the manorhouse has been pointed out to me as a former farmhouse, and so has 49, St. Leonard's Terrace.

It now remains to discuss the two most important farms, Wolborough Barton (where the former manor court was held and where William de Bruera may have lived) and Forde Grange, formerly Keyberry. At the first, some very stout banks surround the farmland, and they may mark the old demesne boundaries. They extend along Coach Road to Gamekeeper's Lane, turn down the lane, appear to cut across country to the Abbotskerswell road, and so back to the Barton. Some fine stretches are to be seen in Gamekeeper's Lane, but the farmer tells me that a bank has recently been demolished between here and the next lane. According to Domesday there was 1 virgate involved, and the area concerned does seem a little small for this. More demesne land, however, may have lain north and west of the church.

We have already mentioned the old boundaries of "Cauebiri": the charters suggest that this ancient holding consisted of at least 100 acres or 4 ferlings. It was in those days an important farm and I do not hesitate in locating its farm buildings as at Forde Grange. This old farmhouse is in the centre of the locality to which the name of Keyberry is still attached; within a stone's throw there is Keyberry Park, Keyberry Mill and Keyberry Road.

"Forde" only occurs in the charters as Milburneford. The ford was on the Aller Brook near the modern "Penguin". and the old road to Combe-in-Teignhead and St. Marychurch went across it. But by 1543 there is mention of the "hamlets of Forde". When the present Forde House was built it adopted the new name, and so the older name of Keyberry was superseded.

There is still a spacious farmyard at Ford Grange but the outbuildings are 19th century. The walls of the old farmhouse seem to be still there in part, though much modernised, and a later house has been attached to the southern end. One of the old millstones, doubtless from Keyberry Mill, is to be seen in the garden.

It is sad to record that, owing to flooding, the mill leat was filled in in 1970, and in 1972 the mill itself was demolished. So after a nonstop run from Saxon days yet another building formerly owned by the Abbots of Torre vanished. The boundary of the old farm would extend eastwards from Gamekeeper's Lane and probably follow the same outline as the woods beyond Decoy do today. To the north the farm would stretch towards the town. In 24 " the road to Cawbiry" is mentioned. This is clearly East Street, which, continuing by way of Church Road, leads straight to Forde Grange.

Before leaving the subject of the mediaeval farms mention must be made of Rydon. On the Tithe Map it is shown as an outlying pocket of Wolborough. In 32 a David de Rydon is one of the witnesses; again in the Lay Subsidy of 1332 David and Luke de Rydon are mentioned under Newton Abbot. So in all probability this was yet another monastic farm.

Turning now to the town, we have to go to East Street and Wolborough Street to look for buildings of antiquity. They are unfortunately fast disappearing, which is a pity, for everything which points back to the origin of the modern town is quite irreplaceable. Though the Canons owned property in the towns of Exeter, Dartmouth and Totnes, yet this is the only town which they actually owned and fostered.

The most conspicuous of the old buildings is, of course, St. Leonard's tower which stands in complete isolation at the junction of the principal streets. In the early 19th century old St. Leonard's church, of which it was a part, was pulled down to make room for redevelopment. The church was rebuilt further up the street; fortunately the tower was allowed to remain. It is a simple, unbuttressed building of two stages with a marked batter. It is of the local limestone, with here and there a piece of sandstone, and is an almost exact replica of Wolborough church tower. Its battlements, belfry openings and west door all appear to be original. The door and its foot-long key, too, are also of great age. The bells, however, are modern. There is one pleasing architectural feature, unseen from the road, and this is a slender pointed arch of sandstone at the foot of the stairway. Church dedications are always worth considering, and in this case the dedication to St. Leonard seems to point to an early origin for the chapel. St. Leonard was the patron saint of prisoners, and in the time of the Crusades this dedication was particularly popular. One can imagine that it was to this old chapel that the women of the town went to pray for the safe return of their absent menfolk. If church dedications are interesting, so, too, are the names of inns. We often forget that the old inn which nestles beneath the shadow of the church tower is often as old as the church itself. Close to St. Leonard's is the "Turk's Head". No doubt this was the trophy which the ladies of Wolborough hoped their husbands and sons would bring back with them from the Crusades.

Rhodes, in his "History of Newton Abbot", says that the new church was built on the site of the old parsonage. Whether this was the monastic priest's house one cannot say. Lying a little back from Wolborough Street is the manorhouse. It is dated 1567, but this date would mark a rebuilding. At first it may seem a little odd that there were two manor houses, for the first was unmistakably at Wolborough Barton; but it is quite clear from various sources that at the time of the dissolution there were two courts in Wolborough—a civil and ecclesiastical one. Like other surviving courthouses which the Canons built, an L shaped plan was followed here, although the original design is heavily disguised. The present house has a fine plaster ceiling upstairs of post-monastic times;

this is one of the gems of Newton Abbot. Here, surely, is a building which the town ought to rescue and restore. It is unfortunate that it is so completely smothered in stucco, for many old features may yet await discovery beneath it. One feels it is a house of many secrets yet to be revealed. In its heyday it would be the most important secular building in the town, and here the business side of the manor would be transacted. In King Henry VIII's reign we find in "Valor Ecclesiasticus" that there is mention of both courts—the Rectorial and Manorial—which represented the spiritual and temporal sides of the Abbey's possessions here. The manor of Wolborough was worth £47.18., the Rectory £20.10.10., and "Newton Abbot", possibly referring to the toll on the market, £10.17.7. This brought in £79.6.8.—a very large sum. There is also mention of the perquisites of courts both at Newton Abbot and Wolborough.

Wolborough Street at rear of Manor House, 1968.   *D. Seymour.*

One of the best remaining corners of Wolborough Street, where old buildings still survive, is Pound Place. Here the former "Tudor House" (now offices) takes up one side, whilst at the end is "Woodbine Cottage" which has attractive old chimneys and much good timber work upstairs. The "Tudor House" is an excellent example of a small two-storeyed merchant's house with a yard, stable and store above. Its frontage suggests a 15th century date, but its narrow spiral stair with its slit window and pointed arch must be a century earlier. This is built into the massive chimney breast, and it is unfortunate that the old hearth has been covered in. There are also two good doorways with shoulder arches.

Woodbine Cottage, 1968.   D. Seymour.

    Deeds going right back to monastic days possibly existed until the time of a former owner—a very old lady. She is reported to have said, "Us 'ad all they deeds, but they was so turrible old they was in a vurrein language, so us burnt all they". So perished in the flames what may very well have been documents going right back to the time when the house belonged to the Abbot of Torre.

    There are other houses in Wolborough Street which, though showing a general style of a later date, are probably mediaeval in origin and retain their old walls. To climb the hill behind the town is to be rewarded with the sight of houses far older than their street frontages suggest. Here old chimneys and steep-pitched roofs show that the properties are many centuries old.

    In East Street were tenements of a larger kind, which on the south side extended up the hill, covering a considerable amount of ground. Unfortunately these houses are fast disappearing. One particularly good red brick house with a frontage of the Queen Anne period has been demolished. Though showing no ancient features, it obviously followed the plan of a far older house on the same site. On the north side of the road is humbler property, and here an inn or two and a few long passages tell of older times. The main streets of Newton Abbot are unmistakably 19th century in style; that is why it is such a relief to find Wolborough Street and East Street with their reminders of the time when all was in the hand of the Abbot of Torre.

The Charters

16. A confirmation from William, son of Antony de Bruera, made to William Briewere of the vill and advowson of Wlveburga for 40 marks in silver and for the service of 1 knight; also the tenement which he held from Ingelramus, son of Odo, for a 9/- rent:

also the fishing rights of Wulveburga on the Teyngne. All this may be given to the church of St. Saviour of Torre. Clause of Warranty.
Date: c. 1196.   MS: Folio 13.

17.   A confirmation by William de Bruera to the Canons of Torre of William Briewere's gift to them of the vill and advowson of Wlueberga and of all the concessions made in Charter 16.
Date: c. 1196.   MS: Folio 14.

18.   Henry, son of Count Reginald of Cornwall, quitclaims to the Canons of Torre suit of court and payment of 12 pence in his hundred of Haitorra.
Date: c. 1196.   MS: Folio 14.

19.   A confirmation of William de la Briwere's gift of Wlveburga to the Canons of Torre made by Robert de Courtenay, lord of the fee. He also quitclaims the service of 1 knight.
Date: c. 1210 (Robert de Courtenay succeeded his father in 1209).   MS: Folio 15.

20.   A confirmation from Matilda de Cortenay of 1 knight's fee in Wlveburgh made to St. Saviour's of Torre.
Date: c. 1220.   MS: Folio 15.

The Elizabethan House, Wolborough Street, from Pound Place.   *D. Seymour.*

21. W. de Ralegh, sheriff of Devon, testifies that William de Bruera confirmed the Wolvebugh charters which he had given to William Briwer and the Convent of Torre before the full council.
Date: The Morrow of the Feast of St. John the Baptist, 1228. MS: Folio 15.

22. A confirmation from Bishop Henry Marshall of the gift of the church of Wlveburga to the religious men of Torre. They are to maintain a chaplain there.
Date: Given at Cheddelegh, July 15th, 1206/7. (The 12th year of Bishop Marshall's episcopate). MS: Folio 15.

23. A concession made by Geoffrey de Bruera to the Canons of Torre whereby they may have the right of free transit through his land of Teyngne for horses, wagons, millstones and all kind of wheels.
Date: c. 1220. MS: Folio 15.

24. A quitclaim from Walter the barber of Tavystoke of a messuage at Newton made to God, St. Mary and the Church of St. Saviour of Torre. It lies between the messuages of Eliot, son of William the forester, and Thomas le Pil, on the south side of the road to Cawbiry. It came to him on the death of his brother, William the painter, who had it as a gift from the Abbot of Torre. The Abbot has given him 31/- for its return.
Date: Probably 13th century. MS: Folio 15 & 16.

25. A gift of his land of Maynbogh to the Church of St. Saviour of Torre from Geoffrey Giffard.
Date: c. 1240. MS: Folio 16.

26. Luke, son of John, lord of the manor of TeyngWike, gives the whole tenement of Maynbogh to Geoffrey Giffard. Rent, a pair of gilt spurs at Easter.
Date: c. 1230. MS: Folio 16.

27. A confirmation of the land of Maynbogh made by Theobald de Anglica Villa to the Canons of Torre.
Date: Mid 13th century. MS: Folio 16.

28. A confirmation of the land of Maynbogh from Theobald de Anglica Villa to Geoffrey Giffard: also of the land given to him by Robert Burnage and Thomas Northlane.
Date: 1235-1245. MS: Folio 16.

29. A gift of a 2/- rent, together with his body, made to the Canons of Torre from Osbert pictavensis. The rent is from the tenement which Emelot Bughweren holds from him at Wogewille.
Date: post 1224. MS: Folio 16/17.

30. A grant from King Henry III of a Wednesday market at Schireborne Nyweton made to the Canons of Torre. A fair may also be held on the Eve, the Feast of and the Morrow of St. Leonard's Day.
Date: Mid 13th century. MS: Folio 17. Witness: William de Valencia, our brother.

31. A gift by Thomas le Peytevyn to the Canons of Thorre Briwere of a 2/- rent from a tenement at Woggewille. Clause of Distraint.
Date: Mid 13th century. MS: Folio 17.

32. A confirmation of the land of Ellacome in the manor of Wolleburgh made by Richard, Abbot of Torre, to Nicholas Clov(u)esworthi. Service: one twentieth of a knight's fee. Rent: 10/-
Date: Thursday, the Morrow of the Feast of St. Luke, 1301. MS: Folio 17 & 18.
Witnesses: Roger de Cokyngtone, knight, William de Comptone, John Alneto, Thomas Weryng, John Elys, David de Rydone, Stephen Bokeyete.

33. A gift from Robert ffrelard, son of Ralph, to the Canons of Torre of the whole of his land at Kavebiri. The Abbot has given him 10 marks in recognition and undertakes to provide for his mother.
Date: 13th century. MS: Folio 18.

34. A gift to the Church of Torre from Gervase, son of Odo, of a 9/- rent at Aulre. He also confirms William Briwere's gift of Aulre with its men and appurtenances. Abbot Adam gave him 40/- as recognition.
Date: 1196-1200. MS: Folio 18.

35. A quitclaim of the 9/- rent at Aulre from W. de Boteraus to the Canons of Torre, given at the instigation of his wife, Avelina. Each had one mark in silver as recognition from Abbot Roger.
Date: c. 1200-1205. MS: Folio 18 & 19.

36. A confirmation of 35 from Avelina de Boteraus after the death of her husband, William. Abbot R(oger) gave her 1 mark in recognition.
Date: c. 1207. MS: Folio 19.

37. A quitclaim from Ralph de Curiford of the 9/- rent at Aulre which his Uncle Engeram, son of Odo, and his mother, Avelina, gave to the Canons of Torre. Abbot R(obert) gave him $\frac{1}{2}$ a mark in recognition.
Date: 1225-1230. MS: Folio 19.

38. A confirmation of a rent of 2 pence (which Richard de Aulre used to pay him) made by Richard de Karra to the Canons of Torre.
Date: 13th century. MS: Folio 20.

39. A quitclaim from John Guril to the Canons of Torre of the meadow of Stamford and one (a blank) adjacent, and four acres.
Date: c. 1250. MS: Folio 20.

40. A confirmation to Robert Guril from Robert ffrelard of one curtillage where there is an orchard called Laxin, all Laigahaie as far as Benorharigge, Slade and Hallond as far as the stream; all of which his father, Geoffrey, gave to him. Rent: a pair of white gloves worth a penny on the Feast of All Saints.
Date: Mid 13th century. MS: Folio 20.

41. A gift from John of Cavebiri to William taberum of Jakeford (who married his daughter Gillotta) of all his land at Cavebiri and Little Aulre: to hold from the Abbot of Torre in chief: on condition that William provides him with all necessaries of life as long as he lives. He also gives him all his goods and furniture and promises to help William and work for their common good.
Date: mid 13th century. MS: Folio 20 & 21.

42. A quitclaim from Richard, son of William the archer of Kavebiry, to the Canons of Torre of his land and tenement at Kavebiry.
Date: Given at Torre Abbey on Sunday, The Feast of St. Augustine the Confessor, 1286. MS: Folio 21. Witnesses: Richard de Aulre, Johanne Paz, Eustachio le Baron, Robert Coffyn, William Bernhous, William de Stontorre, Nicholas de Karswille, clerk and others.

43. A Final Concord in the Court at Exeter between William the Archer and John Guril concerning 4 ferlings and 4 acres at Cavebiri. John recognises William's right of ownership; William then gives him the southern half of the land at a rent of 6/-. After John's death the land reverts to William.
Date: The Feast of St. Martin, 1257. MS: Folio 21.

At the time of the Abbey's foundation, Wolborough was in the hands of William de Bruera, who had married Lord William's sister, Engelesia. So the selling of Wolborough to Lord William was a family arrangement. The object was that a manor close to the new Abbey should be made available as a gift. The ensuing charters are routine confirmations of this gift.

In charters 25-28 the Maynbogh property is dealt with. Situated near Forches Cross, it was an outlying "parcel" of Wolborough. The modern spelling of Mainbow still appears on the map, but the old farm has in the last few decades been given over to market gardening and the house has been demolished. What must once have been a boggy spot, as the name implies, has now been drained to good effect. These charters are undated, and the only guide is the fact that Theobald de Anglica Villa occurs in the Book of Fees in 1236, and 1242/43. Theobald appears to have been of Norman origin; his name in its French form was Englischville. Luke was the grandson of another Luke who was "boteler" to King Henry II.

The Keyberry or Cavebiri charters are for the most part not dated, and it is difficult to get them in chronological order. We may be sure, however, that the ones which do not mention the Abbey are the oldest. These were retained by the Canons simply to clarify their title to the lands later given to them. Such a charter is 41 where John of Cavebiri makes over all his land to his son-in-law William, the taverner of Jakeford—surely a delightul spelling of Chagford. The ffrelard family and also the Gurils farmed Keyberry. In 43 there is mention of the extent of the farm as being 4 ferlings and 4 acres, so it consisted of over 100 acres.

Dublin Cartulary contains two charters which concern this district (folio 135b). The first concerns William the Archer and Abbot Richard, so it will date from c. 1270. It deals with land to the east of Aller Brook which was in the parish of Combe-in-Teignhead. It was called Lateyngeshalre. This word is really three—La Teynges Halre. In other words it was that part of Aller which was in Combe-in-Teignhead. This farm can still be traced without much difficulty. It began at Richard de Alre's land in Upperalre (no doubt near where Manor Farm stands today) and followed the brook to Kavebiry as far as Milburnford (the old ford close to the "Penguin"). It ascended the hill of Milberdoune by the boundary of Roger de Mule's land (the present road to St. Marychurch), went along Greneweye, going south as far as Richard de Alre's boundary at Horscumbe and so down to the brook. Greneweye must have been the track over Milber Down which leads to Coffinswell, and Horscumbe the name of a shallow valley which runs down from Milber to the main road. It is Aller Brake Road today, but I can remember when not a house had been built there. A track ran up the little combe, amid gorse and heather. This marked a parish boundary, and would do so in the 13th century most probably. This, then, was the feudal holding of Teign Aller. Further evidence was made available to me by the late Mr. Jimmie Aston, formerly of Coffinswell. At the age of 94 in 1970, he told me that the land concerned never belonged to the Haccombe estate as might have been supposed, but was always the property of the Earls of Devon. This was striking proof that this farm in post-dissolution times was still a part of the former monastic estate of Wolborough which passed eventually into the hands of the Courtenay family. Its boundaries Mr. Aston confirmed just as I had surmised, and some of its stalwart boundary banks are still extant. He also said that there used to be a tunnel under the main road, close to Aller Cottages through which he used to drive cattle up to Milber Down to graze. So the old farmhouse must have been close by.

The other Charter (folio 157b) between Abbot Simon and John Guril is slightly earlier than the one just discussed. It deals with a considerable amount of land which was leased to John. Boundaries mentioned are "from Samforde by way of the cart track to the "pep" of Blackburge, thence to Scurvehille and so along the moors to the turf tyes in the northern part as far as the ancient boundaries of Cavebiri". Pep or peep may mean a hilltop lookout, and the hilltop should be the summit of Black Ball Copse, where there is a prehistoric tumulus.

Charter 30, wherein King Henry III grants a Wednesday market, is the most important charter so far as the town is concerned. How amazing to find the market still being held on a Wednesday over six centuries later! St. Leonard's Fair, however, is no longer held. Rhodes dates this charter as 1220/21 but gives no reason. I would suggest a much later date—1247/51, because it is witnessed by William de Valencia, the King's half brother. William was the son of Isabella of Angouleme, King John's widow by her second marriage. He did not come to England at all until 1247. Quickly marrying the heiress of the first Earl of Pembroke, he styled himself Earl of Pembroke by 1251. It seems that the charter ought to date from 1247/51.

The tenement at Ogwell mentioned in 29 & 31 was possibly a farm known as "Tor Barton" which stood north east of East Ogwell church. It has now been built over, and and the old house has recently been demolished. Osbert, the donor of the 2/- rent to the Canons, bequeathed his body for burial at the Abbey. He is mentioned in "Devon Feet of Fines" (138, p. 72) in 1224. Thomas was probably his son, and I do not doubt that they lived in the snug little manor house which still stands beside the church.

The Wolborough charters, none of which are later than 1301, give a vivid picture of 13th century life in both town and country. The occupations mentioned are those of the archer, forester, barber, painter and taverner, whilst many others are mentioned as working on the land. The running of the market at the abbot's new town would absorb others. When all is said and done, however, it was agriculture which must have employed the bulk of the people. It is the Latin word "terra", the land, which is the keyword of the Cartulary. It was cultivation of the soil and the care of the sheep and cattle nourished upon it which dominated the lives of the people of 13th century Devonshire.

Further References

Taxation of Pope Nicholas 1288
   Assessed at £4.4.8., the highest of all the Torre Abbey properties.

Devonshire Lay Subsidy, 1332

Only 14 names mentioned—those of interest being "Richard Forester Senior 2/-, David de Rydon 12d., Luke de Rydon 12d.

A.O., Particulars for Grants

There is a very full account of leases at Wolborough, the most important being:—
"To John Gaverock of Newton Abbot and Joan his wife, 1st Sept. 1545, the manor of Wolborough, late of Torre Abbey (LP. xx, pt. 11, 214).

m. 2. Manor of Wulborrough: Free rents, 34/8: customary rates £22.17.3., farm of Wulburrow meade, 113/4; court profits, 40/-; less the fee of John Gaverocke bailiff, granted to him for his life by the crown, 60/- (c) 30/-:—£30.15.3."

m. 3. "Woods at Wolburghe: Wolborough Wood and a grove, 24 ac; Weste Wood 26 ac; Henbury Wood 6 ac,:—56 ac. wherof all except oaks and ashes let to John Gaveroke and William Hylhay as part of their farms on 8th Oct., 1538 and 12th March, 1536 respectively etc. . . . (A.O., Particulars for Grants 472).

To Thomas Yarde of Bradley, Esquire, and Vincent Calmady of Lew Trenchard, gentlemen, 2 August, 1557, the manor and borough of Newton Abbot, late of Torre Abbey (C.P.R.Ph. and Mary iv, 174; the grant also includes lands in Cornwall and Somerset and Devon Chantry Lands).

m. 3. "Manor and borough of Newton Abbot: Free rents £14.2.2¼; customary rents and rents of tenants at will, 43/-; court profits, 3/4 (less 13/4 the fee of John Gaverock, bailiff £6.18.6¼)." (A.O., Particulars for Grants 2180).

To William Riggs and Leonard Brown, 17 August, 1544, property in the parishes of Highweek and Buckland in the Moore and Widecombe in the Moor, part of the manor of Wolborough, late of Torre Abbey (LP. xix, pt. 2, 72).

m. 24. "Part of the manor of Wulborrugh: Copyhold rents of a tenement called Maynebow in the parish of Highweke held by John Leyker, 13/4; of another in Buckland in le More held by Alice Berde 6/8; of another in Widecombe held by William Trend 6/8; court profits, fines etc. 4/-, 39/8d." (A.O., Particulars for Grants 936).

21

Hennock

Few parishes in South Devon can show such a grand panorama of hill scenery as Hennock. The village, which stands some 600 ft. above sea level, commands extensive views of the Haldon hills and Teign valley. To the west lies a wild plateau of granite, rising to 1,000 ft. and more, where are situated Torquay's extensive reservoirs. Hennock is still off the beaten track, but in mediaeval times, standing as it would beneath uncultivated moorland, it must have been looked upon as a bleak and desolate spot. It is not surprising to find, therefore, that all the Abbey property lay among the warmer slopes below the village. Beadon is the only hilltop holding mentioned, but it never belonged to the Canons.

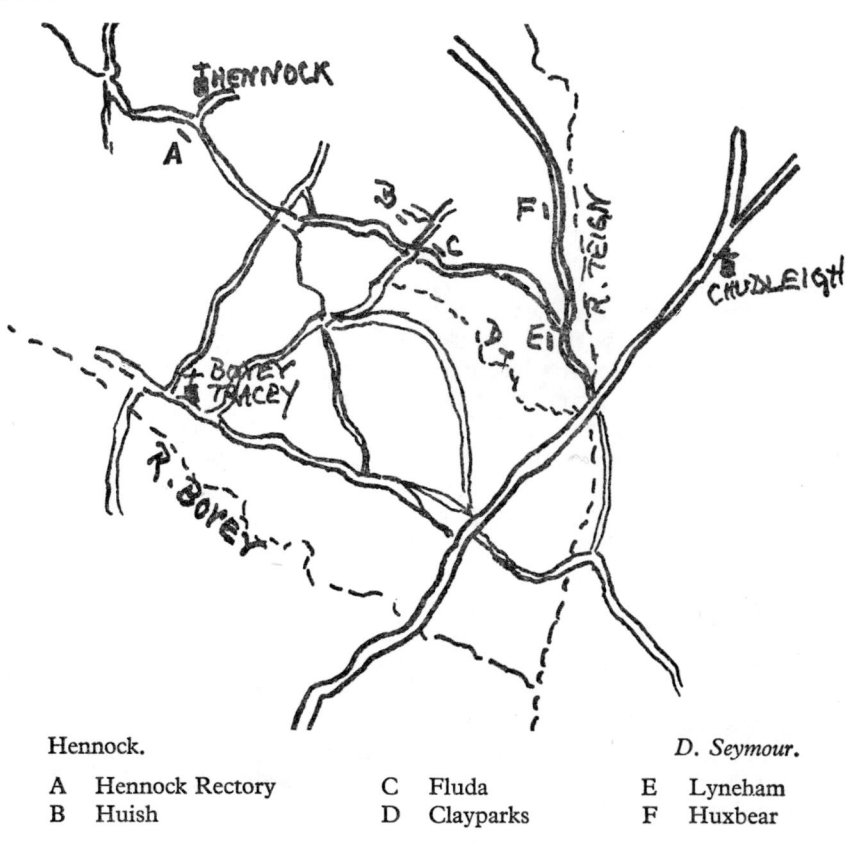

Hennock.   D. Seymour.

A Hennock Rectory   C Fluda   E Lyneham
B Huish   D Clayparks F Huxbear

Prehistoric man, however, braved the elements, and there is evidence of early settlements around the hill-top near Bottor and above Hazelwood. By Saxon times there was a considerable community, farming no doubt on the slopes below the village. The Exchequer Domesday states that:—"Baldwin has a manor called Hainoc and it rendered geld for 1 hide. This can be ploughed by 13 ploughs . . . . Roger has in demesne 3 ferlings and 2 ploughs, and the villeins have 3 virgates and 1 ferling and 6 ploughs . . . . 9 villeins, 6 bordars, 5 serfs, 1 packhorse, 69 sheep".

About 130 years later we read of Hennock in the Cartulary when the church was given to Torre Abbey by Philip de Salmonavilla and his wife, Beatrix (44). What is thought to be the original charter is preserved in Powderham Records 413. It is in an excellent state of preservation and the names of the witnesses, omitted in the Cartulary, are fortunately appended. They were:—William Briwere, the lady Beatrice la Raueleise, Peter de Scudimore, William Seinzaver, John the chaplain, Walter the chaplain, William de Rotomago, Ralph de Brai, Walter filio Juonis, Alan de Boclaund, Roger Burnel, Nicholas de Torre. Like Shebbear this church seems to have been given during the Interdict (1206-1214) for it was not confirmed by the Diocesan until the time of Bishop Simon of Apulia who took over in 1214. The church must therefore have been given between 1206, when his predecessor died, and 1214. Judging from the dates of some of the witnesses and other charters, a date between 1207 and 1208 would be a reasonable one to assume.

Philip de Salmonavilla also appears as Sarmunville, and this may very well have been a Norman place name. His wife, Beatrix, confirms her husband's gift in 45, apparently during his lifetime. She describes herself as daughter of William, the son of Roger, as though they were well known at Hennock—indeed Pole styles them "de Hanok". It is most likely therefore that she had inherited Hennock. She married for a second time Sir Girard de Clist, and their son, Sir William de Clist, again confirms the gift of the church (47). In 46 his son, another William, confirms his grandparent's gift.

Bishop Simon in his confirmation of the church to the Canons safeguarded the rights of Benjamin the vicar, guaranteeing the church to him for the remainder of his life. He had to pay half a mark each year to the Abbot, however. The only thing remaining at Hennock today which Benjamin would recognise is the old square font which he must constantly have used. He is the first recorded incumbent and together with Nicholas, vicar of Chudleigh, and Adelard, the chaplain at Beydon, is one of a group of three 13th century priests which the Cartulary brings to light.

It is surprising how much remains to see at Hennock of later monastic times. First there is the squat tower of the church, belonging to the latter part of the 13th century. It contains two bells which still produce week by week actual sounds which the Canons of Torre heard when they did duty here. The treble is by William Norton of Exeter, dating from the first half of the 15th century. The third bell of the ring is by his successor "J. T.". Its inscription is "protege virgo pia quos convoco sancta maria".—a stock inscription which Norton introduced.

The church, apart from the tower, is a handsome perpendicular rebuilding, all of granite. The most glorious thing which the interior has to show is the splendid ceilure over the rood. It is in perfect condition and has recently been restored to its former colouring. There has been a good rood screen with its lower panels adorned with paintings of saints, but it has lost its cornice and groining. A fragment of stained glass depicting cherubim remains in a window in the north aisle. All these lovely things the Canons saw and no doubt they supervised their making.

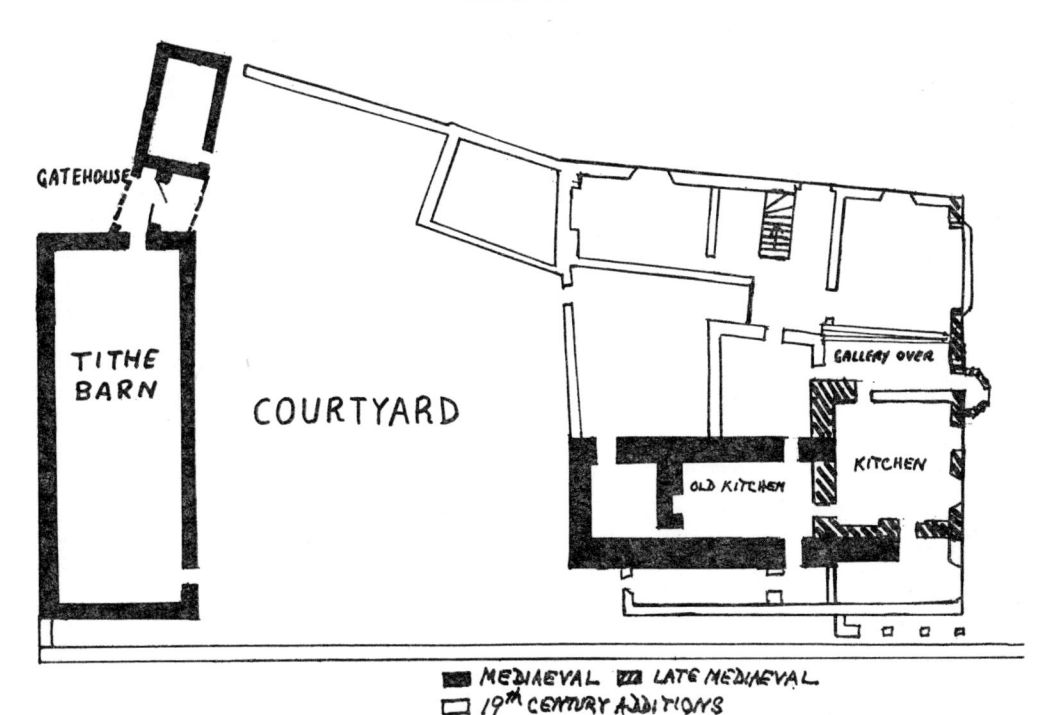

Hennock Rectory.   D. Seymour.

Churches such as this fortunately abound in Devon, but the most remarkable survival at Hennock is the Rectory. It still retains the core of a mediaeval house, and the remains of a gatehouse and tithe-barn. Here and at Buckland Brewer are the only examples of priests' houses to survive, whereas all the Canons' churches are still to be seen; and except at Skidbrook, are in constant use. The west wing of the Rectory contains the thick walls of an early house. They are constructed of moorstone and are rough and irregular like many of the old farmhouses in the district. Then in later times the house became L shaped, and would include the present kitchen and screen. Probably in the 16th century an upper floor would be inserted, but even then the level of the old gallery which overlooked the hall or kitchen was maintained and is still in situ. Finally in Victorian days there were ambitious additions making a new east frontage, all in a most whimsical style. The house is now U shaped and charmingly thatched. The tithe barn is plastered and it is hard to assess its age. With the roofed-in gateway and little porter's house beside it, we have a group of old buildings whose erection the Canons undoubtedly supervised, and which in their completeness form a most satisfying survival of those times.

The Charters

There are 31 charters dealing with Hennock. They concern the gift of the church to Torre Abbey and the business arising from the secular gifts of the farms of Huish, la Flode, la Cley and Lyneham.

Henok

44. A gift of the church of Hanoc from Philip de Salmonavilla to the Church of St. Saviour of Torre; on behalf of his own soul and that of Beatrix, his wife.
Date: c. 1207/08.   MS: Folio 22.

45. A confirmation of above by Philip de Salmonavilla's wife, Beatrix, daughter of William the son of Roger.
Date: Possibly later than 44.   MS: Folio 22.

46. A confirmation of his grandparents' gift of the church of Hanoc from Sir William de Clist, son of William, son of Girard de Clist.
Date: Mid 13th century.   MS: Folio 22.

47. A confirmation of his mother, Beatrix's, gift of the church of Hanoc by William de Clist, son of Girard de Clist.
Date: 1225/30.   MS: Folio 23.

48. A confirmation of the gift of the church of Hanoc by Simon, Bishop of Exeter. The Canons are admitted to the Rectory: Benjamin, the vicar, is to hold the vicarage for life, paying $\frac{1}{2}$ mark annually to the Abbot of Torre.
Date: c. 1214.   MS: Folio 23.

49. A gift by Girard de Hennok to Nicholas, vicar of Chudelegh, of half a ferling of land at la Flode in the manor of Hanoc which Alan formerly held. Rent—a pair of white gloves at Easter. Clause of Warranty.
Date: 1225/30.   MS: Folio 23.

50. A confirmation made to N., chaplain of Chuddelegh, by W. de Clyst of the wardship and dowry of the heiress of Richard de la fflode in William's manor of Hanok. Two parcels of land at la fflode are involved just as stated in the cirograph between Nicholaus and Richard. Clause of Warranty.
Date: mid 13th century.   MS: Folio 23/24.

51. A quitclaim by William, son of Robert de Uppehom, of a rent of 3d which the Abbot of Torre used to pay to him for land and tenements at Hywis and la fflode. William Lanceyn gave these to the Canons in a charter which William has seen and ratifies. He renounces all claim to the rent, lands and tenements.
Date: Torre, Thursday, the Morrow of the Feast of St. Hilary, 1294.   MS: Folio 24.
Witnesses:— John Tremeneth, Richard de Gatepath, Roger Samercy (?), Richard Whytewaye, Alward Homans. (Date and witnesses from "Powderham Records", 196).

52. A quitclaim from N., vicar of Chuddelegh, to Adelardus, chaplain of Beydon, of half a ferling of land at la fflode which Girard de Hanok used to hold.
Date: mid 13th century.   MS: Folio 24.

53. A quitclaim from Nicholas, vicar of Chuddelegh, to Adelardus, the chaplain of Beydon of the wardship and dowry of the heiress of Richard de la fflode: also of half a ferling of land at la fflode. Adelardus gave him 5 marks, three shillings and fourpence in recognition.
Date: mid 13th century.   MS: Folio 24.

54. A confirmation from Richard de la fflode, son of Walter, given to William Parmenter and Alice, Richard's sister, of nine acres which were her dowry. Six lie next to Edward Hockbeare's hedge and three next to Coldeswillesmore. Rent—a pound of wax. Grazing rights given throughout la fflode. Clauses of Distraint and Warranty.
Date: 1215/30.   MS: Folio 24/25.

55. A quitclaim by Walter Parmenter, son of William Parminter, with the consent of Alice, his wife, to the Abbot of Torre, of land at la fflode which his mother, Alice, gave to him. The Abbot gave 2 marks to him and one to his wife in recognition. Clause of Warranty.
Date: c. 1240.   MS: Folio 25.

56. A concession of a ferling of land as a dowry for his daughter, Mary, made by Richard de la fflode. It is half of the land above the road which goes to the north. Rent—a pair of gloves at Easter.
Date: c. 1230/40.   MS: Folio 25.

57. A quitclaim to the church of the Holy Trinity at Torre of a ferling of land at la fflode given by Mariota, daughter of Richard de la fflode. It lies east of the land which the Canons already have.
Date: mid 13th century.   MS: Folio 25.

58. A confirmation given by Alice, daughter of Walter de la fflode, of her dowry made to her son Walter. Conditions as in 54.
Date: mid 13th century.   MS: Folio 25/26.

59. A gift made by Richard de la fflode, with the consent of his wife, Odelina, to Girard de Hanok of a half ferling at la fflode. Rent—half a pound of cummin at Christmas.
Date: c. 1215/30.   MS: Folio 26.

60. Richard de la fflode gives to Aillardus, the chaplain, half a ferling with a garden at la fflode in exchange for the half ferling which Richard gave to Girard de Hanok.
Date: c. 1230/40.   MS: Folio 26.

61. A confirmation from Richard Treymenet made to Adelardus, chaplain of Beydone, of the wardship and dowry of the heiress of Richard de la fflode, which William de Clist formerly made to Nicholaus, chaplain of Chuddelegh. Adelardus gave him 40/- in recognition.
Date: mid 13th century.   MS: Folio 26.

62. Martin de Babbecombe quitclaims to Adelardus, chaplain of Beydone, the dowry of his wife, Johanna, which is land at la fflode. He is to hold it just as Robert de la fflode, her former husband did, by indenture between her father, Nicholas, vicar of Chuddelegh, and Richard de la fflode.
Date: mid 13th century.   MS: Folio 27.

63. A quitclaim of her dowry made to Adelardus, chaplin of Beydone, by Johanna, daughter of Nicholas, vicar of Chuddelegh,
Date: mid 13th century.   MS: Folio 27.

64. A gift to the Canons of Torre from Adelardus, the chaplain. It consists of all his land at la fflode which Richard de la fflode gave to him.
Date: mid 13th century.   MS: Folio 27.

65. Richard de la fflode (junior) confirms to the Canons of Torre his father Richard's gift of his land at la fflode: also the ferling which his sister, Mariota, gave to them. The Canons gave him 6/- in recognition and a free meal daily at their house of Torre.
Date: mid 13th century.   MS: Folio 27/28.

66. A confirmation from Richard Tremeneth of Richard de la fflode's gift of his land at la fflode to the Church of the Holy Trinity at Torre.
Date: 1241/42.   MS: Folio 28.

67. A gift to the Canons of Torre from William, son of Robert Lancelyn, of all his land at Hywys. Clause of Warranty.
Date: early 13th century.   MS: Folio 28.   Witnesses:—Martin de Fishaker, Robert de Morcell, Steven de Haccumbe, John le Barun, Ricd. Tremeneth, Peter Aubeman, Robt. de Woggewil (From "Powderham Records" 197).

68. Richard de fflode, son of Walter de la fflode, gives the whole of his land of la fflode to the Church of Torre. Clause of Warranty.
Date: Given at la fflode on the Morrow of the Feast of St. Gregory, 1241/2.   MS: Folio 28.

69. A confirmation from Richard Tremeneth of Richard de la fflode's gift of all his land at la fflode to the Canons of Torre. (Although the wording is almost the same as 66, yet the charter may have been given by a later Richard Tremeneth.)
Date: Possibly c. 1260.   MS: Folio 28.

70. A quitclaim from Nicholas Burdun of suit of court and service due from the Canons of Torre for the land of la fflode: this Richard de la fflode used to make at Nicholas's court in the free hundred of Teyngebrigge.
Date: 1241/42.   MS: Folio 29.

Cley

71. A gift in perpetual alms from Amelota de Beydona to the Canons of Torre of all her land at la Cleye which came to her from her father, Roger. To be held for the third part of 6d. And for the third of a ferling at Lynicombe, the third part of a pair of spurs worth 3d.
Date: No evidence, probably mid 13th century.   MS: Folio 29.

72. An agreement between Edward de Bydon and his wife, Cecilia, and the Abbot of Torre whereby they give all their land at la Cleye to the Abbot for a rent of 20d. until the death of Cecilia. Clause of Warranty.
Date: The vigil of the Feast of St. Mary Magdalene, 1270.   MS: Folio 29/30.
Witnesses:—William de Fishacre, Herbert de Morcell, Walrand de Cirencestre, knights; Ives de la Were, Richard de Gatepathe and others.

Hennock: Parish Church. *Photo by G. Court Jones.*

Hennock Parish Church: The mediaeval font. *Photo by M. Leach.*

Hennock Parish Church: Panel of rood screen. *Photo by Mrs. F. H. Crossley.*

Hennock Parish Church: The ceilure. *Photo by Mrs. F. H. Crossley.*

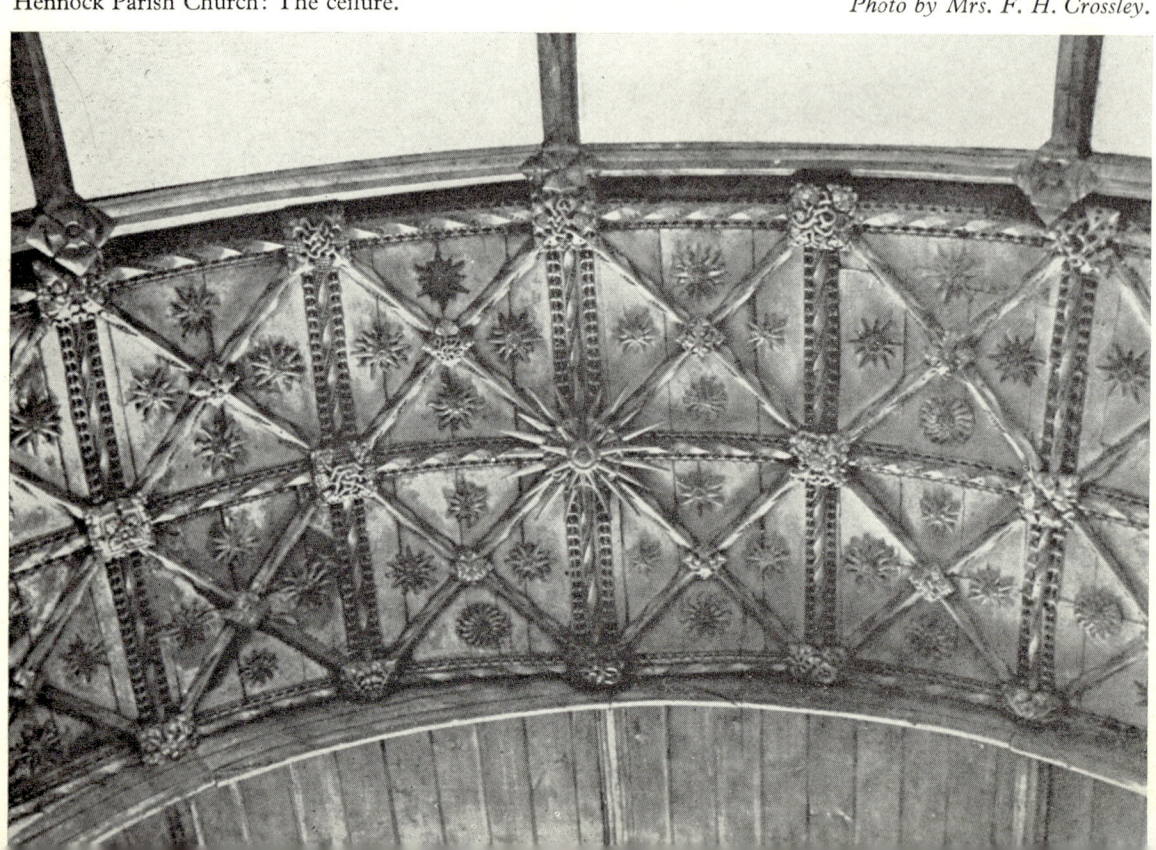

Hennock: Tithe barn and remains of Rectory gatehouse. *Photo by G. Court Jones.*

Hennock: Monastic boundary between Fluda and Huxbear. *Photo by G. Court Jones.*

Hennock: Charter giving Hennock Church to Torre Abbey. (From Powderham collection).

Photo by courtesy of Devon Record Office.

Cley et Lynicombe

73. Ralph de Nova Villa and Edith, his wife, sell to the Church of Torre all their land at la Cleye and Lynicombe for 100/-. Clause of Distraint. Sworn upon the Sacrament upon the altar at St. Saviour's.
Date: April 5th, 1270. MS: Folio 30.

74. A quitclaim of land at la Cleye by Edith, wife of Ralph de Nova Villa, made to the Canons of Torre.
Date: Probably post 1270. MS: Folio 30/31. Witnesses:—Sir Herbert de Morcell, Sir William de ffishacre, Roger de Punchardon, Walter de Aleburne, John Paz and others.

75. A quitclaim to the Canons of Torre Briwer from Osbert de Holcumbe of the land of Lynihuse: this he might have inherited through his wife, Mariota, on the death of William de Lynihuse, her father.
Date: possibly c. 1280/90. MS: Folio 31. Witnesses:—Ives de la Torre, Richard de Gatepathe, John de la Torre, William de Halshang', Richard Humaz and others.

During the 13th century the Canons acquired a block of property formed by five farms which stretch in an almost unbroken line down to the Teign valley. The nearest to the village is Huish. We are told in 67 that "Hywys" was given to the Abbey by William Lancelyn, probably about 1240/50. By the end of the century 51 shows that the Abbot was paying a rent of 3d. for it to a certain William Uppehom. In that charter the latter quitclaims the rent, after seeing the original charter, in 1294. The old thatched farmhouse of Huish still stands, together with its fine outbuildings. It is a simple building in the style of a longhouse, running downhill in a picturesque manner. It has of late been divided into two houses. All the farms in this vicinity have been purchased by the company which owns the quarries in the valley below. Huish has stood empty since this purchase—probably for the first time since the Conquest. The land is farmed from Frost—an adjoining farm. It will therefore be understood that at the moment of writing its future is most uncertain. In the 13th century it consisted of 1 ferling of land ("Powderham Record" 202), but by the 19th century the Tithe map shows 63 acres, or about 2½ ferlings.

Close to Huish and just below the road to Riley are the scanty remains of Fluda—this is "la fflode" in the Cartulary. All that is to be seen today is a barn, traces of a deserted farmyard, and a windswept orchard where half a dozen gnarled and weatherbeaten apple-trees speak of former habitation here. Older people remember the house in ruins, but no-one remembers it intact. A fire destroyed the barn early in this century, but it was fortunately rebuilt with the old stones; it is this solitary building which keeps alive the name of Fluda. That this was a house of consequence in the 13th century is proved by the fact that we have about 20 charters concerning it. Indeed it looks as though it became a sub-manor of Hennock, for there is evidence that there was a court held here—a field adjacent to the house being "Court Meadow". Again in 60 there is mention of Richard de la fflode's "camera". In a word list in her "Latin for Local History", Eileen Gooder gives one use of "camera" as "an ecclesiastical lawcourt, especially when held in a private house". This exactly fits the case here, for the Abbot no doubt was entitled to his own court in which to conduct the business of the five farms which he held eventually in Hennock. In Dublin Cartulary (f. 5a) Torre Abbey is recorded in 1291 as making tax returns from various manors; amongst the list is the "manor of Floode cum pertinenciis" which paid 11/8. After the dissolution the properties would be split up and the sub-manor would become redundant.

The charters concerning this property are nearly all concerned with the de la fflode family and their leasing of land. From them one gets the feeling that la fflode was a large holding with several ferlings of land to spare for daughters of the house; yet by the 19th century the Tithe Map shows a small farm of only 26 acres or 1 ferling. Even today its boundary banks are so clear on three sides that it is unlikely the holding was ever larger. It is possible, of course, that by the period we are considering more land had been acquired, and so what we see today are far older boundaries even than the 13th century. On the eastern side the boundary with Huxbear is one of the most impressive things to be seen there today. It consists of a broken down bank, formerly of great girth, studded with ancient trees. With the passing of the centuries the bank has all but slipped down the steep slope. Another fine bit of earth and stone banking is to be seen in the corner of the field to the N.E., where the old church path comes up from the Teign valley.

Perhaps the most interesting landmark still to be seen is the spring by the willow trees, mentioned in the full version of 60. There can be no doubt at all about the identity of this vigorous spring, for it is the only one on the farm in the required position. Even to this day willows still encircle it.

The old approach road to la fflode was by way of a lane which leaves the valley just south of Huxbear. It is still in use as a woodland path, but almost dies out as it reaches the farm. It reappears at the entrance to the farmyard, however, and is flanked by excellent moorstone walls which suggest a mediaeval origin. The actual position of the dwelling and its shape are at the moment conjectural. One would like to see an excavation here to establish the site of this once important house.

The family of de la fflode seem never to have distinguished themselves in any way, for they appear nowhere outside the Cartulary, and all efforts to track them down from the usual sources of the period have proved in vain. They seem to have been peaceful yeomen who indulged in no litigation and seldom descended from their hills. In the 14th century de Lappeflodes appear, but this family would hail from Laployd Barton in Bridford.

None of the charters dealing with la fflode are dated, with the notable exception of 68 wherein Richard de la fflode in 1241/42 gave the farm to the Abbey. The charters dealing with the wardship of his heiress may reasonably be expected to be later than this, but the rest should be prior to 1241/42.

The terms of the corrody granted to Richard de la fflode are of decided interest, if only to show how a wife was treated when her husband became a resident at the Abbey. We have to go to the Dublin Cartulary in this instance, for the later Exchequer version was not compiled until Richard had been dead and buried for over a hundred and fifty years; so the terms of the corrody were then no longer pertinent. Now a corrody at a convent in the middle ages was a right to reside there, either permanently or occasionally. Such a privilege was only granted to benefactors. In this case Richard, evidently an old man, was given food, lodging and clothing in return for his gift of la fflode. His son (65) appears not to have wanted to run the farm, or was incapable of it, so he was granted a free meal a day at the Abbey and perhaps worked there. But Richard's wife, Odelina, was treated in a most kindly fashion. As women were not allowed to enter the precincts she was provided with a house and various comforts. For instance, each quarter she was provided with 2 quarters of wax and one of barley. At Easter there was 2/- for her, and at

Christmas a basket of fruit and a basket of beans. At Michaelmas she got a quarter of oats and each year a cartload of wood or turf for her fire. So the old couple ended their days in comfort, while Richard junior consoled himself in the Abbot's pantry.

Flitting through the charters concerning la fflode are two priests—Nicholas, the vicar of Chudleigh, and Adelard, the chaplain at Beadon. Of these two Nicholas seems to have been the elder. He makes over land at la fflode to Adelard and also a wardship, rather as though he were too old to cope any longer. It would seem that he flourished from c. 1225 onwards, and by the mid century he would be getting on in years. Now Chudleigh church was dedicated by Bishop Bronescombe in 1259. But these charters prove that this vicar lived long before that. It would be also far too late a date for the building of Chudleigh's first church. So the ceremony of 1259 perhaps marked a rebuilding of the first church. Possibly the low Norman tower is all that remains of this church, but Nicholas no doubt knew it well. It is the only surviving building which Richard de la fflode would recognise if he were to look across the valley from his farm today.

At Beadon no trace of Adelard's chapel is to be seen now, though foundations of older buildings are showing. This must have been yet another important house in the 13th century. Even now the core of the old house survives, heavily disguised under a coat of stucco, a new roof and Victorian windows. The former approach road which Adelard used was by way of an overgrown lane climbing from the valley. Now the farm is reached from above through fields. Set amid rolling hills and just below the top of the plateau, Beadon still has a splendid setting, and it is good to think that after over 700 years the farm is still active.

Nearly all the la fflode charters deal with land and wardships. The Tremeneths appear twice in 61 & 66 where Richard Tremeneth gives confirmations as lord of the fee. He evidently obtained Hennock through his wife, Isabel, daughter of Sir William de Clist. The only other families mentioned are those of Parmenter and Babbecombe. The latter must have come from the fine old house of that name at Ugbrooke Park which still stands.

Leaving la fflode, and slipping a little way down the hill, we come to the next property which the Canons acquired, viz., Clayparks, known in the Charters as "la cleye". It stands below the bleak hills of Hennock and its land consists of a gentle downward slope to a point where a stream separates Hennock from Bovey Tracey. Here are the remains of the old house and farmyard. It is a quite remarkable survival of a cottage type of farmhouse where human beings and animals dwelt under one roof until the 1930's, divided by the thinnest of wooden partitions. Here conditions obtaining four centuries ago lasted well into the present century. Yet the last farmer to live in this damp, three-roomed dwelling is said to have raised a prodigious family.

Careful study will show that the house is probably a 19th century rebuilding done with old materials, and preserving the mediaeval design even down to the wooden screen, which would be a copy of a far older one. A partial excavation, made possible through the kindness of the Stokelake Estate, has shown that the shippen has a fine drain running down its centre. So this would be the animals' end of the house; it could very well be that the style and extent of the house in mediaeval days was much as we see it. Further excavation has not been possible as the floors are under water for a great deal of the year. Fragments of pottery of Barnstaple ware were found in the floor near the stairs, but the mediaeval levels have not yet been reached.

In an adjacent field called "Square Close" there are signs of strip fields; these are more

The Shippen going to ruin, Clayparks, August 1967. *D. Seymour.*

clearly seen in winter. In Orchard and Orchard Meadow, behind the house, are more strips, but the baulks are fainter.

There are four charters which mention "La cleye" (71-74), and from them we learn that it came into the hands of Torre Abbey in 1270. La cleye and Lynicombe, the next farm going down towards the Teign, are mentioned together in 71 and 73. The property seems to have been divided between the de Beydons and Ralph and Edith de Nova Villa (Newton Abbot). It is interesting to note that whilst Amelota de Beydon piously gave away her land to the Abbey, the more hard-headed couple from Newton Abbot sell out for 100/-. No doubt it was well worth the Abbot's while to purchase this land, for with Huish and la fflode he was beginning to consolidate a block of property in Hennock.

Close beside the River Teign stands Lyneham. Its farm buildings are on either side of the road in complete mediaeval disarray. Although the house does not display any old features apart from its chimneys, yet there can be little doubt that if not the actual building, it will be the successor on the same site of a very old farmhouse. Until the last century pack ponies plied between here and Hennock; the ascent was too steep for carts, and so all goods were taken up by the easiest gradient past Fluda and Huish Cross. The one packhorse mentioned in Domesday must not be forgotten in this connection.

The name of Lyneham has changed somewhat over the years, for in the Cartulary it is Lynicombe. Exactly the same thing has happened a mile or so away where we have the old farm of Crockham; but the woods beyond appear on the map as Crocombe. In

"Devon Feet of Fines" (523) we find that Lynicombe consisted of 5 ferlings divided between three tenants; so it was in the old days a considerable farm of some 130 acres. Evidently it included the modern Stokelake Farm. Ralph and Edith de Nova Villa had a part of it (73), but the Canons do not seem to have had the whole until Osbert de Holcumbe gave it to them.

The next farm up the valley is Huxbear Barton, and although both cartularies make no mention of it, yet on p. 179 of Tot. there is a charter of Totnes Priory (103) dealing, among other things with "Hokesbeare in the parish of Hyanock". In this charter of 1276 the Prior of Totnes quitclaims to the Abbot of Torre all right and claim to the tithe of Hokesbeare and whatsoever other tithe in the parish of Hyanock. Dublin Cartulary (Folio 179b) testifies to the fact that dues were paid to Totnes Priory, for on that page an entry states that 2/- was given to the Prior for a certain royal tax. So it seems clear that there were farms in Hennock which for some reason paid tithe to Totnes Priory and not to their own church. The remission of the Huxbear tithe seems to have been a courteous gesture on the part of the Prior, and I read into it that at about this date of 1276 Huxbear had been leased to the Canons of Torre; it will be understood that they then had yet a fifth farm whose lands adjoined Clayparks and Fluda.

The Hennock charters are of decided value because they give a glimpse of the practical side of monastic economics in the 13th century. Two farms were in the first place given to the Abbey, and with the profits accruing from them an astute Abbot was by 1270 in a position to purchase two more. With the lease of Huxbear there were then five adjoining farms which could be easily and profitably administered by one bailiff.

Vicars of Hennock

c. 1207	Benjamin
1259	Simon de Sancto Laudo
1313	Geoffrey de Hurburtone
1322	John atte Wode
1322	Nicholas de Stourtone
1337	Richard Blaunchard
1342	Henry de Okehampton
1349	Richard de Crowen
1354	Robert Langebroke
1368	Thomas Wenlake
1399	John Smyth
1399	John Cok
1413	William Cok
1435	Geoffrey Schute
1445	John Kelly
1451	Richard Kelwa
1537	Thomas Herle

List compiled by Rev. R. Medley Fulford. The first vicar added through evidence of charter 48.

Further References

Taxation of Pope Nicholas, 1288

"Hanoke in the deanery of Mortone" £5.14.11. The vicariate was worth £1.17.0. Flode entered separately as paying 11/8.

A.O., Particulars for Grants 1962

"To John Southcott of Bovey Tracey, Esquire, 7 April, 1553, the Rectory and advowson of Hennock, late of Torre Abbey.

m. 3 Vicarage of Hennock: Valued on 13th February, 1553, £16.
Certified by Thomas Argall

m. 3d. "The acquitans to be made in John Southcote's name"

m. 4 Rectory of Hennocke: Farm of the rectory, leased on 4th January, 1539, to John Southcote and John Parr for 60 years, £10 (RMC) "xii".

22

Buckland-in-the-Moor

Scobetorre

76. A gift in perpetual alms made to the Canons of Torre by Roger de Bokelonde: it is the land of Scobetorr which his grandfather, William de Bokelonde, gave to the Canons with his body. Grazing rights throughout his land of Bokelonde are given and husbote and haibote in his wood of Hokemore. He binds himself (under the jurisdiction of the Dean of Exeter) to a penalty of half a mark if the tenor of this charter is infringed.
Date: c. mid 13th century.   MS: Folio 31.

78. This and 76 appear identical. 78 might have been given by a later Roger de Bokelonde, for although he refers to his grandfather the word "avus" can mean an ancestor.

79. A confirmation of a ferling of land at Scobetorre from Girard de Spineto to the Canons of Torre: this William de Bokelonde bequeathed to them together with his body. He gives them everything due to the tenant in chief.
Date: c. 1200.   MS: Folio 32.

At Buckland-in-the-Moor we have two remote moorland farms to consider—Scobitor and Ruddycleave—whilst further south the Canons owned much woodland on the spectacular slopes which fall down steeply to the River Dart. Most of this was given to them by the de Bokelonde family who were lords of the manor, and remained so; for although the Abbot of Torre had grazing rights and many privileges throughout the manor, yet he never in this case succeeded in getting the whole manor in his grasp.

It is as well to begin this chapter with a consideration of Scobitor, for it comes first among the Buckland charters. This is a typical Dartmoor holding, lying today just over the parish boundary in Widecombe-in-the-Moor. Situated amid the intractable granite outcrop, it must have taken years of toil and sweat to wrest it from the surrounding moorland which still all but encircles it. Walls and ancient banks surround the farm, and in some places there are ditches as well. This was a Saxon farm and the Domesday account of it is that it belonged to two thegns; and sure enough even now two longhouses stand here side by side only a few yards apart. The best view of them is from the curious roundhouse built upon Scobitor itself. Here the independent rooflines of the two houses stand out clearly. They are now joined by a covered passage to make one house. The outside view is disappointing because no old features remain, but inside the centuries-old walls and great fireplaces remain to tell the tale of centuries gone by.

If there were two thegns, then surely two farms, and the boundaries of these are again best seen from the tor. The acreage of the lower farm is now 21.1 acres, and of the higher just over 23. The former occupies a steep downward slope and is a much wilder and more irregular proposition than the tidily laid out field plan of the higher farm. The splendid moorstone gateposts are a feature of both farms. Some are of the hurdle variety with notches cut in the granite.

The higher farm is on fairly level ground. Its pattern of eight fields is most carefully mapped out. It would be the easier farm to work, and I do not doubt that this was the Canons' ferling. The immediate surroundings can have changed little since their day. Scobitor, throughout its history of a thousand years or thereabouts, has been continually threatened by the moor: if once man's labours had failed, it would have quickly gone back; so far as we know it never has, but remains for us to enjoy—one of the most atmospheric holdings on the Widecombe valley slopes. Not very far away are the ruined walls of another Saxon farm—Houndtor. Why was this deserted while Scobitor on its far bleaker site survived? I think the answer lies in the fact that it was a direct gift to the Abbey, guaranteed by the body of the donor which the Canons accepted for burial in the Abbey church. They would never have broken faith by parting with land thus given.

The original charter granting Scobitor to the Canons is not to be found in either Cartulary; 76 is merely a confirmation of it. None of the Buckland charters are dated. William de Bokelonde (son of Roger) appears in "Feudal Aids" in 1284/6. Working back through various generations of the family we may assume that the original gifts of Scobitor and Ruddycleave date from c. 1200.

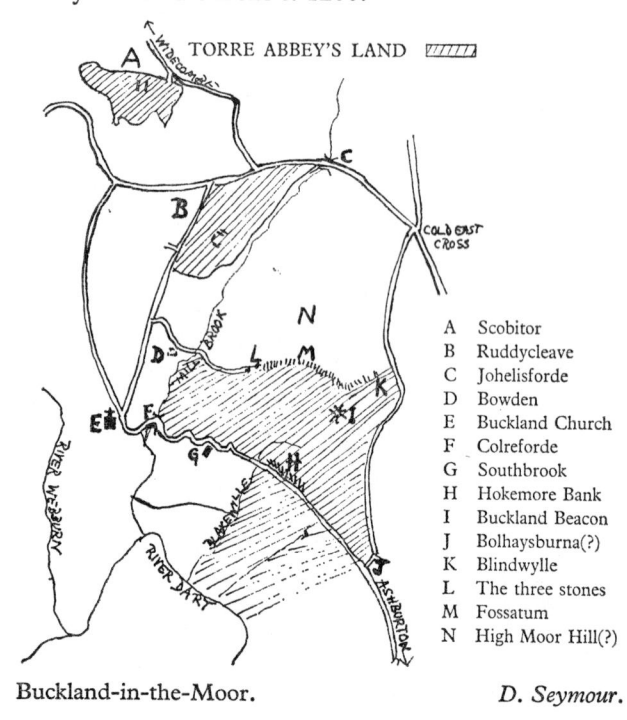

A	Scobitor
B	Ruddycleave
C	Johelisforde
D	Bowden
E	Buckland Church
F	Colreforde
G	Southbrook
H	Hokemore Bank
I	Buckland Beacon
J	Bolhaysburna(?)
K	Blindwylle
L	The three stones
M	Fossatum
N	High Moor Hill(?)

Buckland-in-the-Moor.   D. Seymour.

Radeclyve

77. A gift from William de Bokelonde to the Canons of Torre of the whole of Radeclyve in the manor of Bokelonde. Its bounds ascend by a bank through land formerly

Ruddycleave. *D. Seymour.*

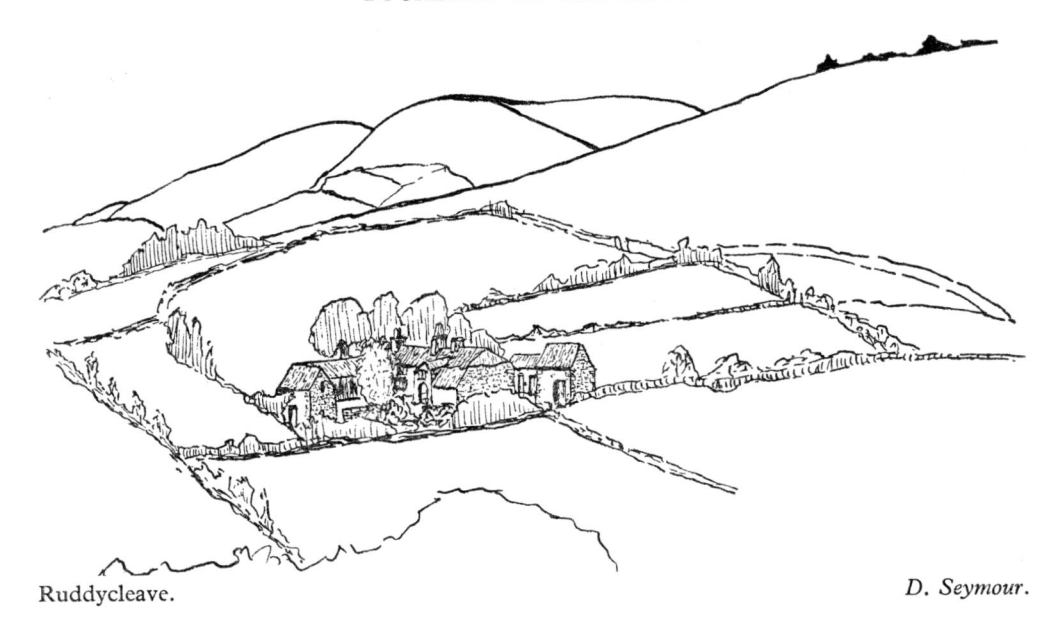

belonging to Aunfridus, as far as the chapel land boundary: thence along the highway to Johelisforde: thence descending beside Millebrok as far as the boundaries of Bughedon. Grazing rights given, also brushwood may be taken from Hokemore wood for fencing Radeclyve.
Date: c. 1200.   MS: Folio 32.

The second charter of the series (77) concerns Radeclyve, today called Ruddycleave—an apt enough name for its pleasing valley seen on an October day when the bracken glows red in the autumn sunshine. The farmhouse stands high above Buckland, a little south of the road from Cold East Cross to Cockingford. Like Scobitor this farm was given to the Abbey by William de Bokelonde, probably about the same time, c. 1200. Its boundaries are stated and they may be followed with reasonable accuracy even yet. Indeed it is doubtful if they ever changed at all because Ruddycleave had a most curious post-dissolution history. It was quickly bequeathed to the parish, with the object that the rent from it should support the poor. It remained parish property right up to the time of the break-up of the Whitley estate in the 1950's. Buckland-in-the-Moor is now a part of the parish of Ashburton, and the vicar there was able to show me a strong-box in which the Ruddycleave Trust papers are carefully preserved. Whilst this is all by the way, yet it does show that it is most unlikely that there has been any change in the boundaries of the farm since the 16th century.

Going back in time we find that in the Exeter Domesday Survey there is a manor of Radecliva consisting of 1 ferling held by Roger of Flanders from Ruald (Adobed). If this was Ruddycleave its boundaries may then have stretched further north into the moor where are the sites of former houses and enclosures which may have been held by the 3 bordars mentioned. It is possible therefore that this farm, like Scobitor, has a history of a thousand years or so, and to trace it through the centuries would form an absorbing study for someone.

Its farm buildings stand in splendid isolation and are an attractive group all in moorstone. They were thatched up to a few years ago. Now corrugated iron replaces the thatch. The farm has been absorbed by Bowden, the next farm, and for a while the house stood empty. At the moment of writing it is occupied again. A house with such an interesting history certainly ought not to be allowed to go down.

Bokelonde

80. A gift in perpetual alms of woodland, glebe and adjacent land made to the Canons of Torre by Roger de Bokelonde. Boundaries: from Colreforde along Millebroke to William de Baldrygtone's wood, thence by his boundaries to the three rocks at Mahimorhilhend: thence by the bank to Blyndwille: thence along the road to Bolhaysburna: thence as far as the road to the north leading back to Colreford. They may embank the land. Clause of Warranty. A gift for his own soul and that of Alice, his wife.
Date: mid 13th century.   MS: Folio 32 & 33.

81. A gift to the Church of the Holy Trinity of Torre from Roger de Bokelonde of woodland in the manor of Bokelonde within these bounds: from Colreforde to the bank of Hokemore: thence by the stream of Blakewille to the River Dart: along the Dart to Millebrok and along it to Colreforde. Free rights of entry and exit given and the right to embank. Clause of Warranty.
Date: mid 13th century.   MS: Folio 33.

82. A gift to the Church of St. Saviour of Torre from Roger de Bokelonde of woodland within these boundaries: from Blakewille to the stream which descends to the Dart and divides the boundaries of the lord Bishop from those of Bokelonde: thence along the Dart to Blakewille: also land extending from the open fields and pastures and wood of Blakewille along the lane leading to Langscore to the stream above Langscore: along the stream to the Dart: along the Dart to Blakewille. Clause of Warranty.
Date: mid 13th century.   MS: Folio 33.   Witnesses: Michaele de Spichewick and Geoffrey de Botryngton.

83. A gift to the Church of Torre from Thomas Chola of that wood in the manor of Bokelonde, together with its glebe and adjacent land, which he had by gift from Roger de Bokelonde.
Date: mid 13th century.   MS: Folio 34.

84. William de Baldryngton, with the consent of his wife and heir, concedes to John le Ram half a ferling at Suthbrok in the manor of Bokelonde. One close is Dodenmanneslond and the other Wlueslond. This Edward Oldman formerly held from Walter Gonnyldesone. Rent 3/-; he must attend two courts a year at Suthbrok. Grazing rights just as other freemen have.
Date: mid 13th century.   MS: Folio 34.

85. A gift of a close in Suthbrok from John Gobet to his son Bricius which William Red formerly held from him. Rent 18d. per annum. John retains a piece of land south of the courthouse there to build himself a house, and a close west of the courthouse called Nywehay. After his death both house and close revert to Bricius.
Date: mid 13th century.   MS: Folio 34/35.   Witnesses: William de Baldryngton, Nicholas de Kyngedon and others.

86. A quitclaim from William, son and heir of Roger de Bokelonde, to the Abbot of

Torre of a 2/- rent for tenements in the manor of Bokelonde; he surrenders all rights in the land which John le Ram used to hold.
Date: 1280/90.   MS: Folio 35.

87.   A confirmation from William de Bokelonde of all his father's gifts to the Canons of Torre, viz:—tenements, houses, gardens, meadows, open fields, pastures, grazing land, woods, rents, turfpits, etc.; all men and their families and cattle he quitclaims to the Canons.
Date: 1280/90.   MS: Folio 35.

88.   A confirmation from John de Stouford to God and St. Mary and to the Church of St. Saviour of Torre of all the gifts which Roger and William de Bokelonde made to that church in the manor of Bokelonde-in-the-Moor.
Date: c. 1340.   MS: Folio 36.   Witnesses:—Master Richard Noreys, Robert Brydeport, Robert at Way, Nicholas Whytyng, Andrew Alliford and many others.

Charters 80-88 concern land nearer Buckland itself. The first thing of interest is the mention of Southbrook as the courthouse. This is mentioned in 84 where William de Baldryngton refers to "my court of Southbrok". Then in 85 John Gobet refers to the close he retains as "south of the courthouse". The present house is obviously a rebuilding of something far older, but no doubt stands on the same site as the mediaeval house.

Trying to trace long-forgotten boundaries is an absorbing occupation, especially as here where the names mentioned in the charters have mostly vanished into the mists of time. One's results, too, can often be so tempered as to produce a happy ending. An open mind must therefore be kept about all my conclusions. Even so, I have been able to make sense of many of the bounds mentioned. In 81, for instance, the gift of land is bounded by Colreforde, the bank of Hokemore wood, the stream of Blakewille, the River Dart and Millebroke. We know from 77 that Millebrok is the stream which comes down from Ruddycleave to the old mill site close to the bridge in the village. It is therefore reasonable to assume that this was Colreforde, the starting point. The full Latin text then tells us to proceed by the road to the bank (fossatum) of Hokemore which runs beside the highway. If we follow the road from the bridge towards Ashburton, we reach modern houses on our left set high on the wooded slope above us. This, from other charters, I believe to have been the wood of Hokemore. Here, beside the road, is a massive bank which continues until just under Buckland Beacon. Though broken in places this is still an impressive bank. Rising behind the houses is an active stream, and the spot where it wells up is now called Stidwell. It crosses the road and then tumbles down into the Dart some 400 ft. below. It is a boundary of Southbrook Farm, and I think this must have been the stream which the charter calls Blakewille. Tracing it to its confluence with the Dart we follow the river to the point where the Millebrok comes down, and follow this stream back to the village at Colreforde. These bounds give a sensible result and a glance at the map will show that we have traced out a roughly quadrangular piece of ground. Another such area is in 82, and adjoins the area we have been following. It also is bounded by two streams falling into the Dart. This time we go from Blakewille (where it crosses the road) to the next stream which falls into the Dart. We are told that it divides the Bishop's land from Bokelonde. Just below Buckland Hall is another stream which rises in a field close by. Following it down to the river and then along it to Blakewille, and so back to the starting point gives us our boundaries.

A further strip in the same charter was land given in the direction of Landscore—the old name for Landscove; but I must admit to failure here, because I cannot find another stream flowing down to the Dart.

Charter 80 gives boundaries taking us well out onto the moor behind Buckland Beacon; it is an extensive area. Once again we set out at Colreforde beside the village bridge and follow the Millebrok (or Ruddycleave Water) as far as William de Baldryngton's wood. This takes us up to a spot below Bowden (Bughedon in 77). Here an old right of way crosses the stream just below the farm where the woodland ends and the enclosures of the farm begin. Being now impeded in the direction in which we were heading it seems logical to turn right up the old road to the moor. We reach this after a climb of about a quarter of a mile, and should now be at what the charter calls "Mahimorhilhend". Stare at this word for a while, then disregard the first syllable, and you will see the four words "high moor hill end". The intrusive "H" in the final syllable is pure Devonian vernacular, but the "ma" at the start is a mystery. Perhaps it was to the scribe, who tried to take down the word from someone speaking broad Devon dialect all those centuries ago. "High Moor Hillend" most aptly describes the spot where we go through the gate onto the steep slope below Buckland Beacon, for here the high moor does end with the start of the enclosures. The next thing to look for is the three rocks or stones mentioned. I was hoping to find a recognisable natural feature, but was disappointed. What I did see, however, was a small mound on which three large stones had at sometime been placed and which have now fallen over. These are easily passed over as they are at the moment buried in bracken. The whole thing is man-made and it is most likely that it was once set up to mark boundaries. I firmly believe that these stones are the ones mentioned in the charter, because just above them the "fossatum", which is the next point, begins. This is a low bank, much spread and broken up in places; but it keeps reappearing on line and runs in a direction a little south of east. It continues up to the wall on the east side of Buckland Beacon, comes out on the other side, but is immediately lost in what was very long grass and gorse at the time of my investigations. Its direction is clear, nevertheless, and walking by the compass one soon reaches a steep hollow where there is a pool and a barn. Water springs up everywhere and this must be Blindwylle—our next point. The name is not remembered now. We are next told to go along the road to Bolhayes burna. The road is close by, just above Welstor, and to get back to the starting point we must go down towards Welstor Cross. Bolhayes is another forgotten name, but the burn could be a springhead below Welstor Cross. We are now told to take the road to the north which takes us back to Colreford. This is the road to Buckland, and it leads us back to the starting point without further trouble. Thus once again an ancient boundary may be followed with some certainty. Here the Canons had a large tract of land consisting of extensive woodland and moorland pasture.

In the final charter (88) we find that Buckland was a part of the fee of the lord of the manor of Stoke-in-Teignhead, of which, in the 14th century, John of Stouford says he is lord. At the time of the dissolution we find that Buckland had become a part of the manor of Wolborough. On p. 45 of "Devon Monastic Lands" we read of a grant made to "William Riggs and Leonard Brown, 17 August, 1544, of property in the parishes of Highweek and Buckland-in-the-Moor, part of the manor of Wolborough, late of Torre Abbey".

Here at Buckland it will be seen that the Abbey had valuable estates, most of which were concerned with forestry. Then, as now, the beautiful slopes of the Dart valley must have been well covered with woodlands and extremely profitable to the Canons.

23

Greendale

To those who have visited Woodbury, walked over its hills and trodden its pleasant lanes, the Greendale charters immediately recall happy memories of a green and smiling countryside, of good red earth, lush pasture and peacefully grazing herds. There are in all 25 charters under the heading of Gryndell, and they mostly concern land at the northern end of the parish; this centred on the present farm of Greendale Barton, where stand considerable remains of the Canons' courthouse. A few charters deal with an overspill of land in the neighbouring parishes of Aylesbeare and Colaton Raleigh; but as the crow flies none of it is more than three miles from the barton, and there is no doubt that the Torre Abbey property in this pleasing corner of Devon was administered from there.

The manor of Woodbury at the time of the Conquest was a royal manor, the Domesday account showing a thriving and prosperous community. Amongst other things there were 30 villeins, 22 bordars and a mill. It consisted of 10 hides.

At the time of the founding of the Abbey about 110 years later the manor was in the hands of the Albamaras who became great benefactors to Torre Abbey. Now Lord William Brewer's mother was a sister of Reginald (1) de Albamara, and in charter 89 he gives Lord William 2 virgates of land in Woodbury; this was Greendale. Lord William in his turn gave it to William de Bruera as his sister Engelesia's dowry. There was a stipulation that if she died childless the property was to return to Lord William. Later on Engelesia and her husband agreed to exchange Greendale for the manor of Houbotone, which may be Halberton, near Tiverton. So by 1196 it was in Lord William's hands again, and it was one of his first gifts to his new Abbey, being mentioned in the Foundation Charter. The Albamaras were still lords of the manor and successive generations confirmed the gift to the Abbey. The family apparently resided at Woodbury and the charters they give have a very local and domestic flavour—particularly the first where, by way of recognition, Lord William gave Reginald a ring and a horse, whilst his son Geoffrey got a hunter. So the leasing of Greendale was an occasion of great rejoicing to that young man. The family later were decidedly generous to the Canons, giving them grazing rights throughout the manor and agreeing again and again to exchanges of land, until in the end Greendale was one of the Abbey's most prosperous farms.

It was obviously a large sheep farm, and one has only to look at the spacious farmyard, which stands as a separate entity and quite apart from the house, to realise its former importance in that respect. It measures 130 ft. x 96 ft. and has a flooring of "popples"—a very common feature in this part of Devon. All the buildings have been of cob and when necessary have been repaired with red brick or popples. On the left of the entry is a rectangular building of cob where lower courses of large red blocks of ancient stone survive. The tithe barn (which may be safely so called, for the Canons had the tithe from

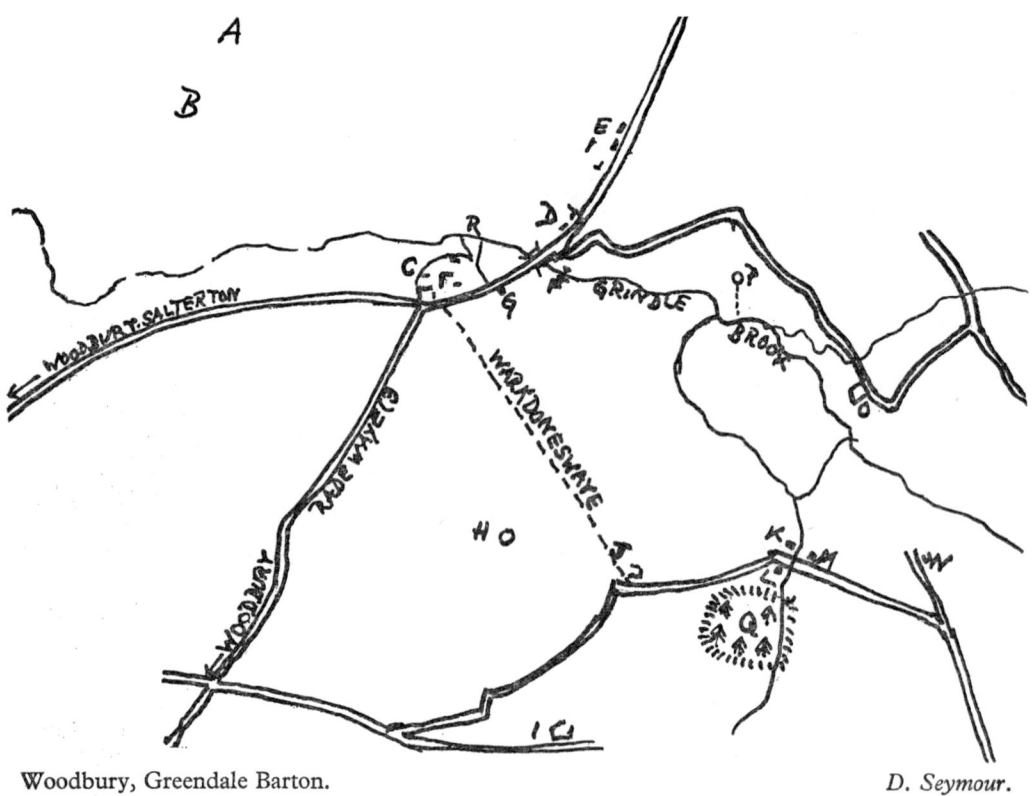

Woodbury, Greendale Barton.   *D. Seymour.*

A	Pyramid	H	Pond (Golden Spring?)	N	Lindhayne (Hr. Hogsbrook)
B	La Segge	I	Cannon Walls	O	Winkley
C	Greendale Barton	J	Hogsbrook	P	Pond at Winkley
D	Higher Greendale	K	Scoarches	Q	Wood of Foxley (?)
E	Cottages of smallholders	L	Whites	R	Cattle Drift
F	Site of Mill	M	Eales		
G	Site of Pound				

Greendale), measures roughly 78 ft. x 27 ft. and has its original cob walls on two sides. One of the outer sides, like the building just mentioned, has blocks of red stone, possibly from Heavitree, for a foundation. This spacious yard has no doubt been put to good use in the sheep-shearing season. It is reminiscent of the Sheepfold on Dartmoor north of Postbridge, but on a smaller scale. Another feature common on Dartmoor is a cattle "drift". Near the farm entrance such a drift is to be seen on a shallow crossing of the Grindle brook. A flock or herd could be placed in the drift until required in the yard. It is so shaped that it is enclosed by high banks on three sides, whilst on the fourth it is narrow enough for a gate to secure it. It is unusual to find a drift complete with a water supply, and to find one at all away from Dartmoor is surely unusual.

The L shaped house is dominated by a fine chimney beside the front door; a show chimney in this position is common in East Devon. The house seems to have kept to its mediaeval plan, yet apart from the front wall and those surrounding the kitchen it is for the most part a 19th century rebuilding in red brick. The dairy wing is built on lower courses of red sandstone which appear old, so the original plan has been followed here. Comparison with the courthouses of Oldstone and Court Barton shows a close resemblance. In each case the courthouse is at rightangles to the main building and separated completely from it by a wall of geat thickness. Here its length is 45 ft.—almost the same as at Oldstone and North Shillingford and a few inches less than at Court Barton. This courthouse wing differs from others in that only half its width adjoins the main house (see plan). Here a modern door has been hacked through the dividing wall. In monastic days there would be none because the business of the courthouse was no concern of the occupants of the house.

Greendale.   *D. Seymour.*

    The house and outbuildings probably formed an enclosed quadrangle, but two sides of this have vanished. Its cobbled flooring may still be seen outside the garden gate, and here one old building—the stable block—survives. An important settlement such as Greendale may very well have had its own chapel, but I have found no documentary evidence of it so far.
    Opposite the entrance stood the old cattle pound, and it is only in the last few years that it has been destroyed. In monastic days there were doubtless many more cottages for the farm labourers clustered round the barton house. On the other side of the bridge is Higher Greendale and a cob and thatch cottage—the typical home of a smallholder. There is also a fine barn of cob and thatch which stands back from the road. Higher Greendale used to be the dairy farm and may always have been so. The house is of decided age and measures 45 ft. x 22 ft. It has what are probably the old roof timbers,

and these seem to come right down through the cob walls almost to floor level. The house is built round a stalwart chimney breast, and formerly there was a spiral staircase built into the thickness of the wall. All this may be seen in the plan which shows this as a longhouse, and I do not doubt that it goes back to the 13th century or even earlier.

The smallholder's cottage has been demolished since I began this book. It showed the same plan as Higher Greendale on a humbler scale. Much good timber work was in it, especially upstairs. No doubt a few acres once surrounded the cottage and tenants mentioned in our charters may have held it. It was entirely of cob.

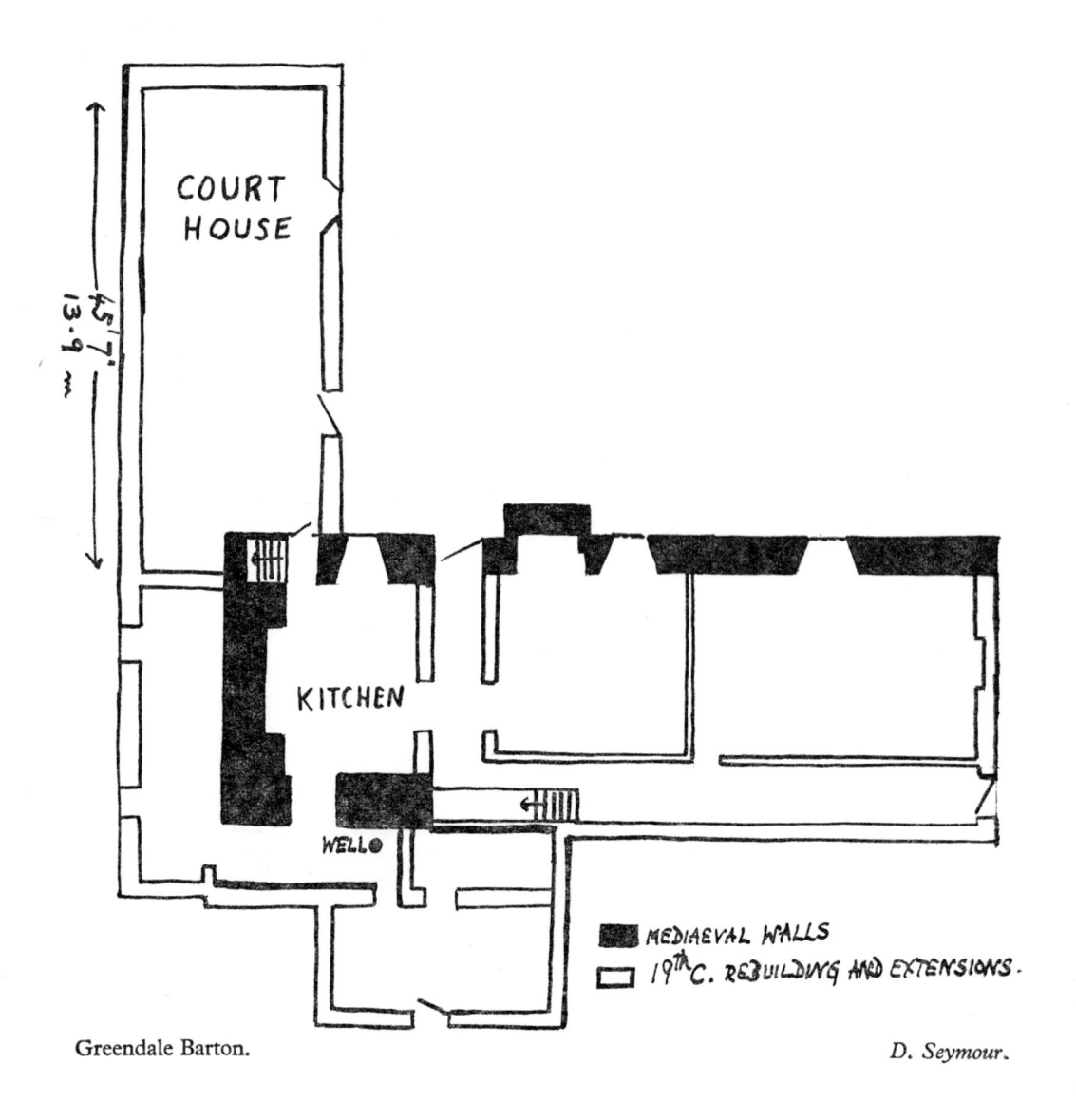

Greendale Barton. *D. Seymour.*

Another important building which must have stood close to the bridge was Gryndell Mill. A field opposite the barton is named Mill-Park. In 113 Brother Richard, Abbot of Torre, quitclaimed to Michael de Wynkelegh 4 acres of land in exchange for a certain pond which would benefit the mill. Now Winkley is still an active farm not far off on the north side of the stream. Miss Parsons, the present farmer, lives in a 19th century house of red brick; the old house, she told me, had been destroyed by fire. All that remains of it is the huge chimney in the kitchen—a fine survivor of monastic days. It was beside this friendly hearth, in the same spot no doubt where Michael de Wynklegh used to sit

Higher Greendale. *D. Seymour.*

at his ease on winter nights, that Miss Parsons told me of a pond which to this day exists in her old orchard. There, some 300 yards above the Grindle Brook, and upon steeply sloping ground, I found a pond—choked and overgrown, but connected with the brook by a culvert through which water still flows. If it were not kept clear then the pond would become a swamp and a hazard to cattle. It measures about 95 ft. by 60 ft.; it is oval in shape and obviously man-made. The water comes from a spring in the side of the slope.

There is evidence below Hogsbrook Farm of a culvert taken from the stream; this, too, may have been needed to give a good flow of water to work the mill, for the Grindle Brook is rather a sluggish stream.

Higher Greendale—upstairs.   *D. Seymour.*

The Charters

89. A gift of 2 virgates of land in the manor of Wodebiry made to William Briewere, by Reginald de Albamara, with the consent of Avelina, his wife, and Geoffrey his son. To be held for one twentieth of a knight's fee. In recognition whereof William has given him a gold ring and a horse, and his son a hunter.
Date: 1180/90.   MS: Folio 36.

90. (Lord) William Briewere gives to William de la Bruera 4 librates of land in Wodebiry as the dowry of his sister, Engelesia: they came to him through his uncle Reginald de Albamara. Should she die childless the land reverts to the donor.
Date: c. 1190.   MS: Folio 36.

91. William de la Bruera exchanges with (Lord) William Brewer all his land at Grendil (which was the dowry of Iggelesia, his wife) for the manor of Houbotone.
Date: c. 1195.   MS: Folio 36 & 37.

92. Iggelesia, wife of William de la Bruera, returns her dowry of Grendel to her brother (Lord) William Brewer in exchange for the manor of Houbotone. After her death it will revert to her brother.
Date: c. 1195.   MS: Folio 37.

93. A confirmation in perpetual alms from Reginald de Albamara to the Canons of Torre of William Briwere's gift of the vill of Grendel. It concerns the land which his grandfather, Reginald, and his father, Geoffrey, confirmed to the Canons.
Date: mid 13th century.   MS: Folio 37.

94. A confirmation by Geoffrey de Albamara to the Canons of Torre of Grendil. He and his father gave this to William de Briwere. It was a part of the manor of Wodebiry as were the villeins and their lands of the same fee which are at Piria.
Date: c. 1220/30.   MS: Folio 37.

95. A confirmation of an exchange of land at Gryndell between Reginald de Albamara and the Canons of Torre. All the arable lands on the east side of Radeweye, Robert Hoggesbroc's holding of Wodelond, 3 acres on the north side of Warkedunesweye, an acre in vudelhister which Geoffrey the carpenter holds, the land which William de Pont holds above vudelhister and 2 acres in the Canons' close to be exchanged for William the smith's land at Westfoxley and 2½ acres of demesne land there, 2 acres at Cammahilla, all the land on the east side of Withemore, 4½ acres north of Ralph Pope's house and 1 acre and 3 virgates of his demesne land. He gives them 11½ acres at Hoggebroc in exchange for his land in the hills. Clause of Warranty.
Date: c. 1240/50.   MS: Folio 37 & 38.

96. A confirmation of an exchange of land between Reginald de Albamara and the Canons of Torre. They are to have all the meadowland which his men Robert de Hoggesbrok, Roger Perteheie and Walter the Granger held from him, viz:—the meadow with the golden spring, lying east and west of the road from Grendull to Wodebiry; a meadow at Milesteken, and the meadow between the pyramid and a meadow under Ailemundesburga in the west part of la Segge; Morsplot in west part of Warkesdonesweye: all in exchange for the Canons' meadow called Baghemore and a half acre in the east part of Wytemore. He also gives 2 acres and half a virgate south of ffoxleghe wood (which Roger Perteheye held) for 2 acres and half a virgate which the Canons had in Langeham. Clause of Warranty.
Date: c. 1240/50.   MS: Folio 37.

97. A gift to the Canons of Torre from Reginald de Albamara of the wood of ffoxleye. They may enclose it with hedge and ditch.
Date: mid 13th century.   MS: Folio 38.

98. A gift to the church of St. Saviour of Torre from Reginald de Albamara of pasture in the manor of Wodebiry between these bounds: by the road between the Abbot's land and G. Hoggesbroc's house which leads to the hill opposite the firebeacon; thence to the bank above Blachediche. Thence climbing to the high road, going east below the firebeacon, and along the road to Chasteiller (Woodbury Castle), and by the east side of it to the road from the south side of Chasteiller to the large cross between Wodebiry and Otteritune; then along the road to the east as far as his land extends. Here the Canons may graze 40 ewes with their weaned lambs, 25 yearling pigs and 100 grazing beasts. Should they stray into cornfields the Canons must pay damages.
Date: mid 13th century.   MS: Folio 38.

99. An undertaking from William de Ponte to pay the Abbot of Torre 8/- per annum at Grendil for land and messuages formerly held from Reginald de Albamara in Wodebiry

manor; also for a close which the widow Christina held at Wodetone. Suit of court twice annually at Grendel at Michaelmas and Hokkeday. Clause of Warranty.
Date: mid 13th century.   MS: Folio 39.

100.   A gift from Reginald de Albamara to the Church of Torre of all the land and messuages which William de Ponte held from him in Wudetone, and a close which Richard the carpenter once held. William to hold for his lifetime, except the close for which he pays 7/4. After his death whoever holds it to have fuel and grazing in the manor of Wodebiry. Clause of Warranty.
Date: mid 13th century.   MS: Folio 39.

The attempt to trace the old boundaries mentioned in the charters is a rewarding as well as an active pursuit. At Greendale, with the aid of Woodbury's excellent Tithe Map, much has been achieved. For instance the boundaries specified in 98, where Reginald (2) de Albamara gives an extensive area of pasture to the Canons can be quite clearly followed today. It begins by way of the road between Gryndell land and Geoffrey Hoggesbroc's house. Now Hogsbrook is today a farm whose name has been changed to Lindhayne. Above the bridge an old path leads through Millpark to join a stony single-track lane which goes straight to Lindhayne. Near this it joins another lane and so climbs to Woodbury Common. It makes straight for the old firebeacon described in the charter as "Virbecna". The next point is Blachediche, which is a deep gulley, no doubt made to form a barrier between the last enclosed land and the rough moorland of the common. From the firebeacon the old boundary follows the present road to "Chasteiller" which was how the scribe spelt "castle". We are then told that the road proceeded on the south side of Chasteiller, which is interesting because it shows that the banks of Woodbury Castle were not then bisected by the road as now. The boundary proceeded along the road to Four Firs where we are told a large cross stood. This, of course, has vanished and the memory of it has quite died out. Turning east the line continued as far as the Woodbury boundary, which today is a well-defined path running at first north-east and later east across the common. It later turns north-west to reach the road again near The Warren. Thence it makes straight for one of the heads of the Grindle Brook (probably Hogsbrook then), and so by way of the brook to the starting point at Grindle Bridge. This brook is still the Woodbury boundary, and in those days it would be the manor boundary, too. The Canons were thus given ample ground for grazing between boundaries which may still be traced.

In 95 further names occur which can be identified:—first Radeweye, which by its description is the road from Greendale to Woodbury. Robert Hoggesbrook's holding of Wodelond could be an even older name for Hogsbrook Farm, and just as apt. Warkeduneswaye I have identified as a track across a field still called Warkedune on the Tithe Map. Vudelhister cannot be traced, and where, too, was Westfoxley and the wood of ffoxleghe?

Foxley is a name which might crop up anywhere, yet in this locality it is not remembered. Now the Canons were given permission to enclose their wood of ffoxleghe (97) and one may be sure that they took advantage of this privilege. My task, therefore, was to find a wood enclosed by banks, and I found it near Lower Hogsbrook Farm. On the Marker Estate Map of 1918 this was called Hogsbrook Wood. It was remarkable to notice also on the map that the enclosure seemed not to fit into the surrounding field pattern. A reason for this could be that the banks of the wood are far older than the surrounding pattern of the present field hedges. On the 1839 Tithe Map its shape and boundaries are exactly the same. Another point is that in 111 an acre of wood on the east side of the wood was given to the Canons. Why did they want it? Surely the little stream just there was a natural boundary. However, had a bank been constructed there the stream would have been constantly undermining it. The map shows that the wood does continue with a narrow strip just beyond the stream. The 1918 map shows a narrow enclosed strip just beyond the eastern limit of the wood, so there really is about an acre of wood and a strip east of the stream. In this way the Canons made a good job of embanking their wood, and I do think that the evidence is strongly in favour of this being the site of the ancient wood of ffoxleghe.

Just below the wood there stood, according to the Tithe Map, three farms with their outbuildings. These were Scorche's, White's and Eale's—all personal names, it seems. They were undoubtedly ancient small holdings. What is more likely than that West Foxley was here, with East Foxley on the other side of the stream? The third may have been Lower Hogsbrook, because the present house of that name on the hill above is Victorian. All the land now belongs to this farm, and I should imagine that a well-to-do farmer built himself the new house and demolished the buildings of the three old farms. So perished more monastic property.

In 86 there is mention of "the meadow with the golden spring". This is certainly a fanciful title, and quite attractive enough to make one determined to find it. The only clue was that the meadow lay east and west of the road to Woodbury. In those days it was the exception rather than the rule to have enclosed fields, so this meadow lay on both sides of the road. I examined the country carefully and found that water was only to be found in one place near Greendale in this direction. This is about a third of a mile from the Barton on the left, in the second field up from the road. Here there is a pond, and in its centre a small island. A semicircular depression is to be seen just above it, and has the appearance of an abandoned sand pit. Perhaps the pond was once a similar pit and a spring was allowed to fill it to make a pond. At any rate there is a spring here in the right locality and more cannot be said.

Close by is the farm of Cannonwalls, which was Cammahill in our charters. Its old buildings have gone, and nothing remains but the name. Fieldnames which can still be identified are Morsplot, La Segge, Withymore (now Whitemoor) and Pyramid.

Huntisbere

So far all the land mentioned has been in Woodbury, but there was more outside the Woodbury manor bounds, which was near enough to be administered from Greendale. Charters 101 and 102 deal with a ferling now in the parish of Aylesbeare. It was described as at Ailenewode or Ailevewde—both variants of the same name, for "beare" means wood. Later the manor seems to have been simply Wood. This ferling was a gift from Alexander, son of Angerus de Hunteba, for which the Canons paid 7/- to the lord of the fee. Now Hunteba immediately suggests Houndbeare of which it seems to be an attempted Latin form. It was therefore easy to assume that this ferling was a part of either Great Houndbeare or Little Houndbeare Farms; but a glance at the Tithe Map showed that both were outliers of Woodbury. The charters tell us that the land was in Ailenwode. Moreover there is evidence that the Houndbeare Farms belonged to the Vicars Choral of Exeter Cathedral. Where, then, was Alexander's ferling?

I found it between the lane from Aylesbeare and Little Houndbeare; it is a small triangular holding called Huntisbere. This name is far closer to Huntiba than Houndbeare, though both names may have had a common origin. Moreover this property is in Aylesbeare. The Tithe Map shows about 15 acres here and 10 on the other side of the road; so the ferling consisted of 25 acres. The western boundary of Huntisbere is most unusual for it is a ditch some 15 ft. in depth which continues for some distance and then turns east. It is so impressive and unlike other boundaries which I saw in my researches that I feel it may very well antedate monastic times; further study as to its extent and age might be rewarding.

The house and outbuildings are old in design, but there has been a good deal of rebuilding. There are remains of a pond and wells near the house; the land is good and dry and is situated on the south-west slope of Aylesbeare Hill. The house was once a simple longhouse, which has been enlarged. Its salient features are its stalwart chimneys at each end. Some good timber work remains downstairs, but not on the upper floor. So perhaps a fire may have destroyed the old roof at some time. Altogether Huntisbere is an excellent survival of a mediaeval smallholding. The two charters concerning it are as follows:—

101.   A gift from Robert, son of Walter, (with the assent of his wife Eufemia) made to Angerus de Hunteba of a ferling at Ailenewode which William de la fforde formerly held. A rent of 7/-. In recognition Angerus has given him 20/-, his wife, Eufemia, 2/-, and his daughters, Margaret and Cicely, 12d. Clause of Warranty.
Date: 1230/40.   MS: Folio 40.

102.   A gift in perpetual alms to the Canons of Torre from Alexander, son of Angerus de Hunteba, of all his land in the vill of Ailvewde. 7/- to the lord of the fee.
Date: c. 1240.   MS: Folio 40.

St. Kalixtus's Fair

103.   The Lady Johanna de Valletorta, in her widowhood, grants the toll on all merchandise bought and sold at St. Kalixtus's Fair to the Abbot of Torre. For the souls of her father, Thomas Passet, her lord, Reginald de Valletorta, and for herself.
Date: mid 13th century.   MS: Folio 40.

The Greendale charters have already shown us a picture of great activity among the Abbot's tenants, but they also tell us about a great number of people—in all over 30. It is surprising after a while how one begins to feel on quite friendly terms with Robert and Geoffrey Hoggesbrook who are mentioned so much in our charters. Some, however, are just passing figures which we hear of in perhaps one charter only. Such a one was the lady Johanna de Valletorta who in 103 gave the Canons the toll on goods bought and sold at St. Kalixtus's Fair. This she did for the benefit of her own soul and those of her former lord, Reginald de Valletorta, and of her father, Thomas Passett. Now this fair was held on Oct. 14th at Colyton; it had been granted to her father by no less a person than King John. But why is this stray charter among the business activities of Greendale? I like to think that Lady Johanna perhaps ended her days in one of those snug little thatched houses in which east Devon abounds. Maybe the Abbot of Torre gave her one; this could have been her reason for confirming the toll from the fair to him.

The Manor of Blackberry

It now remains to discuss land in the parish of Colaton Raleigh which was in the manor of Blackberry; this was referred to in the charters as Blakeburga or Blachebrigg, and it belonged to the family of Budeyn or Baucan—the name is spelt in many ways. They were certainly lords of the manor, for in 104 and 105 Walter Budeyn refers to his demesne land. In his manor there were two pieces of adjacent land which the Abbey eventually acquired. 104 and 107 deal with previous ownership, but in 107 and 292 (a charter unaccountably placed among the Daccombe Charters) it is given to the Canons for a rent of a pound of cummin.

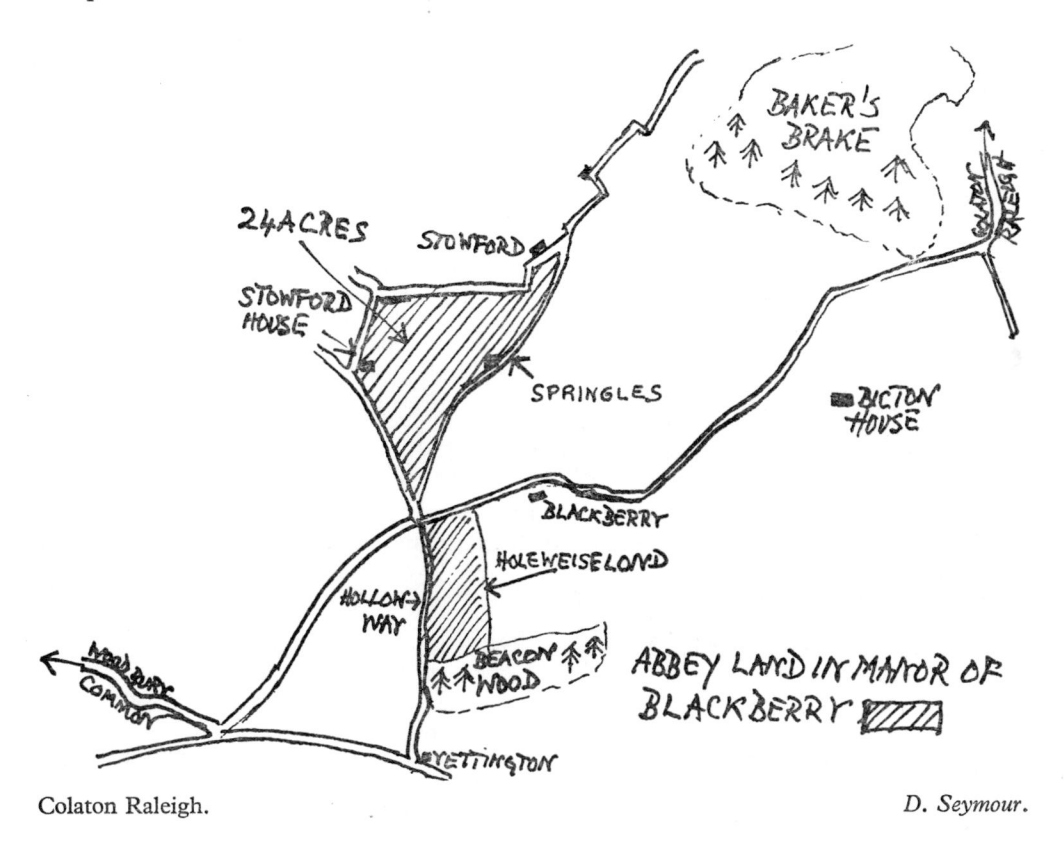

Colaton Raleigh. *D. Seymour.*

The first strip of land was 10 acres of meadow from the demesne land which was at Holeweislonde. No such name exists now and no help was forthcoming from the Tithe Map. It was not very hard to see that in "Holewei" our scribe was trying to spell "Holloway"—a name very common in Devon for a lane which is sunk below the level of the surrounding land and with steep banks on either side. There is a splendid example of this about a quarter of a mile from Blackberry Farm (which was probably the manor house) on the road to East Budleigh. Here, near Beacon Plantation, the lane is sunk in a deep hollow. It was easy to see on the Tithe Map that what had formerly been a large meadow had in the course of time been divided into five fields. Strangely enough these dividing hedges have now been bulldozed away and Holeweislond is once more a large meadow, evidently looking very much as it did in the Canons' day. The huge banks on the east side of the lane will surely be the old demesne bounds of the manor of Blackberry.

The other piece of land given was 24 acres south of the road from Stowford to Blackberry. Today there is a direct road which runs north and south, so no land could be described as to the south of it (104). But there is an older, more indirect road between the two farms which begins by running west. Here, south of it, is a triangle of land comprising 28 acres. 4 acres have been gained since the time of the charters by the disappearance of Springles. This was a smallholding consisting of only two strip fields.

Set amid this triangle of land is the old farmhouse—Stowford House. This is a well-thatched longhouse measuring 52'6" x 20'. It is of cob, with one fine chimney still intact. A spiral stair is a part of its construction. An air photo shows its former outbuildings. These acres which came into the Canons' hands are, according to the present farmer, Mr. L. J. Carter, unusually fertile. So successful has his work been there that I.C.I. has brought out a pamphlet about them entitled "Profit from 28 acres". This soil is a deep, sandy loam and is free draining. In the mild Devon climate it is ideal for early and late grazing. It is curious how this piece of old church land should have become of such interest to the farming community. The Canons were certainly well advised over the lands they acquired. The charters concerning land in the manor of Blackberry are:—

104. A gift from Walter Budyn to his brother Ralph of all his demesne land of Holweielonde and 24 acres south of the road from Stauford to Blakeburga, and the meadow of la Pitte, with the service of Jordan Barnage.
Date: mid 13th century.   MS: Folio 40.

105. Walter Budyn gives his kinsman Jordan 10 acres of his demesne land of Holeweislonde, with the entire meadow below the demesne and next to the church's meadow. Grazing rights given.
Date: mid 13th century.   MS: Folio 40.

106. A quitclaim from Jordan Barnage to Ralph Buty of 10 acres with the meadow of Holeweislonde.
Date: mid 13th century.   MS: Folio 40.

107. A gift to the Canons of Torre from Ralph Budyn of all the land in his manor of Blachebrigge which his father, Walter, gave to his uncle Ralph. Grazing rights given.
Date: 1270/1300.   MS: Folio 40 & 41.

108. A confirmation from Abbot R(ichard) to John and his son, Philip, of Holeweyeslonde. They are to hold it as Ralph and Walter Buty held it. Rent 8/-.
Date: late 13th century.   MS: Folio 41.

292. For the health of his soul and those of his parents, ancestors and successors, Ralph Budeyn gives to the Canons of Torre all of Holeweyeslonde, which his brother gave to him: also 24 acres which Henry, son of William used to hold: also 10 acres which he bought from Jordan Barnage. Rent, a pound of cummin.
Date: mid 13th century.   MS: Folio 98.

THE FINAL GREENDALE CHARTERS

109. Geoffrey de Albamara, lord of Wodebiry, and son of William de Albamara, declares that he has inspected the (charters of) the gifts which Geoffrey and Reginald and his other ancestors have made to the Canons of Torre at Grendil and confirms them. The tithe of Grendil is also theirs.
Date: Given at Grendil, Sunday, the Feast of St. Michael, 1296/97. MS: Folio 41.

110. A Final Concord between the Canons of Torre and Reginald de Albamara: he concedes grazing rights etc. as in 98. If either side defaults over the agreement they shall forfeit a vat of wine or 40/-.
Date: mid 13 century.

111. A quitclaim from Abbot S(imon) to Geoffrey de Albamara of the rent and homage of William de Ponte: except the curtillage which he holds at Grendil for 6d. Geoffrey may plough 10 acres of their pasture, and after the corn has been carried the Abbot may use it for grazing. For this Geoffrey concedes the exchange of a meadow: also 1 acre ad acent to the east part of the wood of ffoxleghe, and a rent of 12d. from a close of land at Wodetone which Gervase le Pope holds. Clause of Distraint.
Date: 1252/63. MS: Folio 42.

112. A confirmation of permission to embank their wood of ffoxlegh given to the Canons of Torre from Fulk de Albamara, son of Reginald, given at the instigation of his lord and brother, Geoffrey: in exchange for an acre which Geoffrey has given him.
Date: mid 13th century. MS: Folio 42.

113. A quitclaim from brother Richard, Abbot of Torre, to Michael de Wynkelegh of 4 acres of land. They lie east and west of John le Kyne's land: in exchange for a pond, which will supply Grendil Mill.
Date: 1270/1300. MS: Folio 42. Witnesses: Sir Ralph de fferdone, Robert de Uppecote, William de fferdone, Robert de Grendil and others.

In 94 there is mention of villeins and their lands which are at Piria in the same fee as Gryndell. No place of that name exists in the district now, and if such a farm name is to be found I shall be surprised. Yet Piria exists as a surname in "Devon Lay Subsidy", appearing there under several headings as Pirie, Piria and Pyrie. There are nine instances of it, some with the prefix "atte"; so the next thing was to discover what "atte Piria" could mean. Now "piria" is the Latin for a peartree, and furthermore there is a drink made from pears known as perry. That this was brewed in monastic days, just as cider was from apples, there can be little doubt. The answer to the riddle seems to be that in the days we are considering there were pear orchards at Greendale in the hands of the villeins. The climate just here is so good for pear growing that I am told on good authority that wild peartrees are still to be seen in Woodbury not far below the Common. So to the list of occupations which the charters show us we can add peargrowing as a serious occupation.

I have pointed out elsewhere how the witnesses to the charters are nearly always the local gentry. In Dublin Cartulary there are two further leases mentioned and the witnesses are nearly all from nearby farms. There is Michael de Winkley whom we have already met, and W. de Feradone who doubtless lived just over the hill at Farringdon.

L

Nicholas de la Wythe came from Aylesbeare where the farm of Within still exists. Then there was William de Opham or Hopham, which is Upham today: it is a fine old house, said to have been the manorhouse of Farringdon. Nicholas de Ponte would live at Greendale Bridge, and is the same person as Nicholas atte Bridge. Robert de Uppecotte would come from Upcott in Rockbeare. All this helps to demonstrate the age of our Devon farmsteads, proving that all these farms go back at least to the 13th century.

The Greendale charters, and indeed the whole locality, are so pleasing that it is with real regret that this chapter is brought to its close. The 13th century was politically a turbulent one, but these charters show that life at Greendale went on its own sweet way, undisturbed by the main stream of events.

Further References

Taxation of Pope Nicholas, 1288
Taxed at £3.1.8.

Devon Lay Subsidy, 1332
William Daumarle taxed at 3/-. This shows that the de Albamaras were still in residence at Woodbury.

Valor Ecclesiasticus
Valued at £17.11.2.

A.O., Particulars for Grants 1390
"To Thomas Goodwin of Plymtree 10th August, 1546 . . . . the manor of Grendon and Salterton in the parish of Woodbury, late of Torre Abbey . . . .
m.9. Manor of Grendon and Salterton in the parish of Woodburye: Free Rents, 32/1; customary rents £13.17.11.; court profits, fines etc., 33/4: £17.3.4.
Certified with declaration by Mathew Colthurst".

24

Dunnyngestone

The Domesday manor of Dunnyngestone was in the parish of Clayhanger. Set amid the Exmoor foothills, a few miles from Bampton, it came to the Canons in the first part of the 13th century. They held it until the suppression of their Abbey.

There are two Domesday manors with similar names, "Donicestone" and Dunuinesdone". The former is probably the manor with which we are concerned because the "c" in the name is a sound which has persisted, later becoming a "g". Then again a mill is mentioned and even today we can point to Denscombe Mill. The Exeter Domesday account tells us that this manor consisted of $3\frac{1}{2}$ virgates and $\frac{1}{2}$ a ferling. There were 12 villeins and 6 bordars, 36 sheep and a mill worth 7/6. At first it was hard to decide upon the whereabouts of this manor, for the name, later Dunston, only survives at Denscombe, which is an isolated building. But there must in the 11th century have been a population of well over 100, and by the 13th century this would have increased. So there is a lost village to discover somewhere in the parish of Clayhanger. There was a chapel, too, at Dunnyngestone and the Cartulary of Bath Abbey (vol. 7, pp. 60/61) shows that c. 1107 it was an appurtenance of Bampton Church, together with chapels at Petetona, Deopeford and Lasela. By 1233 we find Bishop Brewer of Exeter in 120 confirming services at Dunnyngestone Chapel on 3 days a week— the parson of Clayhanger having to provide them. The position of the chapel seems to have been that it never belonged to the Canons of Torre but was entirely dependent upon Clayhanger church by the 13th century.

Now Denscombe Mill is the one solitary building to survive from this period, and it is on the Clayhanger side of the little river Batherm. Its position seems to point to the fact that the lost village lay between it and Clayhanger. The old mill was still working at the beginning of this century, and the present tenant remembers the overshot wheel in position. The walls of the mill could well be mediaeval, but the millhouse looks like a rebuilding of an older house. If this is the Domesday mill, then it worked for 850 years at least. Between it and Clayhanger the only house is Nutcombe Manor. The pleasing 16th century house here is considered to be a rebuilding on a far older site. The general feeling is that Nutcombe is a complete homestead in itself and quite independent of Clayhanger. Moreover, at some time, probably in the 18th century, the Nutcombe estate has been "landscaped". That is to say the surrounding farm land has been made into a tidy park. There are set avenues approaching the house, and the remains of formal clumps of trees. As one walks down from the village one feels that it is too tidy for Devon. The typical, irregular pattern of hedges and small fields is missing. I think that by the 17th century the village was decaying, and some vigorous squire went in for alterations on a large scale; he swept away the former village and its chapel, so that small holdings, cottages and farm buildings have been ruthlessly liquidated.

Mention must be made of an old right of way from Clayhanger which passes through

Nutcombe and then descends to the Batherm close to the mill. Beyond the river it continues through fields above Waterhouse and North Hayne and becomes a lane leading to Bampton. I believe that this was the old approach road to Dunnyngestone which fell into disuse when the village decayed. The present road to Clayhanger takes a very indirect route, winding right round the Nutcombe estate.

Now Nutcombe Manor took its name from the post-Reformation family of Nutcombe. Notice, too, that the house has always been styled "manor"; yet there has never been a manor of Nutcombe. Is not this proof of a deeprooted remembrance in the locality that a manorhouse has always stood on the site? Must it not have been the manorhouse of Dunnyngestone? But better evidence still comes from Lysons (p. 112) who writes "This estate, with the barton of Nutcombe and the manor of Doningston or Dunston, which had long been in the family of Nutcombe . . .". It is easy to see how after this period of the early 19th century the old name of Dunnyngestone became forgotten through disuse. I suggest, therefore, that the old village was west of Clayhanger, and that it probably lay around Nutcombe.

The Charters

114. A gift of the manor of Dunnyngestone from William Briewere to Henry de fferendon. William de Bruera and his wife Angalisia quitclaimed it to him for forty marks. Rent–a pair of gilt spurs or 6d. at Easter. Clause of Warranty.
Date: 1200/20.   MS: Folio 43.

115. A gift from Henry de fferendone to the Canons of Torre of the land of Dunnyngestone, so that a Canon may be deputed to say mass for himself, his ancestors and all the faithful departed.
Date: 1200/20.   MS: Folio 43.

116. William Briwere the Younger gives to the Canons of Torre the whole land of Dunnyngestone which William de Bruera and Ingelesia, his wife, quitclaimed to him as the nearer heir for 50 marks. With it is given the service of Petetone. For his own soul and that of his wife Johanna.
Date: 1224/32.   MS: Folio 43 & 44.

117. A Final Concord in the King's Court at Exeter, between Henry de fferendone and William de la Bruera and his wife Ingelesia. They agreed that a carucate of land at Dunnyngestone was the property of Henry and returned it to him.
Date: Wednesday after the Feast of St. Barnabas the Apostle, 1228/29.   MS: Folio 44.

118. A Final Concord in the King's Court at Exeter between Nicholas de fferendone and Laurence, Abbot of Torre. Nicholas quitclaimed to the Abbot all claim to two carucates of land at Dunnyngestone. In return prayers would be made for Nicholas and his successors for ever.
Date: The Vigil of St. John the Baptist, 1238/39.   MS: Folio 44.

119. A quitclaim from Reginald de Moyun of the homage and service of Gervase de Petetone and his heirs for ever.
Date: mid 13th century.   MS: Folio 44.

120. A confirmation from William (Brewer), Bishop of Exeter, of three services a week to be held in the chapel of Dunnyngestone and provided by the chaplain of Clehangre, viz. on Tuesdays, Thursdays and Saturdays. Given at Cumbe.
Date: June 18th, 1233/34.   MS: Folio 44.

121. A statement from King Henry III to the Sheriff of Devon saying that he has inspected William Briwere's charter given to the Canons of Torre wherein he gave them the whole land of Dunnyngestone. As William's heirs have other lands in which they can distrain for the rendering of scutage, he orders that the Canons are to be left in peace with regard to scutage for the moor of Dunnyngestone.
Date: mid 13th century.   MS: Folio 44 & 45.

There are seven charters dealing with Dunnyngestone and they show that in the early 13th century the manor was in the hands of William de la Bruera and his wife, Engelesia. We have met this couple before in the Wolborough and Greendale chapters. As Engelesia was Lord William's sister, this happy couple no doubt basked in the sunshine of the great man's affluence. Any spare manors, of which he owned legion up and down the country, were liable to be passed on to relatives to be administered.

The charters show how Dunnyngestone came to the Canons as a gift from Henry de fferendone. As a result, a chantry was granted to him at Torre Abbey, and a priest assigned to it. Just how much land went with the gift is obscure. For instance, in the Final Concord of 1228 between the Brewers and de fferendone, only 1 carucate is mentioned (117), but another of 1238 mentions two.

Reginald de Mohun's quitclaim of the service of Gervase de Petetone and his heirs (119) opens up the question as to whether Petton may not have been a part of the manor of Dunnyngestone. It lies on the other side of the River Batherm, and with its old chapel of St. Petroc is not far from Denscombe Mill. As the service of the men of Petetone is given in 116 it is tempting to think of Petton as in the manor of Dunnyngestone at that time. It was always a part of Bampton parish, however; but again it might have been an outlying part of the manor of Clayhanger of which Reginald de Mohun was lord. Was it included in Dunnyngestone by the time of the second Final Concord, and did it form the extra carucate of land? Perhaps a charter giving it to Torre is missing. The final charter from King Henry III excuses the Canons from scutage for the moor of Dunnyngestone. Maybe this refers to grazing land which went with the manor on the Exmoor hills. Is this the land in Somerset mentioned below?

It is strange how all memory of the Canons of Torre has died out. They worked the land for some 300 years, yet not a vestige of that work remains. The chapel, the houses of their men and the small fields in which they toiled have vanished without a trace. Only the mill where they ground their corn remains to tell of the ancient manor of Dunnyngestone.

Further References

Taxation of Pope Nicholas, 1288
   Dounyngestone paid £2.0.0.

Devon Lay Subsidy, 1332
   Mention of Batecok de Doningston under Clehangre. Also Edith atte Pirye suggests pear orchards and perry-making as at Greendale and Blackawton.

Valor Ecclesiasticus

Valued at £7.6.4. This is one of the lowest values among the Canons' properties. Rents £7.3.11½., fines etc. 2/5.

A.O., Particulars for Grants 135

p. 9 no. 11. "To Roger Bluett of Holcombe Rogus, 10 march, 1540 . . . . and the manor of Donningston in the parish of Clayhanger late of Torre Abbey . . . ."

"Donnyngston in the parish of Clayhangar: Free and customary rents £7.2.4½, court profits etc. according to the book of the tenth, 2/5½.:—£7.4.10. Property in Somerset 56/-.

Certified by Mathew Colthurst."

25

Haggelegh

Haggelegh, Haclega or Haggeleya is in the parish of Milverton, Somerset, and ecclesiastically it is in the diocese of Bath and Wells. Its name has quite died out in the district, and were it not for the Tithe Map it would have been impossible to identify its site; but there it appears as Hagleys and Bicnells, with an extent of 52½ acres. By that time both farms were insignificant and were soon to be swallowed up by Grove Park Farm—indeed, there may have been no more than barns remaining even then. The site is a mile or so south-west of Milverton and looks towards the Blackdown Hills and the Wellington Memorial. When I visited it in 1967 the field where the buildings formerly stood had been ploughed for the first time in living memory. On the surface there were many quite large pieces of reddish stone, one of which I brought away as a

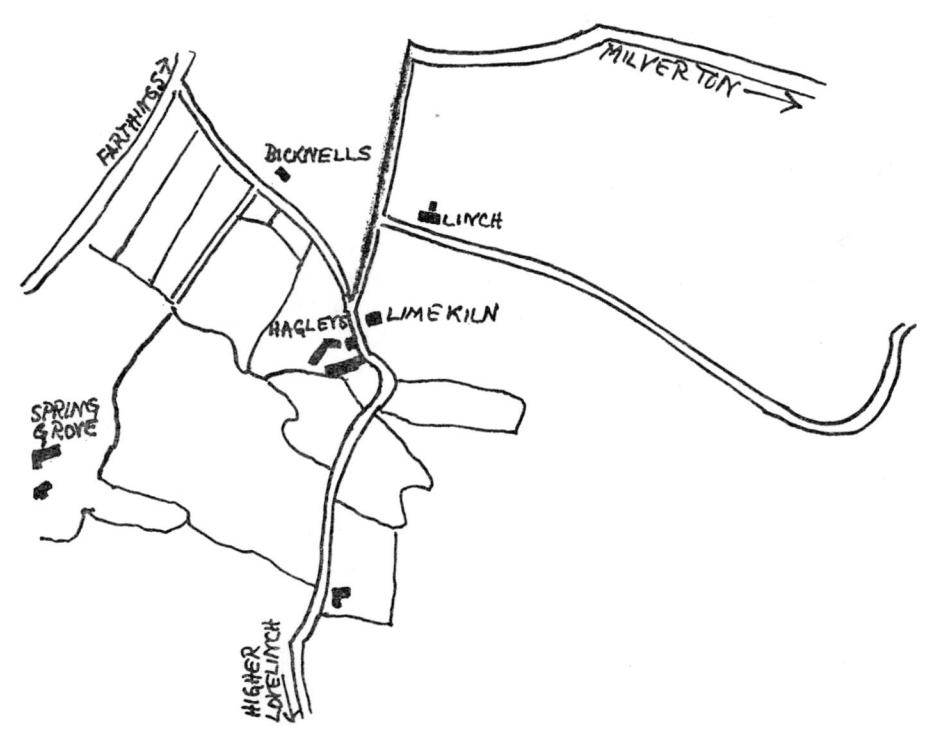

From Milverton Tithe Map 1842, showing position of Haggelegh.   *D. Seymour.*

souvenir. I had little doubt that this was the site of the former farm buildings. To clinch matters a springhead bubbled up just there, and that would have ensured a water supply.

This, then, is all that is to be seen of Haggelegh and its vill, which was given to Torre Abbey by John de Toritone early in the 13th century. There are two charters concerning it:—

122. A confirmation from William de Toritone to the Canons of Torre of the gift of the vill of Haggeleya, which his father, John de Toryntone, made to them. It is to be held with its privileges and free customs just as is stated in his father's charter which the Canons have.
Date: c. 1224/25. MS: Folio 45.

123. An agreement between the Canons of Torre and P., the perpetual vicar of Milverton, over the tithes from the demesne of Haggeleya. After discussion with Master Walter de St. Quintin, Archdeacon of Taunton, P. quitclaimed the tithes to the Abbot in the presence of the Dean of Exeter. Should Hageleya fall into lay hands the tithe will revert to P. The Abbot of Torre gave him 20/- for this quitclaim: the document was signed and sealed by himself and the Dean.
Date: Given at Exeter Cathedral, on the Vigil of the Feast of St. Martin, 1244. MS: Folio 45.

There are only two charters concerning Haggelegh, and the first is a confirmation of the original gift of John de Torrington by his son, William. As he died in 1224 (Tot. 1119) the charter can therefore be no later than this year. The gift is mentioned as early as the first Papalia document, which dates from 1214/23, so it was one of the very early gifts to the Abbey. John de Torrington's charter is not in the Cartulary, however.

In the second charter (123) there is mention of the demesne of Haggelegh, thus intimating that it was then a manor. The document is rather pathetic, and tells the story of poor P., the perpetual vicar of Milverton, who has to surrender his tithe from Haggelegh to Torre Abbey. Evidently there had been squabbling about this, but eventually P., intimidated by the Archdeacon of Taunton, was taken before the Dean of Exeter in whose presence he had to sign away his Haggelegh tithes. Walter de St. Quintin, the Archdeacon, who was sometime vicar of the neighbouring parish of Sampford Arundel, must have lived in the old Archdeacon's house beside Milverton Church; it is now known as "Old Parsonage". I hope it kept fine for P., as he set out for his long ride to Exeter, on the Vigil of St. Martin, 1224.

Two charters such as these can bring to life a facet of local history which would otherwise have been lost for ever. The railway line between Taunton and Whiteball Tunnel is enlivened for me now, for whenever I travel that way I always give a thought to P., and his lost tithes and to the pleasant mangold field where once there lay the demesne of Haggelegh.

Further References

Taxation of Pope Nicholas, 1288
    "Haggelegh £1.2.0. (in the diocese of Bath)".

Valor Ecclesiasticus
    Haggelegh was worth £4.4.9.

26

Ashclyst

The charters headed "Ayssclist" deal with a Prebend of that name attached to the former castle chapel of St. Mary at Exeter. This was said to have been a collegiate church, which until the 18th century stood within the castle walls. Its function seems to have been an attempt to combine the military with the ecclesiastical. It belonged to Plympton Priory but the advowson was in the hands of the Courtenay family, for it was attached to the Barony of Okehampton. Those interested in reading further about this unusual foundation will find notes on it in "Historic Towns—Exeter" by Freeman. In 1228 there were four Prebendaries attached—those of Heghes, Cotetone, Estclyst and Carswille. The number was later reduced to three, but the Prebend of Carswille actually survived the Reformation and the later demolition of the chapel. The last Prebendary to be instituted took office in the 19th century at a ceremony held in the open air within the castle walls.

The Prebend with which we are concerned derived its income from the manor of Ashclyst or Estslyst—there are numerous spellings—which is situated a mile or so south-east of Broad Clyst. The farm today is a part of the Killerton estate and so belongs to the National Trust.

The Charters

AYSSCLIST

124. Robert de Curtenay surrenders to the Abbot and Convent of Torre the advowson of the Prebend of Ayssclist.
Date: 1237.   MS: Folio 45.

125. A confirmation from William Brewer, Bishop of Exeter, made to the Abbot and Convent of Torre of the right to appoint to the Prebend of Asseclist after the death of Master Thomas, the present Prebendary. No exemption given from customary service at Exeter Castle Chapel. Given at ffynetone.
Date: March 31st, 1237.   MS: Folio 45.

126. Final Concord at Westminster whereby Abbot Laurence quitclaims to Robert de Curtenay the advowson of Chauuelegh. Robert then conceded the advowson of the prebend of Aysseclist to the Abbot.
Date: 1238.   MS: Folio 46.

127. A confirmation from Abbot Richard whereby he leases land at Assclist to William le Muchele at a rent of 5/-.
Date: 1298.   MS: Folio 46.

128. A confirmation made to the Canons of Torre Brewere by Hugh de Curtenay of his grandfather's gift of the advowson of the prebend of Asseclist.
Date: 1276. MS: Folio 46.

129. An agreement between William de Werplisdone, Canon of Exeter, and the Abbot of Torre whereby he conceded his manor or prebend of Asseclist to farm at 20 marks for three years.
Date: The vigil of the Feast of the Invention of the Cross, 1284. MS: Folio 46/47.

130. A confirmation from Peter, Bishop of Exeter, admitting the Abbot and Canons of Torre to the prebend of Ayssclyst vacant through the death of William de Werplisdone. It is to be employed for the support of the poor at Torre Abbey.
Date: February 28th, 1284. MS: Folio 47.

131. A confirmation from Pope Martin IV of the Prebend of Aysseclist and its advowson to the Abbot and Convent of Torre.
Date: November 15th (?), 1283/84. MS: Folio 47.

132. A licence in mortmain from King Edward I permitting the Abbot and Convent of Torre to hold the prebend of Aisseclist and its advowson.
Date: Westminster, 1284/85. MS: Folio 47/48.

133. Pope Martin IV orders the Abbot of Westminster and the Precentor of Salisbury to ensure that the Abbot and Convent of Torre are not deprived of their privilege in holding the prebend of Asseclist.
Date: November 10th, 1283/84. MS: Folio 48.

134. A confirmation from Andrew, Dean of Exeter, and the Cathedral Chapter of Bishop Peter's letters.
Date: November 4th, 1288. MS: Folio 48.

The first charters show how the Courtenay family gave the advowson of the prebend of Ashclyst to the Canons of Torre. The Bishop of Exeter confirmed the gift in 125. A year later there is a Final Concord at Westminster where Abbot Laurence quitclaims his right to the advowson of Chawleigh. The Cartulary shows that Torre was never endowed with this living, so either the Canons had procured it by other means, or else it was in some way attached to the Prebend.

All did not go smoothly for Torre Abbey, however, for in Bishop Bronscombe's Register (p. 139) a certain William de Stanfere is appointed to the Prebend of Ashclyst with Sir John de Curtenay as patron, on Feb. 7th, 1260. This entry is quite inexplicable unless for some reason the Abbot had never appointed to this Prebend in the meantime. So in some way it seems that the Canons were being deprived of their rights. In 1276, however, Hugh de Curtenay confirms his grandfather's gift of the Prebend. Then in 1284 the Prebend is again confirmed by Bishop Quivel (130). He was further backed by Pope Martin IV who in 131 breathes anathemas against any who would dare to deprive the Canons of their rights.

Nevertheless in 129 we find that a certain Canon of Exeter, William de Werplisdone, leased the manor of Ashclyst to the Abbot of Torre at 20 marks for 3 years. This makes it clear that the Canons of Torre had never got possession of the manor which went with the Prebend of Ashclyst, and so had not enjoyed the income from it. Even now we find that they had to rent the manor. William, evidently an old man at the time, feeling that he might not live for the three years, made provision for the continuance of the lease should he die in the meantime. This gives a clue to the fact that he had held on to the Prebend for a very long time. The situation, however, was quickly cleared up by the death of William before the following February. Bishop Quivel now saw to it that Torre Abbey at long last stepped into the vacancy. In 130 he arranges that, as the Prebend was a sinecure —i.e. no cure of souls was attached to it—the Abbot of Torre would always be the Prebendary of Ashclyst. The profit from the manor was to go to the maintenance of the poor and needy at the Abbey.

In the same year King Edward I gave a licence in Mortmain permitting the Canons to enter into possession of the manor (132). Finally in a letter to the Abbot of Westminster (133) Pope Martin IV commands the Precentor of Salisbury to see that the Canons of Torre are not deprived of their privileges in connection with Ashclyst, whilst Andrew de Kilkenny, Dean of Exeter, adds his confirmation (134). So after a wait of nearly 50 years the matter was at last settled and the Abbots of Torre were undisturbed in their possession from 1284 to 1539.

The Manor of Ashclyst

Turning now to consider the fine old farm house at Ashclyst, which was formerly the manorhouse, we are rewarded by the sight of a large L shaped building with four stalwart chimneys of red brick. It seems to be only in part mediaeval. At first what I saw was difficult to interpret. However, when once a plan had been drawn I came to the

Ashclyst. *D. Seymour.*

following conclusions. The front of the house is not nearly so old as the west wing and contains none of the old chimney-stacks. Its walls are of considerable thickness, but its back wall is missing, being a jumble of lean-to additions. This wing, I think, might be dismissed as late 17th century. This, too, may be about the date of the roof.

It looks, then, as though this house does not follow the usual pattern of L shaped courthouses such as I found at Coffinswell, Greendale and Oldstone. In these cases the courthouse was at rightangles to the house and separated from it by a very thick wall. We can be quite sure that there was a courthouse here, however, for a grant for 1543 mentions a profit of 5/5 derived from the court that year.

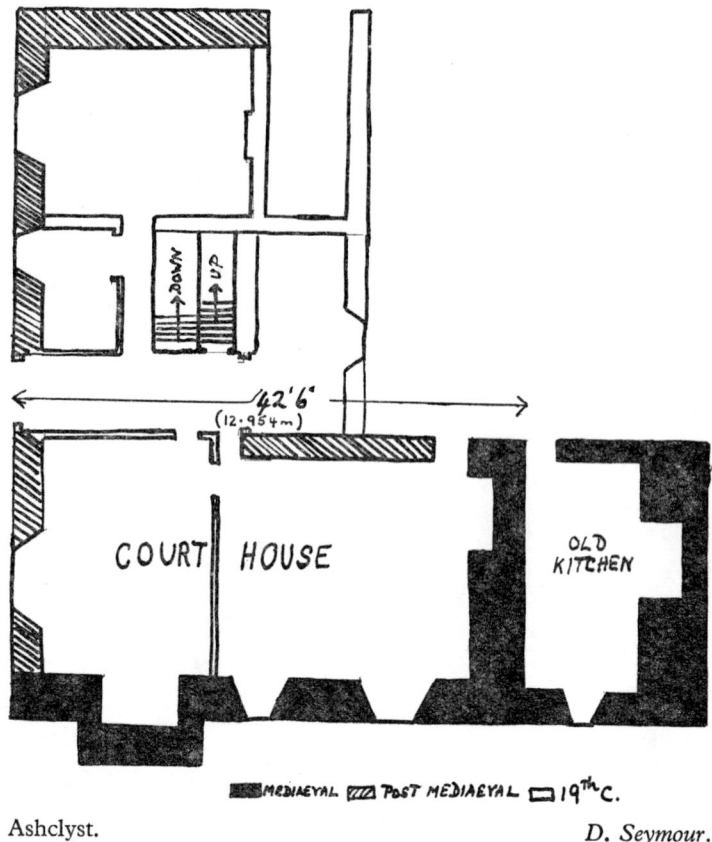

Ashclyst.   D. Seymour.

The only likely place for this courthouse to have been is in the west wing which is undoubtedly mediaeval. Here we have the fine old chimneys with their great hearths now filled in. A glance at the plan will show that between B and C there is a mere partition which, if removed, would result in a court room of reasonable size, though somewhat smaller than those found in the other examples. Moreover, it is separated from the old kitchen by a great wall six feet thick. There is still no communicating door between it and the rest of the house; and this is just what happens elsewhere. The courthouse then would have no intruding first floor, but would be open to the roof. In plan it closely resembles Underhaye where courtroom and house are in a straight line.

The old kitchen, with its great hearth undisturbed, is a fine sight. It may have been the only room in the old farmhouse, unless a whole wing to the east of it, and on line with the present yard enclosure walls, has completely disappeared. If this were the case then Ashclyst followed the more usual lines and was an L shaped house. With its steep-pitched roof and chimneys of mellowed red brick, it is still a house of character, but it does not betray its mediaeval origin to the casual observer.

Outbuildings include some of cob in the farmyard, but it is not possible to assess their age. In the orchard south of the house is a nicely built rectangular building, measuring roughly 10ft by 14ft. It appears old and I wonder if it may have been an ash-house.

There is mention of eight tenants in 1529, so it is probable that there were eight households at Ashclyst in addition to the courthouse. Of the extent of the manor we know nothing; but there is little doubt that it extended beyond the River Clyst, for the extensive Forest of Ashclyst is on the north side of the river. There must have been a forest there for centuries, for in 1529 there is mention of "10 woods at Asheclyste and 300 oaks of 100 years growth". So there is little doubt that the Canons had made the most of the timber-growing possibilities of the manor.

All traces of the old holdings have unfortunately vanished and so have their names. It has not been possible here to trace boundaries as has been done elsewhere on the Canons' estates.

Further References

Devon Lay Subsidy, 1332
Ashclyst was rated at 2/- which the Dean of Exeter paid. Four others paid.

Valor Ecclesiasticus
Ayssheclyst, £12.10.10.

A.O., Particulars for Grants 495
"Grant to Thomas Godwin of Plymtree and London, 26th August, 1543 . . . the manor of Ashclyst in the parish of Broad Clyst, late of Torre Abbey . . . ."
m. 11 "Manor of Aishecliste in the parish of Brodecliste: Free rents 16/-, customary rents £7.16. Farm of the chief messuage called Ayshecliste Farm, with demesne lands called barton lands "(terris dominicalis vocatis Barton Landes"), leased on December, 1529, for his life to William Adam £4: court profits 5/5; less 6/8 to the Prebendary of Hayes £12.17.5. . . . . . .
"Certified with declarations, including "Moreover the manor of Aishecliste aforesaid was stayed for Sir Thomas Seymour knyghte before his departure beyond the see at his own requeste" by Matthew Colthurst.
m. 10. Woods at Asheclyste: 300 oaks of 100 years' growth "polled and cropped" and sufficient only for repairs etc., for the farmer of the demesne John Adam and eight tenants. . .
Certified by William Cowper".

Exeter Castle Chapel (From J. B. Swete's water colour). *D. Seymour.*

In concluding this chapter it is a happy thing to be able to include John Swete's sketch of the chapel in Exeter Castle to which the Prebend of Ashclyst was attached, and also Norden's drawing of the Castle Yard. If Swete's drawing is accurate, then two of the windows have lost their old tracery. A Norman window and door survived, however.

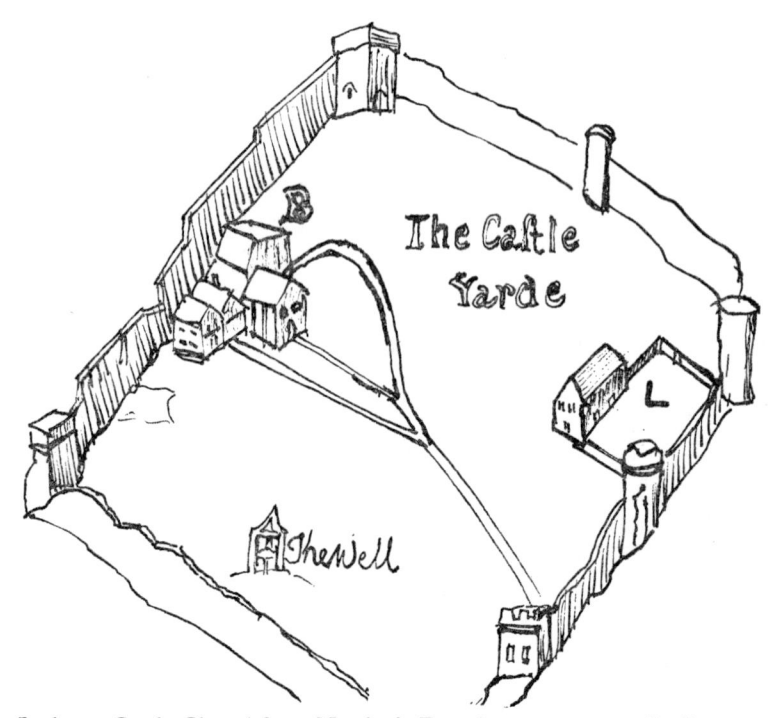

L shows Castle Chapel from Norden's Drawing. *D. Seymour.*

There seems also to be an upper storey at the west end, and this shows, perhaps, that there were living quarters there. The chimney should also be noted in this connection. It is difficult to assess a period for the intriguing bell turret. Norden's drawing shows that the site of the chapel was to the right as one entered the castle, and a little way up the hill. It stood in its own enclosure. The drawing dates from 1617, and its accuracy with regard to the disposition of windows etc. is (like many drawings of the period) much in question. However, these two illustrations are of value as showing the position of the building and its size and proportions.

The link between this old chapel and the farmhouse at Ashclyst is a fascinating one. The former was demolished in 1797, but the pleasant old farmhouse still stands.

27

Bampton

The Charters

135. A gift of a burgage from Fulk Panyel to Robert, the priest of Bamptone. Edward the cobbler used to hold it, and it is next to the church of St. Mary. The rent is 12d. per annum. Robert gave him two golden talents in recognition.
Date: c. 1200.   MS: Folio 49.

136. A gift from Robert, the son of Walter, and chaplain of Bamptone, to Matilda Prilla of all his land and houses between St. Mary's church and the parson's garden. Rent of 12d. to the lord (of Bampton) and to Robert a pair of white gloves at Easter all the days of his life. Clause of Warranty.
Date: early 13th century.   MS: Folio 49.

137. A gift of a burgage made to the Canons of Torre by John of Oxtone. It is next to the church of St. Mary at Bampton and Edward the cobbler used to hold it. The gift is for his own soul and those of Geoffrey the carter and Matilda Prilla, his wife. Rent 12d. per annum to the lord of Bampton for all services etc.
Date: mid 13th century.   MS: Folio 49.

It sometimes happens that the Cartulary, in two or three charters, give us a glimpse of a pleasant spot which came the Canons' way just because someone wanted to give it to them. Glascombe is one example and Bampton another. Very often these quick glances into life in the 13th century are full of interest, and for a moment penetrate the obscurity which for us surrounds those times. Here in these three charters we are allowed to see into the lives of Robert, the chaplain, Geoffrey, the carter and Matilda Prilla. The impression we gain is a pleasant one, and it is all about a burgage in this rather remote little town, set amid the Exmoor foothills. The very word burgage comes as a surprise, and we learn from it that Bampton must have been a borough at an early date. No doubt the burgesses were proud of their status.

In 135 Fulk Paniel, evidently lord of Bampton, leases this particular burgage to a priest named Robert for 12d. The property stood between St. Mary's church and the parson's garden. There are to the north of the spacious churchyard several old houses; and although they have Georgian frontages, yet at the back they betray features of much older style. It was here, then, that Robert lived, close to the vicar's house and the church, where he was probably an assistant. In the second charter he makes the property over to Matilda Prilla, possibly a relative who had just married Geoffrey the carter.

Several years must have elapsed before the final charter. In this we learn that Matilda is dead and Geoffrey, too; the new owner, John of Oxtone, gives the burgage to the

Canons for the salvation of his own soul and those of Geoffrey the carter and Matilda Prilla, his wife. John of Oxtone may be the same person as one of that name who was Praepositus of Exeter between 1200/74. This is a long span of years and a father and son may be referred to; so it is hard to date this charter.

A few interesting facts emerge from these three charters:—

(1) Bampton had burgesses as early as c. 1200 (Fulk Panyel's son, William is mentioned in "Devon Feet of Fines" in 1221, so c. 1200 is a reasonable date for his father's charter).

(2) A burgess was quit of all services and demands due to the lord of Bampton on payment of 12d. per annum.

(3) The old dedication of the church was clearly to St. Mary, and not to St. Michael as at present.

Bampton's fine church contains much ancient work, particularly its 13th century chancel which Robert the chaplain would have known. Its situation, set amid the green hills which encircle the town, make it a pleasant spot to visit at any time of year. The old houses adjoining the churchyard look just the sort of place wherein to end one's days in peace, attended by the friendly ghosts of Robert the chaplain, Matilda Prilla and Geoffrey the carter, who, no doubt, are buried somewhere here.

28

Skidbrook

Skidbrook church was the most distant of all the Canons' many possessions, for it is some 300 miles from Torre, and situated in the desolate marshes on the east coast of Lincolnshire. Richard and Beatrix de Parco gave this church to the abbey between 1196 and 1200 for the salvation of their souls and that of Roland Haket, Beatrix's father. It may in the first place have been their intention to give it to Newhouse Abbey in Lincolnshire, but it is quite possible that the Abbot there, thinking of the recently founded Abbey of Torre, persuaded the donors to divert their gift to this new Premonstratensian house in Devon. This suggestion is of course no more than a conjecture, but it does offer a reasonable explanation of a point on which the Cartulary is silent. It is a remarkable thing that the Canons held on to Skidbrook throughout the centuries, for communication between the two places must always have been difficult. We shall see later on that the tithe from Skidbrook was a valuable one, bringing in over £52 each year. Its wealth lay chiefly in its fishery at Saltfleet.

Bishop Hugh (1) of Lincoln (1180-1200) confirmed the de Parco's gift in 141. Both the de Parco and Haket families were well established in the district by this time. In the "Book of Fees" (p. 174), 1212, we find that the heirs of Roland Haket held 3 carucates of land in Schitebroc from Conan de Britannia for nine tenths of a knight's fee. The de Parcos took their name from Louth Park some eight miles to the southwest. In the "Register Antiquissimum" of the Cathedral Church of Lincoln (vol. V, 1940, pp. 167-193) Roland Haket is stated to have given 3 acres of land to the Cathedral c. 1200. Indeed, this same volume bears witness to the fact that the bulk of the land at Skidbrook must have been given to the Cathedral, for there are no less than 36 charters therein recording gifts of land at Skidbrook in the 13th century from various donors. The "Book of Fees" (p. 1053) shows Walter de Parco, Richard's son, as holding 1 knight's fee in the vill of Skitebroc from Peter de Sabandra, and on p. 1071 his heir is stated to hold ½ a fee in Skytebroc.

The appointment of the first vicar by the Canons of Torre did not take place until 1223/4, the reason being that in 1199 the living was held by four priests, Osbert, Walter, William and Richard, the son of Harvey. Bishop Hugh (1) stipulates in 141 that these four were to hold the living for the duration of their lives. By 1223 only two of the four priests were still living—William and Richard. By this time the Canons of Torre evidently thought that it was time they asserted their rights and made an appointment to the vicarage. William must have been an old man and he seems to have been willing to surrender his quarter share for ten marks. This was the subject of a Final Concord at Westminster (146). Trouble arose, however, in the case of Richard, the son of Harvey, who still held on to his quarter share when the Canons appointed Roger as vicar (144). Two others came forward to see if they also could get a share in the living: Ralph, the son of the priest, William, and a Philip Galle. Who he was we cannot tell—possibly another son. Their claim was dismissed, however, and in a Mandate to the Bishop of Lincoln, King Henry III reports that they have both quitclaimed any right or claim which they might have had in the quarter share of the living of Skidbrook. Later, in 1253, the matter was the subject of a Final Concord. So it took over fifty years for the Canons to get the living entirely in their own hands. Thereafter the controversy which arose through the living having been in the hands of four priests was at an end. So far as we know peace reigned over the marshes for the next 300 years.

The Charters

138. Richard de Parco gives the church of Skidebrok in perpetual alms to the church of St. Saviour of Torre. It is given for the soul of the donor and his wife, Beatrix, daughter of Roland Haket.
Date: 1196/1200.   MS: Folio 50.

139. Beatrix, daughter of Roland Haket, gives the church of Skidebrok to the Canons of Torre, for the souls of herself, her father and her husband, Richard.
Date: 1196/1200.   MS: Folio 50.

140. A confirmation of the church of Skitebrok from Walter, son of Richard de Parco. Given with the consent of his mother, Beatrix.
Date: post 1210.   MS: Folio 50.

141. A confirmation of the gift of the church of Skidebrok from Hugh, Bishop of Lincoln. The priests Osbert, Walter, William and (Richard, the son of) Harvey are to hold the living for their lives. (Words in brackets are in D.C. only.)
Date: 1196/1200.   MS: Folio 50.

142. Hugh (2), Bishop of Lincoln, confirms his predecessor's charter admitting the Canons of Torre to the church of Skitebrok.
Date: January 6th, 1215/16.   MS: Folio 50.

143. Dean Roger and the Chapter of Lincoln confirm Bishop Hugh's charter, which they have inspected.
Date: 1215/16.   MS: Folio 50.

144. A presentation of Roger to the vicarage of Skitebrok by the Abbot of Torre; a quarter of the vicarage belongs to Richard, however. It consists of all the altarage and half the fishery which belongs to the Abbot for ever. There are 2 acres of meadow, 2 of arable and $\frac{1}{2}$ for a toft.
Date: 1223/24.   MS: Folio 50.

145. A confirmation of the appointment of Roger to the vicarage of Skitebrok by Richard de Bradewell, the Bishop's Official.
Date: April 13th, 1279.   MS: Folio 51.

146. A Final Concord at Westminster between William the son of Robert and Robert, Abbot of Torre, wherein William quitclaimed his quarter share in the living of Skitebrok. The Abbot gave him 10 marks in recognition.
Date: The morrow of the Feast of the Ascension, 1223.   MS: Folio 51.

147. A Final Concord at Westminster between Ralph, son of William de Skitebrok and

Symon, Abbot of Torre (represented by Richard, one of his Canons), wherein Ralph quitclaimed all claim to a quarter share of the living of Skitebrok. Ralph was received into the company of those for whom special prayers would be made for ever.
Date: Feast of St. John the Baptist, 1253/54.   MS: Folio 51.

148.   King Henry III, in a mandate to Robert (Grosseteste), Bishop of Lincoln, states that at the Court of Westminster Ralph, son of William de Skitebrok, and Philip Galle quitclaimed to the Abbot of Torre any right to a quarter share in the living of Skitebrok.
Date: July 16th, 1248/49.   MS: Folio 51.

149. THESE ARE THE SANCTUARY LANDS BELONGING TO THE CHURCH OF SKITEBROK.

viz. at Wolfow 5½ acres of arable. At Coketrigges 2 acres. At ffolsigg 2 acres of arable. At Outgangrig ½ acre of arable. At Wolbyncroft ½ acre of arable. At Genwordegne ½ acre of arable. Attached to the house and toft 2½ acres of arable.

Total: 13½ acres.

In Brothercroft 2 acres of meadow. In the same to the west ½ acre of meadow. In Skitebrokwra 2½ acres of meadow. In Houdales ½ acre of meadow. At Cotestede in the meadowland of Somercotes 2 acres of meadow. In Somercotewra 4 acres of meadow. In Petpole in Somercote 1 acre of meadow.

Total: 12½ acres.

Item, William Be holds ½ acre for himself and his heirs for ever. Rent due at Christmas for all services, sixpence. Robert Godrik holds 1½ acres just as William has done.

Total: Rent 12 pence.

Note that neither the land nor the meadow which the vicar holds as his own portion is reckoned in the foregoing writing.

SKIDEBROK

Valuation made there through Nicholas of Dunstorr on the Monday after the Feast of St. John before the Latin Gate, A.D. 1312, by the verdict upon oath of John de la Churche, Thomas, the Vicar's son, Robert de la Havene, Roger de Bideford and Walter of the same town. They say that the value of the Court and houses is 10/- per annum. Item, they say that there are 13 acres of arable land and one perch and they are worth 12/- per annum. There are 13 acres of meadow and they are worth 3/- per annum.

Total: 62 shillings and threepence.

Fruit. They say that in an average year there is 100 quarters of fruit from the tithe and it is worth 4/- per quartern.

Beans and Peas. They say that in an average year it is possible to have 80 quarters of beans and peas at 3/- per quartern.

Barley. They say that it is possible to have from the tithe 20 quarters of barley in an average year and it is worth 3/- per quartern.

Fishery. They say that the Abbot's share in the tithe of the fishery is worth 20 marks in an average year.

Tithe of Meadowland. They say that the parish dues for each acre at 2d. an acre brings in a tithe of 30/-.

TOTAL: £49.16.8.
GRAND TOTAL: £52.18.11.

Date: Monday after the Feast of St. John before the Latin Gate, 1312.
MS: Folio 51 and 51a.

Before describing the church about which the charters have so much to say, the locality in which it is situated must be considered. The vanished village of Skidbrook stood on flat fenland interlaced with an endless number of dykes. Besides draining the marshes they provided the boundaries which hedges do elsewhere. The sea is only about a mile away to the east, but so flat is the landscape that it cannot be seen. There is a wide, muddy foreshore, and to the south is Saltfleetby Haven, dating, so I was told, from Roman days. Here the population accumulated until a small town came into being, but by the Middle Ages a drift inland began—possibly because the harbour was silting up, or perhaps successful drainage had made agriculture profitable. This was the beginning of Skidbrook; and by the times of the Domesday survey there were at "Schitebroc" 3 carucates of land, 24 sokemen, 3 villeins, $8\frac{1}{2}$ teams and 60 acres of meadow. It was therefore quite a thriving place by 1086. As there were four churches within a radius of a very few miles the population must have been considerable. This may also explain the four priests who shared the living early in the 13th century.

Then in the 16th century the plague hit Skidbrook and the population began to drift back to the sea. The village then began to decline, and both it and the manorhouse (which is known to have stood near the church) fell gradually into decay. Today a few bricks mark its site, otherwise nothing is to be seen of the former village but the church, the old Rectory (a Georgian House) and Grange Farm.

Elsewhere boundary hedges and banks, which may be of great antiquity, can vanish in an hour before the onslaught of a ruthless bulldozer, but here, with dykes instead of hedges, boundaries do not change. We thus inherit a perfect mediaeval field system which has come down quite unchanged over the centuries. A good many fields mentioned in the Cartulary as sanctuary land are recognisable on their acreage alone; even when their old names have been long forgotten. Mr. A. J. Michael of Grange Farm, and Mr. Sheals, a shepherd of the locality, were able to identify land mentioned in 149. For instance, immediately north of the ruined church of St. Peter is a half acre which has recently become part of a new burial ground. This is Outgrangrig. Petpole, Mr Sheals identified as a meadow of 1 acre in South Somercotes. Howdales is also remembered.

It is quite amazing also to find how the vicar's own portion which 144 states to be $2\frac{1}{2}$ acres of arable and 2 of meadow is just where it ought to be—in the enclosures beside the old Rectory. The map shows that they consist of 4 acres 1 rood and 2 perches. If the house and grounds are added in then $4\frac{1}{2}$ acres is the total; and this is just as it was in 1312.

The memorandum (149) on the tithe and sanctuary lands of Skidbrook is one of the most absorbing things in the Cartulary. It tells us all about the acreage of the sanctuary lands and what the tithe on fruit, beans, peas and barley yielded in an average year. Then there was the tithe on meadowland and the fishery which yielded 20 marks. No doubt this was based on the haven of Saltfleet. The arithmetic of the period is always suspect, and the Grand Total, given as £52.18.11, was witnessed upon oath by John de la Church, Thomas the vicar's son, Robert de la Havene, Roger de Bideforde and Walter of that place, on Monday after the Feast of St. John before the Latin Gate, 1312; and who are we to argue with their total!

From this delightful memorandum the cost of living in 14th century Lincolnshire may be assessed. It is interesting, too, to read of the vanished courthouse.

St. Botolph's Church, Skidbrook, Lincs. 1970. D. Seymour.

Skidbrook Church

The only mediaeval building to survive the centuries is St. Botolph's church. It is unlikely that it will be there much longer, for in 1970 it was closed for worship and is slowly going to ruin. Standing as it does far from the present day population it has become redundant, and the Rector, the Rev. D. Lambert, closed it accordingly. The wall of the north aisle is also falling outward, and when it does fall the whole structure will be seriously weakened. This is all the more distressing because from an architectural standpoint the church is a gem—particularly the exterior. The low, sturdy tower is a fine sight rising above its surrounding belt of trees, for master craftsmen have been at work upon it, from its beautiful recessed west window and doorway to the elegant belfry lights, with their shapely tracery. Four lively gargoyles look down from the corners of the tower, brooding over the fen as they have done for centuries.

Much red brick has been worked into the clerestory and indeed into other parts of the fabric. Little remains to see of the old Norman church except, perhaps, the walls of the small, low chancel and the wall above its arch. When the rest of the church was enlarged and widened in later times it is interesting to see how the Canons of Torre shirked their responsibilities as Rectors with regard to the chancel; so it was never rebuilt. This is a common occurrence up and down the country.

There is a simple piscina in the chancel, and on each side of the east window a projecting shelf with grotesque heads supporting. They were no doubt meant to hold lights and will go back to the monastic era. The interior of the church is not quite up to the excellence of the exterior, but of course we see it denuded of all fittings. Its main characteristic is its width which gives it an air of spaciousness. There is no hint that there were ever altars at the ends of the aisles, although of course there must have been. If there were ever chantries for the de Parco and Haket families they have long since been forgotten.

The three bells are not mediaeval, but the tenor bell has lettering upon it which is pre-15th century in style: it reads "Sancta Georgi" and is probably the work of Henry Dand of Nottingham and will date from 1570-1600. I am indebted to the Rev. J. Scott who drew my attention to a most interesting quotation from "Church Bells of Lincolnshire (North)" published in 1882. The parishioners, it relates, had sold two of their bells in 1552 because they had been "openly preached against" and affirmed to be "superstitious and abominable". With the money they repaired the church "then sore decayed" and scoured "one haven called Saltfleethaven then also being sor decayed and ruinous and in effect warpt upe so wt sande that the freshe wateres was not able to have full course to the See ne shippes or bootes have eny passage into and frome the said haven whiche is nowe right well amended". In the reign of Philip and Mary the unfortunate parishioners were told to replace the bells. They then prayed their Majesties' Commissioners to be let off "or else thay would be driven to forsake the parish, for they were poor and not able to bear the said charges". Proof was shown of the truth of their statement and so they were excused (Land Revenue Records, Church Goods, Lincs., Bundle 1392, File 81, PRO).

These events are just outside the period of monastic rule at Skidbrook, but how well they demonstrate the difficulties which could arise as soon as the steadying hand of the Church had been withdrawn and a parish cast upon its own resources. Only 13 years after the suppression of Torre Abbey the church was "sore decayed", and the haven upon which the flourishing fishery depended had become silted up and useless. In other words the whole economy of Skidbrook had been upset.

Those who have visited Skidbrook never forget it, for the solitary old church on the fen is a most atmospheric building mellowed by the influence of past ages.

Vicars of Skidbrook

The following clergy are recorded in Lincoln Cathedral Charters prior to the gift of this church to Torre Abbey:—

Hugh the priest of Skitebroc c. 1200 (charter 547).

Ralph, cleric of c. 1200 (541a).

Thomas, priest of c. 1200 (550).

William the parson (Rector of mediety of S.) c. 1200.

Walter the parson (Rector of mediety) (540).

Richard holding one fourth part of the church c. 1224.

Vicars appointed by Abbots of Torre

1224 Roger de Scitebroc.
1265 Robert de Suthfeld.
1299 Gilbert de Mandeville.
1311 Laurence de Wydbury.
1315 Thomas de Wydbury.
1329 Robert son of William de Skydbroke.

Woodbury: Greendale Barton, ancient foundations of courthouse. *Photo by M. Leach.*

Aylesbeare: Huntisbere. *Photo by M. Leach.*

Colaton Raleigh: Stowford House. *Photo kindly supplied by F. J. Carter.*

Clayhanger: Denscombe Mill. *Photo by M. Leach.*

Skidbrook (Lincs.): St. Botolph's Church. Photo by M. Leach.

Skidbrook (Lincs.): St. Botolph's Church. Photo by M. Leach.

Skidbrook (Lincs.): Church tower, detail of West side. *Photo by M. Leach.*

1337	William de Bollesdon deacon (alias William, son of Simon de Saltfleetby).
1348	Robert son of John atte Kirke.
1377	Thomas de Birmingheham.
1387	William Hardy.
1395	John Cook B.A.
1401	John Thorseby.
1413	William Croftes.
1451	John Croftes.
1478	Richard Whissley B.A.
1489	John Wra B.A.
1507	William Oldham.
1537	Thomas Thorneton.
1537-1539	Robert Slade (patrons Oliver Smythe cleric, Robert Howe and John Slaede "by grant of Abbot of Torre").
1539	William Garbney (Patron Hugh Pollard Knt, by grant of Abbot of Torre dissolved).

29

Bradworthy and Pancrasweek

In his excellent booklet, "The Parish and Church of Bradworthy", Cecil Collacott describes the village as "situated in a somewhat remote corner of north-west Devon, in a quiet hinterland, 8 miles north of the old market town of Holsworthy, and about 7 miles from the sea". From the earliest days of Torre Abbey's existence the Canons had considerable possessions both at Bradworthy and at Pancrasweek, and it is these which we will next consider.

In 1086 the Exeter Domesday account of "Brauordina" is as follows:—"Radulf has a manor called Brauordina which Alward (Toui) held on the day etc. . . . rendered geld for 3 hides and one virgate. These can be ploughed by 12 ploughs. Of them R. has in demesne 1 hide and 1 virgate and the villeins have 2 hides and 7 ploughs. There Radulf has 20 villeins and 10 bordars and 9 serfs and 40 head of cattle and 10 swine and 30 unbroken horses and 120 sheep and 5 goats and 40 acres of meadow and 3 leugas of pasture in length and one in breadth. It is worth by the year £8 and it was worth 100/- when he received it".

This, of course, does not take into account other manors in a parish which even in those days was very large, for it included Pancrasweek. Just about 114 years later the charters in the Cartulary begin, and it is from them that we get our next glimpse of Bradworthy. Under the heading "Braworthi" they are as follows:—

150. A gift in perpetual alms from William Brewer (lord of the fee) of the church of Bradeworthi with the chapel of Pankradeswike and all other appurtenances to the Church of St. Saviour of Torre.
Date: 1198/99.   MS: Folio 52.

151. A gift in free and perpetual alms from William Brewer to the Canons of Torre of a ferling of land in the manor of Braworthi. It lies next to the church sanctuary land on the north-west side of the road which leads to the church as far as the land of fford; and on the east side of the road as far as land belonging to Leye, and thence to the ford called Presteforde.
Date: 1198/99.   MS: Folio 52.

152. A confirmation of a gift in perpetual alms made to the Church of Torre by Henry de Pomerio of the church of Braworthi with the chapel of Prankradiswike. He also gives water (for the millpond) from springs in Estecumbe, molture such as William Brewer had in the manor and a ferling of land called Hidesburga.
Date: 1196/98.   MS: Folio 52/53.

153. H(enry), Bishop of Exeter, confirms the gift of Lord William Brewer of the church

of Braworthi to the Canons of Torre. They are to pay 4 marks annually to the church of St. Mary de Valle and provide for a priest to serve the church.
Date: November 6th, 1198. Given at fferendon. MS: Folio 53.

154. A confirmation from S(imon), Bishop of Exeter, of the findings of the General Chapter of the Premonstratensian Order with regard to Braworthi church discussed before him by the Abbots of Torre and St. Mary de Valle.
Date: c. 1219. MS: Folio 53.

155. Abbot Gervase of Prémontré determines that Braworthi church shall be in the hands of the Canons of Torre who must pay 4 marks in silver for it annually to the church of St. Mary de Valle on the octave of St. John the Baptist in Exeter Cathedral. If their messenger be delayed in England through nonpayment he shall have 12 pence daily. This decision was made by Abbots N. de Falese, W. de Luskes, Bartholomew de Valle, Christiana, Adam de Marchasio and Ralph. Community seal of the General Chapter appended.
Date: 1219. MS: Folio 53.

156. A renunciation of Braworthi church and its appurtenances made by W., Abbot of St. Mary de Valle; given at the General Chapter.
Date: 1219. MS: Folio 53/54.

157. William, Bishop of Exeter, states that the vicar of Braworthi shall pay 7 marks in silver, pence, or their equivalent for the two houses in the churchyard.
Date: 1224/44. MS: Folio 54.

158. A quitclaim from Henry Tirel of any right to three services a week at the chapel of Alfaresworthi which he considered ought to be provided by the mother church of Braworthi. Once a year, on the Feast Day of the chapel, shall a celebration be provided. Given before the full Chapter in Exeter Cathedral.
Date: 1315/50. MS: Folio 54.

159. An Obligation given by Sir Richard de Langeforde to pay tithe from the new mill at Bradworthy to the Abbot of Torre. The Canons are to have the second best beast on the death of a parishioner and the offerings on All Saints' day from himself and his men. Given on his sacramental oath under penalty of 60/-.
Date: Vigil of St. Thomas, 1240. MS: Folio 54/55.

160. A confirmation of two ferlings of land at Weika in the manor of Suretone given to the Canons of Torre by Baldewin de Wike, son of Robert de Blakeford. Royal service due to William Talebot. Abbot Roger gave him one mark in recognition.
Date: 13th century. MS: Folio 55.

161. A confirmation in perpetual alms of the gift in 160. Given by Edith, sister of Baldewin de Wike.
Date: 13th century. MS: Folio 55.

162. A confirmation in perpetual alms from William Talebot to the Canons of Torre of all the land which Baldewin Turnerard gave to them and which Henry de Parco also confirmed. It consists of 2 ferlings in the vill of wike, 4 at Blaccheforde and 1 at Sudelegh.
Date: 13th century. MS: Folio 55.

163. An undertaking from Henry de Parco to pay 3/- per annum to the Abbot of Torre for all services due from Blaccheforde, Wike and Horaldesdone. Clause of Distraint.
Date: 13th century. MS: Folio 55.

164. A quitclaim of a tenement and adjacent garden at Bradworthy from Richard le venur and Alice his wife made to the Church of the Holy Trinity at Torre. For all services 3d. is to be paid annually for a light for (the shrine of?) the Blessed Virgin Mary in St. Peter's church, Bradworthy. Clause of warranty. Witnesses: Adam de Esse, Thomas de Horton, Richard de Rihille, Jordan Penuer, John of the court of Bradeworthi and many others.
Date: c. 1310. MS: Folio 55.

165. Sir Gervase de Horton undertakes to pay 5 marks annually to the Abbot of Torre in St. Peter's church Bradeworthi for the mill of Braworthi. Clause of Distraint.
Date: c. 1250. MS: Folio 55/56.

166. A Final Concord given at Westminster between Laurence, Abbot of Torre, and Richard de Langeforde. Suit of mill was agreed as owing to the Abbot at his mill in the manor of Braworthi. The Abbot then gave the mill to Richard at a rent of 5/-. Clause of Distraint.
Date: The octave of the Feast of St. Martin, 1239/40. MS: Folio 56.

167. A Final Concord given at Exeter between the Abbot of Torre and Roger de Parco. The Abbot claimed that 9/- arrears of rent was owing for the free tenement of Blachcheforde(sic), Wike and Harolesdene. Roger agreed to recognise a rent of 3/- and paid 6/- arrears.
Date: Octave of the Holy Trinity, 1244/45. MS: Folio 56.

168. A gift in perpetual alms from Robert le Deneis, lord of Wike St. Pancras, to the Abbot and Convent of Torre Briwere: it is a house and garden at la Burg', and six acres of land in exchange for 5 acres in his demesne. For this the Abbot grants a daily mass for his soul in the chapel of Wike St. Pancras.
Date: Probably mid 14th century. MS: Folio 56/57.

169. An agreement between R., Abbot of Torre, and Robert de Bosco whereby he may build a chapel at his courthouse of de Bosco and have a chaplain to celebrate mass only. The rights of the parish church and the chapel of Wike Pancras to be reserved.
Date: Feast of St. Laurence the Martyr, 1284. MS: Folio 56b.

Charters 159-169 of the Exchequer Cartulary are devoted to Bradworthy and Pancrasweek under one heading. The first charter in chronological order is no doubt 152 where the church and chapel of "Prankradiswike" are given to the Canons of Torre by Henry de Pomerio. His gift included molture from the mill of Bradworthy and water to work it, also a piece of land called Hidesburga. Reference is made to the fact that Lord William Brewer formerly had the molture from this manor which he eventually purchased in 1198. We must also remember that his wife, Beatrix de Valle, was a cousin of Henry de Pomerio; and when this has been understood it will be seen that the selling of the manor to Lord William was a family affair, enabling him to endow his new foundation with a church, a mill and some land.

Charters 153-156 bring to light a matter which must have caused the Pomeroys some little embarrassment, for the family had founded an abbey in Normandy at Bayeux. It was known as St. Mary de Valle, and it seems quite clear from the charters that the Pomeroy family had endowed it with Bradworthy church. At first it seems that this Convent was pacified with the sum of 4 marks per annum, for in 153 Bishop Henry Marshall concedes the church to the Canons of Torre providing this sum is paid. This was in 1197/8. But Torre Abbey did not get away with things quite so easily, for later the whole matter was referred to the General Chapter of the Premonstratensians. An important charter (155) from Gervase, head abbot of the Order, and dating from 1219, tells how the matter had been referred to six other abbots of the Order. They persuaded the Abbot of St. Mary de Valle to waive all further claim to Bradworthy. In charter 154 Bishop Simon of Exeter states that he has discussed things with the abbots of Torre and St. Mary de Valle and has arranged that 4 marks is to be paid in Exeter Cathedral before two or three of the Canons on the Octave of St. John the Baptist. One can imagine the anxiety with which the messenger from Bayeux was speeded on his way, for the Canons of Torre had to pay him 12 pence for every day's delay in England.

Nothing remains today, so I am told, of the Abbey of St. Mary de Valle—even its site is not remembered. Beatrix de Valle, Lord William's wife, possibly had connections with this abbey before her marriage on account of her name. This chapter in the Abbey's history came to an end with a formal renunciation of Bradworthy church in 156 by Abbot W.

The next local family to be mentioned are the Tirels of Alfardisworthy, and 158 concerns their chapel which is still standing. Dating probably from mid 14th century this charter is a quitclaim from Henry Tirel whereby he waives all claim to three services a week at his chapel at "Alfaresworthie". These he thought the mother church of Bradworthy should provide. But in front of the Chapter at Exeter he had to say he would be content with one mass a year on the feast day of the chapel. It is unfortunate that we do not know its dedication. Henry was probably trying to avoid the expense of paying a chaplain of his own, but his schemes went awry.

Another influential family with which the charters deal is that of Sir Richard de Langeford. Charters 159 and 166 tell of his dealings with Torre Abbey concerning two mills in Bradworthy. The earlier charter (166) tells of a Final Concord given at Westminster. Sir Richard acknowledges in it that molture is due to the abbot for grinding at his mill at Bradworthy. Abbot Laurence then leases the mill to Sir Richard for five marks to be paid annually in the church. He also surrenders Lord William Brewer's charter recording the gift of the mill. In order to understand the meaning of 159 it must be understood that Bradworthy is a very large parish and that the Tamar is its western boundary. Just across the river stands Sir Richard's old home—a fine old longhouse which still bears his name. He and his men must have found the long journey to the Abbot's mill most tedious, so it seems he built a mill not far from Langeforde. This, I believe, still stands and is known today as Moreton Mill. It is on the banks of the Tamar, on the Bradworthy side of a bridge across the river. Even today the O.S. map marks the beginning of an old path between it and Langeforde. Moreton Mill is a tall three-storeyed building and it is most difficult to asses its age. Its filled-in leat may be traced for some way through the fields. I spoke in 1968 to an old man, Mr. F. Colwill, who had worked there in his youth; so the mill was still active in this century.

Now 159 shows that Sir Richard had not only built his mill but was pocketing the proceeds as well. He was taken to court for this, however, and at Exeter on the Vigil of St. Thomas, 1240, had to give a solemn undertaking upon his sacramental oath that the tithe from the new mill was to go to the Abbot of Torre, who also claimed the second-best beast when a parishioner died. On All Saints' day the offerings of the good knight and his men were also to go to the Abbot. The humble and penitent tone of this interesting charter shows how in the 13th century a local tyrant could be humbled effectively by a powerful Church.

The scene next shifts to Pancrasweek, at that time the home of the de Wikes. In 160 two ferlings of land are given to the Abbey by Baldewin de Wike. He describes himself as son of Robert de Blakeford. This is probably another form of Blacheford; Baldewin's sister, Edith, also confirms the gift in 161—evidently her brother had died meanwhile. William Talebot gives a further confirmation in 162. He was lord of the fee. He refers to Baldewin Turnerard and not de Wike. This shows how fixed surnames had not established themselves in the 13th century. Baldewin must have later given more land for there is mention of 4 ferlings at Blacheford and one at Sudelegh. William also gave the Canons relief and wardship and all profits due to the lord of the fee.

By the time of 163 (undated) this land was leased to the de Parco family. It would be interesting to discover if they were the same family who gave Skidbrook church in Lincolnshire to the Abbey. Henry de Parco in 163 undertakes to pay a 3/- rent for Blaccheford, Wike and Horaldesdone. In 1244 a Final Concord given at Exeter marked the end of a squabble between Abbot Laurence and Roger de Parco. He was accused of owing 9/- in rent for the same land which he had disputed. He had to promise to pay 3/- per annum and arrears of 6/-.

The Denises were the next family mentioned, and in 168 Robert le Deneis, lord of Wike, gives land to the Abbey. It was given in honour of God, St. Mary and the Chapel of Wike St. Pancras which belongs to St. Peter's church, Bradworthy. All this is discussed later.

Charter 164 takes us back to Bradworthy and records an interesting bequest. Richard le venur and his wife, Alice, give a tenement and adjacent garden in Bradworthy. From it 3 pence is to be paid annually for a light for (the shrine of) the Blessed Virgin in the church of St. Peter. This is one of the all too rare occasions when the scribe has copied in the names of the witnesses. From them we can assume that the charter dates from c. 1310. Among the witnesses is the name of Horton. This family lived in the bleak north-west corner of the parish and their old house is still to be seen, though partially destroyed by fire in 1969. It is thought that Horton was a sub-manor in Bradworthy. In 165 we find Bradworthy mill being leased to Sir Gervase de Horton for a rent of 5 marks to be paid in St. Peter's Church twice annually. The date will be 1249/1259—at least ten years after the lease to Sir Richard de Langeforde. So far as we know Sir Gervase was an exemplary tenant!

The final charter of the series (169) dates from Aug. 10th, 1284. It gives Robert de Bosco the right to build a chapel at his courthouse of de Bosco (now Wooda) on account of the distance from the parish church. He may maintain a chaplain to perform the office of the Mass, but no other. Neither the parish church nor the chapel of Wike St. Pancras are to suffer any loss of revenue. If they do then the chapel services will be discontinued. Such a proviso was quite common at the time when private oratories in houses of consequence were the fashion. In this way the parish churches protected themselves from loss of revenue.

Bradworthy Church

The charters make it clear that the old dedication of this church was to St. Peter; yet today the dedication is to St. John the Baptist. St. Peter's Well, near the south-east corner of the churchyard, still commemorates the older dedication, however. Of all the Canons' churches this is the only one still to be recognisable as a 13th century building. All the others were rebuilt in the grander perpendicular style. The simple, aisleless plan with Norman walls of great thickness still remains here. Such rugged, irregular walls certainly owe nothing to the trim correctness of the 14th century builders who tidied up the exterior. Standing in the nave it is easy to imagine the building as it was when the Canons of Torre first saw it. The ancient font which they used is still there, and on the south side of the chancel is a somewhat unusual piscina of E.E. style which William Norton and Thomas Dyare (later to become Abbots of Torre) must have used every time they celebrated Mass. On either side of the chancel are two priests' doorways which they constantly used.

This sturdy old building which has stood up to the buffeting of Atlantic gales through the centuries has twice had the misfortune to be all but destroyed. It was in ruins in 1395 after lightning had severely damaged it. Then in the 18th century it was extensively damaged by fire. This explains the absence of all mediaeval woodwork.

Perhaps the oddest feature in the church is a deep recess in the north wall of the nave, which in Victorian days was a family pew. It is surely too insignificant to have been the beginnings of a transept as some have suggested—for one thing it is not even on line with the south transept, which is much more ambitious. It seems to me that it may have been a chantry chapel, for in its exterior treatment it exactly resembles the small chantries on both sides of the Canons' church at Wolborough. In both churches the roof is continued to cover the small extensions outward. If this was indeed a chantry it would be interesting to speculate as to which local family was commemorated here.

Bradworthy Church, South-East Corner. *D. Seymour.*

Piscina in Bradworthy Church. D. Seymour.

The splendid tower which dominates the church and village is thought to have been built c. 1500. With its elegant octagonal pinnacles it is a landmark for miles around. It contains a ring of six bells, three of which were recorded in 1552. These were recast in 1757 by Abraham Rudhall of Gloucester. These three may have been ancient bells, so it is quite likely that much of the metal in the present peal dates from monastic times. The church with its fine belt of surrounding trees, spacious churchyard and lofty tower, beneath which the thatched inn has sheltered for so long, is a fine sight, adding much to the interest of the spacious village square.

Hidesburga

Henry de Pomerio in 152 gave the Canons a ferling of land in the manor of Bradworthy called Hidesburga. This name has vanished from local memory, but a clue as to its whereabouts is to be found in 151 where it is stated to lie next to the sanctuary land of the church. Now the gift of the church, mill etc. is mentioned in the Abbey's Foundation Charter as coming from Lord William Brewer, and Henry de Pomerio is not mentioned. This seems to me to confirm that the date of the giving of the Foundation Charter was after the sale of the manor which was in 1198 (Feet of Fines 8). So the gift of Hidesburga from Henry must date from 1196/98.

The ancient sanctuary land of a church was often adjoining it or else very close. In this case I do not doubt that it consisted of the present spacious churchyard, for in those days the cemetery would be quite small. But the sanctuary land would extend around it and be bounded on the south and east by the same lanes as the churchyard of today. By means of 151 it has been possible to trace this ferling of land and to be rewarded by the discovery that the whole extent is for the most part surrounded by superb banks so wide that, in the words of a local inhabitant, "You could drive a horse and cart along them".

178   TORRE ABBEY

In many places I certainly walked along the top of these banks which are in no way to be confused with hedges. The banks were surely meant to be important boundaries and may be of great age.

One section lies immediately south of the Square; it is described as being north and west of the road to the church and extending as far as the land of fford. Now the main approach road from Holsworthy just before entering the village makes a right-angled turn and so land to the left of it is aptly described as being to the north and west of it. Littleford is the name of a farm just south of the village, and so to come up to its boundaries makes sense. This western boundary today is a right of way through fields, and on its east side is the first of the banks. It extends from behind the houses in the Square to the road near the new Cemetery. Unfortunately a considerable portion of the bank abutting on the highway has recently been demolished. One wonders how much more of it will have disappeared by the time this book is published. This section of the ferling is a small outlying part, as a glance at the diagram shows.

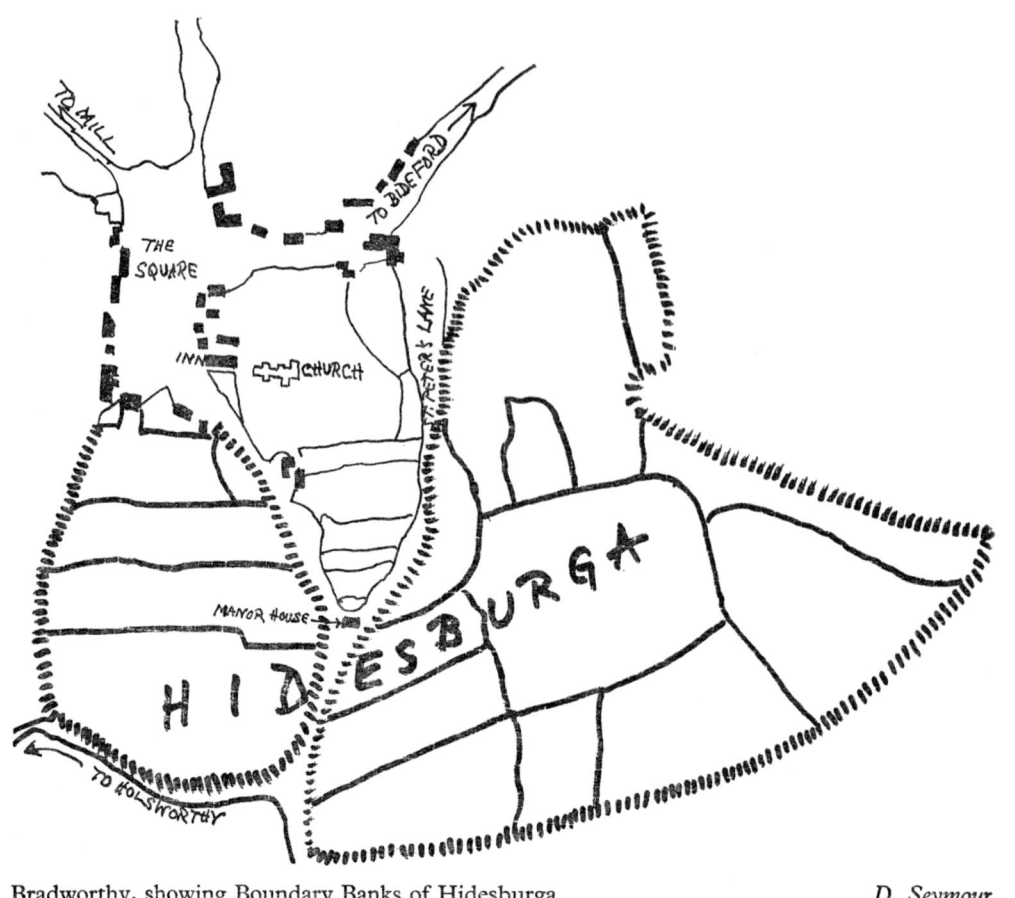

Bradworthy, showing Boundary Banks of Hidesburga.   *D. Seymour.*

The charter then goes on to say that the land lies on the east side of the road as far as Leye. This is a farm which has kept its name through the centuries and is known today as Leyland. Behind its buildings we pick up the boundary line which is a broad bank running downhill through four fields to a stream. Here Presteford must have been. Old maps show a crossing-place, and higher up, I am told, there were stepping-stones; but the position of these has long been forgotten, and I found the bottom illtended, swampy and overgrown. From here the bank turns northwest towards the village and later north to join a cul-de-sac which runs east. Following this for a short way it next turns south to join the east bank of St. Peter's Lane, which forms the rest of the boundary. This final stretch lacks the impressive embankments which we have seen hitherto, and what remain have been much disturbed.

It remains to mention a small triangle of land just south of the churchyard. At its southern tip is a 19th century house called "The Manor House". I cannot but wonder whether it may not occupy the site of the old manor house where the Courthouse of the Manor would stand and all business be transacted. Behind it and close to the churchyard are the scanty remains of a farmyard. Its principal building is a shippen whose west wall in particular looks to be mediaeval. The old south approach to the church ran past this farmyard but is now blocked by a bungalow.

This little triangle of land, consisting of just over an acre in extent, was probably church land, and it seems more than probable that these old buildings mark the position of the farmyard of the land we have been considering. The total acreage is 27.79—rather more than might have been expected, but if we subtract the 1.13 acres taken up by the triangle then we get 26.66 acres which compares well with the 26.8 acres of the ferlings at Coffinswell. I consider it likely that the triangle was already a part of the sanctuary land when Henry de Pomerio made his gift, on account of its position.

So the search for Hidesburga proved most rewarding, giving us fine boundary banks and a reasonable acreage. But the reaction of an old inhabitant of Bradworthy was even more remarkable, for he said, "You have been walking the boundary of the old church glebeland". He went on to tell how a former vicar even in this century had farmed it himself. Most of it has been disposed of now, but the church still retains some of it. So for nearly eight centuries these same acres have been church property. At the dissolution of Torre Abbey Henry VIII evidently agreed to their becoming the parson's glebeland. He held on to the advowson, however, and Bradworthy has been a Crown living ever since.

Monastic Connections in the parish

The Dublin Cartulary gives a list of farms in the parishes of Bradworthy, Pancrasweek, and Buckland Brewer; Watkin considered it to date from the late 13th century. It takes the form of a tithe return, and I am told on good authority that with one or two exceptions all these farms are going concerns today.

The list is as follows:—

Decima ecclesie de Braworthy

Bradeworthiford	XXII sol.
Wrangesworthi	XXII sol.
Instapel	IIII sol.
Instapel moltone	XI sol.
Nywelond	XIII sol.

Alfarsworthy	XXXXIII sol.
Kymeworthi	XXXI sol.
Walstaddonne Stoforde et Duoworthy	XLII sol.
Lovenscote Brithnesworth	XXII sol.
Westerblacburge	XXI sol.
Trentworthi	IX sol.
Rihille cum Blacburge	XXXs. VId.
Durehulle et Whitedonne	XIIIs.
Polkesdonne	XXXIIIs. VId.
Nywelond	XIIs.
Herdesworthi	XXIs.
Hortone cum duabus Gratedonne	XXXIIIs. IIIId.
Overdonnesworthy	XVIs.
Radfenford	XXXIIs.
Donne	XXXs.
Hele	XVIIIs.
Attaworthy	XIIs.
Sother donnesworthy	XLIIs. VId.
Spitel	IIIs.
Berdoune	VIs.
Esteresse	XVs.
Westeresse	XVIs.
Heth	IXs. Vd.
Overwiteley	IXs.
Turille et Selleworthy	XVIIs.
Estercumbe	IIIs.
Cleverdonne	XIIs.
Deaulonde	Xs.
Braworthy	XXXIIs.
Decima le Wyte	IIIIs. VIIId.
Water et leie	IIIIs.
Dounesworthy	XXXVIIs.

The reader will have realised by now that we are dealing with a remote corner of Devon, where farms and their boundaries will hardly have changed at all over the centuries. It is a wonderful thing to record that the mill of Bradworthy, or at any rate its ruins, can still be seen. This is the mill given to the Canons in the Foundation Charter by Lord William Brewer, and it stands at the bottom of the hill which leads from the village to the River Waldron. Here on the right-hand side stands an old house which was formerly the millhouse. The mill adjoined it at right-angles, and its scanty ruins are still to be seen. It was a working mill up to the time of the first World War; older residents can remember the millwheel surviving until recently. The mill was built up against the face of a small quarry on top of which was the millpond. This is still distinguishable, though very overgrown. Its leat, now dry, can be traced for some distance in a northerly direction. So this is the pond and leat for whose construction Henry de Pomerio gave permission in 152. The mill had a long innings of over 700 years, but happily the name of Bradworthy Mill is still proudly born by the old house.

In 157 there is mention of two houses in the churchyard. Of these there may be one survivor—the inn. The thatched part of this is a house of decided antiquity, and one end of it is within a few feet of the church tower. There are said to be the foundations of another house in the garden on the other side of the path to the church. The regularity of the churchyard has certainly been intruded upon by the inn and its garden. Two houses on this site could certainly be described as in the churchyard.

In the 13th century Richard le venur and his wife Alice gave a tenement and garden to the Church and Canons of Torre. The Tithe Map shows an isolated piece of sanctuary land in the north-west corner of the Square, bounded on one side by the road to the mill. Was this the tenement concerned, and did the church manage to hold on to it for all those years?.

Apart from the churches, only one other ecclesiastical building of monastic days can be said with certainty to be extant. This is the chapel at Alfaresworthy mentioned in 158. The farm stands some ¼ mile above the Tamar Lake and the farmyard is on a steep slope. The chapel is the highest of the buildings, and below it stands the L shaped farmhouse—formerly the mansion of the Tirels. A holy well is thrown in for good measure on the west side of the farmyard. The fact that this little outbuilding was once a chapel seems never to have been forgotten. It may be recognised by its large east window —now blocked except for the upper part which serves as a doorway to the intruding top floor. In the roof some of the original moulded beams survive and below is a stone bracket in the east wall near the altar site. It may have been meant to hold a light. The chapel is correctly orientated and the floor is cobbled. There is a fine mediaeval door in one of the outbuildings which does not fit its present position. It is tempting to suppose that this was the chapel door. The walls are of the local rubble, with cob under the eaves. This charming little chapel was one of my happiest finds in my survey of the former properties of Torre Abbey, and it was all the more rewarding to find it so well preserved. How one would like to see the intruding floor removed and the chapel restored to something like its former self.

In 169 the de Boscos of Wooda settle a dispute about the number of services to be held in their chapel. I have made an exhaustive search among the farm buildings there, and eventually found one which might have been a chapel. Its shape, style and orientation are right, but no recognisable features remain, and all that can safely be said about it is that it resembles the chapel at Alfaresworthy. So the chapel site here is forgotten, but there is the memory of a "monks' path" from Wooda to Bradworthy church, about which I was told.

Further References

Taxation of Pope Nicholas, 1288

"Bradeworthe with the chapel of Pancraswyke in the Deanery of Holsworthy 20 li., vicariate £4-0-0". On folio 169b of Dublin Cartulary "Brawirth 30 marks with vicariate".

The Devonshire Lay Subsidy of 1332

42 names recorded, the most important being:—Richard Tyrel 2/-, Robert de Parco 20d., John de Horton 2/-, Richard de Bosco 2/6, Henry Deneys 14d., William de Ferariis 40d., Robert de Horton 2/-.

A.O., Particulars for Grants 1485

"To Richard Chamond Esquire and Roger Prideaux, gentlemen, 2 May 1553, property at Waterland in the parish of Bradworthy, late of Torre Abbey. . . . . . .

m.5. Parish of Bradworthye: Farm of a piece of land or agistment called Waterlonde, leased it is said to Thomas Cole esquire and William and Richard his sons for their lives, 53/4 (RM) XXV".

Certified with declarations, 25 January 1553 by Henry Loke."

Vicars of Bradworthy

1271-80	Thomas Prigge
c. 1280	R. de Bosco
1328	John Battyn
25.9.1336	John de Wynscote
16.6.1349	William Rayshleghe
27.8.1373	William Nortone (later Abbot)
14.7.1382	Richard Sele
12.12.1382	John Dalkyn
25.2.1405	John Yerde
27.9.1413	Nicholas Botburgh
21.12.1442	Robert Dybbe
25.12.1446/7	John Benford
c. 1470	Thomas Dyare (later Abbot)
1486	Roger Lagg
27.9.1499	John Durke
9.9.1523	William Sherwell

Pancrasweek

The parish of Pancrasweek seems to have been separated from Bradworthy c. 1400. At about this time the rebuilding and enlarging of the church would take place. Hitherto it would have been just a small chapel entirely dependent upon the mother church. The two churches formed one living, however, until quite recent times.

There is no village here, and the hilltop church stands out in splendid isolation. Whether this has always been the case is hard to say. The manorhouse, for instance, must have stood close to the church, and in the field to the north are banks and much uneven ground which certainly points to the fact that buildings may have stood there. The large field to the north is called "Borough" on the Tithe Map, and this must be "La Burg" mentioned in 168. In this charter Robert le Deneis gives land to Torre Abbey which lies between the road on the west side of his house and "La Burg". He further gives land to the north of his house and his meadow of "La Burg" and the same road. There is, therefore, good evidence that the manor house did stand just north of the church. From there it would be but a step to the chantry chapel in the church which the Deneises founded.

At the beginning of the Abbey's connection with Pancrasweek it was the de Wike family who owned the manor, however, and it was Baldewin de Wike who made the first grant of land in 160. Also mentioned in 160 is land at Sudelegh, but it is disappointing to record that so far I cannot trace it. Horaldesdone, mentioned in 163, can be identified as near Puckaland where on the Tithe Map field 542 is named Horill's Moor.

At the dissolution the church did not manage to hold on to nearly so much land as at Bradworthy, for the Glebe land according to the Tithe Map only consisted of 7 acres. Of course the church may have parted with more land here in the period between. This Glebe land would no doubt have formed a part of the 2 ferlings at Wike just discussed. It lies about half a mile north of the church on both sides of the road. Glebe Cottage and its outbuildings were the farm buildings from which this small holding was worked. At first sight the cottage seems chopped in half, but there are other cottages in this locality which have this strange appearance, and I wonder whether it may be just a local peculiarity in building. Glebe Cottage, in its inelegant way, has great charm, and is a humorous little house with never a straight line anywhere. It consisted originally of one room downstairs and two up. There is a fine old hearth still in situ, and the massive chimney stack passes through the bedroom above quite undisguised. The present owner, Mr Craig, tells me that this little house was mentioned in church deeds four centuries ago.

St. Pancras' Church, Pancrasweek. *D. Seymour.*

It was also known as "Parsonage" until recently. Thus it has undeniable church connections over the centuries, and I do not doubt that it served as a priest's rest house as well as the farmhouse from which the church sanctuary land was farmed. I feel that the rest of the 2 ferlings of land given to the Canons may very well have centred on Glebe Cottage, and that research may yet reveal surrounding banks as at Bradworthy.

Pancrasweek, Glebe Cottage.   D. Seymour.

As Pancrasweek was served by the vicar of Bradworthy, it is most likely that there was a direct path between the two villages. I was told at Wooda that there was the memory of a monk's path between there and Bradworthy. A direct line would pass through Lana, Wooda, Aldercott and Virworthy. A glance at the map will show quite a few stretches of actual road on this line, whilst a footpath between Aldercott and Virworthy is marked on the 1 inch map. This book has been overlong in production, and if the writer had devoted yet more time to exploring such fascinating byways then it would never have seen print. However, it would be on some such route as this that William Norton and Thomas Dyare, both later to be Abbots of Torre, travelled from Bradworthy to the chapel at Pancrasweek. Coffins, too, must have been carried along this path, for there was no burial ground at Pancrasweek until 1403.

The Church of St. Pancras

We can be quite sure that there was a Norman chapel at Pancrasweek prior to 1200, for it was mentioned in the Abbey Foundation Charter. It was not a private manorial chapel, but a parochial chapel dependent upon Bradworthy. All that remains in the present fabric of those far-off times are fragments of a Norman window and doorway in the North wall. Today we see a graceful perpendicular church with a south aisle separated from the nave by a granite arcade of five bays. The original tracery remains in many of

Bradworthy: Parish Church.   Photo by M. Leach.

Bradworthy: Boundary bank of Hidesburga. *Photo by M. Leach.*

Bradworthy: Chapel at Alfaresworthy. *Photo by M. Leach.*

Bradworthy: Roof of Mediaeval Chapel at Alfaresworthy.

Bradworthy: Alfaresworthy, outline of east window of Chapel. *Photo by M. Leach.*

Bradworthy: Old door at Alfaresworthy. *Photo by M. Leach.*

Shebbear: South doorway at St. Michael's Church.   *Photo by M. Leach.*

the windows, and very fine it is. The screen has vanished, but much mediaeval work remains in the richly-carved wagon roofs. The building is lofty, spacious and light when compared with the rugged old mother church at Bradworthy. A link with Torre remains in a finely-carved monk's head which acts as a stop to the hood moulding of the east window on the south side. On the other side is a female head with distinctive head-dress but it is hard to say whom it is meant to portray.

Four bells were listed in 1552, and of these old bells one remains. Its inscription "Voce mea viva de pello cunta nociva" is one of the stock Exeter inscriptions. It probably dates from mid 15th century. It is possibly by William Yorke or Robert Russell. Two other bells were recast in the 17th century, and the last in 1741 when a fifth bell was added. It is possible that the two trebles of 1741 were cast out of the old tenor, if the four old ones were not part of a major scale. So, quite apart from the one 15th century bell still surviving, the metal from the bells of the Canons' day is retained in the present peal.

Who can doubt that the north transept was built to house the chantry chapel of the Deneis family? It would be here that the daily Mass was said. I have remarked elsewhere, that the Deneises got their chantry without endowing the Abbey with anything very spectacular; but I much wonder whether the spacious church of today was not rebuilt at their expense. This was a much smaller and poorer parish than Bradworthy, containing, according to the 13th century Tithe List, only 19 farms against its neighbour's 40. The Deneises seem to have been the only family of consequence, apart from the de Boscos of Wooda. I think everything points to the fact that they were the great benefactors of the church, and so for this reason the Canons undertook to provide a chantry priest to say a daily Mass. Is it too much to assume that he lived at Glebe Cottage?

13th Century Tithe Return from the Farms

Capella de Wike Pancracii

Decima Roberti le Deneis	IIII marci
Decima Roberti de Bosco	XLIII s.
Luffelonde	VI s.
Hermerdesworthy et Slade	XLVI s.
Donestonne Pichard	XIX s.
Lane	X s.
Forda	VII s.
Heddoune	V s.
Kynford Fen et Fennelounde	XXX s.
Swinhille cum Rihille	XIIIIs. XI d.
Brendonne	XXIIII s.
Pukland	XV s.
Bromhulle	XXXI s.
Dearbeare	XLV s. IX d.
Huddesdonne	XXIIII s. vel
Aluinicote	XXV s.
Picteworthy	XII s.
Decima Gayn	XIII s.
Yaldonne	XIIII s.

From Bishop Stafford's Register (folio 49, Vol. I)

"The Bishop having been informed by the parishioners of the chapelry (which was attached to Bradworthy belonging to Torre Abbey) that it was a separate parish as to population and boundaries, possessing its own baptistry and all things pertaining to a parish except the right of sepelture; that roads and streams between them and the mother church were dangerous for funerals, and therefore they praye the Bishop to dedicate the said Chapel and the adjacent ground for a cemetery; he issued a commission directed to the Religious of Torre Abbey and to John Dalkyn, vicar of Bradworthy, to make enquiry into the facts. The result being favourable to their petition the Bishop summoned the Abbot of Torre and the vicar on the one part and the parishioners by their proxies Robert atte Wode and Richard heyne on the other part to appear before him at Chudleigh 8th Nov. 1403, for the determination of the business. The prayer of the parishioners was granted, saving the rights of the mother church; to which they were all bound to repair once a year (on the Sunday next before the Feast of St. Pancras) and offer one obulus; but they were to make their oblations at their own Chapel on All Saints' Day and at Christmas and at Easter; the chaplain to be withdrawn to the mother church in case of default or attempt to evade these conditions (8 Nov., 1403) i, 68".

Further References

None.

Bradworthy and Pancrasweek have been fascinating to explore and results have been rewarding. In such a remote corner of Devon little has occurred over the centuries to bring about a radical change in boundaries. The mediaeval farms are as active as ever, and so are the two churches. Most of the places mentioned in the charters have been pin-pointed, but a few have evaded us.

A glance at a map of the region will show that the remaining property of the Canons in North Devon was not a great way off. There is little doubt that Bradworthy was the focal point, and so Buckland Brewer, Shebbear and Sheepwash would all be administered from there.

30

Shebbear and Sheepwash

Shebbear and Sheepwash are two remote parishes in the triangle of land formed by the towns of Great Torrington, Holsworthy and Hatherleigh. Like Bradworthy, the village of Shebbear surrounds a large square, at the west end of which stands the church. At its gate, beneath an ancient oak, lies the famous stone which is solemnly turned over each year on the 5th of November.

By their very names it may be seen that sheep have been raised in the two villages since remote times on an ambitious scale. Shebbear was a royal manor in the time of Domesday and 500 sheep are mentioned there.

From an ecclesiastical standpoint Shebbear has always been the mother church, with the chapel of St. Laurence at Sheepwash dependent upon it.

The Charters

170. A gift in perpetual alms of the church of Scheffbere made to the Canons of Torre from John, King of England, Lord of Ireland, Duke of Normandy and Count of Andegavie.
Date: Malberg, August 27th, 1207. MS: Folio 57. Witnesses:—W., Earl of Salisbury and W., Earl of Arundell.

171. A confirmation of the church of Schefbere made to the Convent of Torre by Simon, Bishop of Exeter. Vicarage to be held by P., the chaplain, for his lifetime, who must pay 20/- annually to the Abbot.
Date: 1214/16. MS: Folio 57.

172. A confirmation from William Brewer, Bishop of Exeter, stating that the vicar of Schefbere is to pay to the Abbot of Torre $2\frac{1}{2}$ marks annually from the altarage and the church land to the south of the church.
Date: 1224/44. MS: Folio 57.

173. A confirmation from R., Archdeacon of Barnstaple, of the institution of the Abbot and Convent of Torre to the church of Schefbere made by his predecessor, Archdeacon J.
Date: 1207/14. MS: Folio 58.

174. A confirmation from J., Archdeacon of Barnstaple, instituting Abbot W. to the church of Schefbere on the presentation of King John, the See of Exeter being vacant.
Date: 1207. MS: Folio 58.

Shepwayssh

175. A confirmation of a gift of half a ferling of land at Chinrigge and half a ferling at Hocrigge from Ralph de Monte Sorel to Robert Markeros. Rent: a pair of white gloves at

Easter. Robert in recognition gives him a white horse worth 5 marks.
Date: 1225/50 (Donor mentioned in 1249 in "Devon Feet of Fines" 510).
MS: Folio 58.

176. A restatement of 175 but boundaries of second half ferling specified.
Date: c. 1225/50.   MS: Folio 58.

177. A confirmation from Leticia de Pirro, in her widowhood, to Robert de Markeros of half a ferling in Hochrigge and all her demesne land at Brendon. Boundaries from junction of Laket with Michelbrok at Knight's bridge: thence by her boundary to Thorngrave: thence by ditch next to Lady Mary's land to Michelbrok. Rent—a pound of cumin at Michaelmas. Six pigs may graze freely in her wood of Shepwaissch. Clause of Warranty.
Date: mid 13th century.   MS: Folio 58.

178. A gift in perpetual alms from Robert de Markeros of half a ferling at Hocrigge to the Canons of Torre, the church of Schefbere and the chapel of St. Laurence at Schepwaysch to maintain a chaplain there; also another half ferling east of Chimbrigge given to him by Ralph de Monte Sorel and half a ferling at Brendon given to him by Leticia de Pirro.
Date: mid 13th century.   MS: Folio 59.

179. A gift in perpetual alms of the mill of Uppecote given to the Canons of Torre by Sibilla de Alta Villa, together with suit of mill from her men of Uppecote. Leats and a millpond may be constructed. An acre of land beside the mill, providing sufficient timber for repairs, is also given. Clause of Warranty.
Date: No evidence—probably 13th century.   MS: Folio 59.

180. A gift from Matthew, son of Robert, parson of the chapel of St. James, Toritone, to William the carpenter of all his land at Toritone—to wit two houses and a garden which belong to the chapel. Rent 3/-.
Date: ante 1346.   MS: Folio 59.

Charter 174 is of great interest because it establishes the existence of Abbot "W". His position among the Abbots is fully discussed in the chapter "A Consideration of the Abbots". We have another version of 170, King John's gift of the church, for it was copied later onto a document drawn up at Paignton in 1300 which established the title of the Canons to their churches. Here both the date and names of witnesses are included. The date is earlier than might have been expected, for the charter was signed by the King "apud Malberg, August 27, 1207". Witnesses were William de Bryer, Gerard fil' Gerard, Gam. de Nemys, Radulfo de Gerounis, Johanne Capellano, persona de Nobhoure, Bar (?) pro Magistro Hugo de Well, Arthuro Well.

So since Lord William Brewer's name comes first it is clear that this was yet another church which he procured for the Canons of Torre through his influence over the King. The next charter sequentially is 174 wherein J., Archdeacon of Totnes, institutes the Abbot and Convent of Torre to the living because the See of Exeter is vacant. This was during the years of the Interdict (1206/14) and presumably the Pope would not institute a new Bishop. But King John, in spite of the Pope and his anathemas, went blithely on his way and appointed the Abbot of Torre to the church in his royal manor of

Shebbear. It is not until 171 that Simon of Apulia, the newly appointed Bishop, confirms the church of Shebbear to the Abbot. Apart from the sanctuary land south of the church Torre owned no other land at Shebbear.

At Sheepwash the Canons were given $1\frac{1}{2}$ ferlings of land, however, by Robert de Markeros to help maintain a chaplain at Shebbear and Sheepwash. 176/7 concern previous owners of this land. 179 is a particularly interesting charter in its comprehensiveness. Here Sibilla de Alta Villa gives the Canons her mill at Uppecote. They are also given suit of mill from "my men of Uppecote" and from all others accustomed to use the mill. Rights of entry and exit over her land are given, together with permission to construct a millpond and leats. Then she gave them an acre of land hardby from which timber might be taken under the direction of her foresters for repairs to the mill. Altogether she thought of everything, and we do hope she married again, for such a lady would have run a house to perfection—nothing would her lord and master lack from clean rushes on the floor to a pound of cumin in the kitchen.

Alas, her fine house of Upcott Barton is going fast to ruin and was abandoned in 1968; the great hall with its fine moulded beams is a pitiful sight. Amongst the outbuildings I was shown what was said to be a chapel. It has a pointed arch to its entrance and there are windows with their old wood mullions still intact. This building is of two storeys and it reminded me of Neadon at Manaton where the upper floor was for human occupation whilst the animals lived below. This might therefore have been the forerunner of the present more pretentious house where Sibilla probably dwelt.

At a spot some 300 yards beyond the house a monks' cemetery is said to be. One sees a rectangular depression in a large meadow bordered on two sides by sweet-smelling limes. This ground is never ploughed or disturbed in any way, and I wonder what strange memory of some forgotten event lingers there.

The final charter in the Sheepwash series has no connection with that parish, but concerns the Chapel of St. James at Torrington. It was no doubt inserted in the Cartulary just here because Sheepwash was the nearest territory connected with Torre Abbey. St. James's was the castle chapel and it was not finally demolished until 1780. In this charter Matthew, son of the chapel parson, leases two houses and a garden to William the carpenter. They were chapel property. In a "History of Torrington" (author unknown) a list of chantry chaplains of this chapel is given. It is fairly complete from 1346 onwards. Unfortunately Robert's name does not appear, so he must have held office before this date. For some good reason the Canons saw that this charter was copied into the Cartulary. Perhaps they acquired the property at a later date, or in some way became involved in the doings of the chapel.

Sheepwash has so far proved reluctant to yield up its secrets of the past. Apart from Muchelbrook (now Musselbrook) and Laket (now Lake) no other names have been identified. Upcott Barton, of course, is there, and the site of its mill is remembered. It was demolished c. 1960 and already its site is hard to discern. The overgrown watercourses are traceable, however. Hochrigge, Chinbrigge, Thorngrave and the Knight's bridge have died out in local memory, neither are they to be found on the Tithe Map. There are at least three farms in the district called Brendon, but which belonged to Leticia de Pirro?

The Tithe Map of Shebbear shows that in the early 19th century the church owned an amazing amount of land in the parish, and also quite half the property in the village. Apart from the sanctuary land to south of the church our charters do not show the

Canons as owning other land at Shebbear. Then again "Devon Monastic Lands" shows no extra land belonging to Torre; so the inference is that all this church land and property was acquired in post-monastic days.

In conclusion, one may say that the most rewarding thing in my researches here has been the church at Shebbear, for here there is much to see which the Canons would recognise today.

Shebbear Church

The parish church of St. Michael stands at the western end of the ridge on which the village is built. Its large churchyard slopes away steeply to the south, and it is no doubt here that the Canons' sanctuary land was, for a much smaller cemetery would be all that existed then. The Norman origin of the church is attested by the elegant south doorway of this period which is so similar to the one at Buckland Brewer that the same mason may have worked on them. Here, however, the actual archway to the door is pointed whilst the outer arch is rounded in the usual way. In the porch is also a rather unusual stoup which the Canons must have used constantly.

The interior can have changed little since their period, consisting of nave, chancel and south aisle, with a chapel opening into the chancel. The most curious feature of all is the

St. Michael's, Shebbear. *D. Seymour.*

nave arcade which has square piers with chamfered angles and double chamfered arches. When the church was enlarged in the 14th century could it be that the old Norman south wall was cut through in four places to make an arcade? In this ingenious way, perhaps, the Canons saved a good deal of cash. Risdon credits Lady Prendergist of Ladford as the donor of the south aisle, and she is buried there beneath a stately recumbent effigy.

The column supporting the chancel arch on the south side has a small piscina let into it. This probably marks the eastern limit of the former Norman chancel.

The old wagon roofs remain over the nave, chancel and south chapel. This chapel appears to be the latest addition to the church and has two graceful arches with granite capitals opening into the chancel.

The tower is comparatively low, but looks imposing at a distance, for the land falls away from it to the south and west. It contains six bells. There were three in 1552. All were recast—the present six being a five of 1792 plus a later treble. Some of the mediaeval metal therefore remains in the present peal.

The list of vicars is unusually complete. "P"., the chaplain mentioned in 171, may be John de Plasseto; but it was more usual to use the initial of the Christian name. So there may be yet another name to add to the list.

List of Vicars

1204	Alan de Herteglie or Hertleigh
1207	John de Plasseto
1241	B. de Totton
	Walter
1251	Richard de Totton (on death of Walter)
1262	Sywardus, presbyter
1284	Luke de Torritone chaplain
1285	Peter Dierlyng, priest
1309	Martin de Saltcumbe
1311	Jordan de Walcedonne
1314	Sir Robert de Pyworthi, priest
1344	William Alyam
1349	Sir Richard de Welcombe, priest (**recommended**)
1356	William atte Wayte
	John Wayte
1401	John Harry, chaplain
1420/21	Sir John Preston, deacon
1425	Sir John Bultr, chaplain
	Thomas King
1460	Sir Richard Cole, chaplain
1462	Sir John Cranmore
1465	William Smyth
1466	Sir John Dollyng
	William Wyntyr
1480	Sir William Morished, chaplain
	Sir John Bette
1518	Sir Richard Tomlyn, priest

Chapel of St. Laurence, Sheepwash

Nothing remains of the old chapel at Sheepwash except one precious relic—the Norman font. Pevsner describes it as "square, of block capital shape, one of the semi-circular surfaces with foliage, the others plain". The present church was built in 1881, and I have been unable to discover if the old chapel survived until that date. It is said to have been destroyed by fire. As Sheepwash is under a separate heading in the Cartulary it may, like Pancrasweek, have had its own ecclesiastical boundaries, although the church had no parochial status.

Further References

Taxation of Pope Nicholas, 1288
  "Shefber 20 marks with vicariate" (D.C. Folio 169b).

Devon Lay Subsidy, 1332
  26 names mentioned, none of which appear in the Cartulary. 13 names at Sheepwash, including John de Horton.

Tithe of the Church of Scheftbere (D.C. 138a).

Sprei	XIIIs. IIIId.
Durpeleigh	XVIIIs. IIIId.
Bisdoune	VIs. VIIId.
Nortedoune	IIIs.
Baddekweye	XXXIIs.
Lippebeare	XXXVIIIs.
Heie	XLs.
Bery cum Wottonne	XLVIIIs.
Baddeworthy	XXXs.
Lovecote	IXs.
Faddecote	XLs.
More	XXIIIIs.
Bimeworthi	XXIIIIs.
Pilliacnolle	XXXVIIs. VId.
Paddune et furse Bowadoune	Xs.
Luddeforde	XXIs.
Furse	XIIs. VId.
Alinacote (?)	XIIIIs.
Schepwasse	Xmarc. et dim.

31

Buckland Brewer

Buckland Brewer has for its setting the high hills of north Devon. It stands in deep country and is not easy of access; but those who brave the narrow, twisting lanes will be rewarded eventually by the sight of a pleasant hill-top village, dominated by a majestic church which stands on the highest ground. It is surrounded by a spacious churchyard and a small village green, and was given to the Canons of Torre by Lord William Brewer whose name the village still bears.

There is more than one manor under the heading "Bochelande" in the Exeter Domesday, so it is not possible to distinguish with certainty between them. The entry given below is thought to be Buckland Brewer:—"The Earl (of Mortain) has a manor called Bochelanda which Edmar the Black held etc. . . . it renders geld for 3 hides less ½ a virgate. These can be ploughed by 20 ploughs. And now Ansger Brito holds of the Earl. Of them Ansgar has ½ a hide and 3 ploughs in demesne, and the villeins have 2 hides and 1½ virgates and 8½ ploughs. There Ansger has 42 villeins and 5 bordars and 3 swineherds and 7 serfs, 19 head of cattle, 150 sheep, 50 goats, 100 acres of wood, 40 of meadow and of pasture, 1 leuga in length and ½ in breadth. This was worth £7.10s, and it was worth as much when the earl received it". The 42 villeins mentioned correspond well with the 42 farms of the 13th century Tithe return, and the 100 acres of wood suggest the wood of Greatcleave, soon to be mentioned.

It must have been nearly 140 years later that Lord William Brewer gave the advowson of this church to Torre Abbey, and it may have been one of his later gifts to the Canons. There is no mention of Buckland in the Foundation Charter, nor yet in the first Papalia document which dates from 1214-1223. Charters 183 and 184, which are confirmations of the gift of the church from William Brewer, Bishop of Exeter, must date from c. 1224, for the Bishop began his rule in 1224; Lord William made over all his worldly goods to his son in 1224 when he entered Dunkeswell Abbey. The gift of the church should therefore date from c. 1223/24.

The Charters

181. A gift in free and perpetual alms of the church of Bokelonde made by Lord William Brewer to the Church of St. Saviour of Torre.
Date: c. 1223/24.   MS: Folio 60.

182. A confirmation of the above by William Brewer, son of Lord William.
Date: 1224.   MS: Folio 60.

183. A confirmation from William Brewer, Bishop of Exeter, admitting the Canons of Torre as patrons of the church of Bokelonde, so that they can maintain the sick and

poor who come to the Abbey. A suitable vicar to be provided; he will be assessed at 7 marks.
Date: c. 1224.   MS: Folio 60.

184.   A confirmation as above. The vicar to pay 7 marks from 12 acres of sanctuary land and from the corn tithes.
Date: c. 1225.   MS: Folio 60/61.

185.   A Renunciation from the Prioress of Kynkitone to the Abbot of Torre of the church of Bokeland Bret. Surrender of documents from J., Bishop of Exeter, J., Count of Mortell and W. Tirel—formerly patrons. These and papal letters to become invalid.
Date: c. 1228.   MS: Folio 61.

186.   Incomplete charter from Prioress of Kynktone. Preamble only.
MS: Folio 61.

187.   A Final Concord at Wilton between Maria, Prioress of Kyntone, and Robert, Abbot of Torre. She quitclaims advowson of Bokelande church in return for the Abbot's land at Nywenham, Berkshire.
Date: Monday after the Feast of St. Peter ad Vincula, 1228.   MS: Folio 61.

188.   Robert Mile leases half a ferling at Mileford to Henry the priest at 2/- rent. Formerly held by Henry le Horton.
Date: No evidence—possibly late 12th century.   MS: Folio 61.

189.   Brother John, called "le Rous," Abbot of Torre, quitclaims all rights of grazing, husbote and heybote etc. in manor of Northbokelond to Brother William de Comba, Abbot of Donkeswille, lord of the manor. Four acres of growing timber in wood of Gratecleve to be excepted.
Date: Tuesday, Feast of St. Nicholas, 1307/8.   MS: Folio 62.

190.   An agreement between William de Combe, Abbot of Donkewille, and lord of North Bokelonde, and John, Abbot of Torre. The former concedes all growing timber in 4 acres of his wood of Grateclyve for Husbote and Heibote etc., but pasture to belong to him. Grazing rights (except in corn and meadow) for animals which in winter can subsist in church demesne land above Cledone—Reigheye excepted. A rent of 2d.
Date: St. Nicholas' Day 1307/8.   MS: Folio 62.

The first four charters are straightforward and need no comment, but in 185-187 the Prioress Maria of Kynkitone makes an appearance. Her Priory, founded in 1155, was in Wiltshire; its name is also spelt Keinton or Kington. She refers to her claim of the advowson of the church of Bokeland Bret. The suffix "Bret" may refer to the name of previous owners of the manor. It seems that her Priory had been endowed with this church, but she relinquishes it for land at Nywenham in Berkshire. One virgate here had been given to Torre Abbey by Walter, the son of Ives (see 5). As it was some distance from Torre the Canons were no doubt glad to make the exchange, and one hopes the Wiltshire lady was just as delighted.

Charter 188 is of interest, if only because Torre Abbey is not mentioned. Neither is there any further mention of this ½ ferling. Was it a part of the sanctuary land which came to the Canons? And where was Mileford? All these are small points in the Cartulary which so far cannot be cleared up. At any rate in the full text we learn that if the priest Henry fell foul of Robert's court, he was only to be quit on payment of half a sester at least! So Robert was lord of a manor somewhere near, and the former owner was Henry le Horton—probably of the same family as the Hortons of Bradworthy. And that is as far as we can get.

It will be gathered from the charters that the Abbot of Dunkeswell was lord of the manor of Buckland Brewer, whilst the Abbot of Torre held the advowson of the church, sanctuary land, and a few other privileges granted by Dunkeswell.

Buckland Brewer Church

This church is dedicated to S. Mary and St. Benedict. As it seems formerly to have been in the hands of Kynktone Priory one may well wonder whether that was a Benedictine house. If so it may have influenced the rather unusual dedication of Buckland church.

The building is dominated by a stately perpendicular tower, rebuilt in 1399 after being struck by lightning. The oldest thing of all is the lovely Norman doorway in the south porch. The interior of the building has fallen a prey to the 19th century restorer, but the exterior must be very much as the Canons left it. One thing of beauty still remains within the church and this is a delicately-carved doorway which leads from the east end of the south aisle into a passage connecting the church with a small independent building.

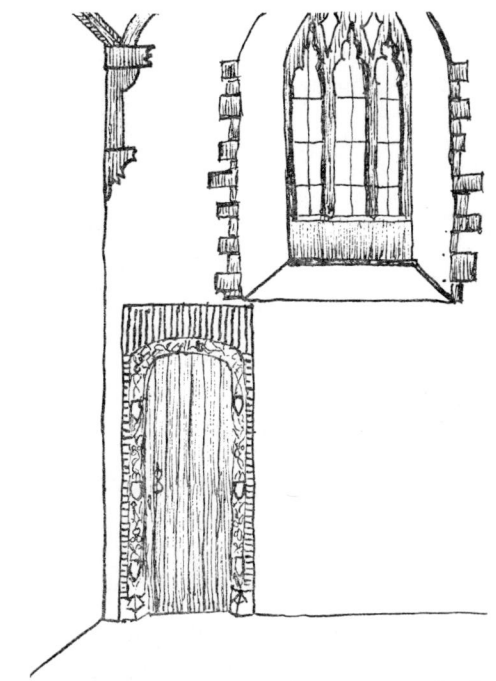

Buckland Brewer, South Aisle Doorway.   *D. Seymour.*

Standing due east of the church, its former purpose is by no means clear. I was told that this was where the monks lived. This is hard to believe, for the building resembles a chapel and certainly not a dwelling house. We know that in the Middle Ages there existed here a Fraternity of St. Michael, which seems to have been a kind of chantry for its members. It is quite likely that this was its chapel. I have wondered, too, whether the carving round the door just mentioned may not be in some way symbolical. Are the shields and twining branches in any way connected with the Fraternity? At first sight the little building appears to be 19th century, but a closer inspection reveals that the window tracery is ancient. It is no doubt a rebuilding of something far older.

St. Michael's Chapel, Bulkworthy. *D. Seymour.*

On the subject of the Fraternity Oliver (p. 480) says, "It appears by the Chantry Roll in the Augmentation Office that there was a Fraternity in this church dedicated to St. Michael, and the lands were valued in 1547 at £8.7.4 per annum". Risdon (c. 1630) says, "The freternyte of St. Michael formed by Thos. Radforde and dyvers others to find a pryst to pray for their sowles".

The Canons had two chapels attached to Buckland church—those at Bulkworthy and East Putford. The former is an intriguing little building. It has a short nave and a south aisle of two bays only. There is a small bell turret at the west end containing two bells, both of which are thought to date from monastic days. Unfortunately they have lost their clappers and so cannot be rung today. A curious feature is a priest's room over the south porch reached by an exterior stair. Standing as it does on a high bank above the road, this chapel of St. Michael is of great charm. A rather unusual font looks as though it is Norman in origin but adapted to the style of a much later period.

Nothing remains of the ancient chapel at East Putford but its mediaeval font, bits of the old rood screen and some tiles in the porch. What we see today is a rebuilding of 1882. It is a well built and attractive small church consisting of nave only. It is sad to record that at present it is unloved and unused, and being allowed to go slowly to decay—or so it seems.

No one seems ever to have undertaken a history of Buckland Brewer, but in spite of this, on my first visit there, I was fortunate in being introduced to Mr. Mantle, then Postmaster. He at once produced a series of newspaper cuttings about a century old which dealt with the history of the village and are signed "Marland". I have not been able to identify the newspaper in which these articles appeared, but it is clear from them that "Marland" was a clergyman. His account of the village is most absorbing. He gives accounts of the witnesses of the Foundation Charter of Torre Abbey and most interesting pedigrees. All this has been of much use to me as it appears to be reasonably accurate.

Through him I am able to identify with a good deal of certainty the old priest's house

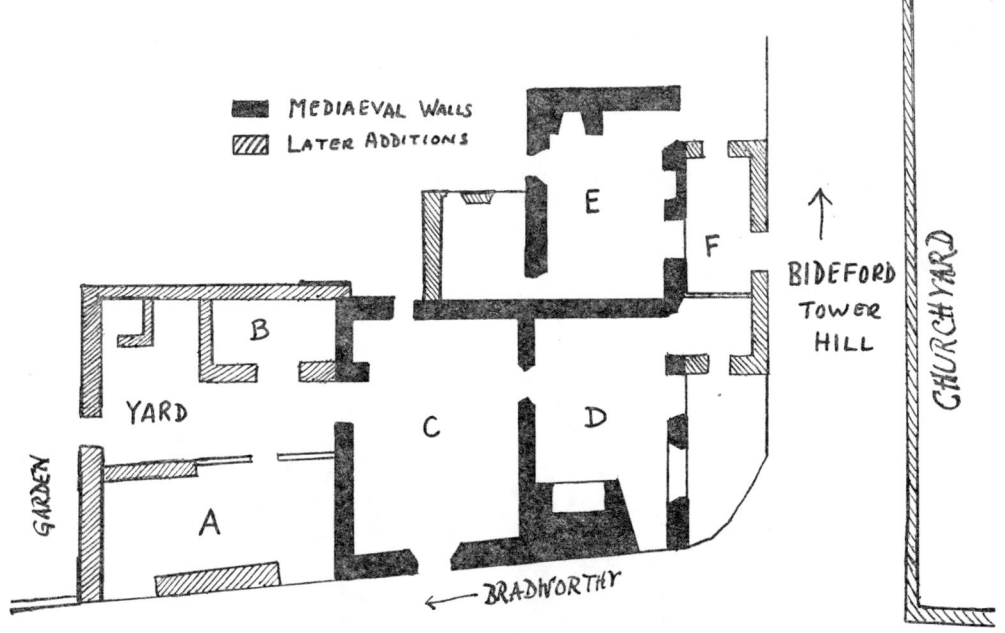

Priest's House, Buckland Brewer, later the Vicarage.   *D. Seymour.*

The rooms mentioned below occur in the Terrier of 1721. The plan of the house (kindly supplied by Mr. & Mrs. I. K. Mitchell) remained unaltered until c. 1975.

A Dairy   B Cellar   D Parlour   E Brewhouse   F Porch with "studdy" over where the Canons' clergy must have lived. It stands immediately west of the churchyard, on the corner, and is an L shaped house of obvious antiquity. A terrier of 1727 quoted by "Marland" from a paper by the Rev. J. I. Dredge is as follows:—"A Terrier for the Vicarage of Buckland Bruer and the two chappels, one is East Putford and the other Bulkworthy.

(1) The vicarage house is builded of mudd walls covered partly with thatch and partly with healing stones. It consists of five under rooms, a parlour floored with lyme ashes, the walls on the inside plaistered; the kitchen floored with earth the walls on the within side plaistered; one cellar, one dairy and one brewhouse, all floored with earth. Over these rooms are four chambers, and over the porch one studdy, all plaistered. The outhouses are one barn of two bays of building, and one stable of one bay, both covered with thatch.

(2) The glebe consists of two fields of 9 acres, bounded toward the east and north by ye highway, on the west by Bartin Moor, and on ye south by a small meadow". The rest is not of interest, but there is mention of a wood tower at the Chapels of East Putford and Bulkworthy. Two small bells at the former and three at the latter. The terrier is signed "Apud Torrington Magnum, 15 die May, 1727".

This account of the vicarage would not be enough to certify the house as mediaeval, but the present owner could show me a plan of the building before recent alterations were made. It had a long, narrow porch filling all the space between the front windows, and it abutted right onto the pavement. A staircase from the porch led to a small room above. This beyond doubt was the "studdy" of the terrier; and so the unusual arrangement of an

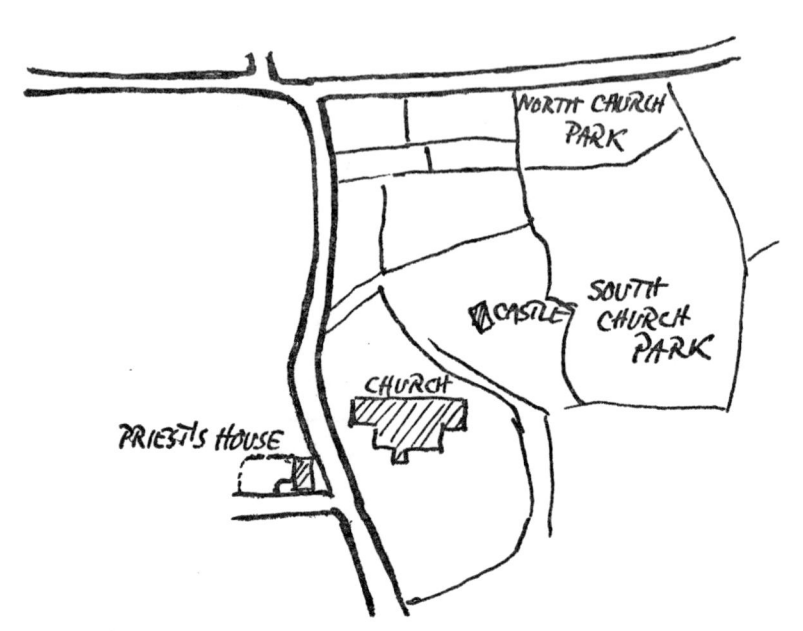

Buckland Brewer, from Tithe Map of 1842.   *D. Seymour.*

independent room over the porch proved that this was the old vicarage. The number of rooms in the house fits also. The barn and stable are also to be seen in old outbuildings backing onto the road at the side of the house. Unfortunately no old features remain but the walls. Whether these are original or a rebuilding on the old site no one can say, but it will have been on this spot that the vicars supplied by Torre Abbey lived.

The Canons were given 4 acres of land at Gretcleve which was, and still is, a fine wood in the valley below the village. It has so far not been possible to identify these acres. Close to the wood is Bearah and here I can identify the field called Reigheye in the Cartulary. Today it is called "Rick". So Rick heye or hedge was in those times no doubt a clearing in the wood enclosed by steep banks. They still surround the field to this day. This field is on the south side of the short entrance lane to Bearah.

So the researches made at Buckland Brewer have shown that many of the former links with Torre Abbey are visible today. They are (1) the parish church (2) the priest's house beside the church (3) the sanctuary land (see map) (4) the field of Reigheye (5) the names of many farms still going strong today, and all of which paid tithe to the abbey as the list below testifies.

13th C. Tithe Return (from Dublin Cartulary) from the farms in the parish:—

Decima ecclesie de Boclond

Yornwiger	XXVIIIs.	Clive	Xs.
Holewille	XLs.	Duockworthy	XXs.
Holelegh	XIIs.	Dune	XXIs.
Boroddoune	XIs.	Tudecote	XXXs.
Quercichene	XVIs.	Guvelandwrang	XIIs.
Hethercichene	XVIs.	Godekingeslond	XIIs.
Bilifford	XXs.	Duogalleshore	XXXVIs. VId.
Kippertonne	XXIIs.	Decima de Bulcworthi	XLs. IXs.
Hele	XIIs.	(should surely be IXd.)	
Yornhele	Xs.	Decima domini de Bulcworthi	
Cranham	XIIs.		XLVIs. VIIId.
Oik (Iip?)	IIIs.	Pucheford	XXXVIs.
Leie	Xs.	Mambiri	XXIIIs.
Heleluveriche	VIIIs. IIIId.	Rennecridua	XXs.
Beare	VIIIs.	Gardine	Xs.
Sulclond	XIIIs. IIIId.	Yornputford	XXXVIIIs.
Vielestoune	XIIs.	Northcote et Nortedoune	XLs.
Orleghe	XXXIIIs.	Witslade	XXXVIIIs.
Schorcterigge	Xs.	Boclond Abbatis	LXXIIIs. VIIId.
Burghe	XIIIIs.	Brendoune	LVIIIs. VId.
Taddepute	XXIIs.	Duogorford	
Bogawode	XIIs.		

Vicars of Buckland Brewer

1279	Sir Walter de Denetone.
1312	Sir Richard de Hurtleghe.
1333	Brother de Elmore.
	Sir John de Copshill ob. 1405.
1405	Sir Richard de Dunste ob. 1433.
1433	Sir Thomas Antred res. 1436.
1436	Sir Richard Chyryton ob. 1444.
1445	Sir Robert Hayman ob. 1458.
1458	Sir Philip Husband.
	Sir Thomas Radford res. 1507.
1507	Sir Robert Horsley.
	Sir John Corck res. 1525.
1525	Sir William Prescott ob. 1532.
1533	Sir Thomas Pearse, Patron then John Coblegh

The next patron was King Henry VIII, and the royal patronage continues to the present day.

Further References

Taxation of Pope Nicholas, 1288
  "Bokland 20 marks with vicariate" (D.C. folio 169b).

Ministers and Receivers Accounts, 1558/59
  Rectory of Buckland Bruer, with the chapels of Wicke, Bulckworthi etc.: Farm of the tithes etc., £39.7s; less 26/8 for a chaplain, and farm of some property, £4.13s:—£42.13.4d.

Sheepwash: Mediaeval building at Upcott Barton. *Photo by M. Leach.*

Buckland Brewer: Parish Church of St. Mary and St. Benedict.

Buckland Brewer: Romanesque south doorway at the Church of St. Mary and St. Benedict. *Photo by M. Leach.*

Buckland Brewer: Guild Chapel adjoining Parish Church. *Photo by M. Leach.*

Buckland Brewer: Font at East Putford Chapel. *Photo by M. Leach.*

Dartmouth: St. Clement's Church, Townstall. *Photo by courtesy of H. G. White.*

32

Townstall, Dartmouth

Before considering the great influence which the Canons of Torre wielded over the port of Dartmouth, it is necessary to understand something of the development of the manors in which it lay. The parish of Townstall, of which Dartmouth forms a part, took its name from the Domesday manor of Dunestal. This was a small manor rendering geld for only half a hide. In 1086 there were five villeins, four bordars and two serfs; it was worth 10/- and would centre round the site of its ancient hilltop church.

Now the manor of Norton, in which most of Dartmouth lay, was four times the size. It consisted of two hides; there were nine villeins, twelve bordars and six serfs, according to the account of the Domesday "Nortona". Whilst some have thought that this was a manor elsewhere in the county, yet it seems most unlikely that the manor in which such an important place as Dartmouth was situated got no mention. There is little doubt, however, that the small manor of Dunestal was practically surrounded by its larger neighbour and became very soon absorbed into it. Certainly it no longer existed by the time Torre Abbey was founded, for there is never a mention of it in the charters we have. Its name survived, strange to say, for ecclesiastical purposes, and as Townstall it has come down over the centuries as the name of the parish in which most of Dartmouth lies.

As the port of Dartmouth began to grow Norton went from strength to strength in its importance as a manor. It stretched from the river inland as far as Hemborough Post. At the time when our interest in it begins it was still largely agricultural, and there is little doubt that its origin was not beside the river at all, but up in the lofty hills above, where, safe from sudden attacks from the sea, the farmer could till his ground in comparative safety. The Kingswear chapter shows how very much the same thing happened there. If anyone wants proof of the place of origin of Norton, let him look at the tithe map of 1841 where he will find no less than four ancient holdings of that name north of Dartmouth. They are Higher Norton, Lower Norton, Hogg's Norton and West Norton. So I think that in Saxon times the old settlement was up here in the hills, just below the old prehistoric earthwork at Norton Park.

We next have to consider the situation of the manorhouse of the FitzStephen family, who in the early 13th century gave Townstall church to Torre Abbey. Several of the charters were signed "at Norton". The family by this time were influential and well-to-do, and they were soon asking for their own chapel at their house at Norton. My own opinion is that this manorhouse stood on the main road to Kingsbridge close beside the old entrance to Norton Park. Here today is an attractive rectangular enclosure with its further wall pierced by the drive to Norton Park, which was built in the 19th century. There seems little doubt that before that time there would be a narrow entrance here, with probably a gatehouse. It is still a narrow entrance, and it is flanked by tall old houses, probably of the 17th century. Beyond, and on the west side, is a long low house which has the proportions of a mediaeval house. This, I think, may quite possibly be the site of the FitzStephens' unassuming manorhouse. The present house has no old features showing, but its shape and thick walls are consistent with a mediaeval origin. It was never added to or enlarged in any way, for the family moved further down the hill to Place in the 16th century.

At the northern end of the house the plan, according to the Tithe map, shows a quadrangular building projecting eastwards from the house. It is correctly orientated for a chapel, and its position in relation to the house is very similar to the chapels at Bradley Manor and Compton Castle. The map shows the east wall as missing, so by that time it was perhaps already a ruin. Its walls may be faintly traced yet on the lawn in front of the house.

On the opposite side of the courtyard stands another old house; this until a few years ago was the farmhouse of Higher Norton. This would be the barton farm. The house has been rebuilt, but the back wall has not been touched, and here there was a fine old chimney stack not long ago.

Higher Norton.   D. Seymour.

The taller houses on either side of the entry tend rather to dwarf the two older houses, but they do not in any way detract from the charm of this secluded courtyard, nor do they mar the plan of the humble manorhouse with its attendant buildings and gateway.

Place was no doubt built when the port of Dartmouth had grown to such a size that it was no longer convenient to conduct the manor business at Norton. It occupied the site of a later house called Mount Boone, which in its turn was demolished when the Royal Naval College was built. There is every reason to think that the manor courts etc., would be held at Place, for its very name gives indication of its importance.

Then in the 19th century a strange thing happened—the owner of the manor decided to build a fine house above the old manorhouse on the summit of the hill. So a return to the former site took place, and the new house was called, very rightly, Norton Park. Surrounding the house were circular banks and ditches, showing that a small, prehistoric earthwork crowned the hilltop. Now that a holiday camp has grown up here, this has all been filled in and is to be seen no more. I feel, therefore, that in early mediaeval days Norton had its origin up here on the hill. Folk memory is a strange thing, but I think that an old lady living nearby was more right than she knew when she said to me, "Norton Park has always been *the* house of the parish".

There were, later on, subdivisions of the manor of Norton of which Clifton and Hardness were two. Indeed the full title of the town became Clifton Dartmouth Hardness. Just south of Clifton was the 14th century suburb of Southtown. The "Devon Lay Subsidy of 1332" shows headings thus:—Norton (14 taxable), Clifton Dertemuth (29 taxable), Sutton Dertemu (16 taxable). Southtown or Sutton was annexed to the borough of Dartmouth as late as 1463 (Russell P. 65). It seems to have obtained manorial status at some time, for Lysons refers to the manor of Southtown (p. 157 pt. 2) as being given at an early period to Fleming by FitzStephen, and it included St. Petroc's and the Castle. Watkin in "Dartmouth" (p. 347) quotes a document of 1437 which refers to the "court of the lord of Southtown". It probably always lay in the parish of Stoke Fleming and continued to do so until recently. The manor existed until 1864 when it was sold by Colonel Seale (Russell p. 155).

The Charters

191. A gift in perpetual alms of the church of Tounstalle from William FitzStephen to the church of the Holy Trinity of Torre. Given for the souls of himself, his wife Isabella and William Berc(t)hele.
Date: c. 1198. MS: Folio 62. Witnesses:—G. de Lucy, Bishop of Winchester, William Brewere, Richard Heriet, Thomas de Ussebarne, Henry de Lapumei, John de Torintone, Matthew FitzHerbert, Richard Fleming, Guy de Aubermarle, William Bevian, Martin the chaplain, Ralph de Brai, Ralph de More, Reginald de Aubermarle and many others. (Names of witnesses from Dartmouth Corporation Deed).

192. Richard, son of William, confirms his father's gift of Tounstall Church to the Canons of Torre.
Date: c. 1210. MS: Folio 62.

193. A confirmation of the gift of the advowson of Tounstalle church by Simon, Bishop of Exeter.
Date: c. 1214. MS: Folio 62.

194. An agreement between John de Berkadone, Abbot of Torre, twelve of the parishioners of Tounstalle and Thomas Burgeis, vicar. Since the parishioners have presumed to build a chapel at Dertemuth without permission, Thomas, Bishop of Exeter, authorises all differences to be settled thus:—As Townstall parish church stands high above Dartmouth it is difficult of access for the aged, women and invalids and is rarely attended in severe winter weather, the Abbot and vicar assent to the building of a chapel with Baptistry and graveyard entirely dependent on the mother church of Tounstall. The

consecration to be at the parishioners' expense; they will also meet the cost of services. Sacraments to be ministered by the vicar or a suitable chaplain elected annually. Tithes go to the mother church, monastery and vicar. Once a year, on St. Mary Magdalene's Day, all to go to Tounstalle church to present their pence or halfpence. The 12 representatives then declared their support for the chapel; tithes, maintenance of the chaplain, book of lauds, chancel furnishings and all repairs to be borne by them. If they neglect worship in the chapel and go to the mother church then the chapel will be closed.
Date: Oct. 4th (at Torre) and Oct. 5th at Dertemuth, 1372.   MS: Folio 62, 63, 64.

195.   A confirmation from William Brewer, Bishop of Exeter, and the Cathedral Chapter made to the Canons of Torre of the advowson of Tounstalle church. They are to provide a suitable chaplain.
Date: Ascension Day 1232/33.   MS: Folio 64.

196.   A confirmation from King Richard II of letters patent made to the Burgesses of Clifton Dertemuth by his grandfather in the 30th year of his reign, whereby the Burgesses were granted the privilege of being brought to court only in their own town and tried before the Mayor and Bailiffs. This was granted because of the damage and loss which they sustain in time of war; also because they are bound to maintain at their own expense two warships always ready to sail anywhere at the King's command; the King therefore grants the Mayor and Bailiffs the right to hear within the town all cases concerning land tenure, tenement tenure, dispossession etc. The Burgesses to elect a Coroner annually; no other to be introduced by the King or his successors. Profits from the court to go to the King. All depends on their maintaining the two ships.
Date: Westminster, Nov. 25th, 1394/95.   MS: Folio 65.   Witnesses:—W., Archbishop of Canterbury; Thomas, Archbishop of York, our Chancellor; J., Treasurer of York and Salisbury; John, Duke of Aquitaine and Lancaster; Edward, Duke of York; Thomas, Duke of Gloucester, our dearest uncle; Thomas de Bello Campo, Earl of Warwick; William, Earl of Salisbury; Thomas de Percy, our seneschal of hospices; Edmund de Stafforde, warden of our privy seal. Date: Given by our hand at Westminster, Nov. 25th, 1394.   MS: Folio 65.

197.   A confirmation from William (Brewer), Bishop of Exeter, of the right of the Canons of Torre to appoint to the living of Tounstalle whenever it is vacant.
Date: Given at Chuddelegh, May 17th. (?), 1224.   MS: Folio 65.

198.   A confirmation from Richard (Blondy), Bishop of Exeter, that Hugh the Chaplain, vicar of Tounstalle, must pay 7 marks annually to the Abbot of Torre from his altarage and all other dues.
Date: Peinton, February 7th, 1274.   MS: Folio 65.

199.   An agreement between Gilbert FitzStephen and the Canons of Torre whereby he may keep the oblations made in the chantry chapel at Norton by himself, his wife and the young men of his family: but all other offerings from freemen or servants to go to the mother church of Tounstalle. For this Gilbert gave the Abbot all the land between his old garden at Tounstalle and Thomas Wodegrene's land. He is also to give a pound of wax annually to Tounstalle church. If he does not, services in the chapel will cease. Gilbert further gives all lands which they (the Canons) rent in the fee of Tounstalle. A pound of cummin is to be paid for the land which Guy Crispin gave to the Canons. He

also renounces all claim in the feofee and houses in Tounstalle which belong to the Abbot: also the spring. He promises to spend 2/- annually on lights in the chapel and other necessaries for the vicar.
Date: Totnes, Monday after Passion Sunday, 1250. MS: Folios 65 & 66. Witness:—
Martin, the priest etc.

200. Richard FitzStephen gives to the Abbot of Torre $2\frac{1}{2}$ acres lying on the west side of Tounstalle in his manor of Norton; it is where there are several parcels of land of which the Abbot was seised and enfeoffed. In exchange Abbot Richard has given him $2\frac{1}{2}$ acres adjoining his vill of Tounstalle.
Date: Given at Norton, the Wednesday before the Feast of St. Gregory, 1288. MS: Folio 66. Witnesses:— Ralph de Lynham, then seneschal, William de Penylls, John ffaukes, Thomas ffynamore, William Man and others.

201. A gift from Richard FitzStephen to Guy Crispin, his kinsman, of a ferling in Tounstalle which Richard de Camera used to hold: also a messuage in Dertemue situated between Thomas Wobe's house and Sibilla Neyvin's.
Date: 1250/80. MS: Folio 66.

202. A gift from Robert Peysim to Guy Crispin of a half ferling in Tunstalle which Richard FitzStephen gave him. If Robert is unable to warrant this land he will give land of equal value at Honewille.
Date: mid 13th century. MS: Folio 66.

203. A gift from Guy Crispin to the Church of Torre of $1\frac{1}{2}$ ferlings in Tunstalle, which Robert Peysim gave to him. Given for his own soul and that of Richard FitzStephen, his lord.
Date: mid 13th century. MS: Folio 67.

204. A gift from Thomas Wambe, the chaplain, to the Canons of Torre of a messuage and garden between the church of St. Clement and the parson's house. Twopence or a pound of cummin to be paid annually to the heirs of Robert Peysim. 60/- paid in recognition.
Date: mid 13th century. MS: Folio 67.

205. A confirmation from Brian, Abbot of Torre, to Peter de ffisacre and his wife, Beatrice, of the land at Lidewichiston which John, Robert and William held. Rent of 8/-. Distraint may be exercised at the Abbot's court at Kyngeswere.
Date: 1264/70. MS: Folio 67.

206. A quitclaim of Tunstalle Church given in the King's court by Gilbert, son of Richard FitzStephen and made to the Abbot of Torre.
Date: Tuesday before the Feast of the Epiphany, 1294. MS: Folio 68. Witnesses:—
Sir Robert Denys, Sir John de Asselegh, Peter heym, Philip Burde, William de Aleburne and others. Given at Tounstal.

207. An exact replica of 200.

208. A cirograph between Richard FitzStephen and the Canons of Torre. Richard gives them $4\frac{1}{2}$ acres in parcels of land in the southwest and east of Tounstalle; in exchange for land which Abbot Richard gave to him and which he enfeoffed to Gilbert de ffawy, Henry FitzStephen and Richard the baker.

Date: Given at Norton on the Vigil of the Feast of St. Vincent, 1285. MS: Folio 68. Witnesses:—Peter de ffisacre, then seneschal, William Man, Walter de Modeworth, Michael the carpenter, Richard the baker and others.

209. A quitclaim from William Damyot, mayor of Clyftone Dartmouth, made to William, Abbot of Torre, of the conditions of the charter of 1372, wherein the Canons had undertaken to provide a chaplain for the new chapel at Clyftone Dertemuth on such days as there would otherwise have been no service. In default of this the tithe was to be sequestrated by the Bishop of Exeter and the Canons were to pay the Mayor 100/-. The Mayor and Community now take upon themselves to provide the chaplain. If the Bishop should sequestrate the tithe, which he will do if the services cease, then the Mayor undertakes to pay the Abbot 10 marks.
Date: February 26th, 1395. MS: Folio 69 & 70. Witnesses:—Edmund, Bishop of Exeter, Lord John Holand Huntyndon and Edward Courtenay, Earl of Devon; John de la Pomeray, William Bonwyle, and James Chuddelegh, knights of the Exeter diocese, and County of Devon; Martin de fferers, Thomas Peverell, William fferers, John Bevyle, John Prescote, William Burlestone and others.

210. Edmund, Bishop of Exeter, confirms the vicarage of Townstall to the Abbot and Convent of Torre. Brother Richard Bradeworthi the vicar or any vicar appointed by the Convent is to pay 20 marks annually. A penalty of 20/- for nonpayment.
Date: 1400/1419. MS: Folio 70 & 71.

There are 19 Townstall charters and some are amongst the most interesting in the Cartulary. 194 and 209 are of formidable length in the original, but relate much that is of importance in the winding up of a long struggle between the burgesses and the Canons on the subject of the establishment of St. Saviour's church. These, too, were days when Dartmouth was the most thriving port in Devon. In time of war it was a perilous place in which to live; two ships of war, manned with their crews, had to be kept at the ready to sail anywhere the King might wish. As the burgesses had to equip these they had special privileges and must have been a thoroughly independent community. Through its foreign trade and the constant coming and going of sailors and ships of all nationalities, Dartmouth must have been an exciting place in those days.

The giving of Townstall church to the Abbey at the very end of the 12th century began a connection which was to last for nearly three and a half centuries. Gradually the Abbot acquired more and more property in the town, as the charters tell, and eventually had considerable influence over local affairs. With the large manor of Blackawton just a mile or so inland, more property on the Kingswear side of the river, Waddeton, and fishing rights on the river, the Abbey was certainly a power to be reckoned with in Dartmouth. Unlike the outcome in other districts over which the Canons held sway, they never managed to acquire the manor of Norton. The FitzStephens were far too astute to let this happen. They seem to have been hard-headed business men who never got into financial straits, and never gave away a thing after the initial gift of the church. Exchanges of land with successive Abbots were common, as the charters show. One senses that succeeding generations resented the early gift of the church to the Canons. In 1294, some 90 years afterwards, Gilbert FitzStephen evidently tried to question the validity of the gift, but he was taken to court by the Abbot and had to give a quitclaim of the church "for ever" as the full text of charter 206 says. The charters concerning the church and tenements in Dartmouth tell their own story and need no comment.

Of all the charters 196 is perhaps the most exciting, for here we are suddenly immersed in affairs of state. It is a document given by King Richard II and witnessed by the heads of state, the two Archbishops, and the Dukes of Aquitaine, Lancaster, York and Gloucester—the King's dearest uncles—the Earl of Warwick and others. In this charter the King renews letters patent given by his grandfather, Edward III, whereby the Burgesses of Dartmouth are given all sorts of privileges in their own town provided that they keep the two ships of war, which we have just mentioned, at the ready. Dated Nov. 25th, 1394, this was evidently considered a charter of the greatest importance on account of its illustrious witnesses. It has apparently no connection with Torre Abbey, so why was it copied into the Cartulary? Possibly because the Abbot may have had instructions from the King to see that the Burgesses were in fact carrying out their part of the bargain and maintaining the two ships properly. The Abbot would certainly have been in a position to employ competent deputies to see that all was as it should be.

Charters 194 and 209 must be considered next. These are, in the original Latin, two of the most tedious and verbose charters in the Cartulary. Yet when once unravelled they tell the story of the beginnings of one of Devon's notable churches. For all their stodginess these charters are not without touches of unintentional humour—indeed the whole episode from which they derive is slightly comic and could perhaps have happened nowhere else but at 14th century Dartmouth.

For all its prosperity Dartmouth had no church in its midst, and the well-to-do burgesses had to climb up nearly 400 ft. to reach their parish church. This was much too arduous to be endured, and so they decided that a chapel in the town centre was a necessity. For some reason the Abbot of Torre must have been against this, but when in 1286 King Edward I visited the town the burgesses besought him to give them permission to build a chapel. A certain William Bacon came forward and offered an acre of ground for the purpose. In spite of obtaining royal approval the Canons and the Bishop of Exeter would not give permission for the building. Matters dragged on over the years and it seems that eventually the burgesses took the law into their own hands and began to build the chapel. Just when this was is not easy to discover, but certainly by 1340 it seems that the chapel was a fait accompli. The actual work was carried out by the so-called order of Hermits of St. Augustine. In 1347 the Court of Rome declared the work illegal and perpetual silence was imposed upon the Brethren.

Prior to this, however, fate played right into the hands of the burgesses, for there landed upon their shores no less a person than Hugh, styled Bishop of Damascus. Now he was nothing but a charlatan and an adventurer, and his fantastic buffoonery may be studied in the Register of the Bishop of Exeter for the period. The one fly in the ointment so far as the burgesses were concerned was the fact that their new chapel was unconsecrated, and they could get no one to perform the ceremony. There seems little doubt that the self-styled Bishop was only too ready to perform the rite, however, and did so. In charter 194 there is mention that the chapel must be "rightly consecrated" and "canonically consecrated", as though the Bishop of Exeter knew only too well what had happened. On account of its position Dartmouth is not easy of access by road even today; so in those days it would have been possible for this impostor to deceive the people for quite a long time. In the end, of course, he was brought to book, but not before he had had a good run for his money.

This was in 1344, but it was not until 1372 that matters between the Abbot, the Burgesses and the Bishop were finally amended as charter 194 demonstrates; a final agreement was reached in 1395. The upshot was that the new chapel was eventually consecrated and set on a legal footing. But the burgesses were entirely responsible for its maintenance and upkeep. The chapel was dedicated at first to the Holy Trinity, but by 1496 there is mention of a chantry chapel of St. Saviour. Eventually the older dedication was superseded, and it is as St. Saviour's that the church has come down to us. Both dedications, of course, commemorate the twofold dedication of Torre Abbey.

The Dartmouth Churches

(1) *The parish Church of St. Clement, Townstall*

There is still much to see in the old mother church of Townstall which the Canons would recognise. There are also three 15th century bells which give forth actual sounds

St. Clement's, Townstall. (From Drawing by A. E. Flint). *D. Seymour.*

which they heard all those years ago. The most conspicuous feature of the building is the tower, which is a landmark from the river nearly 400 ft. below. With its diagonal buttresses and exterior stair turret, it much resembles Cockington tower which the Canons may have built at about the same time.

The church is cruciform, and the great length of its transepts is remarkable. In the south transept is the beautiful tomb of Isabella de Languire, wife of William Fitz-Stephen, the donor of the church. But where is William? One would expect a chantry here for both; perhaps William was buried a few feet to the north and his tomb, being in the way, was despoiled. There is no mention of a chantry, however, in the Cartulary. On the other hand the chapel at Norton was looked upon as a chantry (199).

The Canons would find the old font which they used still doing service; the nave arcade and chancel arch are also of their period. The small Norman church was probably rebuilt c. 1318, for in that year the Bishop of Exeter dedicated a new high altar there.

Of the three mediaeval bells the biggest is by William Chamberlain of London, c. 1480, and bears the five crosses and two shields which he used. The inscriptions are:—

4th, "Wox Augustini Sonet in Aure Dei".
5th, "Santa Katerina ora pro nobis".
6th, "Sit Nomen Domini Benedictum".

A similar bell to the tenor is at Marldon. These bells are three good castings with inscriptions in black letters. There were four in 1552.

As the Canons were patrons of the living it is not surprising to find them as vicars. The 13th century list is unfortunately missing. I am grateful to Mr. and Mrs. M. P. White of Dartmouth for the following list which they have compiled:—

1374	Geoffrey Baroun
1391	Brother Nicholas de Cherleton
1394	Brother Matthew Yurd (later Abbot)
1396	Nicholas de Cherleton
1400	Richard Bradeworthy
1406	William Mychell (later Abbot)
1414	John Burgh (proxy John Lane, clark)
1433	Brother John Lacy (later Abbot)
1442	Sir John Gambone
1442	Brother Richard Cade (later Abbot)
1497	William Cullynge
1499	Roger Legge
1513	Thomas Umfray
1531	Simon Rede (Abbot at the time, on the presentation of Nicholas Kirkham Esq. by reason of the patronage being granted to him by the Abbot and Convent of the Monastery of Saint Salvatore de Torre, the original patrons)

All these vicars were Canons of Torre and several became Abbots. This rather suggests that only the intelligentsia among the Canons were appointed to Townstall. Set in the midst of a thriving seaport, the living was evidently looked upon as the most important in the Abbot's possession.

P

(2) *St. Saviour's*

From an architectural point of view St. Saviour's is a remarkable church, yet it is full of deep contrasts. It has one of the county's most spectacular interiors, yet the exterior is lacking in a single feature of interest. The humble, unbuttressed tower, reminiscent of Torre or Wolborough, was in 1631 heightened considerably, and the result is devoid of character and even good proportions. Perhaps the fact that the aisles were lengthened as far as the west wall of the tower does much to rob it of any dignity. The building stands badly, too, on an awkward site, hemmed in by streets and houses.

The Canons would be pleased to see that the splendid iron work on the south door is intact. The fierce lions there depicted are a part of the town seal, and they undoubtedly reminded all who entered the church that it belonged entirely to the town and was the responsibility of the burgesses.

On entering the church one is immediately beset by the problem of dating the arcade. The two westernmost bays, with their pointed arches, ought to be late 13th century, and why should they not be? Yet the theory always advanced is that the church was built in 1372 when it was consecrated, and in 1972 the 6th centenary was observed. It has already been told how King Edward I visited Dartmouth in 1286, giving permission for a chapel to be built on an acre of land given by William Bacon. I cannot help but think that these arches are remains of this old chapel, and that it was built not so very long after the King's visit. If this point is agreed then the old arcade fits into its rightful period.

A further legacy from the 13th century chapel is the old font which also fits into the scheme of an early date for the church. The magnificent screen and pulpit, and the spacious design of the east end all belong to a Perpendicular rebuilding. We learn that in the 1390's there was talk of the chapel being "enlarged", and this would be about the period when the scheme was carried out. The elaborate roundheaded arches of the eastern bays of the nave are thought by Russell to be part of the debased gothic rebuilding of the 17th century, but Pevsner dates them as 14th Century. From a stormy beginning St. Saviour's, therefore, gradually grew in size and magnificence until it became the most glorious of all the Canons' churches.

Colvin in "The White Canons in England" relates an amusing story relating to a certain Sir John Dabridgecourt who died at Dartmouth when about to set sail for France. He was duly buried in 1415 in the chapel of the Holy Trinity (St. Saviour's). But it was found that he had wished to be buried in Alvaston Church or Dale Abbey. Now the Abbot of Dale, being one of his executors, discovered that he had left 10 marks, a chalice and his best set of vestments to the church where he was buried. Using his powers as executor the Abbot lost no time in sending for the body of Sir John, who was duly exhumed and reinterred in Dale Abbey. So the Canons of Torre lost the legacy!

The close connection between St. Saviour's and Torre Abbey is now quite forgotten, but in the late-monastic period there must have been constant communication between the two over all ecclesiastical matters. For instance, just before the dissolution there is the typical entry among the town's documents:—"1531, To John Hingeston at Mr. Maire's commandment to ryde to Herberton for a clerk 4d., more to him to ryde to Torre for a clerke ageynste Crismas 8d. To the organ player for his being here at Crismas 3s. 4d."

Further References

Taxation of Pope Nicholas, 1288
"Tunstalle in the deanery of Totnes, value 10 li., vicariate £2.6.8. Temporalities:— Tunstalle and Aveton £3.14.4."

Devon Lay Subsidy, 1332
Those families mentioned in charters and also chaplains paying tax were:— Wm. Fynamour 16d., William Persoun 20d., John Chapleyn 12d., John Fynamour baker 7½d., Robert de Fouwy 8d., Adam Muchel 4/6. William Persoun 7½d.

Valor Ecclesiasticus
"Towynstall" was valued at £7.11.7.

A.O., Particulars for Grants
"Grant to George Rolle of Stevenstone and Nicholas Adams of Combe, Dartmouth, 28 Sept. 1545, ... the manor of Townstal and property in the parish of Dartmouth late of Torre Abbey . . . ." (LP. xx, pt. ii, 228).
Rents per annum totalled £7.10.1½.

33

Kingswear

In early times Kingswear was a part of the large parish of Brixham. From a civil point of view this was composed of six manors—Briseham, Galmentona, Locetona (Lupton), Hewis (Woodhuish), Coletone (Coleton Fishacre) and Liewichestona or Levricestone. There is little doubt that Kingswear at that time was a part of the latter and it was a place of little importance. In the chapter on Townstall I have pointed out that the early Saxon settlement on that side of the river seems to have been at Norton—well up in the hills, away from sudden invasion scares. So on this side of the river there was also an early settlement at Levricestone, high up above danger. We see the remains of it round the present-day farm of Boohay, which latterly was the alternative name for the old Saxon manor.

By Norman times a small fishing community must have sprung up at Kingswear. At any rate there was a sufficient population to support a chapel in the 12th century. Now Brixham church belonged to Totnes Priory and so would this chapel, which was dedicated to St. Thomas à Becket. The land, when our story begins, belonged to the de Vesci family, and there is mention of William de Vesci giving half his land to Totnes Priory. By the middle of the next century Kingswear had grown apace, and the Abbot of Torre had a court there (see 205 where Abbot Brian grants Levricestone to Peter and Beatrice de ffisacre; here there is mention of "our court of Kingeswere").

Very little remains to see of this early stage in the town's history apart from the squat tower of the church, one or two old cottages, the approach to Kittery Court and two nicely-pointed sandstone doorways at "The Priory".

The Charters

KYNGESWERE

211. A gift in perpetual alms of all his land at Kyngeswere from Walter de Vasci to the Canons of Torre; excepting the part which belongs to the Prior of Totnes and sixpence which belongs to the hospital of Jerusalem.
Date: c. 1200.   MS: Folio 71.

212. A gift of a messuage with(in) Kittetorra from William de Vascy to Robert Bastard, son of William Buzun. Rent a ¼ lb. of wax at the Feast of the Assumption. In recognition whereof Robert gives him a gold piece, Juliana, his wife a silken wimple and his son, Walter, a silver ring.
Date: c. 1180.   MS: Folio 71.

213. Michael de Restercumbe, son of Oliver, gives 3 acres at Horestone to the church of Torre: they are part of the tenement of Wattersipe where his brother W. was killed whilst defending this land.
Date: early 13th century.   MS: Folio 71.

214. A quitclaim from Guy de Restercumbe of 3 acres of land made to the Canons of Torre. They are above the hill of Kyngeswere between the lord Martin de ffisacre's wood and the land called Watersipe and extend towards the highway to the east.
Date: mid 13th century.   MS: Folio 71 & 72.

215. Lease of an acre of land (which Osbert ffranciscus used to hold) by the Prior of Totnes to the Canons of Torre. It lies beside the road coming down from Kitetorr to Alan de Kyngeswere's tenement in length; in breadth it stretches to the sea. Rent 8d. Also half an acre at Uppetone at 6d.
Date: 1220/30.   MS: Folio 72.

216. A confirmation of 3 ferlings of land made by the widow, Alice de Rotomago, to William ffynamore, her brother. They are at Lydewygintone, and the first two were held by her man William ffuterel, and the third by her man Bolla. Half a pound of cummin at Easter for all services. Grazing rights in Wodehiwis and Liddewigetune. Clause of Warranty.
Date: Mid 13th century.   MS: Folio 72.

217. William ffinamore confirms to the Canons of Torre the 3 ferlings mentioned in 216.
Date: Mid 13th century.   MS: Folio 72.

218. Thomas ffinamore, son of William, confirms the 3 ferlings mentioned in 216 and 217 to the Canons of Torre.
Date: 1275/80.   MS: Folio 72.

219. Thomas de Circestre confirms the same 3 ferlings to the Canons of Torre.
Date: Mid 13th century.   MS: Folio 73.

220. Osbert ffranceys gives all his lands and houses at Kingeswere to the Canons of Torre; also a half acre at Uppetune: for the salvation of the souls of himself and his wife Dionisia. 8d for Kyngeswere property and 6d for Uppetune, to be paid to Totnes Priory.
Date: 1220/30.   MS: Folio 73.

221. Master John, vicar of Brixam, undertakes to pay the Canons of Torre 14d. per annum for a half acre of land at Uppetone.
Date: Mid 13th Century.   MS: Folio 73.

222. An indenture testifying agreement between Abbot Simon and Ives de ffisthacre over customary payments for 2 messuages, a cottage, a mill and 3 ferlings of land at ludewycheton which Ives and his forbears held from Torre Abbey. Ives agrees to hold these for the eighth part of a knight's fee and for 21/4 for all services, demands etc. Clause of Warranty. Given at Torre.
Date: Sept. 1st, 1331/32.   MS: Folio 74.

Witnesses: Thomas de Courtenay, Henry de Pomeray, John Danne, John de Cheverstone, James de Cokynton, knights; Geoffrey Gilbert, William fforest, John Cola, Symon de Newenham, Ralph Tregotz and others.

The oldest of the Kingswear charters will undoubtedly be 212, which antedates the founding of the Abbey. In it William de Vasci gives a messuage and Kitetorra in Kingswear to Robert Bastard, the son of William Buzun. Now Kingswear church was given to Totnes Priory by William de Vasci for the souls of his parents and that of William Buzun, the deacon. So Robert Bastard was evidently his illegitimate son. The name of Kitetorra still survives as Kittery, which used to be the name of the lower part of the town. Kittery Court—a 19th century house with older parts still to be seen—must mark the site of the Canons' courthouse. The photographs show the approach to Kittery Court before the Yacht Club and the house next to it were built; they date from c. 1880. They certainly recapture a glimpse of the monastic period.

Charter 212 may date from c. 1180 because the previous charter in which Walter de Vasci gives the remainder of his land to Torre belongs to the next generation (he being William de Vasci's son). Walter's gift is mentioned in the Papalia document of 1226 as being already given. Altogether 212 is a delightful charter with a whimsical ending, for William de Vasci received a goldpiece, his wife a silken wimple and son Walter a silver ring. As one stands on the road above Kittery Court and gazes down upon this pleasing river frontage, given with its road and paths, water and cliffs to Robert the Bastard, one cannot but envy him; for he had it all for quarter of a pound of wax.

Perhaps it would be assuming too much to hope that the lands given to Totnes Priory and those given to Torre were neatly divided by the precipitous Wood Lane, which was probably the old approach road. Certainly the church must have been on Totnes land. In 215 the Prior of Totnes leases an acre of land to Torre, and its boundaries sound rather as though it is the site of Kittery Court, which would be less in extent then. It was formerly held by Osbert the Frenchman, and in 220 he gives all his Kingswear property to Torre Abbey. In both documents a further half acre at Upton in Brixham is given.

The remainder of the charters concern Lydewichestone—a manor which some writers have confused with Lupton; but that was surely the Domesday Lochetona. At any rate, evidence quoted at the end of this chapter, proves that "Lethewiston" was centred on the farm of Bowhaye or Boohay.

The first mention of Lydewichestone is in 216 where Alicia de Rotomago gives 3 ferlings of land to her brother. Her second husband, Thomas de Cirecestre, confirms this gift in 219. Alice's brother, William ffynamore, next gives the 3 ferlings to Torre (217) and his son, Thomas, gives a quitclaim in 218. Abbot Brian then leases the property to Peter de ffisacre at a rent of 18/-. Finally, in 222, Ives de ffisacre settles a dispute with the Canons over "Ludewychetone". The charter is headed "Boway" and there is mention of 2 messuages, a cottage, a mill and 3 ferlings of land. Later we are told that the messuages consist of a grange, a byre, a gatehouse, a cottage and a mill. This description quite fits Boohay, as it is spelt now. The present house is mostly Georgian, but facing on to the farmyard is a far older wing. It is quite clear, too, where the gatehouse stood, for its narrow entrance is still in use although the upper storey has gone. The farm buildings on either side are decidedly old with narrow slits for windows. Further along the road towards Kingswear are the ruins of a small house and yard. The house was extant 40 years ago, so I was told. This could have been the second messuage. Further along is a cottage. Here, I do not doubt, was the old vill of Boway on which the ancient manor of Lydewichestone centered.

Now the mill has not yet been accounted for, and we have to go further afield to find it. The land belonging to Boohay comes right down into Kingswear, forming one side of the Contour Road. This is not surprising if the extent of the old manor once took in Kingswear. On the opposite side of the road to the farm lands the site of the mill may be seen. It is now occupied by a laundry, but was a mill until recently. Its pond and leat may still be recognised amid a tangle of overgrown vegetation. They were taken from the swiftly-flowing stream which cascades down from Waterhead. There is a tidal creek below the mill, and I do not doubt that in the old days shipping could get up to it.

Two early charters (213 and 214) have now to be discussed. In the first Michael de Restercumbe gives 3 acres of land to the Canons at Horestone, stated to be part of the tenement of Watersipe. He adds dramatically that his brother, William, was killed whilst defending this land which was now given on behalf of his soul. So here is evidence of a local skirmish or raid from the sea. Would that we knew more about it! Now Little Orestone and Lower Orestone are to this day the names of two fields situated just above Nethway. This small holding was called Watersipe, and I suggest that it may be an older name for Nethway.

Uppetone

When Osbert, the Frenchman, gave his land at Kingswear to the Canons he included in it a half acre at Uppetone. This was confirmed to them by the Prior of Totnes (215). Upton—evidently a post-Domesday manor—is in Brixham about ¼ mile south of St. Mary's church. Its manor house has long since vanished, but some of its farm buildings (much knocked about) still stand. They are the premises of Upton Farm Creamery. The present farmer, Mr. J. E. Hosking, has no knowledge of the whereabouts of this half acre, for there have been considerable changes in the old boundaries here. Strangely enough he could tell me that his father always spoke of one of the farm buildings as a monks' rest house. Not far away is Monksbridge; so coming to us over the centuries there is still a memory of monks at Upton.

Master John, vicar of Brixham, paid 14d. each year for his half acre. This was either John Grygge (mentioned 1349) or John Wodeman. There is no mention of Kingswear in the Taxation of Pope Nicholas, probably because it would be included in Brixham. The Devonshire Lay Subsidy mentions Nicholas Foterel, thus proving that the family mentioned in 216 was still going strong in the following century. In "Valor Ecclesiasticus" Kyngeswere was valued at 107/2.

A.O., Particulars for Grants 495

"Grant to Thomas Gale of Dartmouth 22nd Feb?, 1544, the manor of Kingswear late of Torre Abbey (L.P. xix, pt. i. 82).

m.3. Manor of Kingeswere: Free rents, 13/11½; customary rents, £4.7.2; court profits, 5/8; less bailiff's fee, 6/8. c. 3/4:—103/5½. (A. O. Particulars for Grants 466).

p. 69 . . . from Henry Walron and John Holway esquire, for part of the manor of Bowhaye alias Lethewiston 21/4 . . ."

Dartmouth: St. Saviour's Church.

Dartmouth: St. Saviour's Church; 15th century screen and pulpit.

Dartmouth: South door of St. Saviour's Church.

Kingswear: The old approach to Kittery Court.   *Photo by courtesy of Brigadier W. Hine-Haycock.*

Kingswear: Old houses in approach to Kittery Court.   *Photo by courtesy of Brigadier W. Hine-Haycock.*

Waddeton: Tor's, Tor's Wood and piers (left of centre).
Ministry of Defence (Air Force Dept.) Photograph. Crown Copyright Reserved.

Waddeton: The old pier. *Photo by G. Court Jones.*

Ugborough: Torr's Barn, Monksmoor. *Photo by M. Leach.*

Ugborough: Ruins of ancient enclosures at Monksmoor. *Photo by M. Leach.*

34

Waddeton

High above the east bank of the River Dart stands Waddeton Court. In the mid 13th century this pleasant spot was owned by Isabella de Wadeton, as she styled herself. She was the widow of Martin de Fissacre and at that time was probably getting on in years. She evidently thought that it would be a good thing to have masses said for her soul after her death, and so she decided to found a Chantry for herself at Torre Abbey. To maintain this she gave the Canons a ferling of land at the vill of Wadetone and grazing rights throughout her land there. With it went John le Connere and his family. The previous tenant had been Robert de Wichasel, and to make quite sure that everyone knew the piece of land she was giving, she tells us that she bought it from Juliana Marthut.

Isabella made certain stipulations with her gift; first she bequeathed her body for burial at Torre Abbey and then ordained that a lamp should be kept burning for ever before the altar of the Holy Cross in the Abbey Church; and here, day by day and week by week, prayer was to be made for her soul and those of her husband, parents and successors. Should the lamp be extinguished then her gift lapsed immediately. Her charter (D.C. folio 27b) was witnessed by several local gentry—Sir Henry Pomeray, Sir Jordan de Haccombe, Herbert de Morcales, William de Cokintone, Warin de Fissacre, Walter le Bon, Robert de Compton and others. No date is given, but from the witnesses we can assume that the charter was signed between the years 1260-1270.

It was a pleasant surprise on looking at the Tithe Map to find that in the last century this gift had by no means been forgotten, for immediately in front of Waddeton Court was an extensive meadow called "Tors"; it occupied the whole of the narrow spit of land which sweeps down to the river. It was bounded on either side by steep combes. To the east was "Tors Wood" and, near the present house, "Tors Orchard". All this is quite unchanged today and is a repetition of what I found at Monksmoor, Ugborough, where the possessive title Tor's was still remembered. There is, moreover, a strong tradition in the neighbourhood that the monks built the pier below and also constructed the fishponds. The pier acts as a breakwater to the little creek; it is simply constructed of large stones placed one on top of another. Since it is not subject to much action from the river, which is here very wide, it may never have needed rebuilding. It is quite impossible to assess its age with any accuracy, however.

Adjoining the pools and at the extremity of Tors Wood there is a steep quarry. Professor Hoskins in "Devon" states that the splendid red sandstone which went into the building of Totnes church tower came from quarries at Galmpton Creek. If this was the case, then the pier may have been constructed so that boats could come alongside and take their load of stone up the river from this quarry. Mr. Hugh Goodson, the present owner of Waddeton, is a firm believer in the tradition that the monks constructed the pier, and he also mentioned open cast iron mining which was once carried on here.

Waddeton.   D. Seymour.

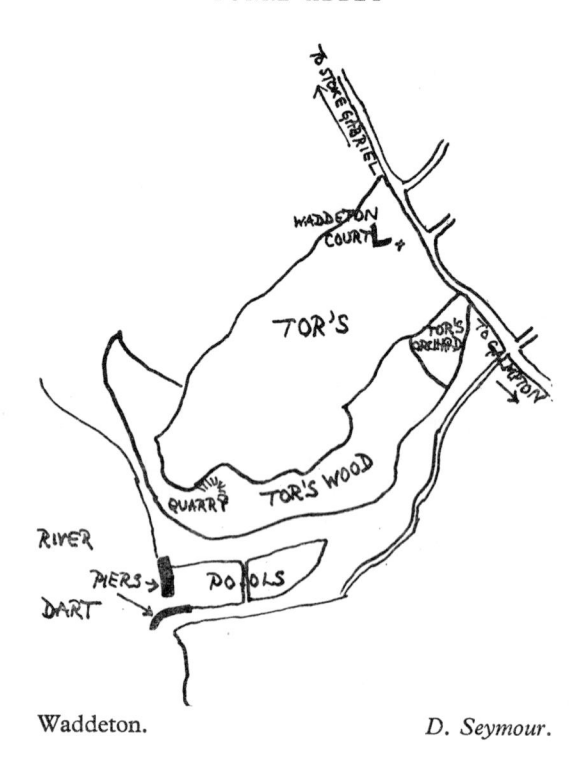

Somewhere in connection with this compact little monastic property there must have been a farmhouse and outbuildings. It is tempting to assume that we see it in the now rather derelict farmyard north of the chapel and former manorhouse. The only building left suggests decided antiquity, and it is annoying to record that all the others were demolished only a year or so before my visit. A rather fine sandstone barn is all that remains now. There are no buildings anywhere else in the original ferling of land, but that is not to say that they did not exist.

According to the Tithe Map the extent of "Tor's" is just over 21 acres, the wood about 14 and the orchard $\frac{1}{2}$ an acre. With the farmyard this makes a total of just on 36 acres—certainly a large ferling. Curiously enough, in the "Book of Fees" there is mention of a 36 acre ferling at nearby Galmpton. So perhaps after all, with the same measure in the next manor, the Waddeton ferling is right enough.

What this little estate lacked in size it made up in charm, for its situation on the banks of Devon's most noted river is delightful. The Canons, as was their wont, put it to good use. Sheep and cattle would be reared here, for they had the right to graze "throughout the land of Wadetone". A fishery, a stone quarry and even, perhaps, open cast iron mining brought in a worthwhile income; whilst from the wood there was adequate timber for repairs. There is no further mention of Wadetone in the Cartularies nor in "Valor Ecclesiasticus". Perhaps it had been sold before the crash came.

35

Blackawton

Blackawton appears in the Cartulary as Avetone or Blachcheavetone; it is a large parish which centres around the waters of one of South Devon's most attractive rivers, the Gara. Its northern tip is the ancient earthwork at Stanborough and in the days of the Canons of Torre it extended southward to Slapton Sands, for Strete was then a part of it. The majority of its old farmhouses are situated high up in the hills which rise steeply on both sides of the river. Almost without exception the farmyard captures a springhead, so the water supply for both man and beast was assured. I believe that the farmhouse sites are of great antiquity and that they were settled first from the sea. It would have been comparatively easy to develop along the gentle slopes on the tops of the 500 ft. ridges which run northward from Start Bay. The valleys were no doubt thickly set with a tangle of undergrowth and so would be left for later development.

Blackawton was the Canons' most extensive possession in South Devon, and when in 1539 it came at last into lay hands it was still intact—"the manor of Blackawton, late of Torre Abbey". The only fly in the ointment was the fact that the advowson of the church was in the hands of Plympton Priory, so the tithes went there and not to Torre. Nevertheless on a capital of a pillar on the north side of the church the arms of the Abbey are proudly displayed.

In Domesday there are two manors entitled Avetone. One was worth £14.10.0 and the other £3., so there is very little doubt as to which was the manor concerned. It was, moreover, a royal manor, and this will explain why King Henry III confirmed the first gift of land here (228). There were 25 villeins, and 22 bordars, making up a complex of 47 holdings; and the present number of farms is very close to this figure. There were 6 hides and 24 ploughs. The demesne had 2½ hides and the villeins 3½ hides. A saltworking is mentioned, and this was no doubt near Slapton.

One of the most fascinating things about the 16 charters which deal with this manor is that all the farms mentioned can be identified with certainty, for their names have changed but little in 700 years. One or two, such as Yanstone and Stanborough, are outside the present parish, but were clearly a part of the old manor. At first I thought that the Canons' territory might not have extended to the west side of the Gara, but that idea was proved wrong, for Wood is mentioned (238), Abbotsleigh has a self-explanatory name (it never belonged to Buckfast Abbey, although its coat of arms is displayed on a slate panel attached to a chimney there!) and Pasture was a farm where there were grazing rights common to Blackawton and East Allington. To all this Strete must be added, for it was not a separate entity then. That the manor had access to the sea is proved by the will of Richard Phillipps (to be found at the Devon Record Office). Dated at Yeanstone in 1654, there is mention of his "wife possessing boates at Blackawton the sixth part of a cellar".

The charters which now follow tell the story of the giving of this large manor to Torre Abbey.

223. A gift of all the principal messuages and whatever else he owns in the manor of Avetone to the Church of the Holy Trinity at Thorre from Peter Fitz Matthew. He also gives his body for burial there. The men of Stoke are bound to make suit at the fulling mill. 10 marks annually to be paid to his brother Roger.
Date: mid 13th century.   MS: Folio 74.

224. A confirmation from John FitzMatthew of his brother Peter's gift to Torre Abbey. Clause of Warranty embracing himself, his heir and whosoever shall hold the manor of Hurdestoke.
Date: mid 13th century.   MS: Folio 74/75.

225. A confirmation in free and perpetual alms from Matthew, son of John, and nephew of Peter, of all the gifts which his uncle Peter made to the Church of Torre.
Date: c. 1275.   MS: Folio 75.

226. A gift from Symon, son of Robert, made to Henry de ffysakre of a ferling of land at Westerhurtlegh in the manor of Avetone. Rent 2/-. Should scutage or any other royal service be demanded, Henry shall be quit of the 2/- rent (and of) 2 ferlings of wood which his father gave to Richard fflandren.
Date: 1200/50.   MS: Folio 75.

227. A gift from John le Barun of all his land at Westhurtlegh to the Canons of Torre.
Date: mid 13th century.   MS: Folio 75/76.

228. A confirmation from King Henry III of 10 librates of land in Aveton which Peter FitzMatthew gave to the Canons of Torre.
Date: mid 13th century.   MS: Folio 76.

229. A quitclaim of the whole of Avetone from Isabella de Fortibus to the Canons of Torre. It is a part of her Barony of Plympton, and suits and services etc., from the two fees in the manor of Hurdestoke are to be made to her.
Date: mid 13th century.   MS: Folio 76.

230. A Final Concord at Westminster between Symon, Abbot of Torre, and John FitzMatthew, whereby it was agreed that the holding of Aveton with its rights, customs etc. belonged to the Abbot. John promised that he and his villeins and heirs would make suit at the Abbot's fulling mill. He quitclaimed his right to 10 marks rent which the Abbot used to pay to Roger FitzMatthew, John's brother.
Date: Easter Day, 1259/60.   MS: Folio 76 & 77.

231. A recognition from Hugh Treverbyn that the freemen and villeins of Strete, ffewthe and Burlawestone should make suit of court, services, etc. at the Abbot's court, just as they did in the time of Herbert FitzMatthew.
Date: c. 1270/80.   MS: Folio 77.

232. A gift to the Canons of Torre from William le Spek, of all the land in his manor of Aveton, viz. Shinrestone, Teritone, Suestone, Olwestone, Hurteleghe and Warth. Clause of Warranty.
Date: mid 13th century.   MS: Folio 77.

233. William le Spek, lord of Wemmeworthi, secures to the Canons of Torre the land which he has given to them in the sum of £30.
Date: mid 13th century. MS: Folio 77.
Witnesses: William de ffysakre, Robert Date, knights; Peter de ffysakre, Benedict de London, Thomas de Gatepathe and others.

234. A quitclaim from Abbot Richard of the lands of Youinstone and Stanburgh made to Andrew FitzMartin. He is to hold at a rent of 20/- and for the fifth part of a knight's fee.
Date: 1270/1305. MS: Folio 77.

235. A quitclaim from Nicholas FitzMartin of a rent of 50 marks from the Abbot of Torre.
Date: 1271. MS: Folio 78.

236. A quitclaim from Nicholas FitzMartin to the Abbot of Torre of a rent of 50 marks and arrears.
Date: Friday after the Feast of the Exaltation of the Holy Cross, 1271. MS: Folio 78.

237. Brother Richard, by God's patience Abbot of Torre, concedes to William de Prestatone all the land which his father Alardus held from him at a rent of 7/-. He and his heirs must grind at the Abbot's mill. Grazing granted on the Canons' land. William gave £4 in recognition.
Date: 1270/1305. MS: Folio 78.

238. A confirmation to Geoffrey de Bosco from Abbot Richard of the land of de Bosco. Richard de Combe used to hold this from the Abbot. Rent 10/- per annum. Grinding to be done at the Abbot's mill. Whenever Geoffrey or his men arrive, their grinding is to be done next. He is not to hinder the Canons from repairing the bank of their park at Avetone.
Date: 1270/1305. MS: Folio 78.

239. A quitclaim from Elias Tylya to Abbot Richard of his title to Westhurtle and Stone in Blakavetone, which John Gambon of Torre, John More and Thomas Gylle formerly held from the gift of Henry Beare. For this remission the Abbot gave him 20 marks.
Date: August 3rd, 1469. MS: Folio 79. Witnesses: William Huddersfeld, Oto Gylbard, Gilbert Yerd, John Meryfeld, William Gambon and others.

It will be seen from the charters that the two principal donors of land at Avetone were Peter FitzMatthew and William le Spek, and the evidence is that these gifts were both made in the mid 13th century. The Final Concord of 1259/60 concerns Peter's brother, John. We can therefore assume that Peter was then dead and his brother dealing with any business which arose over the gift of land to Torre. Richard le Spek, father of William, was dead by 1242/3 (Book of Fees), so his heir would have been free to make the gift to Torre at any time after this date. There seems little doubt therefore that it was about the middle of the century that the bulk of Avetone came to the Canons.

The first charter (223) records Peter's gift of all his lands and capital messuages, and he also bequeathed his body for burial at Torre. There must have been trouble over getting tenants etc. to grind at the Abbot's Mill, because it is stipulated in several of the following charters that they must do so. The reference to Hurdstoke is to Stokenham and not to

Yanstone

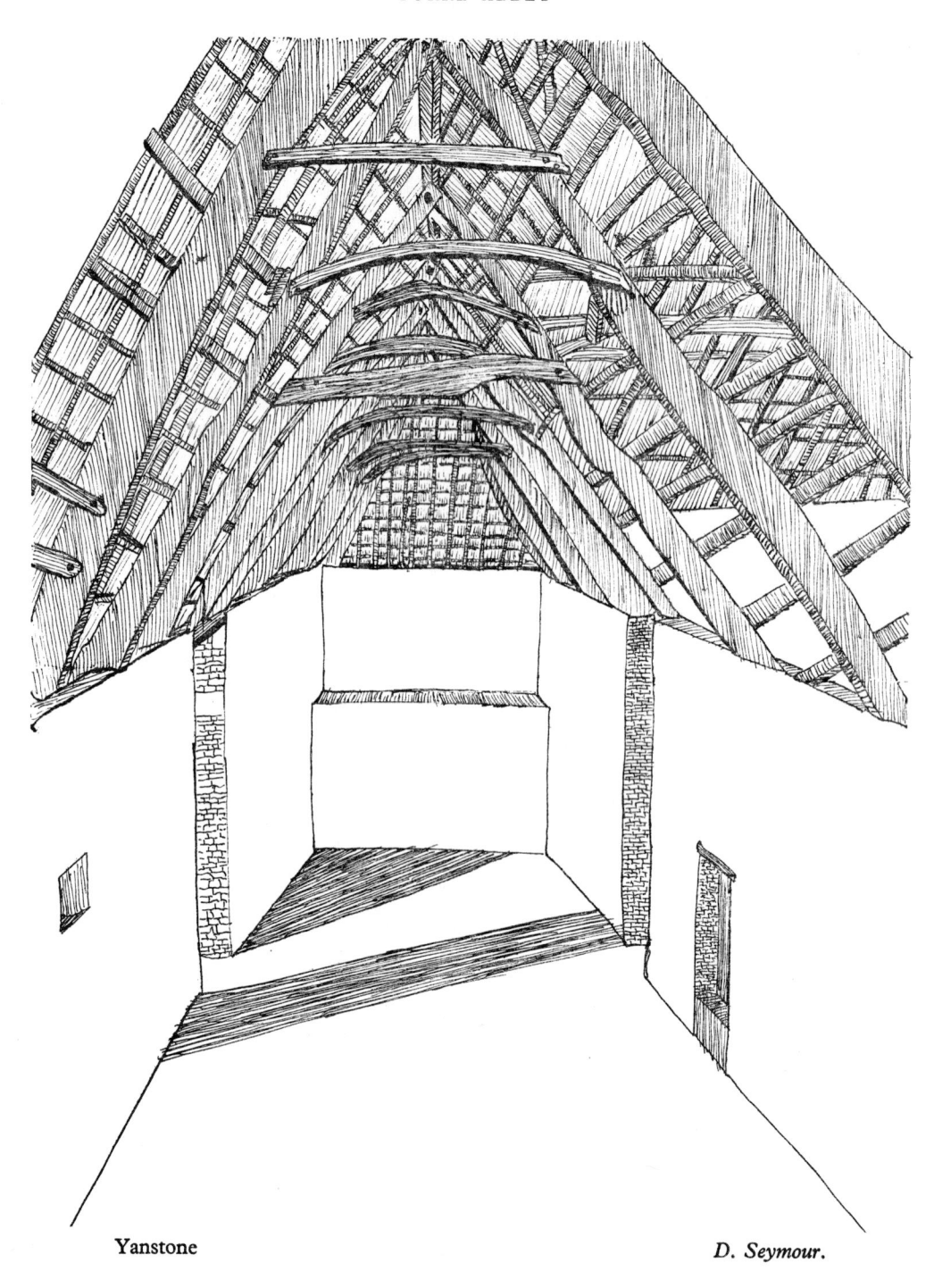

D. Seymour.

Stoke Fleming which was in the hands of the Fleming family at an early date. John, who confirms his brother's charter (224), guarantees it on behalf of "whoever shall hold the manor of Hurdestoke".

The next two charters deal with "Westhurtlegh". The two farms of East and West Hartley are on either side of the road to Blackawton from the Normandy Inn. In 226 Symon, son of Robert, gave West Hartley to Henry de ffisakre. In 227, John le Barun gave it to Torre. He is mentioned in "Devon Feet of Fines" in 1219, and in the "Book of Fees" in 1242/3.

On visiting West Hartley I was shown a map of the farm and had little difficulty in picking out what must have been this original gift of land. It consists today of four adjacent fields on the top of the ridge. It adjoins the farmyard and is surrounded on one side by an old lane, said to have been a mill path, and the north by a steep bank, beyond which the ground falls away. The eastern boundary now is the farm of Langstone—no doubt "Stone" in 239. All other fields added to the farm later show up on the map as an untidy and haphazard mess. The total acreage is only 17.9; but at Monksmoor we found a ferling of similar area. It is worth recording in passing that much of the South Hams was commandeered in the 1939/45 World War by the Americans for training. During this period the land had naturally gone back. When Mr Tope, the present farmer, took over in 1945 the first fields that he broke were those of this very ferling; his reason was that it was the best and easiest land to work. So, after some 700 years of farming, these acres were used again as a starting point.

In 232 William le Spek is very specific about the farms which he is going to give to the Canons. They are Shiurstone (Shearstone), Teritone (Dreyton), Suestone (Sweetstone), Olwestone (Oldstone) Hurtelegh (probably East Hartley, as West Hartley was already given) and Warth (probably Worden, now in Stoke Fleming). This was a very considerable gift, rivalling Peter FitzMatthew's, for it consisted of all the best farms on the east side of the manor. Note that William here refers to Avetone as his manor. He flourished in the 1270's and I wonder if he had acquired the manor of Avetone from the FitzMatthews by that time. If so his gift to Torre could be later than Peter FitzMatthew's.

It is unfortunate that King Henry III's confirmation of Peter's gift is undated. He died in 1272, so 228 must have been given before then. Its great interest lies in the fact fact that it tells us that Peter's gift consisted of 10 librates of land.

In the full text of 229 Isabella de Fortibus, the great heiress in whose Barony of Plympton Avetone lay, releases the Canons from making suit of court at Plympton Castle once every three weeks. This castle has been a ruin for so long that it is quite surprising to find that it really was a going concern in the 13th century.

Charter 231 shows how the men of Strete, Fuge and Burleston had to make suit of Court at the Abbot's court at Avetone. In 234 Yeovinestone and Stanburgh are mentioned. Neither are in Blackawton today, yet in the "Devon Lay Subsidy" of 1332 the first name mentioned is that of Laurence de Vuyngeston. This can only be Yanstone in Loddiswell, and both must have been outliers of the manor of Avetone.

The attractive farm of Wood is mentioned in 238. Here Geoffrey de Bosco gets a most remarkable privilege made to him—when he goes to the mill his grinding is to be done next. Why he was thus allowed to jump the queue we shall never know. Geoffrey is ordered not to interfere with any repairs to the banks of their park which the Canons may wish to make. I have searched for banks of more than usual strength in the neighbourhood, but have gone unrewarded. The only explanation which I can offer is that the next farm in the valley is called "Straypark", so after all the banks may have been nothing more spectacular than those enclosing a pound for strays.

In the final charter (239) we are back at West Hartley and Langstone. It seems that over the century these farms were somehow alienated. Now, however, Elias Tylya quitclaims them to Abbot Richard in 1469.

Having learnt the contents of the charters we come next to a consideration of what is to be seen today of the monastic period. Fortunately for us the South Hams is as deeply involved in agriculture as ever it was in the 13th century. The district has never been opened up. The plans for a railway from Dartmouth to Plymouth never materialised; the line from Brent to Kingsbridge has gone, and no drastic road making has taken place. So the whole wonderful countryside is ours to explore. Single track lanes abound, and those with no metalled surface can scarcely have changed since the days when Peter Fitz-Matthew and William le Spek rode along them.

The most valuable survival, apart from the church, is the courthouse at Oldstone. This holding was a part of the gift from William le Spek. Where the courthouse of the former royal manor stood we do not know, neither do we know where the demesne land was. It could very well have been here at Oldstone, but to digress further into this nice little problem is outside the scope of this book.

Oldstone. *D. Seymour.*

Wherever the royal courthouse may have been, the Canons chose for theirs a most convenient spot from a geographical point of view; for Oldstone stands at a junction of roads from Kingsbridge, Dartmouth, Strete and Blackawton. The old farmhouse which stands behind the ruined manorhouse of the Cholwich family cannot now be reached by way of the imposing entrance and drive on the main road; the approach is by a rough lane off the Blackawton road. The building is a strange example of two houses at rightangles to each other, and so forming an L shaped house. Until recently there was no connection between the two houses, and a great dividing wall nearly 5 ft. thick continues right up to the top of the roof.

Until a few years ago these were two farmhouses, but in the Canons' time such an arrangement would be quite unnecessary because there would be only one farm to serve—the barton farm which consisted of the manorial demesne land. Even now the steep banks of its boundaries may be traced with some certainty. They are roads on the east and south sides, a stream on the west side and a thick bank which comes up from the lakes on the fourth side. Why, then, were there two farmhouses here?

I think the answer lies in the fact that one was the courthouse of the manor and the other the barton farmhouse. The plan shows the shorter wing, which runs roughly east and west, to consist of kitchen, cross passage and dairy. This is the pattern of a later

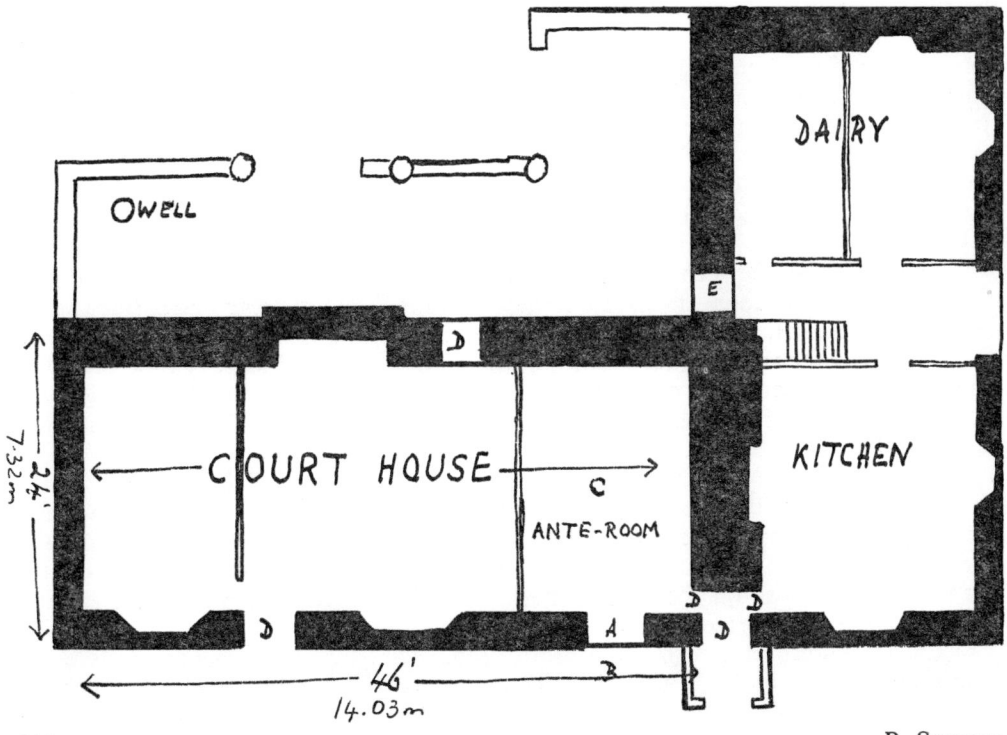

Oldstone. *D. Seymour.*

type of house than the older longhouse where animals and humans lived under one roof.

The other house, however, shows none of these characteristics. There is no sign of there ever having been a cross passage, and the huge fireplace has no oven—surely a sign that it never served a kitchen. After making a plan to scale I came to the conclusion that this was the actual courthouse. It had originally been one simple hall 46 ft. in length (cf. Court Barton, Greendale etc.). Here all the business of the manor would be conducted and the courts held. The partitions making three rooms are of course modern and have no structural importance. In the old days, too, the intrusive upper floor would be non-existent, and the simple, dignified hall would be open to the steep-pitched roof. This still retains old trusses, but it is most difficult to say if the timbers are original.

Another clue to the fact that this was one large hall is given us by the position of the fireplace. If the old entrance was at "A", then what I have called "ante-room" on the plan would have been a kind of lobby separated from the main hall by a wood screen. If this were situated a foot or two to the right of the modern partition between the houses, then the great fireplace was just about centrally placed along the back wall. And this is surely where it ought to have been.

Now the farmhouse has encroached upon the courthouse by one room on each floor. The huge dividing wall was hacked through downstairs immediately behind the front door, and on the next floor at the top of the stairs. But as soon as the dividing wall has been recognised as such then all this modern work can be ignored.

The attractive porch to the front door is a curious case of a rebuilding a few feet from the former position. Its entrance is altogether a refined example and has chamfered edges throughout. It is free standing, however, and not built into the house wall, so it cannot be in situ; then again it faces right onto the dividing wall of the two houses. This has been cut short to make a small entrance hall. It is a fairly recent affair, constructed to give an entrance to C which was taken from the courthouse to become the lounge of the farmhouse. The porch roof is a shoddy affair and clearly the work of an amateur, but the rebuilding of the arch has been done with care. Below the window at B is a break in the outside wall where I consider the porch once stood (at A).

The large flagstones which cover the greater part of the floors in both houses are some of the best things to be seen at Oldstone. They have been taken up in the kitchen and lounge and each was found to have a roman figure incised upon the under side. So far none have been lost, as they are used as steps etc., in the garden. Said to have been quarried locally they are of a brownish yellow. In the dairy are others of a blue-grey hue. They are of great beauty and one can only hope that they will long remain in position. On account of their roughness they are hard to keep clean, however. In the courthouse some are covered by a wood floor.

Since writing the previous paragraphs a visit to Oldstone in 1976 revealed that the courthouse wing has been entirely rebuilt. It had been derelict for years and was fast decaying, so it is a happy thing to be able to record its rescue. The fine open hearth and chimney are retained. An unexpected find was a complete cobbled floor beneath the flagstones. In the wall on the southwest side traces of three older windows were uncovered between the present ones.

Visitors to Oldstone have to be made to understand that the farmhouse site is far older than the ruins of the house below. This is entirely post-monastic in date. Its overgrown and reputedly haunted drive was shared by the farm, which was approached by a left fork. At the old entrance to the farmyard at the back of the house are the fragmentary remains on the north side of something very nicely made, which is more than just a gatepost. A similar projection on the south side has recently been removed. I feel that here there could have been an arched entrance or even a gatehouse.

Two other reminders of the existence of a court here are to be considered; first, at the nearby "Forces Cross" must have stood the gallows where miscreants met their end. This is found elsewhere as "forches", meaning the wooden forks which supported the gallows. Secondly, the name of the next farm to the south is Wadstray; this must surely

The Old Kitchen Fireplace, Middle Wadstray. *D. Seymour.*

be "wardstray", and in the old days I do not doubt that this was a manorial pound for strays. So we have "Straypark" in the south part of the manor and another pound here in the northern sector. By and large Oldstone is an intriguing place for the antiquary, for when he has completed his speculations about Torre Abbey, he can begin on the romantic tunnels, grottoes and hermit's cave associated with the ruin; whilst a quarter of a mile away, on the brow of the hill beside the turning to Strete, there is a mound which has never been excavated.

After the church and manorhouse the next most important building in a parish was the mill. Molture from the mill brought in a steady income for its owner in monastic times. Now at Millcombe the Abbot of Torre had two mills within a quarter of a mile of each other. One was a fulling mill and its name of Washwalk is still attached to the millhouse. The ruins of the other mill is to be seen in the garden of the first house in the lane. A not so very elderly villager told me that he remembered both mills working; further down the valley was Forder Mill, once a flourishing flour mill. The millpond for the lower mill was almost opposite Washwalk Mill, whilst the fulling mill was supplied by a leat which may still be traced. Its pond was much further up the Gara valley below Woodford.

Several old mill paths and rights of way lead to these mills, and the tracing of them would be an interesting study for someone with a bent for using his legs. Such direct paths were very necessary in the old days, for our charters show how the men of Stoke, Fuge, Strete, Yanston etc., all had to use the Abbot's mills. This must have been a sore point, because they would have to pass mills nearer to their homes on the way, and this may be why so many charters insist upon grinding at the Abbot's mill.

The splendid farmhouses of the manor are the next consideration. They form quite an outstanding group, for there is so much to be seen that goes back over the centuries. At the time of my visits to Blackawton I found hardly a case where both house and outbuildings had been entirely replaced by modern building. For the most part the old houses still stand, and the majority of them have developed from simple long houses sometimes into something more ambitious. So numerous are these old houses that it is impossible to mention them by name or describe the many points of interest. Those with an eye for rural architecture will find them well worth a visit.

It ought to be pointed out before we leave the farmhouses that there are two distinct types to be seen: (1) the house that has "grown up" into something quite imposing—sometimes an L shaped house, but certainly a house with a spacious hall at one time, and (2) a much smaller, cottage type of farmhouse. These smaller houses are fascinating in their simplicity and lack of grandeur. They are to be seen at Bowe, Langstone, Barncott, Hr. Cliston (formerly Cheat), the rear part of Seccombe and, I think, at Sheplegh. Lower Cliston and Sweetstone are excellent examples of the other more imposing type of house.

Bowe. *D. Seymour.*

Lower Cliston. *D. Seymour.*

I very much wonder whether these may not be the houses of the villeins of the royal manor of Domesday. On the lower rung of the feudal ladder were the bordars; do the smaller, humbler houses mark their dwellings? No one would claim for these houses that they are the actual buildings, but where rebuilding does take place in a rural backwater such as this, it is very often on the old foundations. So the old plan is preserved and the houses retain their old proportions. I think that among these old houses on the Torre Abbey manor there is much to make us ponder.

It remains to consider a few statistics. In 1288 Avetone was taxed by Pope Nicholas at £3.13.4. In the Devonshire Lay Subsidy of 1332 thirty-seven names are mentioned and an unexpected occupation is mentioned. Robert Pira and John Pirya surely took their name from the making of perry (cf. Greendale, where the same thing occurred). These pear orchards must have flourished in the sheltered Gara valley.

In "Valor Ecclesiasticus" the annual value of the manor was £54.14.8—the highest return from all the Canons' properties. But when one considers that it stretched from Stanborough to the sea its value is not surprising. As elsewhere, sheep-rearing would be the most profitable occupation.

Blackawton was granted to Lord John Russell and Anne his wife in 1539.

Total land in manor of Blackawton (D.C.f.131a).

Strete 16 ferlings, Wood juxta Strete 3, Fuge 6, Burlestone 10, Combe 4, Ford 2, West Down 2, East Down 2½, Sweetstone 2, Preston 3½, Dallacombe 2, Sheplegh 1, Abbotsleigh 5, Millcombe 2¼, Weston Down 1½, Hutcherleigh 2, Hingston Post 6, Avetone 4, Woodford 1, West Hartley and Warthe 3, East Hartley 2, Dreyton 1, Shinerston 2, Cliston 3, Stone 2, Wadstray 4, Cotterbury 3½ Hole 3, Total 99½ ferlings.

36

Monksmoor, Ugborough

In his Foundation Charter Lord William Brewer gave the Canons of Torre a ferling of land at Ugborough with grazing rights on Dartmoor. He is said both by Reichel and Risdon to have acquired the manor in 1190. Like the manor of Torre, Ugborough passed to his daughter Alice de Mohun after the death of her childless brother, and the de Mohuns were still lords of the fee in 1346. In "Feudal Aids" for that year (p. 397) we read ". . . of John de Mohun, one fee in Ugborough of the honour of Plympton from John de Mohun the holder".

The identification of the ferling given by Lord William looked at first as though it was going to be difficult, but it must be remembered that the large parish of the present day was divided into several manors, Ulgeberge, Langeforda, Pech, Coma and Lodebroc. So

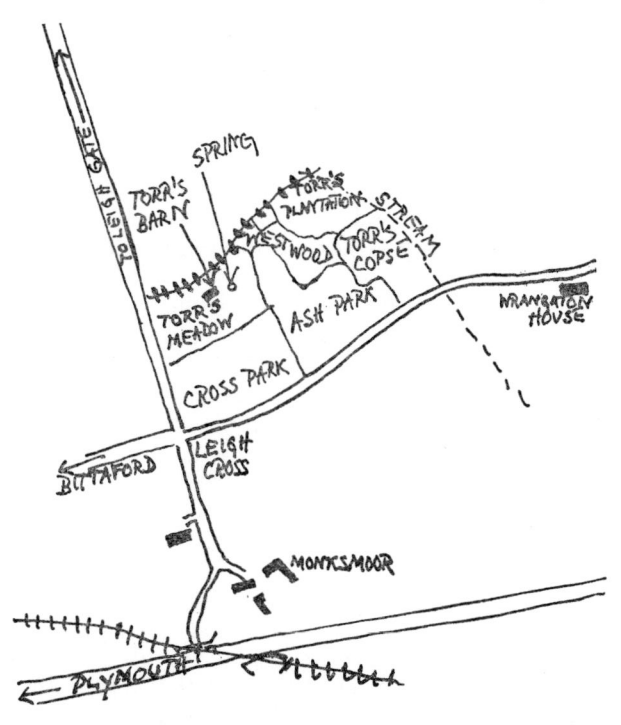

Ugborough, Ferling of Land at Monksmoor.   *D. Seymour.*

the search narrowed down to the actual manor of Domesday Ulgeberge, which must have centered round the church and village. Careful perusal of the map suggested that the farm with the name of Monksmoor might be a likely spot to inspect, for its very name gave authority to a probable ecclesiastical connection. As the crow flies Monksmoor stands about a mile above the village on high ground, and upon the direct road from Ugborough to Leigh Gate, which opens upon the Dartmoor commons. It would be up this old road that through the centuries cattle from the manor wended their way to the rich pasture on the hills above. Further to the east are Wrangaton Gate and Peak Gate, showing how each manor had its own access to the moor. Owley Gate, which may have lost its old name, was the place of access for the manor of Langeforde. Monksmoor stands only a few yards away from the hectic A38 which cuts through the old farm lands; the house, outbuildings and surrounding walls are of obvious antiquity. The present farmer, Mr. Jayne, was able to furnish me with much information concerning the farm. I told him that I was looking for a small farm within a larger one, and he was immediately able to give me the astonishing information that just above Leigh Cross are Torr's Barn, Torr's Meadow Torr's Copse and Torr's Plantation. An old sale catalogue dating from the early 1900's substantiated all that he had said; it also gave the acreage of the fields concerned. Inspection of the site showed a small farm, formerly complete in itself, with one remaining building to mark the farmyard site—Torr's Barn. Beside it is the spring which all those years ago had made the site possible for both human beings and cattle. The boundaries are the stream in Wrangaton Bottom on the east side, the old coach road to Plymouth on the south, and on the west the road to the moor already discussed. Only to the north is there an artificial boundary and it consists of a massive bank of earth and boulders suggesting great age.

The old farm stands on a steep downward gradient, easing towards the south where Torr's Meadow, Cross Park and Ash Park are situated. The rest is a wooded slope in which old enclosures and the fragmentary remains of old walls are yet to be seen. These have long gone to ruin, and the evidence is that the farm was abandoned at an early period for the more hospitable slopes below. What we see now is no doubt the forerunner of Monksmoor; it was allowed to go back and has been no more than a cattle run for centuries.

The survival of the name of Torr's (spelt thus on the map with its possessive apostrophe) is remarkable, yet exactly the same thing occurs at Waddeton Court and is discussed in another chapter. There is very little doubt that the old farm buildings stood close to Torr's Barn. This is a fine building in excellent preservation. It consists of two storeys—advantage having been taken of the steep downward slope. There are excellent tunnel-like dry courses on its north and west sides. The walls may be mediaeval in part— certainly the west wall with its beautiful dry stone walling appears so.

The little farm consists of between 17 and 18 acres, showing that the ferling here was much less than, say, at Coffinswell, where I found it to be 26 to 27 acres. It is my opinion that the ferling in Devon contained a larger acreage in fertile parts of the county than on the barren slopes of Dartmoor. At Monksmoor in 1196 this land would only recently have been reclaimed from the moor and anything but easy to plough.

It has been argued that Monksmoor got its name from the monks of Plympton Priory who were given Wrangaton Manor by King Henry II in 1160. But that manor at the time of Domesday was a part of Langeforde Lestre, never of Ugborough. All the evidence is that Monksmoor has always been in Ugborough. Even in modern times a

Wrangaton Estate map of 1905 does not include it. So the arguments to the contrary are not at all convincing.

Another point which could be brought against my case for Monksmoor is that the manor of Pech (later Torpeak) was owned by the de la Torre family. Could the Torr names at the farm by any chance refer to them? The answer is that the de la Torre's only held Pech for a brief period—1260-1379. It is therefore quite unlikely that their name would cling to fields in another manor.

So, when all the evidence has been sifted, I feel that the case for the little farm around Torr's Barn being the ferling which Lord William Brewer gave to the Canons of Torre in 1196 is a strong one, for nowhere else in Ugborough can another such site be found.

There is no further mention of Monksmoor in the Cartulary, so it seems that the Canons parted with it before the dissolution.

37

Glascombe

The Charters:—

240. A confirmation from William de Lestre to the Canons of Torre of all the land between the east and west Glazebrook and the wood of Glascombe. The boundary extends north to Nywapitte. Grazing rights and all easements etc. are granted on the moor but not the public highway to Dartmoor. All this in exchange for a ferling of land at la Hethe given to the Canons by William's father, Geoffrey. Clause of Warranty.
Date: c. 1250.   MS: Folio 97.

241. A confirmation from Abbot John to William atteffenne of the land of Glascombe for a 5/- rent. Suit of court annually at Avetone. Clauses of Distraint and Warranty. Relief 10/-.
Date: c. 1350.   MS: Folio 97/80.

These two charters concern a small piece of land on the southern fringe of Dartmoor which was a part of the manor of Langeforde Lestre. They describe a pleasant place, for of all the southern approaches to the moor that by way of Glascombe is perhaps the most delightful. The land given was in the shape of a triangle whose apex was Glazemeet and whose base was a wall joining the east and west Glazebrooks. When walking up from Owley the whole farm may be seen at a glance. At the northern end is said to be Nywapitte and this perhaps refers to extensive tinworkings on the western stream. It is interesting to learn that they may be as old as the 13th century. The name suggests that this was a new "pit" at that time. In the Dublin Cartulary a lengthy document on the rights of stannators is included. It dates from this period, and I think we are safe in assuming that through ownership of this land and nearby Monksmoor the Abbot of Torre would consider himself a Stannator, i.e. one with a right to prospect for tin. Further evidence is the ruins of a blowing house lower down the stream at Glazemeet.

William de Lestre (or del Estre) was then lord of the manor, and he occurs in the "Book of Fees" in 1242/43. Mr. H. G. Hurrell tells me that he is also mentioned in a document relating to Owley in 1256. Charter 240 may therefore date from c. 1250. The wood of Glascombe is also mentioned, and whether its extent was similar to what we see today no one can say, but I imagine that very little will have changed with regard to boundaries. Glascombe would be a useful sheep farm. At the northern extremity its boundary is now a massive wall which runs alongside the old road which climbs onto the moor by way of Diamond Lane, passes behind Corringdon Ball and so on to Spurrells's Cross. Grazing rights and turbary within the manor boundaries were given on all these commons.

At the bottom of the hill and beside the west Glaze Brook are still to be seen the

Glascombe.   D. Seymour.

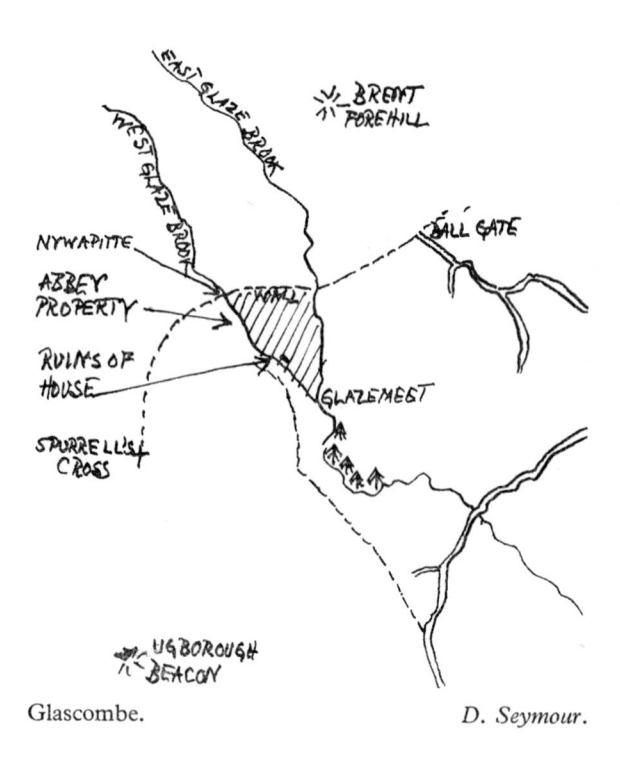

remains of a small farmhouse. An imposing entrance with tall granite gateposts stands beside a ford over the stream. Before the house is a yard, and traces of a former pond; there are also gateways in good condition. A clump of trees shelter the homestead from the prevailing wind. All these signs point to recent occupation and it is probable that there has been continuous occupation here from mediaeval times up to the opening of the present century. An excavation of the house to determine its age would no doubt be rewarding.

Now the charter records that in recognition of William de Lestre's gift the Canons agreed to return to him a ferling of land which his father, Geoffrey, had given to them. It is recorded in the first "Papalia" document and nowhere else; it is referred to as the land of "la Hethe" in charter 240, but there it is said to be at "Inkkeston". Now the manor of Ingsdon often appears spelt thus in this period, and bearing in mind that Heathfield is not far away, we are given the clue to its whereabouts. I am grateful to Mr. R. Wills of Narracombe, Ilsington, who pointed out to me that there were three former "heathfields" on Bovey Heath. They belonged to the three manors of Ilsington, Ingsdon and Bovey Tracey. The Ingsdon field was close to the A38 and not far from the

Stover Golf Course. Heathfields were grazing enclosures much larger than the small mediaeval enclosures, and to find one of about 25 acres in extent would not be surprising. So we may be reasonably sure that the land given to Torre Abbey by Geoffrey de Lestre was in fact Ingsdon Heathfield.

The second of the Glascombe charters is a lease of land to William atteffenne and his heirs by Abbot John. The rent was to be 5/- per annum and suit of court was to be made at Avetone (Blackawton). If the rent was unpaid then the Abbot could exercise distraint throughout la fenne. Venn, situated about a mile from Wrangaton Cross, will be the place referred to. There is still an ancient house standing here. William atteffenne is mentioned in 1346 in "Feudal Aids", so this charter may date from the time of Abbot John Gras in the mid 14th century, and it is a lease of the Glascombe property. Like Monksmoor, there is no further mention of Glascombe in the cartulary.

For the casual visitor who likes a short stroll on the moor a visit to Glascombe can be recommended. It is a little over a mile from Owley Gate whence a track can be followed all the way. This will be the "public highway" mentioned in charter 240, so even in those days it was an important approach road to southern Dartmoor.

38

North Shillingford

About a mile and a half south-west of Alphington is the small village of Shillingford Abbot. It is marked Lower Shillingford on older maps, but a recent vicar, knowing of the Torre Abbey connection with nearby farms, fought officialdom for many years until the name was changed to Shillingford Abbot. The barton farmhouse still stands in part, though the old manor courthouse was destroyed by fire some twenty years ago. In the Cartulary it is always known as North Shillingford. Colvin in his "White Canons in England" mistakes this holding of Torre Abbey for the Shillingford near Bampton. But the Cartulary makes it very clear that these fertile acres on the good red soil of South Devon were in the parish of Exminster.

Shillingford Barton before the Fire. *D. Seymour.*

The gift of this land goes right back to 1199, when it was bought by Lord William Brewer. In the Foundation Charter he says, "Moreover I gave and conceded to the aforesaid Canons all my land of Northschillyngforde.... which I bought from William Traci for 80 marks in silver". There are 16 charters dealing with this property and charters 242-3-7-8-51-52 give the student an excellent idea of legal usage at the close of the 12th century, with regard to gifts of property. As at Wolborough and Greendale Lord William bought the property from William de Traci so that he could give it to the Canons. Then there follows the various confirmations of the gift. The Final Concord was given at Wilton on St. Hilary's Day, 1199, when Abbot Adam gave Drogo de Montgiroun, Lord of the Fee, 32 marks in recognition of the transaction. By this time Lord William must have bought North Shillingford, thus enabling the Final Concord with Drogo de Montgiroun to be made. This all points to the date of the Abbey's Foundation Charter being after January, 1199, when all legal transactions had been concluded and Lord William was free to make his gift to the Canons.

There are two charters which show the previous holders of the land (245 and 256). It had passed from Osmund de Schillyngford to Everard Cole. He in his turn quitclaimed it to the Abbot of Torre. The remaining charters concern the land itself, rents exchanges etc. 249 is of interest for it shows how in 1235 there was a dispute with William de Bysiniano, rector of Exminster. The Abbot claimed that although North Shillingford was in the parish of Exminster, he had the right to the tithes on the gardens, orchards, meadows and pastures, through the gift of Lord William Brewer. He admitted that he was only allowed 200 sheep on the land where he paid no tithes. If he had more then it went to the Rector. This was agreed.

Charters 254/255 concern dealings between Abbot Richard and Henry Pynde of Bowhay. The land of this farm and the Canons' former Courthouse of Shillingford Barton adjoin. The latter charter was to produce one of the most satisfying finds in my researches into the former Abbey lands. 255 is an agreement whereby water is to be shared between the two farms for the purpose of irrigating the fields. Each farm was to enjoy the benefit of the water from a stream for six months of the year, after which it was diverted to the other farm. Some of the watercourses constructed for this purpose are still to be seen, and enquiry at both farms showed that the sharing of the water between the farmers in this shallow valley had gone on over the centuries in much the same way as the charter describes. Indeed it is only in the last few years that the practice has been discontinued.

More surprising still was the fact that I could locate a stream which Henry Pynde in the charter said flowed down between his hall and his kitchen. At first I expected to see a stream flowing under the house, but there was nothing of the sort at Bowhay. There was, however, a vigorous stream to be seen flowing rapidly down beside the house. On the other side of the stream stood a fine barn which at the end nearest the house displayed a magnificent old chimney of sandstone. Inside an open hearth is still in situ; it has, moreover, a nicely constructed oven with a well-shaped apex, all in sandstone. I therefore came to the conclusion that Henry had a free-standing kitchen. This, of course, was not at all unusual at that period. So strong is this chimneybreast that, when the kitchen went out of use, it was retained to become the end wall of the barn. It has been allowed to remain until the present day because steps made in its side give easy access to a loft on the first floor. Unfortunately the stack has been cut off at the level of the top of the gable of the barn. How much longer it will be allowed to remain depends upon whoever is farmer. I could do no more than record it. Whether we see today the actual chimney and fireplace of 1288 or a successor on the same site, who can say? But no one can deny that it exactly fulfils the description given in the charter.

In 1336 Richard de la Leye gave 2 ferlings to the Canons which Philip de Schillyngforde used to hold. The next charter is a licence in mortmain from King Edward III

Chimney at Bowhay. *D. Seymour.*

in which he politely says that he is unwilling that the Abbot or Richard or Thomas de Willeyurd (another tenant) should be inconvenienced by the statute.

Shillingford Barton, the Canons' courthouse, was a large E shaped house with Georgian additions at the rear. This will be considered fully at the end of this chapter. Bowhay is a strange jumble of a house. There are no recognisable features of Henry Pynde's original farmhouse to be seen now. One can only say that it wears an ancient air. The third farm in this remote corner is Pengelly's. It is recognisable as a really old house and has out-buildings, too, of decided age. Sometimes a farm loses its old name and takes the name of the farmer, perhaps a strong personality, who once resided there. The old name then becomes eclipsed, as it were. My own opinion is that this farm is the Willeyurd mentioned in 258, and for which 3/- was paid to the Abbot by Thomas de Willeyurd. For one thing the name tells its own tale, for in the yard at Pengelly's there is a more than usually active "wille" or spring—quite enough to give the place a name. Again, on the Tithe Map, adjoining the stream below the house is "Winnard's Meadow". Surely the similarity between Willeyard and Winnard can hardly be an accident.

Another lost property is Uppleye which is mentioned in 253, 257, 258. I consider that it was a holding now vanished which was at the rear of Bowhay. Here the Tithe Map shows adjacent fields called Higher, Middle, Lower and Back Ley. I wonder, too, whether this may not give a clue as to the whereabouts of the Domesday manor of Leia which

R

in the Exeter Domesday precedes "Selingforda". It consisted of half a hide. Could it be that it comprised all the land to the north of the road outside Shillingford Barton as far as the road on top of the ridge? If so, Bowhay and Willeyurd may have been a part of it. This presents a nice little problem for someone to solve. Then again there is no manor of Northshillingford in Domesday, so was it also a part of the manor of Leia in Saxon days? It seems that Richard de la Leye was lord of the fee. (257).

The Charters

242. A confirmation of all his land at Northschillyngforde from Drogo de Monte Giroun to the Canons of Torre. They are to hold it free and quit from William de Tracy for a ¼ of a knight's fee.
Date: c. 1199.   MS: Folio 81.

243. A confirmation of all his land at Northschillyngforde from William de Traci, son of Gervase de Curteny, to the Canons of Torre who gave him 80 marks in recognition. Given at Wilton on the Sunday after the Feast of the Epiphany, 1199.
MS: Folio 81.
Witnesses:— G. Wintone, episcopo, W. Briwere, magistro T. de Usseburne etc.

244. A quitclaim from Evarard Cole, made to the Abbot of Torre, of his entire holding of Schyllyngford which belonged to Osmund.
Date: c. 1199.   MS: Folio 81.

245. A grant of half his land at Sillyngforde made by Osmund de Schillyngforde to Everard Cole at a rent of 6/-. Given before Drogo de Mungerun, lord of the fee, Gellanus de Pomeria, Ralph ffanuel, and Herbert de Boslay.
Date: pre 1196.   MS: Folio 81.

246. A confirmation from Drogo de monte Geroldi to the Canons of Torre of all the land of North sillyngforde. To hold for ¼ of a knight's fee from tenant in chief.
Date: c. 1199.   MS: Folio 81.

247. A quitclaim from Henry, son of Count Reginald of Cornwall, to the Canons of Torre of suit of court due from Northsillyngforde to the Hundred court of Bradeneyse.
Date: 1196/99.   MS: Folio 81/82.

248. A quitclaim from Richard, Earl of Cornwall, to the Canons of Torre of suit of Court due to the Hundred court of Bradeneys.
Date: Given at London, July 16th, 1248.   MS: Folio 82.   Witnesses:—William Wyntone, bishop, William Sarum, bishop; G. de Lucy, Peter de Mara, Giles of the Chancellery, Alexander Giffard, Roger de ffrinille, John, son of Thomas, knights; Philip de Eya, William Blundel, clerics and many others.

249. Since a dispute has arisen between William de Bysiniano, rector of Exeminister, and the Abbot of Torre over the tithe, the Canons declared before the Lateran Council that by gift from William Brewer they have right to tithes in Exeminister and also the tithes on their gardens, orchards meadows and pasture. William has therefore conceded these rights to them for the duration of his life. If the Abbot, however, has more than 200 sheep on this land then he pays tithe to William. But on all the others tithe is to be paid

to the mother church whether they are in a close or not. Exception: those in the old close near the house. The Abbot pays William 2/- per annum at Midsummer for this agreement.
Date: The Vigil of St. Barnabas, 1235. MS: Folio 82.

250. A Letter of Testimony from the Prior of St. Nicholas', Exeter, to R., Bishop of Salisbury; he has examined the evidence above. They (the Abbot and Rector) both appeared before him and agreed to the terms which are placed in the Bishop's hands. Signed by Thomas, Archdeacon of Totnes.
Date: 1235. MS: Folio 82/83.

251. A Final Concord made in the court at Wilton between the Abbot of Torre and Drogo de Mungirum whereby the latter quitclaimed the manor of Schillyngforde to the Abbot in the presence of G., Bishop of Winchester, and the Justices, William Brywer and Thomas Usseburne.
Date: Saturday after the Feast of St. Hilary, 1199. MS: Folio 83.

252. A Final Concord made in the court at Wilton between the Abbot of Torre and William de Tracey whereby the latter quitclaimed the manor of Northschillyngforde in favour of the Abbot.
Date: Saturday after the Feast of St. Hilary, 1199. MS: Folio 83.

253. A Final Concord in the King's Court at Exeter between Robert, Abbot of Torre, and Adam, the son of Peter, whereby the former recognised that a ferling of land at sillyngforde was Adam's by right: to hold from the Abbot at 8/-. A quarter of a ferling to be held by Roger de Uppelegh from Adam for 12d. After his death it was to revert to Adam. For this agreement Adam gave the Abbot a messuage which William de la Hulle held in exchange for $2\frac{1}{2}$ acres of demesne land in Ulvescroft.
Date: Thursday before the Feast of St. John the Baptist, 1228. MS: Folio 83.

254. An agreement between Brother Richard, Abbot of Torre, and Henry Pynde of Northschillyngforde whereby the Abbot gives Henry 6 acres in the northern part of Somermore and $\frac{1}{4}$ east of Henry's house, in exchange for 5 acres in la Suburgehaye. Clauses of Warranty on both sides.
Date: Friday before the Feast of St. George, 1275. MS: Folio 83/84.

255. An agreement between Brother Richard, Abbot of Torre, and Henry Pynde of Schillyngforde whereby they agree to irrigate and water their fields by means of a stream which flows into Henry's close called Widehay, and by another flowing down between Henry's hall and his kitchen. They will be made to flow through the middle of the close to take water through the Canons' land: this it will irrigate for six months between Michaelmas and April 1st. After this the water to return to its old course. The Canons give Henry land to help this scheme at a rent of 4d.
Date: The Feast of St. George the Martyr, 1288. MS: Folio 84. Witnesses:—
Philip de Schillyngforde, Walter de Braynton and many others.

256. A recognition from Drogo de Moungiroun that Odelina, daughter of Osmund de Schillyngforde and wife of William de Schillyngforde, shall inherit 3 ferlings of land there which were her father's. Rent 12/- per annum. William and Odelina then gave Drogo 3 marks in silver.

Date: pre 1196. MS: Folio 84/85. Witnesses:—William, then chaplain of Exemynster, Robert the tumbler and others.

257. A gift to the Canons of Torre from Richard de la Leye of 2 ferlings of land which Philip de Schillyngforde used to hold from him in chief for 1d. with his homage. The Canons to hold on the same terms. Clause of Warranty.
Date: Feast of St. Margaret the Virgin, 1336. (from D.C.). MS: Folio 85. Witnesses:— William de St. Helena, William la Moygne, William de Deneforde and many others.

258. A licence in mortmain from King Edward III granted to the Abbot of Torre and enabling him to receive 1d. rent from Richard de Upley and a 3/- rent at Willeyurd from Thomas de Willeyurd.
Date: None given, probably mid 14th century. MS: Folio 85.

Shillingford Barton

This chapter would be incomplete without a description of the Canons' former courthouse. An extensive Georgian house was built onto the back of the old house and became a part of it. After the disastrous fire this became the inhabited part of the house. The lower courses of the walls of the burnt out house were fortunately retained as garden walls, so it was possible to make a plan. A kitchen and offices have been constructed in the part marked A. The kitchen is entered by the old cobbled porch which was once the main entrance. Here the original front door remains. It somehow survived the fire and is the only thing about the house which the Canons might recognise.

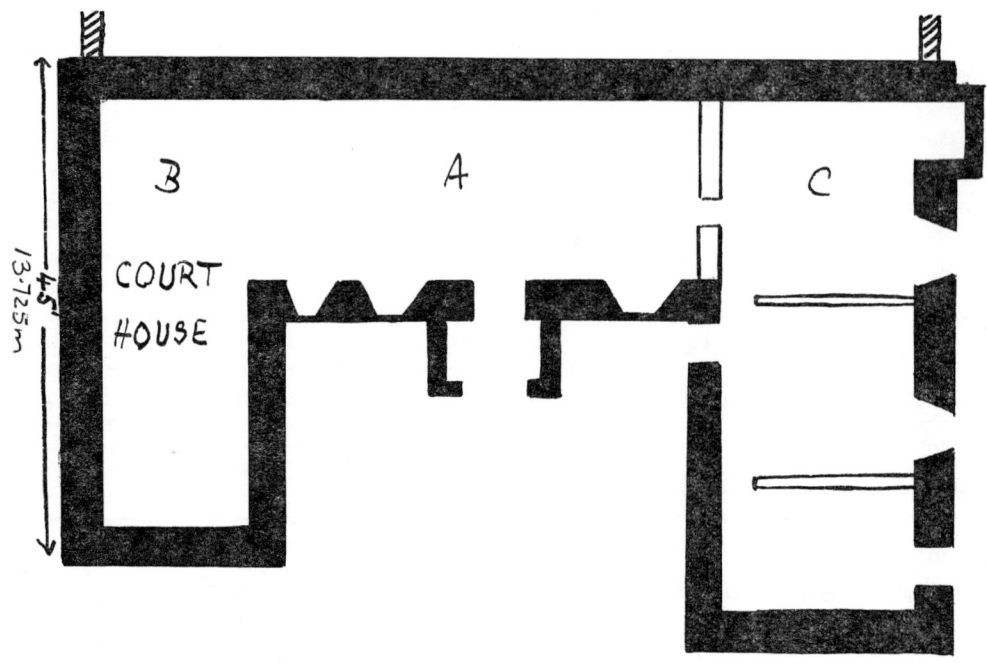

Shillingford Barton. *D. Seymour.*

Fortunately an excellent photograph of the old house is in existence and shows it to have been E shaped. If the whole house was mediaeval then it was a far grander house than the other courthouses which the Canons possessed. What probably happened here is that an L shaped house has had an extra wing added to make the courthouse. This could have been either at B or C. But in wing C is the old kitchen which has a massive fireplace and chimney; and I consider it most unlikely that the position of the old kitchen would be changed. It would be far more likely that an entirely new wing was added at B when a courthouse was required. This wing is nearly 10 ft. shorter than C, but it measures 45 ft. which is just about the same measurement as the Canons' other courthouses.

There is little doubt that a chapel existed here in monastic times. The large meadow east of the house is "Chapel Meadow". The Tithe Map shows it as a much smaller enclosure close to the house. I have made a diligent search for any signs of the old chapel, but there is nothing to be seen.

The Tithe Map also shows "Mill Meadow" beside the stream below the house. A right of way crosses the stream below the house, and there is remembrance of a water mill standing there long ago. Many of the barton outbuildings are of great age. They form an impressive group all in red sandstone. The tithe barn, however, is of cob. Its walls are crumbling in places, but it is still a fine sight. The position of the old gatehouse can easily be discerned from the lie of the buildings near the entrance.

Mr and Mrs Paul, the present owners, told me that there are water courses beneath the yard. About half a mile W.N.W. are two small ponds. They are artificially made and must once have been the main water supply of the farmyard and house. Although water was close at hand in the stream below the house, yet this could not be brought up to the much higher level required unless a leat was made higher up the valley on land belonging to Bowhay. Did the Canons, I wonder, make the ponds? If so, they must then have had a really adequate water supply.

Shillingford Barton is a place of great charm where the spirit of the past clings persistently, and it was a pleasure to visit it and work there.

In the village of Shillingford St. George there stands a good example of a mediaeval cross of sandstone. I am told that this was once in the garden of Shillingford Lodge, a little to the east of the barton; and there is a distinct possibility that it was a boundary mark of the Torre Abbey property there. The late Mr. G. P. Earwaker, formerly of Shillingford Lodge, told me that in the early part of this century there was a gate across the lane just outside his house. Thus the lane which leads to Shillingford Barton, Bowhay and Pengelly's could be shut off, as though leading to private property. It suggests that these farms may have come down through the centuries as one property almost to the present time.

Further References

Taxation of Pope Nicholas, 1288
"Shillyngforde" paid £2.4.8.

Devonshire Lay Subsidy
No names under Exminster suggest a connection with the Canons' property.

Valor Ecclesiasticus
Shillyngforde was valued at £12.2.0.

A.O., Particulars for Grants 856

From grant to John Southcott of Bovey Tracey, 23 Dec. 1540:—"Manor of Shillyngford Abbates in the parish of Exmynster: Free and customary rents, £6.10d.; farm of the chief messuage called North Shillyngford ...... 53s.4d. Court profits according to the book of the tenth 36s.4d.:—£10.10.6.

Certified by Mathew Colthurst.

"Sir the woodes growing upon the premysses be not yet surveide wherefore I pray you take recognysaunce of the partie:

Yours Tho. Pope".

39

Cockington

The Cockington charters may be divided into three groups:—(1) Torre Abbey's relations with St. Dogmael's Abbey, Pembrokeshire. (2) Grants of water given by the lords of the manor of Cockington. (3) Privileges granted to the Canons.

It always comes as something of a surprise to those interested in the history of Cockington Church to learn that it once belonged to an Abbey in Wales—yet such was the case. In the early 12th century Robert FitzMartin, lord of Dartington, was also lord of Cockington. He founded the Abbey of St. Mary and St. Dogmael (or St. Domuel) in Pembrokeshire, one mile west of Cardigan. It stood in a region known as Cameys or Kemys, and was possibly built on or near the site of a far older Celtic monastery. Those interested may read E. M. Pritchard's "The History of St. Dogmael's Abbey". Robert FitzMartin founded his Abbey c. 1113/15 for a prior and 12 monks, and it was a daughter house of the French abbey of Tiron. He endowed it with certain lands and churches among which were the church of Rattery and the chapel of Cockington; so when Torre Abbey was founded in 1196 the Welsh abbey had owned Cockington chapel for over eighty years. The earliest charter which we have dealing with the subject is 262, which was given by Bishop Bartholomew Iscanus c. 1162/65.

The charters dealing with St. Dogmael's Abbey are as follows:

259. A confirmation to R(oger), Abbot of Torre, from A., Abbot of St. Domuel's of Kamasia, of a gift of all the land at Cokyntone which they (St. Domuel's) have by gift from Robert FitzMartin. A rent of 5/-.
Bishop Bartholomew's charter (262) surrendered.
Date: 1203.   MS: Folio 86.

270. Under the seals of the Priories of Pembrok, Averforde and Kardikun, R., Abbot of St. Dogmael's, sends to R., Abbot of Torre, a transcript of the original charter of Robert FitzMartin, their Founder. In it he gives to the church of St. Mary of Cameys the Churches of Treygrut and Rattre; also the chapel of Kokyntone.
Date: c.1203.   MS: Folio 90.
(Misplaced in the original, this charter is now placed among those dealing with the same subject).

260. A quitclaim of the chapel of kokyntone from Master Walter de Pembrok, Rector of St. Mary's, Rattrew. He has seen the charter (259) signed by Abbot R. (a mistake for A.) of St. Domuel's, bearing the Abbey seal; he understands that Torre Abbey pays a rent of 5/- annually.
Date: October 8th, 1203.   MS: Folio 86.

261. A confirmation from W(illiam), Bishop of Exeter, stating that as the Abbot and Convent of St. Domuel's and the Rector of Rattrew, have ceded the chapel of kokyntone to the Abbot and Convent of Torre, it is placed under the jurisdiction of the parish church of Torre.
Date: January 19th, 1203.   MS: Folio 87.

262. A confirmation from Bartholomew, Bishop of Exeter, of a quitclaim made in his presence by Roger de Cokyntone to Abbot Roger of St. Mary of Cammeis, of the secular service known as hutibannus on 2 ferlings of sanctuary land at kokyntone.
Date: 1162/65.   MS: Folio 87.

316. A quitclaim made to Richard, Abbot of Torre, from Philip, Abbot of the monastery of St. Mary and St. Dogmael in kemys, of the chapel of St. George and St. Mary at Cokyngton, together with the tithe and all offerings there: also all lands, tenements, rents etc. at Cokyngton.
Date: July 1st, 1469.   MS: Folio 107/8.

317. A sealed indenture testifying that Richard, Abbot of Torre, delivered the sum of £63.6.8 to Thomas Kermerdyne, Prior of Caldey, David John and John Apprys for Philip Saunder, Abbot of St. Mary and St. Dogmael at Kemys: it is for the quitclaim given by Abbot Philip of any further rights that he might have in the chapel of St. George and St. Mary at Cokyngton or its tithes and appurtenances. Sealed by both sides.
Date: July 18th, 1469.   MS: Folio 108.

318. A quitclaim from Philip, Abbot of St. Mary and St. Dogmael at Kemys, to the Abbot of Torre of any kind of action, demand or dispute which he might make against the Church of Torre.
Date: July 1st, 1469.   MS: Folio 108.

319. A document in which the Abbot of St. Mary and St. Dogmael, of the order of Tiron, and in the diocese of Menevia (St. David's) rehearses the ancient claims which his Abbey has to the chapel of Cokyngton. He introduces John Prise, Bachelor of Laws, as his attorney and special messenger. Given in the chapterhouse of St. Dogmael's.
Date: January 18th, 1467.   MS: Folio 108/9.

Charter 262, the oldest of the St. Dogmael's series and possibly one of the oldest in the Cartulary, resolves a dispute between Roger (1) de Cockington and the Abbot of St. Dogmael's. Both were summoned before Bartholomew Iscanus, Bishop of Exeter, because the case had apparently been referred to him by the civil court. Roger maintained that he was entitled to the royal service from the Abbot known as "hutibannus", but admitted that his uncle, Robert FitzMartin had given the Abbot 2 ferlings in perpetual alms. He produced a charter from King Henry 1st confirming the gift. The Abbot then said that for thirty years and more his Abbey had enjoyed the gift free and quit of all service. Eventually Roger agreed to remit any further claim to this service. So there was much activity at Cockington long before Torre Abbey came on the scene, and the full Latin text of this charter of which I have given a resumé is full of interest.

There is little doubt that the chapel and land at Cockington soon became an embarrassment rather than a boon to St. Dogmael's on account of its distance from Pembrokeshire. It is not surprising therefore to find in 259, the first charter of the group, that St. Dogmael's wished to lease Cockington chapel and its two ferlings of land for

5/- per annum. 260 is a quitclaim of the chapel given in 1203 by the Rector of Rattery, Master Walter de Pembrok. Now Rattery church was also given by Robert FitzMartin to St. Dogmael's, and the Rector states that he has seen charter 259, leasing Cockington to Torre Abbey. He must have been quite glad to get rid of it if he was responsible for arranging the services there and perhaps riding over to take them himself sometimes. In January, 1203, (the same year as 260 by the Calendar then in use) episcopal approval was given to the transfer of the chapel to Torre Abbey. Bishop Brewer's name appears at the beginning of the confirmation in 261, but this must be a mistake on the part of our scribe, for Bishop Brewer did not assume office until over twenty years later. Bishop Henry Marshall was clearly meant on account of the definite date given. The scribe also made an error in 260, mentioning Abbot "R." of St. Dogmael's when Abbot "A.", who gave the previous charter, is being referred to.

So in 1203 Cockington Chapel was placed under the jurisdiction of the parish church of Torre. How amazing it is to think that this arrangement worked for nearly 679 years, for until the year 1882 Cockington had no more status than a chapel of ease to Torre; after 1882 it at last became a parish church. In monastic times the Canons would be responsible for the services as they were at Torre church.

There is no more mention of St. Dogmael's Abbey until the final four charters of the Cartulary which date from the 1460's, when some sort of trouble seems to have flared up. Whether the payment of the 5/- rent had lapsed over the years or whether Torre Abbey got weary of paying it we cannot tell. All that the charters reveal is that in 1467 St. Dogmael's attorney, John Prise, arrived at Torre with a lengthy document from his Abbey, rehearsing its claims and ancient privileges with regard to the chapel of Cockington. Two years later Abbot Richard Cade sent the sum of £63.6.8. to the Abbot of St. Dogmael's by John Prise, David John and the Prior of Caldey. This was a very large sum at that time, and through paying it the Canons of Torre had Cockington chapel, its tithes and the 2 ferlings of sanctuary land in their possession for good. Abbot Philip of St. Dogmael's made a final quitclaim of Cockington on July 1st, 1469, and that was the last that the Canons heard of St. Dogmael's Abbey.

There are five charters concerning the gift of water to the Abbey by the de Cockington family; they are as follows:—

264. A gift in perpetual alms from Roger de Cokyntone to the Church of the Holy Trinity at Torre of the stream of ffuleforde. It is on behalf of his own soul and that of M., his wife., and all his forbears and successors. The canons may repair and clean the watercourse four times a year. At the source they may have (a channel) 4 ft. in width, but where it crosses Roger's land, 2 ft. in width. His right to water cattle at the stream to be preserved. The Canons may quarry stone in the east part of Corvenasse below Tynaldclive. They may take nothing beyond Grungnium nor damage the two rock pillars there; they may not take away millstones. Pigs from the Abbey may have the run of the quarry, but may not go beyond towards Livermead. etc.
Date: mid 13th century.   MS: Folio 88.

265. An agreement between Roger de Cokyntone and brother Richard, Abbot of Torre, whereby he gives all the water below the millrace at ffuleforde mill which begins at Schirewelle. Roger reserves his right to all water flowing into the millrace. The Canons may take the water to the Abbey over Roger's land at Twynbrok. Rights of access, cleaning, repairing etc. Clause of Warranty.

Date: Wednesday, the Feast of St. Katherine, 1293. MS: Folio 88/89. Witnesses: Robert le Denys, Richard de Kirkham, knights, William de Sciresestre, William de Comptone, John Bitelgate, Guy de Restercombe, Robert de Doddescombe and many others.

266. A confirmation of water from Schirwelle and adjacent streams made to the Canons of Torre by Henry de Cokyntone, son of Roger, formerly lord of that manor, and brother of W. who made the gift.
Date: 1330/45. MS: Folio 89. Witness: Walter de Nimeth.

267. A gift from William, lord of Cokyntone, to God and St. Mary and the Canons of Torre, made on behalf of his own soul and that of Johanna, his wife. It consists of his body for burial and the water from Schirewelle brook which, after it has passed the mill wheel, is to be conducted under the centre of ffulforde bridge and thence to the Abbey by the old water course. Rights of entry etc. The Canons to maintain a chaplain to celebrate mass on Wednesdays at Cokynton chapel for their souls. If a Feast day, then the mass to be said the day before or the day after. On other days the mass will be at the altar of St. John the Baptist at the Abbey church. Clause of Warranty.
Date: 1330/45. MS: Folio 89. Witnesses: Walter de Nymet, Richard de Lumena, Jordan de Haccombe, William de ffissacre, Johel de Bukynton, knights, Herbert de Morcell, Walrond de Cirencestre, Roger de Punchardon, Robert de Cumpton and others.

268. Brother Symon, Abbot of Torre, undertakes to maintain a chaplain to say mass at the altar of St. John the Baptist in the Abbey church for William de Cokynton and his wife Johanna; for it was he who gave the water from Scirewelle, confirming it by a charter displayed above the altar in the chapel where his body lies. Conditions as in 267. Should the water be diverted the terms of this charter will be annulled.
Date: 1330/45. MS: Folio 89/90. Witnesses: Richard de Lumena, Herbert de Morcell, Walrond de Cirencestre, Robert de Cumpton, Roger de Punchardon, Jordan the clerk, Roger de Stantorr and others.

It is quite clear that in the early days the Abbey had a rather inadequate water supply. The Foundation Charter gave the Canons the right to make ponds and a fishpond at "Northwille de Torre" and to construct a leat to the Abbey. Northwille may have been so called because it was north of the other spring in Torre—St. Petroc's well. It might have been on the fairly level piece of ground near Torquay Police Station. Near here a mediaeval well was discovered not long ago during alterations to the Torbay Inn. Certain 19th century maps also testify to springs in this locality; so it should have been possible to make ponds here.

The next gift of water was from St. Petroc's spring which flowed down beside the courthouse kitchen, and was given by William Brewer the Younger (11). This was between 1226 and 1232, so the Canons then did a little better, but the swift-flowing streams which they must have coveted were all on the land of the lord of Cockington. By the mid century they must have been on good terms with Roger (2) de Cockington who in 264 gave them water from Fulleforde brook and the right to conduct it to the Abbey over his land. Now Fulleforde brook rises above Torre Station near Lowes Bridge and flows down what is now called the Torre valley. It was the boundary between Torre and Cockington manors and was a swift-flowing stream. We see it today beside the King's Drive. The mill after which Old Mill Road and Mill Lane are named, was Fulleforde Mill, and it stood very near the railway bridge in Old Mill Road. The mill was worked with water from it, but after this gift Roger seems to have used the Sherwell Brook as well.

But the Canons were desirous of getting even more water, perhaps to work a mill within the precincts. At any rate in 1293 Roger and Abbot Richard made an agreement whereby Roger granted him the water which had worked the mill wheel and came from Sherwell Brook. The water was to be taken to the Abbey by way of Twynbrok—the name for the open space now known as Torre valley north. It used to belong to the Devon Rosery, and I can remember when the Fulleforde Brook and the Sherwell Brook both flowed through it.

But an even better gift was made by William de Cockington in 267, for he gave the Abbey all the water from Sherwell Brook. The Canons now had the combined waters of Fulleforde and Sherwell, and this at last worked their mill in the precincts (see 281). The Sherwell Brook was made to bypass the mill after water had been drawn off to work it, and it merged with the Fulleforde Brook, flowing along the old leat to the Abbey which used to take the latter stream only. William and his wife were granted a chantry, and he at any rate was buried in the Chapel of St. John the Baptist, where his charter giving the water was displayed over the altar. Now the date of this gift must be about 1330/45 (the dates of Abbot Symon mentioned in 268), and this tallies with the probable date of the extension of the north aisle of Cockington Church, which was surely built to house William de Cockington's chantry chapel.

The final arrangement of the Abbey water supply was made unexpectedly easy for me when a map of Torquay, dating from the 1860's, turned up at Torquay Town Hall. No building had then taken place in the vicinity of the streams, and I found a double avenue of trees marked in Avenue Road. The leat occupied the easternmost avenue and the road the other. Fulleforde Mill still existed under the title of "Cockington Mills". The water flowed behind it, and then under Fulleforde Bridge (which was at the four cross roads at the bottom of Mill Lane) and so reached the leat which then flowed along to the Abbey on level ground. The footpath in Avenue Road, which is exceptionally wide for its period, is now explained for it spans the filled-in leat. Where the two lodges at the Abbey gate now stand there was a pool, evidently the old millpond, whilst the subsidence in the soil beside the wall beyond shows the line of the filled-in channel taking the water to the house. It seems from this map that, until the advent of main water, Torre Abbey was using its old mediaeval water-courses well into the middle of the last century.

This is as good a time as any to consider the whereabouts of Efrideswille, which was mentioned in the Foundation Charter. The boundaries of Rowedone came up from the sea along the causeway known now as the King's Drive as far as the road from Cockington, passing through land where the Spring of Efrideswille was. There has been much speculation in the past as to where this spring or stream might be. A clergyman of the last century thought that it was St. Petroc's Well and so the drinking fountain outside Torre church had "Efrideswille" incised upon it. The road in which it stood was then called St. Efride's Road. This, of course, is complete nonsense, for there never was any such saint. "Efrides" means "ever ready", or in this case "ever flowing"; this is a most apt name for Fulleforde Brook; through over half a century I have never known it to dry up. I think it an older name for the brook, which later took the name of the full ford at the crossing place below Mill Lane. The boundary of Rowedone followed it up the valley, and that is why it was mentioned.

MONASTIC
WATER SUPPLY
(from map of c. 1860)

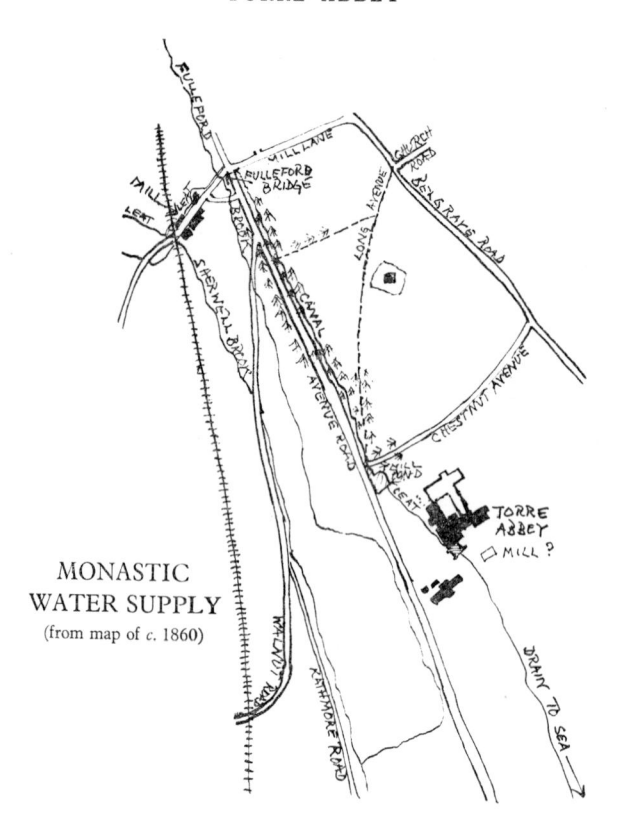

The third section of the Cockington charters deals with gifts and privileges granted to the Canons within the manor of Cockington. The charters are:—

263. A confirmation of an exchange of land between Roger de Cokyntone and the Canons of Torre. Twenty one and one sixth acres of arable land on the hill of La Windiete and a certain meadow next to the stream in the meadow of Chilleston in exchange for a meadow and sanctuary land belonging to the chapel of Kokinton. Clause of Warranty.
Date: 13th century. MS: Folio 87/88.

269. An agreement between James de Cokyntone and the Abbey of Torre whereby he confirms fishing rights at Levermede to the Canons. They may spread and dry their nets below the cliff on Cockington land.
Date: March 3rd, 1327/28. MS: Folio 90.

281. A confirmation made to the Canons of Torre from Sir Thomas Bourchier, lord of the manor of Cokyngton, of the charter which Henry de Cokynton made to Abbot John. In it the Canons were given 24 ft. of land throughout the length of the Abbey walls on the west side. He further confirms the gift of William de Cokynton, Henry's brother, giving

water from Shorewyll and fulford brooks which have been channelled to the mill in the Abbey.
Date: October 6th, 1471/72.   MS: Folio 94.   Witnesses: Oto Gylbert, Gylbert yerd, Joge merifeld and others.

In the second half of 264 Roger (2) de Cockington gives privileges to the Canons in the vicinity of Corbyn's Head, which was in the manor of Cockington. Here they were given quarrying rights. The mention of a tunnelled cliff deserves consideration. The scribe called it "tynaldclive" and until the 1930's one of the salient characteristics of Corbyn's Head was a rock standing a little way from the headland. It had a large hole in it and was much beloved by artists on account of its picturesque appearance. It was eventually washed away, and I much wonder if this was not the tunnelled cliff mentioned in the charter. No quarrying was allowed beyond "grungnium"—evidently another landmark, and there is also mention of rock pillars which must not be damaged. Quarrying was carried on here by the lords of the manor until well on into the 19th century. Upton Parish Church has records showing that when that church was built in the 1840's it was suggested that sandstone might be purchased from the quarry at Corbyn's Head.

I like the picture of monastic pigs straying about the quarry, and trust that the venturesome ones who strayed round to Livermead did not get mixed up with the Canons' nets. Charter 269 is in French, and in it James de Cockington gives rights to trawl and fish and dry nets below Livermead cliff.

In the final charter (281) we find that the de Cockingtons have gone and Sir Thomas Bourchier is lord of the manor. He confirms a gift of which we have no record in either Cartulary; it was a grant of 24 feet of land outside the Abbey wall on the west side. It was originally given by Henry de Cockington. After so many changes in the Torre valley it is quite impossible to guess why this land was given.

This chapter has shown how important to the Canons the grants and privileges made by the lords of the manor of Cockington were. The water supply, the fishing rights and the quarrying for stone all affected the daily lives of the Community to a marked degree. Without the friendly co-operation of successive lords of Cockington the monastery could not have been run so smoothly.

The Parish Church of St. George and St. Mary

The venerable old church at Cockington, said to be one of the most visited in England, has far more to show of monastic days, than the mother church of Torre. Of its ancient origin there can be no doubt, for even in the early 13th century charters it is referred to as "the ancient chapel of Cokynton".

There are two roundhead Norman doorways remaining: one is the west door to the north aisle, and the other is in the north porch. Both are survivors of the Norman chapel. The thirteenth century tower is the next oldest thing, and the Canons no doubt supervised its building. It is built of the local rubble and its walls are of great strength and thickness. The polygonal stair turret on the north side is a most attractive feature, with its slit windows and battlements. The chamber in the tower with a fireplace etc., is clearly meant for human habitation, and no doubt the Canon in charge of the services lived and slept here at times, in spite of being so near his Abbey. The officiating priest also had a

Cockington Church.   *D. Seymour.*

room over the former south porch, and here the business side of the church was probably transacted. A parvise in this room overlooks the north aisle.

Our pilgrimage in the steps of the Canons is well rewarded at Cockington, for there is much to see both within and without which can scarcely have changed since their day. Practically all the 18th century and Victorian work has been removed and the modern work, such as the new roofs and restoration of the rood screen, are in excellent taste.

The north aisle is unusual in that there is a join in the wall, showing two periods of building. I often wonder whether its two westermost bays are not the remains of the original chapel of Norman days. My reason is that it has a west door of that period. Moreover, it is the only door in the church which enters it at ground level. The other west doors all have an awkward entry by downward steps. Then again the north-east diagonal buttress of the tower does not fit symmetrically into the aisle. Such joins were usually carried out with skill and a reason for this imperfection might be that the west and north walls of the old chapel were retained when the tower and nave of the new church were built alongside; it would have measured about 27′9″ x 13′3″.

When in the 14th century the aisle was extended eastwards it would be to house the new chantry of William de Cockington. Here, too, is the small door by which the chantry priest entered and left the chapel after saying his mass on a Wednesday. After the suppression this chapel would become the squire's "pew". As a boy, the writer can remember seeing the Misses Mallock of Cockington Court enter by this north door for the Sunday services. They sat in the old chapel in a pew facing south. Thus, some six centuries after the founding of the chantry, the connection between the squire's family and this spot was perpetuated week by week.

In 1825 the two misericords in the sedilia were brought from Torre church where doubtless the Canons used them; the misericord on the wall of the chancel, however, is said to have come from Torre Abbey itself. Other things which the Canons knew are the fragments of ancient glass and the 15th century font.

Now there was a path connecting the Abbey with Cockington, reputed to have been almost in a straight line. A fragment of it still remains, according to an oral tradition handed down by Hugh Watkin; it is immediately outside the Vicarage gate, where there is a grassy verge. When the Vicarage was built, why was not the garden wall built right up to the pavement? The answer given was that it would have encroached upon this old right of way. The path ended just here, for it joined the lane down to Cockington, descending into it through a gap in the hedge and down a steep bank. This was all much clearer thirty years ago, and the bank has now been supported by a wall. The railway must have come into being long before the old path disappeared, and I very much wonder whether the footbridge crossing the line between Rathmore Road and Solsbro Road may not in the first place have been an accommodation bridge built to take this old right of way over the line.

In about 1938 I remember visiting the church and being fortunate enough to see a cobbled path exposed at a depth of about 10 feet. It had been stumbled upon by accident when workmen were digging near the east wall of the chancel; it was covered in again next day. It came right up to the south-east corner of the chancel, and ran in a S.W.— N.E. direction. It was about four feet in width and would be the old direct route to the church from the village, and also the end of the path from Torre Abbey.

Further References

Taxation of Pope Nicholas, 1288
    Cockington paid 12/-.

40

Daccombe and Coffinswell

In the time of the Domesday Survey the present parish of Coffinswell was divided into two manors. Both are called Willa in the Exeter version, but in the Exchequer version they are entitled Welle and Wille. In the next century this same distinction was to be made in the Cartulary; but Welle soon became Coffinswell, when the family of Coffyn began to have influence there. The name of Wille, which referred to the easternmost manor, died out as Daccombe developed in importance. There was even a transitional stage when in 1303 there is mention of Daccombe Wille in the "Book of Fees".

Domesday shows two manors of the same extent. Both rendered geld for 2 hides. Welle, the Abbot of Tavistock's manor, consisted of 10 villeins, 12 bordars and 4 serfs, whilst Wille had 16 villeins, 2 bordars and 7 serfs.

Further early evidence of the title of Daccombe for the eastern manor is to be found in 1159 in the document recording the founding of Coffinswell church. Here the manor of the lord of Daccombe is said to come right up to the church. There is therefore little difficulty in finding the dividing line between the two manors because running past the church is a very ancient road, thought to have been a salt track. It is today known as Ridgeway Lane. Coming up from the salt marshes beside the River Teign at Combe Cellars, it climbs the ridge behind Combe-in-Teignhead, passes through No Man's Land and continues above Haccombe. It then descends to Coffinswell, passing straight through the farmyard of Court Barton where there are still three gates on line. It crossed the orchard beyond the churchyard wall, ascended the steep hill opposite, known as Churchway, and so reached Kingskerswell. From thence it continued through Marldon and Berry Pomeroy towards Totnes. The importance and antiquity of this old way cannot be questioned; in Saxon times, therefore, it would form the most likely dividing line between the two manors. Daccombe would extend eastwards, and its remaining boundaries would be those of the old roads above the horse-shoe shaped valley in which it lies, which were manor, and later parish, boundaries. Coffinswell would be bounded on the west by the manors of Aller and (Kings)kerswill and to the north by the ridge road coming up from Milber Camp.

We are now in a position to consider the Charters concerning the two manors, and the varying headings in the Cartulary will be followed.

Welles

271. A quitclaim to the Canons of Torre from Robert Huppetone and his wife, Margaret, of all their land at Welles. To be held free and quit from the lord of Welles. Date: Early 13th century.   MS: Folio 91.

272. A quitclaim to the Canons of Torre from Margaret, daughter of Seward, of all her land at Welles.
Date: Early 13th century.   MS: Folio 91.

273. A quitclaim to the Canons of Torre by the widow Odelina, daughter of Seward, of all her land at Welles.
Date: Early 13th century.   MS: Folio 92.

274. A gift in perpetual alms to the Church of Torre from Sampson ffoliot of 3/- per annum to be paid to the reeve from his "Gagbulagium" on the Feast of St. Peter's Chains. The gift is for his soul and those of his parents and forbears, so that wax may be provided to light the altars where masses are sung. When he dies the Canons have promised that they will give their full service to him as though he were a Canon of the house.
Date: Early 13th century.   MS: Folio 92.

275. A confirmation to the Church of St. Saviour of Torre from Richard ffoliot, son of Sampson ffoliot, of a ferling of land in his vill of Welles. It is the land which Seward and his daughters Odelina and Margaret used to hold.
Date: mid 13th century.   MS: Folio 92.

276. A gift to the Church of the Holy Trinity of Torre by ffulc de fferrars, with the consent of his wife, Lucia, of all his land, messuages, meadows and pastures in Welles. William Bugge, the tenant and his family are included. Clause of Warranty.
Date: 1240/50. (ffulc de fferrars men. 1238/54 "Devon Feet of Fines").   MS: Folio 92/93.

277. A confirmation from Richard ffoliot of the gift which ffulc de fferrars made to the Church of Torre. William Bugge, or whoever is tenant, to have grazing rights throughout his land of Welles.
Date: 1240/50.   MS: Folio 93.

278. A confirmation of the ferling of land at Welles as in 275 by Richard ffoliot, son of Sampson. He also confirms ffulc de fferrars's gift of half a ferling.
Date: mid 13th century.   MS: Folio 93.   Witnesses:—Reginald de Mohun, William de Mohun, Martin de ffisacre, Hameline de Dealdone, Roger de Cokyntone, Roger de Puncherdone, John le Barone and others.

279. A chirograph given at Exeter between the Abbot of Torre and ffulc de fferrars in settlement of a dispute. The Abbot agrees that when due, royal service shall be made by his villeins William de Wyndsore and Edward the Hound, just as is made by ffulc's villeins. For this concession ffulc agrees to pay the Abbot 6d. per annum. Clause of Distraint.
Date: The Feast of St. Agatha, the Virgin, 1285.   Witnesses:—Alan de Daucombe, Walter de Breyntone, William de Seyntmarichurche, Richard de Alre, Philip de Comptone and others.   MS: Folio 93.

Charters 271/79 concern land in Coffinswell and are under the heading of the older name of Welles. Both Welles and Daccumbe until 1277 were under the jurisdiction of the Abbot of Tavistock as lord of the fee, and formed 2 fees. In the "Red Book of The

Exchequer" p. 250, Tavistock Abbey is said to have had 16 fees, William de Tribus Minetis holding two at Coffinswell and Daccombe. Although this Abbey held Coffinswell in 1086, they do not seem to have acquired Daccombe until c. 1135. The le Speks were later tenants in chief, but the preceding charters make it clear that they had been followed by the ffoliots.

Charters 271-2-3-5 concern a ferling of land which had belonged to Seward. It was inherited by his daughter, Margaret, who married Robert Uppetone. They both gave this ferling to Torre Abbey. Evidently they died childless, for Margaret's sister Odelina, apparently after the death of Margaret and Robert, again confirms their gift. It is finally confirmed by Richard ffoliot.

Sampson ffoliot's gift of 3/- per annum for candles to the Abbey gained him the promise of being made a confrater after his death; and the Canons promised to pray for him just as they would for one of the Canons of the house. This was a high honour for an apparently small gift; but Sampson may have been a lifelong benefactor in ways of which we know nothing.

In 279 we hear of two of the Abbot's villeins, William de Wyndsore and Edward the Hound, who had not been giving royal service when required, whilst ffulc's villeins had. This was the cause of a dispute which was settled at Exeter, probably just as court proceedings were imminent.

Seyntmarichurche

280. A gift of a ferling of land in her vill of Seyntmarichurche from Avicia, the lady of Seyntmarichurche, to the Canons of Torre. It was given for her own soul and that of her deceased husband, Maurice de Rotomago. It is the same ferling that Symon Burnestaburge used to hold, and with it she gives Walter de ffonte and his family. Grazing rights throughout her land.
Date: post 1252. (Maurice de Rotomago men. 1252, Devon Feet of Fines 535).   MS: Folio 94.

This is a solitary charter concerning a ferling of land at St. Marychurch. It is no doubt placed among the Daccombe and Coffinswell charters because they lay in the parish of St. Marychurch; but from an ecclesiastical point of view they were not the concern of the Abbot of Torre, whose Canons never made themselves responsible for services at Coffinswell, so far as we know.

Alicia (or Avicia) de Rotomago appears again in 216 where she gives 3 ferlings at Lydewichestone to her brother. Her husband, Maurice, was living in 1252, and this is the only date we know in connection with her. She was married again to Thomas de Cirecestre.

Unfortunately we cannot identify the whereabouts of the ferling given in St. Marychurch. Hilda Walker, however, has pointed out that there were two Domesday manors at St. Marychurch—a fact not always realised. One was the Church of St. Mary, and the other St. Marychurch. The former, she considers, later became the manor known as Combe Pafford. If this is so, then Avicia's manor would lie mostly to the south of the church and would extend in that direction. Now the Cary family in post-monastic times owned much of this manor and may have bought back the ferling of land which formerly belonged to the Abbey. Cary Park bears the family name, and ancient fields are known to have existed there prior to the building which took place toward the end of the last century. Close by is the old name of Furrough Cross which marked a right of way across the furrows. The farm in which all this land lay was Babbacombe Barton, which existed up to the time when building swamped all its agricultural land. At the time of the charter this old farm may very well have consisted of about 25 acres. It is therefore not beyond the bounds of possibility that Avicia's ferling lay near Cary Park.

281, which follows next, is a stray charter concerning Cockington and will be considered under the chapter of that heading.

Daccumbe

282. Richard le Spek salutes his men, both Norman and English, stating that he has given Daccumbe and Wille to Ibert ybro and his brother, Michael, for the service of two knights. He wishes him to hold it just as Michael's brother, William, did in the year and on the day when he died at Jerusalem.
Date: c. 1190.   MS: Folio 95.

283. A gift from Jordan de Daccumbe to the Canons of Torre of all his land at Daccumbe. In return the Canons will assign a chaplain to say mass in the Abbey church for the souls of himself, his wife, Cecilia, and all his ancestors and successors for ever.
Date: c. 1239.   MS: Folio 95.

284. A Final Concord given at St. Bride's, London, between Laurence, Abbot of Torre, and Jordan de Daccumbe, whereby the latter recognises that the manor belongs to the Canons of Torre through his gift. With it go the homage and service of Warin, son of Johel, Hugh Coffyn and Stephen Baucan. The service of Davyd de Holrigge also given. The Abbot is to pay Jordan 20 marks per annum for his lifetime. In the presence of Warin and Hugh.
Date: The morrow of the Feast of St. John the Baptist, 1239/40.   MS: Folio 96.

285. A charter dealing with Holerigge and discussed in that chapter.

286. A gift from Jordan de Daccumbe to Stephen Baucan of the land of la ffunteyne in exchange for the ferling which Robert Buvy held, and also for Robert Martyn's holding in the same vill. Rent—a pair of white gloves at Easter. Stephen gave him 5 marks in silver and his wife a gold ring. Clause of Warranty.
Date: 1230/40.   MS: Folio 97.

287. A quitclaim from Thomas de Daccumbe, son of Jordan, to the Canons of Torre of the land of Daccumbe.
Date: mid 13th century.   MS: Folio 97.

Charters 285, 288, 289 and 290 concern Holrigge and are placed among the charters of that chapter.

291. Stephen Bauceyn gives to the Canons of Torre 2 ferlings of land at Welles Coffyn which he had by gift from Jordan de Daccumbe.
Date: Mid 13th century.   MS: Folio 97 & 98.

292. This charter concerns the chapter on Greendale and is placed there.

293. A Final Concord between Symon, Abbot of Torre, and Robert Coffyn whereby the Abbot recognised that a property at Welles, which Robert had from Adam de la siete is his by right.
Date: Given at Torre on the Feast of St. Dunstan the Bishop, 1254. MS: Folio 98.
Witnesses:—Martin de ffisacre and others.

294. The same confirmation as in 291.

295. A quittance from Alan, Abbot of Tavistock. He has received £10 from Abbot Laurence of Torre Abbey, which is relief paid from the two fees of Daccumbe and Welles in the Barony of Tavistock on the death of Jordan de Daccumbe. This would have been paid to William le Spek, tenant in chief, but he is under age and so cannot receive it. Clause of Warranty.
Date: Feast of St. Peter and St. Paul, 1245/46. MS: Folio 98/99.

296. A quitclaim to the Church of Torre from William le Spek of two knights' fees in Daccumbe and Welle Cophin.
Date: 1277. MS: Folio 99.

297. A chirograph between Robert, Abbot of Tavystok, and Richard, Abbot of Torre, whereby the former quitclaims to the Church of Torre two knights' fees in Daccumbe and Wellis Coffyn. 10/- annually for all services etc. Clause of Distraint.
Date: The morrow of St. Dunstan, the Bishop, 1277. MS: Folio 99. Witnesses:—Peter, Prior of Plympton, Sir William de ffisacre, Thomas de Bokelonde, Adam de Middletone, clerks, Stephen Stoil, Richard de Mewy, Henry de Castlewike and others.

298. An agreement between the Canons of Torre and Robert Coffyn whereby his villeins may grind at Robert's mill at Welles Coffyn. For this Robert is to pay 4/- per annum. Clause of Distraint.
Date: Feast of St. Valentine, 1282/83. MS: Folio 99. Witnesses:—Martin de ffisacre, Hugh Peverel de Sampforde, Sir Jordan de Haccombe, Sir Richard de Pultemore, Sir John de Valle torta, William de Cirecestre, Eustace Date.

299. A quitclaim made by Abbot John to Robert de Scobehille and Roger de la Hulle (heirs of Robert Coffyn, formerly lord of Welle Coffyn) of the whole of the north part of the manor with boundaries agreed: also of the park with its banks to the south of these boundaries. In return Robert and Roger quitclaimed to the Abbot all the land south of the boundaries agreed: the park and its banks excepted.
Date: Given at Exeter, Tuesday before the Feast of the Holy and Blessed Virgins, 1309. MS: Folio 99 & 100. Witnesses:—Sir William Martyn, Sir Stephen de Haccumbe, Sir Thomas de Cirecestre, Sir James de Oxtone, Sir John de Bikebiri, William de Strete, Henry Pinkenay, John de Bittelsgate, William de Nywetone and many others.

300. A memorandum stating that Coffynwille is one knight's fee, and relief due on the death of the heir to the manor is 100/-, except on the land held by the Abbot of Torre; this must be subtracted from the whole. There are $524\frac{1}{4}$ acres in Coffynwille and the Abbot holds 94. Total 616 acres. Relief is 1d. per acre so the heir receives 13/8 from the Abbot. So the true relief paid to the Abbot is £4.6.3.

Robert Coffin had three sisters:—

(*a*) Roysa, the eldest, who married Adam de la hille. Their son, Roger, quitclaimed to the house of Torre all his possessions and those of his heirs.

(*b*) Christina, who married Alan de Colbrok; their son, Stephen, also quitclaimed all his possessions to the house of Torre.

(*c*) Margery, the youngest, married Thomas de Scobahille. Their son was Robert de Scobahille.

Beatrix, Robert's sister, was betrothed to William Chivaler who had a daughter, Agnes, by her; Agnes was betrothed to John Mare whose son was Luke Mare Peter (?). His father migrated whilst his son was living, but soon died. The son had no heir. Afterwards Beatrix, in her widowhood, had an illegitimate daughter called Agnes who married John Mare.

301. A licence in mortmain from King Edward II permitting the Canons of Torre to possess 91 acres of land and 3 of meadow in the fee of Robert de Skobehille and Roger de la hille at Coffinswille. They acquired this without licence, but this transgression is now pardoned. Witnessed by the King himself at Westminster.
Date: October 25th, 1314/15.   MS: Folio 101.

Charters 282-301 deal with land in both manors, whilst one or two concerning Holrigge are thrown in for good measure. There is even one dealing with land in the manor of Blackburga, which should be among the Greendale charters, and another isolated charter concerning Cockington. The result is confusing for the charters are by no means in chronological order, neither do they deal with the same subject consecutively.

Charter 282 is unusual in the way Richard le Spek begins it by greeting his men, both Norman and English, in right royal fashion. He gives Daccumbe and Wille to Ibert Ybro and his brother Michael for the service of two knights. (Note that he has confused Wille and Welle). He wishes Michael to hold it just as his brother William did, and then states that he fell at Jerusalem. This must have been in 1189, so the charter dates from a little later than that and is definitely a pre-foundation charter. The two fees came to the le Spek family through an heiress of the Tremeneth family; she married William le Spek, who held them in 1162 (see "Collectanea Topographica et Genealogica", 1834, p. 62, no. 28).

Jordan de Daccumbe, who gave the whole manor to the Canons in 283, was probably grandson of that Nicholas described as lord of the manor in the Coffinswell church foundation charter of 1159. Risdon says he held South Pool from 1154-89, styling himself de Pola. He had two sons, William and Stephen, one of whom may have been Jordan's father. The family having established itself in Daccombe soon styled themselves "de Daccumbe".

Jordan's gift was evidently looked upon by the Canons as of great importance, for he and his wife Cecilia were granted a chantry at the Abbey. In the Final Concord of 1239 the homage of Warin, the son of Johel, Hugh Coffyn and Davyd de Holrigge was made to the Abbot in the King's Court at St. Bride's, London. Those three men, who possibly could neither read nor write, thus travelled to London specially to take part in a typical feudal ceremony. To their dying day they would never forget the excitement of the journey, nor the fact that their homage and service was due to the Abbot of Torre always. And everyone in Daccombe and Coffinswell would know that in future whoever held that land was the Abbot's man. In this way illiterate men were made to understand the importance of such a transaction as the change of ownership of the manor in which they lived.

Another family who held land at Coffinswell were the Baucans or Bauceyns. They also held land at Blackburga, and we read of them in the Greendale group of Charters. The land of "La ffunteyne" mentioned in 286 was possibly near Doddawell which is the main spring in Coffinswell.

In 1277 the Abbot of Tavistock quitclaimed his two fees at Daccombe and Coffinswell to the Canons of Torre for 10/- per annum. So, bit by bit, they were getting more and more influence in the two manors. Daccombe Mill, which was of course in that manor, is indirectly referred to in 298. This would be the Abbot's mill, but in the charter Robert Coffyn and his men are given permission to grind at his own mill. Now there is no memory in Coffinswell of any other mill than Daccombe Mill and Robert's mill has quite disappeared. The only other stream which could have worked it is a feeder of the Aller Brook which flows down below Manor Farm. It must have stood somewhere on this stream.

The three final charters of the group deal with the squabble which arose when Robert Coffyn died towards the close of the 13th century. He seems to have been childless, and the manor descended to his three married sisters; the memorandum given in 300 shows how the sons of two of them, Roger de la Hille and Stephen de Colbrook, quitclaimed everything to Torre Abbey. Robert de Scobahille, however, the son of the third daughter, did no such thing. Yet a fourth unmarried sister Beatrix, had an illegitimate daughter who might have caused trouble in a dispute over the inheritance. What actually happened is obscure but it is quite certain that Abbot John le Rous tried to take possession of the manor and dispossess Robert de Scobehille and Roger de la Hulle. He did not succeed, however, and in 299 had to quitclaim to the two cousins the whole of the north part of the manor. Although the memorandum says that Roger de la Hille and Stephen de Colbrok quitclaimed all that they had, (presumably meaning their land in Coffinswell), yet in the Cartulary the vital charters giving it in the usual way are not to be found. Somehow there had been a slip between the cup and the lip. On the other hand, whilst Abbot John's action in seizing the manor appears to us high-handed, yet he was surely not so badly advised as to act as he did unless he had a good title to the manor. However it may have been he had to make terms with Robert and Roger in 299, which dates from 1309. The boundaries agreed upon then are of considerable interest, for they are still for the most part in use today. The cousins were to hold the north part of the manor, and this roughly corresponds to the land held by the farm of Court Barton right up to the present day. In addition they were to hold the park and its banks in the south part of the manor.

The time has now come to speak of Manor Farm. An estate map of 1942 gives its acreage as 110.25. It occupies most of the southern part of the manor, but includes Herpin's Break (8.6 acres) which is in the next parish, and probably was in the next manor in mediaeval times. This reduces the acreage to 101.65. Now we know from 300 that the Canons held only 94 acres in Coffinswell; if this is subtracted from 101.65 it leaves nearly 7 acres to account for. This may have been the extent of the "park" which Robert and Roger still had in this southern part of the manor. Remembering that at Blackawton we found a similar park mentioned which was an enclosure for strays, so here the "park" may have been put to this use. The deduction from all this reasoning is that in Manor Farm we see the original holding of the Canons. This comprised $3\frac{1}{2}$ ferlings as the various charters show. The ferling here can, therefore, once again be calculated and works out at 26.8 acres.

The two sections of the old manor were divided in 1309 by the road which goes through the village, and this is still the dividing line between Court Barton and Manor Farms in the lower part of Coffinswell. The Canons, of course, never gained an acre by their dispute with the heirs of Robert Coffyn and simply kept the 94 acres which they had previously.

In 1933 the Rev. Keble Martin, the celebrated botanist, wrote "A Short History of Coffinswell" whilst he was Rector there. It was revised in 1955 and is contained in vol. 87 of the "Transactions of the Devonshire Association". He advances the theory that there were three manors here—Wille, Welle and Daccombe. He was not of course aware of the contents of the Cartulary which, as we have seen, make it abundantly clear that there were only two in the early days. After 1309, however, there is every reason to suppose that people very soon looked upon the Canons' property as a separate manor; and at a later stage, long after the dissolution, the small holdings would be merged into one farm which took the title of Manor Farm. It is a tradition that the Canons' courthouse was at Court Barton, which its name implies. The northern manor, however, had its manor-house on the site of "The Linnay". This is in part an old building and I can remember when it was a nicely-thatched house. During the rebuilding a good, open hearth was uncovered which had two ovens. Unfortunately it was destroyed. The fine, mullioned windows at Court Barton are said to have come from the other manor house. I certainly have seen an old print of the house when the present windows were not there, so there seems to be truth in this suggestion.

Coffinswell is fortunate in possessing a good deal of cob and thatch, but it is difficult to assess the age of such buildings. Such items as the circular stair at Osmond Cottage and the fine door at Willa Cottage obviously go back to the monastic period. So does the excellent barn in the western range of the farm buildings at Manor Farm. The small L shaped house beside it is possibly the old farmhouse, for the present house is 19th century. Many of the cottages in the village are remembered to have been farm houses once, but at Coffinswell all the small holdings, of which there must have been a good many, have merged into the two present-day farms at one time or another. The estate map already mentioned showed a network of lanes north of the village. These today are cul-de-sacs, but I am quite certain that formerly they all led to the vanished small holdings of which the Domesday Survey gives indication.

Court Barton is without doubt the most interesting of the old properties to be seen today. Not only was it a farmhouse but it was also a courthouse as well. Just as at the Canons' other courthouses at Greendale, Oldstone etc., we have an L shaped plan with the courthouse at rightangles to the main house, and separated from it by a stout wall four feet in thickness. It is at a lower level than the house and today is entered by two or three descending steps. Its length of about 45 ft. compares well with the other houses.

The courthouse may have been added after 1309, for it does not appear to be so old as the house. The plan of the house at first sight seems a little curious because it has two kitchens. There is a break in the front wall, and I interpret this as the fact that the kitchen and dairy are older than the rest and once formed a simple longhouse. Where the break occurs the plan shows the remains of a return wall which would be the outside wall of the first house. This older house would consist of kitchen and byre only. I think that the next stage was the extension of this house eastwards, and then the present kitchen was added, probably at first the hall of a more ambitious house. The courthouse may have been built at the same time. It was at this period an important house where the

Glascombe: Abbey land occupied triangle left of centre.   *Photo by M. Leach.*

Glascombe: Remains of farmhouse.   *Photo by M. Leach.*

Cockington: Parish Church of St. George and St. Mary.

Coffinswell: Court Barton c. 1950. *Photo by Nicholas Horne.*

Coffinswell: The Courthouse wing at Court Barton. *Photo by Nicholas Horne.*

Ideford: Charter from William de Holrigge giving his large garden to the Abbot of Torre.
Photo by kind permission of Exeter Cathedral Library.

Canons' bailiff would live and administer the affairs of both Coffinswell and Daccombe.

In post-monastic days there would be big changes again. The courthouse itself was no doubt made into four rooms—two upstairs and two down. The hall of the house became the kitchen and the old kitchen would be abandoned and separated from the house as it is now. The courthouse wall would be broken through to give access to the present kitchen. The end wall of the old house was also broken through to connect the byre with the new kitchen, so that the byre became a dairy. Lastly a wall was built disconnecting the former kitchen which was no longer needed. But it should be noted that the only real structural changes since monastic times have been a drawing-room and bedroom over, added in Victorian times when a prosperous squire lived here in great gentility.

The L shaped house and its outbuildings formed at one time an enclosed quadrangle. The buildings on the south-west side have now gone, their place being taken by a high wall. All the windows and doors of the old house faced onto this quadrangle and the entrance was by way of a gatehouse at the north-west corner. The present tunnel-like entrance is possibly a rebuilding of this on the same site. The house in olden times was therefore well protected. The outbuildings have all been restored within the last century —very probably with old material. Much old sandstone was used, and built into an outside stair is a millstone.

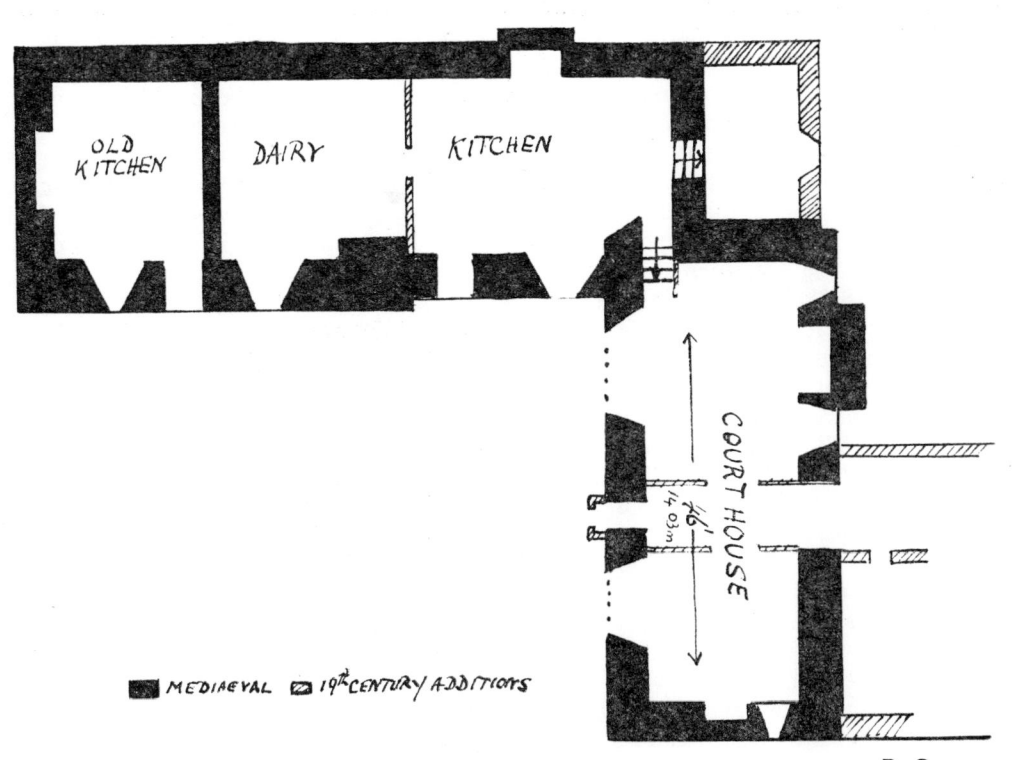

Court Barton. D. Seymour.

If the farmhouse is a fine relic of the monastic period, so is the rest of the extensive farmyard. There are two other groups of buildings, and I consider that in times past each had a separate function. It must be first understood that the church and the buildings stood at the intersection of crossroads. It has already been mentioned how Ridgeway Lane passed right through the yard from north to south. An intersecting road came up from Welle to the church, and from the top of the tower its impression can be seen quite clearly coming through the field opposite the farm entrance on the west side. It is significant that this is still the official entrance to the church. This road would continue across the garden of Court Barton to Daccombe.

It is easy to see how, when all three groups of buildings came under one owner, these roads would be discouraged and alternatives made on the other side of the farm buildings. With the landlord of Coffinswell residing at Court Barton very little opposition would be made. And so the farmyard gradually became enclosed and the crossroads went out of use.

It is most probable that the buildings immediately west of the church belonged to it, and the splendid barn would be the tithe barn. Two wings run out from it to make a little courtyard. All the buildings are thatched and undoubtedly form the most attractive group at Court Barton. Keble Martin mentions another tithe barn which stood close to a spot where the Aller Brook crosses the Daccombe road. This may have been Daccombe's barn as there is no memory of a tithe barn in the village there.

The third group of buildings just west of the farmhouse is the most extensive and forms a double courtyard, with every indication that they formed a separate entity in themselves. All were thatched until recently when a fire destroyed one wing. There is no sign of a former dwelling house here. Willa Cottage is reputed to be an old farmhouse, and these may have been its outbuildings; or again they may have been at one time those of the northern manor house.

Turning now to present day Daccombe, we find here a pleasing group of old dwellings, for the most part better maintained than they were, say, twenty-five years ago. A good deal of cob and thatch is still to be seen. The village shows its antiquity in the pattern of its farms. These are not isolated units, but like the surrounding old villages of Upton, Cockington, Stoke and Combe-in-Teignhead, the farmhouses are all in the main street, and the land attached to them is to be found in scattered parcels on the surrounding hills. So the farmer of today, like the villein of old, still goes forth from the village to his appointed strips of land. The tithe map shows many small strip fields. Their pattern suggests many more small holdings than there are now. In 1086 there were 16 villeins and 2 bordars at Wille. In the village today there is the Manor Farm, Drews Farm, Balls Farm, and Home Farm. Aynells is half a mile away, towards Coffinswell, and does not seem to fit into the old plan. It is first heard of in post-monastic days in the 16th century. Being a later development it may well contain two or three older holdings. In the village itself there are one or two more houses said to have been farmhouses early in the present century. But all this only represents about half the Domesday quota of farms.

The house at Manor Farm does not appear to be the original courthouse; it is a spacious one, probably dating only from the 17th or even 18th century. In the orchard on the opposite side of the road, however, there are banks and mounds at the northern end which suggest the former existence of considerable buildings. Beside them, too, are the fragmentary remains of Daccombe's mediaeval chapel. I think it far more likely that the former manor house, courthouse and chapel stood here, quite independent of the barton farmhouse. In "Devon Monastic Lands" p. 95 there is mention of "Lez Courteplace" and "Courtegarden" in 1539, and it is quite probable that this orchard is the place meant.

The chapel remains comprise the east wall only, and a very small fragment of the south wall. Built onto the east wall is a much later farm building, which has undoubtedly saved the chapel from being completely demolished. This chapel is mentioned in a charter of c. 1225 (Exeter Cathedral Library no. 2084) and it is still known to old villagers as "the chapel". This would be a parochial chapel served in the monastic period by St. Marychurch clergy; for it never had any connection with Torre Abbey. To discuss this remarkable survival further would therefore be outside the scope of this book.

The Canons, it will be seen, held in Daccombe and Coffinswell a complex of adjacent farms which could be simply and easily administered from Court Barton. The charters form a pleasing group, telling us a great deal about the successive owners and tenants of the two manors. Happily, both villages at the time of writing are still agricultural and there is little development. There is still time, therefore, for research to be done with regard to the lost small holdings which must once have existed. The site of the Daccombe courthouse and chapel would also surely repay excavation. The preservation of Court Barton and its adjacent thatched farm buildings ought to stand high on the list of secular buildings to be preserved. Such relics of the past are too precious to be allowed to fall into decay, for they are the rightful heritage of all who love the Devon countryside.

Further References

Taxation of Pope Nicholas, 1288
    Taxed at £2.15s.

Devon Lay Subsidy, 1332
    No reference.

A.O., Particulars for Grants 120
    Mention of "Lez courteplace" and courtegarden" in farm of the chief messuage to John Goderige and Joan, his wife for their lives 11/8.
    Mention of 2 closes Brode parke and Lordes meade to John Ridgeway for 21 years 60/-.
    Manor of Daccombe: Free rents 28/4, customary rents £13.6.4½., Rent of barton land leased to tenants £8.13.4½. Total £26.19.6.

41

Holrigge

The position of the ancient vill of Holrigge has confused some writers; for since some of the Holrigge charters are placed among those of Daccombe, it has been asserted that Holrigge was a forgotten name for a farm in that manor. This was not the case, however, because it was in Ideford parish, where the old farm of Combe Holeridge still exists. The charters were placed with the Daccombe charters in the Cartulary simply because in the early days the de Daccumbe family held Holrigge, and so the story of the two places became interwoven.

More serious was the mistake of confusing Holrigge with Horridge in Islington. The similarity in the names naturally caused trouble. Careful perusal of the "Book of Fees", "Feudal Aids", and "Devon Feet of Fines" should prevent any further confusion, for according to "Feudal Aids" (p. 347) Holridge was held by the Abbot of Torre for one third of a knight's fee, whilst Horridge was held by Thomas Horridge and two others for half a knight's fee (ibid p. 484). The latter was in the Honour of Braneys, whilst Holrigge was a part of the Honour of Plympton. It was also a part of the Hundred of Teignbridge, whilst Horridge was in the Hundred of Wonford. But the compiler of the index of "Feudal Aids" had not grasped that two different places were involved and there places both under Ilsington.

Further evidence is provided in Pole's "Devonshire", where on p. 268 is the statement "Holridge in Ideford parish William Worth held in King Richard II's tyme". In Exeter Cathedral Library there is a receipt of the 15th year of King Henry VI given by William Abbot of Torre, for the annual rent for Holrigge. It amounted to 20/-, and was paid by William Werthe.

A licence in mortmain from King Edward I (302) describes Holrigge as a vill. Having established Holrigge in Ideford we have yet to locate the position of the ancient vill. I have found this no easy task, for the name survives only at the farm of Combe Holeridge, which, apart from one or two fairly modern cottages nearby, stands alone at the bottom of the valley of the Moor Brook. But on the other side of the brook, further up the valley, are Combe Farm and Combe Mill. Both are old buildings. Behind the farm house, which has a Georgian frontage, there is an older house, dating from earlier days. The mill adjoins two cottages of later date. Both these old buildings may have had their origin in monastic days, but they could hardly be said to constitute a vill. There are, moreover, no indications of vanished homesteads just here, for the valley bottom is wet and marshy.

The charters themselves are perhaps our best guide, for they record three gifts of two ferlings of land apiece. Now on the western slopes of the valley are four farms in close proximity to each other consisting of about 25 acres apiece, or multiples of it. So here we have the old mediaeval measure of the ferling, and this leads one to suppose that these are old holdings whose boundaries may not have changed over the centuries. Doubtless, soon after the dissolution, they became a part of the Clifford Estate, and still are. They are Well, Sedgwell, Olchard and Underhaye. Now Well was held from the Abbot of Torre for a pound of wax and the homage of the tenant, but the others are not mentioned by name in the Cartulary. The interesting point, however, is that three of the farmhouses are quite close to each other, and there are two old cottages beside Olchard. Altogether we have here the beginnings of a small village, and the old title of "vill" would fit very well. I feel reasonably confident that this is the Holrigge of monastic days, but it is strange that its name has died out. The buildings are all of ancient origin, too; and their sites may go right back to the days of the charters. The mill is possibly the most interesting of the group, for it is built of stone throughout and was evidently free standing at one time. The Tithe Map shows another mill close by, but that has quite vanished although the water courses are clear enough. One mill must have been a fulling mill, for in the charters are several mentions of William the fuller of Holrigge. He was a benefactor of Torre Abbey, but never parted with his mill. The mediaeval house at Combe, where William may have lived, seems later to have been enlarged and so became an L shaped house. There are 25 acres attached, and this was possibly one of the ferlings given to the Abbey.

Sedgewell has 50 acres; it has old outbuildings and the farmhouse contains a massive old chimney breast. Coming now up the valley to the old vill of Holrigge, we find the fine 17th century house of Well, now a farmhouse. Below it are the remains of a really old house with a fine chimney and open hearth; it is now used as a barn. This would be where Walter de la Wille, mentioned in 308, lived.

The old house at Olchard was demolished in 1969, but fragments of it survive in the house which is built on the site. The delightful cob-and-thatch cottage just below is a fine example of a dependant's cottage. The third house—Underhaye—is a much more pretentious building. It has altogether the air of a house of importance and is presided over by a stately chimney. I should imagine this was the home of David de Holrigge and

Underhaye. *D. Seymour.*

his daughter, Petronilla, who was such a generous benefactress to the Abbey. These three adjacent farms all consisted of 50 acres apiece, so it is possible that Olchard, Well and Sedgewell were the three gifts of 2 ferlings apiece given to the Abbey by William de Holrigge, William the Fuller and Petronilla de Holrigge. They are mentioned in 302—a licence in mortmain from King Edward I. If Underhaye was the principal house, then no doubt Petronilla would continue to reside there in her widowhood; then she gave all her land to the Canons and perhaps went elsewhere.

Charter 308 gives conclusive evidence that there were, in all, five holdings at Holrigge; for in it Okelina de Holrigge gives all her land at Holrigge to Susanna, niece of Richard the parson of Alfynton, with the homage and service of Richard de (name omitted) William the ffolour, William de Cavilswere, Walter de la Wille. So it is clear that each, including Okelina, held one of the five farms which we have been considering. We can thus be reasonably sure of the extent of Holrigge.

I do not consider that Combe Holeridge was included in the Torre Abbey property, for its land is all on the east side of the valley; until recently it was a large farm of 200 acres. To include it would also give us one farm too many. Until evidence to the contrary can be produced, I consider that the Holrigge charters deal with the five farms of Combe, Sedgewell, Olchard, Well and Underhaye.

As at Hennock this compact group of farms under ecclesiastical ownership came to be regarded as a manor. In Dublin Cartulary (folio 5a) there is reference to the "manor of Holrigge" in 1291.

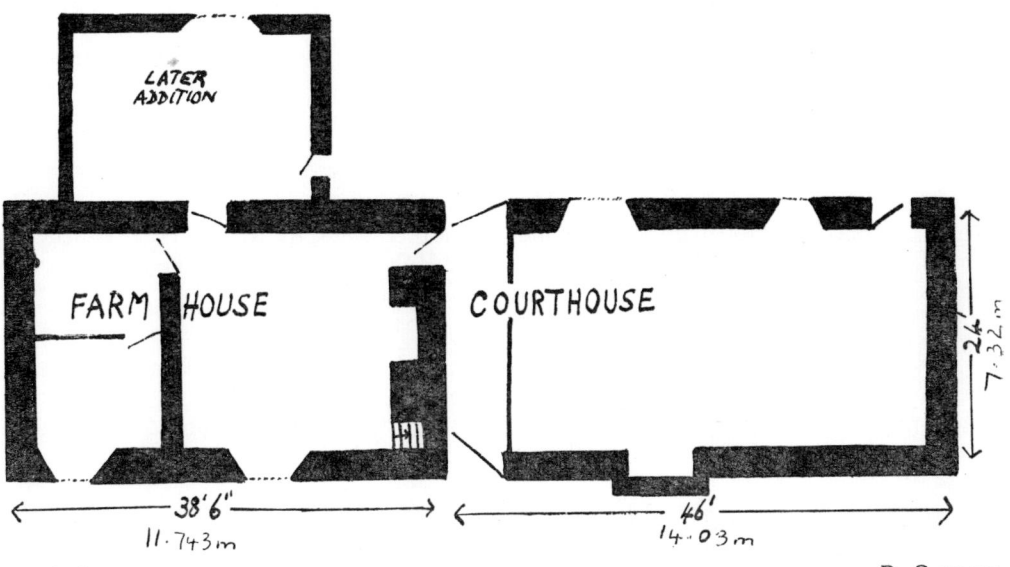

Underhaye. D. Seymour.

It is not surprising, therefore, that yet another courthouse came to light at Underhaye, the principal house. This time the courtroom is in a straight line with the main house (see plan). Its exterior length is 46 ft. and it is separated from the house by a wall nearly 5 ft. in thickness. It is carried right up to the roof, as at Oldstone. The central placing of its fireplace also recalls Oldstone. Again there are no dividing walls, only flimsy partitions. The final bay on the first floor has never been made into a room, but has been used over the centuries as a loft. It is still open to the roof. The walls are of rubble, surmounted by cob.

The Charters

Among the Daccombe and Coffinswell Charters:—

285. A quitclaim of the homage and service of Davyd de Holrigge given by Jordan de Daccumbe to the Church of Torre. It is made for the salvation of his soul, that of his wife, Cecilia, and for those of his forbears and successors. Clause of Warranty.
Date: Early 13th century.   MS: Folio 96.

288. Nicholas de Pola greets all his men, both French and English, bidding them know that he has given the land at Holrigge to Michael de Daccumba who is to hold it just as Robert de Daccumbe held it, for one third of a knight's fee.
Date: 1160/90.   MS: Folio 97.

289. A quitclaim from Agatha de Holrigge, widow of William Chamberlayne, of a messuage at Holrigge with its lands, meadows and gardens: it is made to the Abbot of Torre who gave her 40/- in recognition.
Date: Mid 13th century.   MS: Folio 97.

290. A quitclaim from Thomas de Daccumbe made to the Canons of Torre of the homage and service of Davyd de Holrigge for the tenement of Holrigge. This he used to hold from Thomas's father, Jordan.
Date: Mid 13th century.   MS: Folio 97.

Holrigge

302. A licence in mortmain from King Edward I whereby William de Holrigge, Petronilla de Holrigge and William the ffolour of Holrigge may each make a gift of two ferlings in the vill of Holrigge to the Canons of Torre.
Date: Given at Langleye, April 20th, 1286/87.   MS: Folio 102.

303. A quitclaim of all his land at Holrigge which he had through Susanna de porta, given by William Russel to the Church of Torre.
Date: mid 13th century.   MS: Folio 102/103.   Witnesses:—John de Witewei, Richard de Babbecumbe, Richard de Gatepathe, Robert de Grendil, Richard Gayer and others.
   (Original in Exeter Cathedral Library).

304. The same gift as in 303 with slightly different wording.
The same witnesses.

305. Petronilla de Holrigge in her widowhood gives her large garden at Holrigge to the Canons of Torre. They have given her 100/-. Clause of Warranty.
Date: Late 13th century.   MS: Folio 103.   Witnesses:—Sir William de ffissacre, William de Comptone, Richard de Babbecumbe, Philip de Cumpton and others.

306. A gift of a messuage in Holrigge, with its curtillage, made to the Canons of Torre by the widow Petronilla, daughter of David de Holrigge. Clause of Warranty.
Date: Late 13th century. MS: Folio 103. Witnesses:—Sir William de ffissacre, Sir Jordan de Hakkumbe, Richard de Gatepathe, Richard de Babbecumbe, John Witewie, Randolph de la Were, Alfred de Harecumbe and others.

307. A gift in free and perpetual alms from William Chaulesway to the church of Torre of all that land at Holrigge which was the dowry of his mother, Matilda. Clause of Warranty.
Date: Late 13th century. MS: Folio 103/104. Witnesses:—Sir William de ffissacre, John de Witeway, Randolph de la Were, Richard de Gatepathe, William de Holrigge and others.

308. A gift from Okelina de Holrigge made to Susanna, niece of Richard the parson of Alfyntone, of all her land at Holrigge, with the homage etc. of Richard de? (a blank) William the ffolour, William de Caveliswere, and Walter de la Wille. A rose at midsummer is to be the rent. Clause of Warranty.
Date: Late 13th century. MS: Folio 104. Witnesses:—Ives de la Were, Richard de Babbecumbe, Richard Galier, Richard de Holrigge, Richard de Gatepathe and others.

309. A confirmation of all her land at Holrigge made by Susanna, niece of Richard the parson of Alfyntone, to William Russel de la Gata. With it go the service etc., of Petronilla de Holrigge, William le ffolour, and Walter de la Wille.
Date: Late 13th century. MS: Folio 104. Witnesses:—Ives de la Torre, Richard de Babbecumbe, Richard Wayer, Richard de Gatepathe, John de Witewie, William de Hircy, Robert Tudde and many others.

310. William de Chetelisbeare (son of Roger de Bagatorre) and Matilda his wife give all their land at Holrigge to Richard, the parson of Alfyntone. Clause of Warranty.
Date: Late 13th century. MS: Folio 104. Witnesses:—Thomas le Gras, Richard Treymenet, Roger de Bagatorre, Ives de la Were, Richard Gayer, Adam de la Leye, John de la Leye, Richard de Babbecumbe and others.

311. A quitclaim from William Russel de la Yate to William Chauleswaye of all the land at Holrigge which he had from Richard the parson of Alfyntone.
Date: Given at Holrigge on the Thursday after the Feast of St. Gregory the pope, 1278/79. MS: Folio 104 & 105. Witnesses:—Richard de Babbecumbe, Richard de Gatepathe, Yves de la Torre, Richard Gayr, Davyd le ver and others.

312. Richard the parson of Alfyntone quitclaims to William Russel de la Gate all his land at Holrigge which he holds from William Chetelisbeare and his wife Matilda.
Date: 1270/80. MS: Folio 105. Witnesses:—Ives de la Torre, Richard de Babbecumbe, Richard Gayr, Richard de Gatepathe, John Witeweye, William de Hyerti, Robert Tudda and many others.

313. A confirmation from Petronilla de Holrigge, widow of Richard de Plimtrii, to the Canons of Torre of all her land at Holrigge. Clause of Warranty.
Date: Late 13th century. MS: Folio 105. Witnesses:—Robert de Beldermerse,

Richard de Gatepathe, Osbert the clerk, Martin de la Torre, Randolph de la Were, William the fuller of Holrigge, William of that place and others.

314. An agreement between William Russel de la yete, and William Chamberlayne and William the fuller of Holrigge whereby William Russel lets all his land, gardens etc., at Holrigge to the other two for 10 years. Rent 8/- to be paid at Alfynton, and 1lb. of wax to the Abbot of Torre for la Wille. They may not sublet nor dispose of the trees. Clauses of Warranty and Distraint
Date: The Feast of St. Benedict the Abbot, 1277. MS: Folio 105 & 106. Witnesses:—Richard de Babbecumbe, Ives de la Torre, Richard de Waye, Richard de Gatepathe, Davyd le ver, William Chamberlayn, William the fuller of Holrigge and many others.

315. An agreement between William, son and heir of William and Matilda de Chaulesway, and Roger the physician of Axemue, whereby he leases all the land in Holrigge which he had from William Russel de la Yeta to Roger on a six month lease. Clauses of Distraint and Warranty. On the security of Andrew de Halchewille.
Date: Thursday before the Feast of St. Edward, King and Martyr, 1277. MS: Folio 106. Witnesses:—Richard de Babbecumbe, Ives de la Torre, Richard Wayer, Richard de Gatepathe, Davyd le ver, William Chamberlayn, William the fuller of Holrigge and many others.

The earliest of the Holrigge charters is undoubtedly 288 where Nicholas de Pola, evidently lord of the fee, gives his land of Holrigge to Michael de Daccumbe for one third of a knight's fee. Robert, who previously held it may have been Michael's father, but we cannot be sure. The date of this transaction might be as early as the middle of the 12th century. 285 has the first mention of Torre Abbey, and here Jordan de Daccumbe quitclaims the service of Davyd de Holrigge to the Canons. In a Final Concord of 1239 Jordan grants this to Abbot Laurence together with other concessions concerning Daccumbe. In 290 Thomas de Daccumbe, Jordan's son, gives a similar quitclaim to 285, no doubt after Jordan's death c. 1246.

Now Davyd de Holrigge had a daughter called Petronilla who was a great benefactress to the Abbey. She married Richard de Plymtrii whom she evidently survived by many years. Her gifts seem all to have been made when Holrigge was hers to dispose of. In 305 she gave the Canons her large garden at Holrigge for which they gave her 100/-. The original charter survives in Exeter Cathedral Library with her dark-green seal still intact. The words "Petronilla de Holrigge" can just be distinguished on the obverse side. Unfortunately no date is attached. Her next gift was a messuage with adjacent curtillage —would that she had mentioned it by name—then in 1286/87 she gave a further 2 ferlings. Lastly she gave all her land at Holrigge. Probably this was near the end of her days.

Another generous donor was William Russel who adds "de la Gate" or "de la porta" after his name. The name today is Gappah, meaning "gate path". As the old ridge road through Gappah leads straight to the large prehistoric earthwork above Ugbrooke Park, the name may have originated in this way. In 303 William gives to the Abbey all his land which came to him through Susanna de Porta. Perhaps she was his wife and the land her dowry. 310, 311, 312 show how the land had come to her through her uncle, Richard, parson of Alphington.

307 is a further gift of land to the Abbey, this time from William de Chaulesway. It

had been the dowry of his mother Matilda. 314 is a lease of this land before it came to the Canons; so is the final charter, 315. Does the fact that there was a physician at Axemouth show that in those days it was a considerable town?

These last two charters, dated 1277, show how late it was in the century before all Holrigge came to the Canons. The Licence in Mortmain dates from 1286. It took the Abbey about 60 years to acquire the whole property, and the result was a very compact little group of farms above the valley of the Moor Brook. The whole procedure of gifts followed exactly the same pattern as the giving of land at Hennock. Once more the Canons could run a group of adjacent farms most economically.

As in the Hennock charters the names of witnesses are all from local houses. Those who know the district well will appreciate this fact and realise what close neighbours they all were. Unlike other series of charters in the Cartulary, all the Holrigge ones have the names of witnesses recorded.

In 1291 £1 was paid under the Taxation of Pope Nicholas. In the "Devonshire Lay Subsidy" of 1332, under "Yudford," is the name of Ralph de Holrigge who paid 16d. But there is no mention of the estate in "Valor Ecclesiasticus", which looks as though the Canons may have sold out to the Worth family who were tenants. Soon after the dissolution Holrigge became a part of the Clifford Estate, in whose hands it still remains.

KEY TO FACING PAGE

A. Torre Abbey
B. Ilsham
C. Cockington
D. Daccombe and Coffinswell
E. Wolborough
F. Kingswear
G. Waddeton
H. Norton and Townstall
I. Blackawton
J. Buckland-in-the-Moor
K. Monksmoor
L. Glascombe
M. North Shillingford
N. Greendale
O. Blackberry and Stowford
P. Huntisbere
Q. Houses in Exeter
R. Pancrasweek
S. Hidesburga
T. Buckland Brewer
U. Shebbear
V. Sheepwash
W. Dunnyngestone
X. Haggelegh
Y. Coleton
Z. Ashclyst
KK. Hennock
LL. Holrigge
MM. Skidbrook (Lincs.)

THE DISPOSITION OF TORRE ABBEY PROPERTY

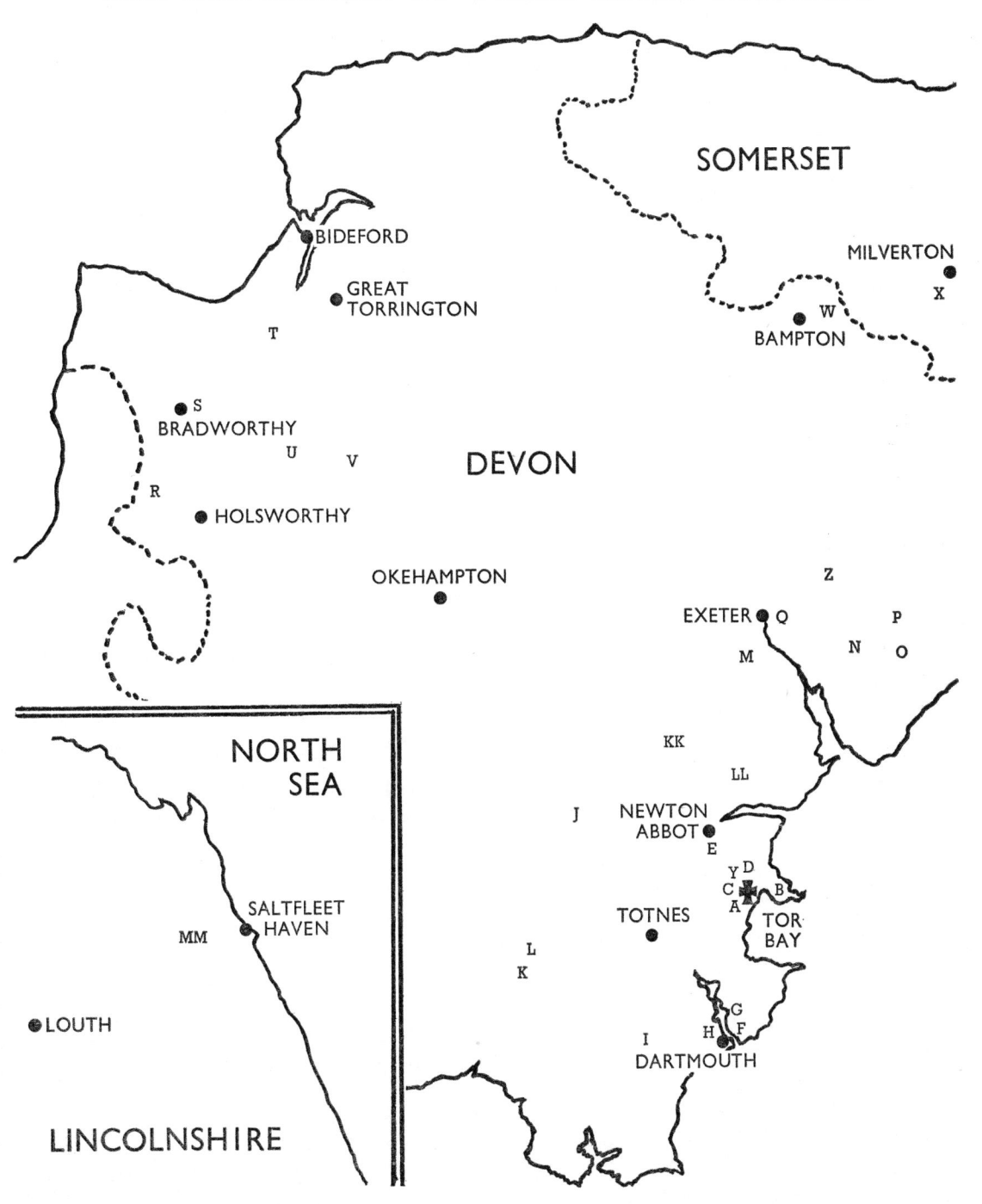

Addenda

(1) The Abbey Library

Whilst the Premonstratensians were educated men with a working knowledge of Latin, yet they did not produce any of the great scholars who were characteristic of English monasteries in early mediaeval times. They were ascetics rather than scholars. They were nevertheless encouraged to read, and each day time was allotted for this pursuit. There were two periods, one between sext and dinner, and the other between vespers and supper. In winter the early afternoon was chosen for this second period, but in summer this was a time of rest.

We have only scanty knowledge of the contents of the various libraries of the Order, but information as to the number of books in some of them is available. Titchfield, for instance, had about 224 books, and as well as the usual books on theology there were others on Grammar, Law, Surgery and Medicine. The Canons would do their reading in the Cloisters where the light was best; the copying of the choir books and cartularies would also be carried out there.

A few facts have come to light with regard to the Library at Torre Abbey. Oliver (Mon. Dioc. Exon. p. 171) says that in 1532 a certain Devonshire vicar, Hugh Bruselegh, vicar of Ilsington and Widecombe-in-the-Moor, left to Torre Abbey in his will a Bible in 6 volumes "cum Postilla magistri Nicholai de Lira glossa ordinara et interlinearia". Books were permitted by the Order to be loaned with the Abbot's permission, and a certain William Donne, Archdeacon of Leicester, made provision in his will for the return of a book which he had borrowed from Torre (See "Notes on the Will of a Mediaeval Archdeacon" by A. P. Moore in Ass. Arch. Soc's. Reports and Papers 27, 1903/4, p. 516).

(2) The Alleged Execution of Symon Hastynges

It is the unfortunate way of the world that the good is so often forgotten whilst things that are bad and macabre are meticulously recorded for succeeding generations. So it was with Torre Abbey. Its daily round of prayer and ministration to the sick and needy goes unmentioned whilst scandals are meticulously recorded in Rolls and Registers.
In 1390 rumours were rife to the effect that Abbot Norton had beheaded one of the Canons, Symon Hastynges. So persistent and troublesome was the gossip that Bishop Brantyngham suggested that the Canon should show himself publicly both in the Abbey and elsewhere. This he did, and the Bishop issued sentence of excommunication against those who had spread such a malicious report.

(3) The Retreat of John Harreys

In 1455 we are allowed a glimpse into the life of a certain Canon called John Harreys, and it is quite surprising to learn that life at Torre Abbey was too much for him. He wrote to the Pope (Calixtus III) asking permission to go to a safer spot. On Dec. 21st of the same year the Pope granted his request, permitting "John Harreys, a Canon of the

Premonstratensians of the Holy Trinity, Torre, in the Diocese of Exeter, to leave it and go to a safer place, as it is situated on the sea-shore in a place dangerous on account of invasions, so that the Canons have sometimes to have recourse to arms for the defence of themselves and the monastery, wherefore he fears to reside longer therein".

(4) *Recorded gifts in papal letter to Bishop Simon*

The Exchequer Cartulary contains at the very beginning two incomplete and undated papal letters. The first is to Simon of Apulia, Bishop of Exeter, and must therefore date from 1214/23. It was written either by Pope Innocent III or Honorius III, and in it the gifts of land and churches with which Torre Abbey has been endowed are rehearsed. What is of considerable interest is the fact that no less than four churches are mentioned which are not recorded elsewhere. They are those of Morton, Dupeforde, Trendelhou and Brenok. It is, of course, quite certain that these churches never came to the Canons of Torre, for there is no further mention of them anywhere. Whether the entry was an error in the first place, or whether these were promised gifts which never materialised, we cannot tell.

Bibliography

The Premonstratensian Order in England.
Colvin, H. M., "The White Canons in England" (Clarendon Press, 1951).
Gasquet, F. A., "The English Premonstratensians" Transactions of the Royal Historical Society, v.s. XVII, 1903.
Gasquet, F. A., "Collectanea Anglo-Premonstratensia" (ed.), 3 vols., Camden Society, 3rd. series, vols. VI, X, XII, 1904/6.

Torre Abbey
Blewett, Octavian, "Panorama of Torquay" (1832).
Dugdale, W., "Monasticon Anglicanum" (1817) pp. 855-945.
Ellis, A., Chapter on Torre Abbey from "An Historical Survey of Torquay" (Devonshire Press, 1930).
Hope, W. St. J., "Archaelogical Journal", LXX (1913, pp. 546/7).
Oliver, G., "Monasticon Dioecesis Exoniensis" (1846, pp. 169/91).
Russel, P., "A History of Torquay", pp. 19/21 (T.N.H.S. publication, 1960).
Walker, H., "Torre Abbey's Story began 770 years ago" (Devonshire Press, 1966).
Watkin, H., "The Abbats of Thorre", T.N.H.S. Transactions 1936/7.
Watkin, H., Pamphlet—"A Short Description of Torre Abbey" (Fleet Printing Works, 1909).
Watkin, H., "The Manor of Tormohun", T.N.H.S. Transactions 1923/4.
White, J. T., "The History of Torquay" (pp. 15/37), 1878.
Ewings, J., Various references from "Devon Monastic Lands", (Devonshire Press, 1955).

Bradworthy
Collacott, C. T., "The Parish and Church of Bradworthy". (Polypress Ltd., Bideford).

Cockington
Ellis, A., "An Historical Survey of Torquay" (chapter on Cockington).
Lang, J. F., "Old Cockington", vol. 1 (Western Litho Co. Plymouth, Ltd. 1971).

Dartmouth
Watkin, H., "Dartmouth Mediaeval Town", (Devonshire Press, 1935).
Russell, P., "Dartmouth", (Batsford, 1950).

Kingswear
Russell, P. and York, G., "Kingswear and Neighbourhood" (T.D.A. vol. 85, 1953).

Upton
Seymour, D., "Upton—the Heart of Torquay". (Townsend, 1963).

Wolborough
Rhodes, A. J., "Newton Abbot—its History and Development".

Index I

Places and People

Figures in heavy type refer to charter numbers, the rest to page numbers. e.g. **63** 199 will mean Charter 63 on page 199. Where possible, members of the same family, or bearing the same name, have been placed in chronological rather than alphabetical order. Dates have also been inserted when available.

A.

A., Abbot of St. Dogmael's, **259** 247.
Abbotskerswell, 101/3; Priory of St. Augustine, 102/3
Adam, Abbot of Torre, **34** 110, 12, 25/6/9, 30; s. of Peter, **253** 243
Adelard (Aillardus), chaplain of Beydon, **52/3** 118, **61-4** 119/20, 116, 123
Ailemundesburga (Greendale), **96** 139
Ailenewode (Ailvewde), Aylesbeare, manor and vill of, 141, **101/2** 142; Robert of, **101** 142; his w., Eufemia, **101** 142
Alan, Abbot of Tavistock, **49** 118, **295** 261
Alardus, **237** 221; his s., William de Prestatone, q.v.
Albamara (Aubermarle, Daumarle), Guy de, **191** 203; Reginald (1) de, u. of Lord William Brewer, **1** 83, **89** 138, **94** 139, **191** 203; his w., Avelina, **89** 138; their s., Fulk de, **112** 145; and Geoffrey, (1), **1** 83, **93/4** 139; Reginald (2), s. of Geoffrey, **93-100** 139/40; Geoffrey (2), s. of William, **109** 145, **111/12** 145; Isabella de Fortibus, Countess of, see Fortibus
Alburne (Aleburne), Walter de, **74** 121; William de, **206** 205
Alfaresworthy, chapel at, **158** 172, 96/7, 181
Aller (Alre, Halre, Aulre), **34/5** 110, 25, 30/1; burn, 104, 266; Little, **41** 110; manor of, 257; Teignaller (La Teyngeshalre), **111/12**; Upper, 111; Richard de, **38** 110/11, **279** 258; William de, 33; his w., Johanna, 33
Alliford, Andrew, **88** 131
Alneto, John de, **32** 110
Alphington (Alfyntone), 239; see also Richard, the parson of
Alta Villa, Sibilla de, **179** 188/9

Andrew (de Kilkenny), Dean of Exeter, **134** 154/5
Anglica Villa (Englischville), Theobald de, **27/8** 109/11
Anjou, Margaret de, 11
Anselm of Haverburg, 10
Apprys (Prise), John, **317/9** 248
Apulia, Simon de, Bishop of Exeter, **48** 118, **154** 172, **171** 187, **193** 203, 60, 74, 116, 278
Archbishops: see Canterbury, York
Archdeacons: see Barnstaple, Totnes, Taunton
Archer, William the, **42/3** 111; his s., Richard, **42** 111
Arundell, William Earl of, **170** 187
Ashclyst (Asseclist, Aissectist, Ayssclist) in Broadclyst 153-9; Barton of, **43**, 155/6; courthouse of, 156; Forest of, 157; manor of, **129** 154, 34, 43; prebend of, **124-6** 153, **128-134** 154, 32; connection with Exeter Castle Chapel, 34, 153, 158/9; prebendaries of, see Thomas and William de Werplisdone
Asselegh, Sir John de, **206** 205
Aston, Jimmie, 112
Attefenne, William, **241** 235
Aubeman, Peter, **67** 120
Augustine, St., Hermits of, 207
Aunfridus, **77** 129
Averforde, see Haverford
Avetone, see Blackawton
Avicia, lady of St. Marychurch, wife of Maurice de Rotomago, **280** 259; see also her second husband, Thomas de Cirencester
Axmouth, Roger de, the physician, q.v.
Aylesbeare, see Ailenewode

B.

Babbacombe Barton, 260
Babbecombe (Babcomb, Babbcumbe, Babbekumbe), Martin de, **62** 119; his w., Johanna, **62/3** 119; Richard de, **303-15** 272-4
Babidon, Henry, 67
Bacon, William, **207/10**
Bagtor (Baggatorre, Baggetorre), Roger de **310** 273; his w., Matilda **310** 273

Baldryngton (Baldrigton, Baldrynton), William de, **80** 130, **84/5** 130
Bampton, 147-9, 161/2
Barbere le, Walter, **24** 109
Baron (Baroun, Barun), Eustace le, **42** 111; Geoffrey, Canon of Torre, 39; John le, **67** 120, **227** 220, **278** 258
Barnage, Jordan, **104/106** 144, **292**
Barnstaple, Archdeacons of, see John de Bridport and Ralph de Werewell
Bartholomew (Abbot of St. Mary de Valle), **155** 172
Bartholomew Iscanus (Bishop of Exeter), see Iscanus
Bartletts (Wolborough), 104
Basset, see Passet
Bastard, Robert le, **212** 213/5
Batherm, River, 147/9
Baucan (Bauceyn), Stephen, **284/6** 260, **291/4** 260/1
Bayham, Abbey of St. Mary, Kent, 14, 18
Be, William, **149** 165
Beadon, see Beydon
Beare, Henry, **239** 221; William, 40
Bedall, Robert, Prior of Shap Abbey, 69, 70/1
Beeleigh, Abbey of St. Mary and St. Nicholas, Essex, 18
Beldermerse, Robert de, **313** 273
Bellastone, Baldwin de, **1** 83
Benjamin, vicar of Hennock, **48** 118, 116
Berchele (Berthele ?), William, **191** 203
Berkadone (Bercadone), John de, Abbot of Torre, 25-27, **194** 203, 39/40, 64
Bernhous, William, **42** 111
Beverley, Convent of Friars Preachers, 55
Bevian, William, **191** 203
Bevyle, John, **209** 206
Beydon (Beadon, Bydone), Adelard, chaplain of, q.v.; Edward de, **72** 120; his w., Cecilia, **72** 120; Roger de, **71** 120; his d., Amelota, **71** 120
Bickington (Bukynton), Sir Johel de, **267** 250
Bideforde, Roger de, **149** 165; Walter de, **149** 165
Bigbury (Bikebiri), John de, **299** 261
Bingham, Robert de, Bishop of Salisbury, **250** 243
Bitelgate (Bitelsgate), John de, **265** 250, **299** 261
Blackball Copse (Wolborough), 104, 112
Blackawton (Blakeaveton, Avetone), 219-229; manor of, **231/2** 220, **239** 221, **241** 235; Domesday mention of, 219; courthouse of, 225/6; ferling, extent of, 223; mediaeval holdings at, 223-8; mills of, **223** 220, **230** 220, **237/8** 221, 33, 227/8
Blacheforde (Bradworthy), **162/3/7** 172/3/5
Blackberry (Blakeburga, Blachebrigge), manor of, **107** 144, 143
Blakewille (Buckland-in-the-Moor), **82** 130

Blewett, Octavian, 4, 86
Blondy, Richard, Bishop of Exeter, **198** 204
Blundel, William (clerk), **248** 242
Blyndewille (Buckland-in-the-Moor), **80** 130/2; (Torre), 93
Boclond, Thomas de (clerk), **297**, 33
Bodeyn (Budyn, Buty), Walter, **104/5/7/8** 144; his b., Ralph (1), **104** 144, **292** 144; Walter's s., Ralph (2), **106/7** 144
Bodmin, Prior of, 33
Bokeyete, Stephen, **32** 110
Bolhaysburna, **80** 130/2
Bolla, **216** 214
Bon, Walter le, 217
Bonville (Bonwyle), Sir William, **209** 206
Bosco, Geoffrey de, **238** 221; Robert de, **169** 173/5, 181
Boslay, Herbert de, **245** 242
Boterau, William de, **35/6** 110, 25, 26; his w., Avelina, **35/6** 110, 25, 26
Botryngton (Baldrygtone?), Geoffrey de, **82** 130
Bourchier, Thomas, Lord of Cockington, **281** 252
Boohay (Bowhay), Kingswear, **222** 214, 213-6
Boway, Thomas, 40
Bowden (Bughedone), Buckland-in-the-Moor, **77** 129/30, 132
Bowe (Blackawton), 228
Bowhay, (Shillingford Abbot), 34, 240/1
Bradninch, Hundred of, see Index II
Bradewelle, Richard, (Official of diocese of Lincoln), **145** 164
Bradeworthi, Richard, vicar of Townstall, **210** 206
Bradworthy (Bradworthi), 171-186; church of, **1** 82, **150-156** 171/2, **164/5** 173, 40, 43, 79; advowson of, **150-6** 171/2; description of, 176/7; sanctuary lands of, 177; Manor of, **151/2** 171, 81, 83; Domesday mention of, 171; boundaries in, 99, 177/8; mediaeval holdings in, 179/80; mill of, **1** 180, **152** 171, **165/6** 173, 32, 82; vicars of, 182; vill of, **1** 82
Brai, Ralph de, 116, **191** 203
Brantyngham, Thomas de, Bishop of Exeter, **194** 203, 39, 40, 277
Brayntone (Breyntone), Walter de, **255** 243, **279** 253
Brendon (Sheepwash), demesne land of, **177** 188
Brenok, church of, 278
Brewer (Brewere, Briegwere, Briwere, Bruera, Brywere), Henry, 47; his s., Lord William, Founder of Torre Abbey, 1-5 82/4, **6/7** 85, **8-10** 95, **16/17/19** 108, **34** 110, **89-94** 138/9, **114** 148, **121** 149, **150/1/3** 171, **181/2** 193, **243** 242, **251** 243, 7, 47-50, 74, 81/4, 95/9, 116, 188, 193, 203, 239/40; his w., Beatrice de Valle, **6** 85, **8/9** 95, 49, 95/9; their sons

INDEX I PLACES AND PEOPLE

(1) William the Younger, **7** 85, **8** 95, **11/12** 85, **116** 148, 47/8, 51/2, 63, 83/5, 96/9, 193; his w., Johanna, **7** 85, 51, 95; (2) Richard, 51; their daughters (1) Engelesia, w. of Wm. de la, q.v. **90/2** 138, **114** 148, **116/7** 148; (2) Isabel, w. of Baldwin de Wike, q.v. 26; John, **1** 83; Richard, parson of Torre, **1** 82, 81; William de la, (s. of Antony), **16/17** 107/8, **21** 109, **90/2** 138, **114** 148, **116/17** 148, 101, 111, 133; William, Bishop of Exeter, **15** 85, **120** 149, **125** 153, **157** 172, **172** 187, **183** 193, **195/7** 204, 74; Geoffrey, g.s. of Wm. de la, **23** 109
Breyse, Ralph, 32
Brian, Abbot of Torre, **205** 205, 26, 33/4, 213
Bricius, s. of John Gobet q.v.
Bride's, Court of St., see Index II
Bridgewater, Hospital of St. John the Baptist, 49
Bridport (Brydeport), John de, Archdeacon of Barnstaple, **173/4** 187; Robert, **88** 131
Brixham, John, vicar of, q.v.
Bronescombe, Walter, Bishop of Exeter, 26, 32-4, 154
Bruselegh, Hugh, 277
Bryene (de Bryan), Guy, 39, 54
Buckfast, William (1), Abbot of, **1** 83, 30; William (2), Abbot of, 32
Buckland (Bokelonde), Guy de, **9** 95, 99; his s., Alan de, **1** 83, **9** 95, 51, 116; William de, **76/7** 127/8; his g.s. Roger de, **76/7** 127, **80/3** 130, **86/8** 131; his w., Alice, **80** 130; their son, William (2) **86** 130/1, **88** 131; Thomas de, men, 1277, **297** 261
Buckland Brewer (Buckland Bret, North Bokelond), 193-200; church of, **181-7** 193/4; advowson of, **183/4/7** 193/4; description of, 195/6; Fraternity attached to, 195/6; sanctuary lands of, 198/9; old vicarage of, 43, 197-9; manor of, **189** 194; Domesday mention of, 193; mediaeval holdings of, 199
Buckland-in-the-Moor (Bokelonde in la More), 127/32; manor of, **81/3** 130, **86/8** 131; courthouse of, 130; Domesday holdings of, 127/9
Budyn (Budeyn, Buty), Ralph, **104/5/7/8** 144, **292** 144; his b., Walter, **104/5** 144; Ralph (2), s. of Walter, **107** 144
Bugge, William, **176/7** 258
Bughedone, see Bowden
Bughweren, Emelot, **29** 109
Bulkworthy, chapel of St. Michael (Buckland Brewer), 43, 196/7
Burde, Philip, **206** 205
Burdun, Nicholas, and his w. Margery, **70** 120
Burg', la (Pancrasweek), **168** 173, 182
Burgeis, Thomas, vicar of Townstall, **194** 203
Burlawestone (Blackawton), **231** 220
Burlestone, William, **209** 206
Burnage, Robert, **28** 109

Burnel, Roger, **1** 83, 116; his s., Walter, **1** 83
Burnstaburge, Symon, **280** 259
Buvy, Robert, **286** 260
Buzun, William, **212** 213/5
Bysinianus, William de, rector of Exminster, **249** 242, 240
Bydon, see Beydon
Byggode, Richard, 66
Bytton, Thomas, Bishop of Exeter, 74

C.

Cade, Richard, Abbot of Torre, 25, 27, 41/2, 65/6, **239** 221, 73/4, 77/8, **316/7** 248
Calixtus 111, Pope, 277
Caldey, Thomas Kermerdine, Prior of, q.v.
Cammeis (Cameys, Kemys), Pembs., see St. Dogmael's Abbey
Campo, de Bello, Thomas, Earl of Warwick, **196** 204
Cannonwalls (Cammahilla), Greendale, **95** 139/41
Cantelupe, William de, 32; his w., Eva, 32
Canterbury, Archbishops of, see William Courtenay, Walter de Hempsham, Stephen Langton, Hubert Walter
Cardigan (Kardikun), Priory of, **270** 247
Caretarius, Geoffrey, **137** 161
Carpentarius, see Geoffrey, Michael, Richard, William
Cary, Sir George, 3; family of, 259; Colonel Cary, 52
Casteiller (Chastiller, Casteilleir), see Woodbury Castle
Castelwike, Henry de, **297** 261
Cavebiri, see Keyberry
Cervus, Robert, **256** 244
Chamberlayn, William, **289** 272, **314/5** 274; his w., Agatha, **289** 272
Chard, Thomas, Suffragan to Bishop Veysey, 27, 43
Chaulesway (Caueliswere, Cavileswere), William, **315** 274; his w., Matilda, **307** 273, **315** 274; their s., William (2), **307/8/11/15** 273/4
Chaumpeaus, Robert de, **1** 83
Chawleigh (Chauulegh), advowson of church of, **126** 153
Chelston (Chillestone), meadow of, **263** 252
Chetelisbeare, William de, **310/12** 273; his w., Matilda, **310** 273
Cheverstone, Sir John de, **222** 215
Chinrigge (Chimbrigge), Sheepwash, **175/6** 187
Chivaler, William, **300** 262; his d., Agnes, **300** 262
Chola, Thomas, **83** 130
Christiana, a Premonstratensian Abbot, **155** 172
Christina, a widow, **99** 140

Chudleigh (Cheddelegh), 33, 55; church of, 123; Nicholas, vicar of, q.v.; Sir James, **209** 206
Churche, John de la, **149** 165
Cirencester (Cirecestre), Thomas de, **219** 214, **299** 261; his w. Alice (Avicia) de Rotomago q.v.; Sir Walrand de, **72** 120, **267** 250; William de, **265** 250, **298** 261
Clarus, Chapel of St. (Dartmouth), 37
Clayhanger (Clehangre), **120** 149, 57, 147-50
Clayparks (la Cleye), **71-74** 120/1, 123/4
Cledone (Buckland Brewer), **190** 194
Clifton (Dartmouth), 203
Clist, Bishop of Exeter's manor of, 73
Clist, Girard de, **46/7** 118, 116; his w. Beatrice (widow of Philip de Salmonavilla q.v.); their s., William, de, **47** 118, 116, **50** 118, **61** 119; their g.s., Sir William de, **46** 118, **50** 118, 116; his d., Isabel, wife of Richard Tremeneth, 123
Cliston, Lower (Blackawton), 229
Clov(u)esworthi, Nicholas de, **32** 110, 102
Cockington (Cokyntone, Kokyntone), 87, 247-55; chapel of, **260/1** 247/8, **270** 247, **316-9** 248, 25, 37, 42; description of, 253-5; chantry at, **267** 250, 58; link with St. Dogmael's Abbey, **259/62** 247/8, **270** 247, **316-9** 248, 42, 248/9; later parochial status, 249; path to, 255; manor of, 89; wood of, **1** 83, **10** 95, 83, 99; Roger (1) de, **262** 248, 32 (see also his u., Robert FitzMartin); Roger (2) de, **263** 252, **264** 249, **278** 258; his w., M., **264** 249; Sir Roger (3) de, **32** 110, **265** 249; his s., William, **266-8** 250, 58, 217; Wm's w., Johanna, **267/8** 250, 37, 58; his b., Henry de, **266** 250, **281** 252; Sir James de, **222** 215, **269** 252
Coffinswell, (Coffynwille, Welles Coffyn), 87, 257-67; courthouse at, 264/5; manor of (Welle), 36; Domesday mention of, 257; ferling, extent of, 263; mill of, **298** 261/3; lords of fee, 258/9, 263
Coffyn, Hugh men. 1239/40, **284** 260/2; Robert, men. 1286, **42** 11, **293/8/9** 261, **300** 262/3; his d., Christina, **300** 262/3 (see also her h., Alan de Colebrook); Margery, **300** 262/3 (see also her h., Thomas de Scobahille); Roysa, **300** 262/3 (see also her h., Adam de la Hille)
Cola, John, **222** 215
Colaton Raleigh, 133, 143
Cole, Everard, **244** 242, 240
Colebrook, Alan de, **300** 262/3; his w., Christina Coffyn, q.v.; their s., Stephen, **300** 262/3
Coleton, see Shiphay Collaton
Colreforde (Buckland-in-the-Moor), **80/1** 130/2
Colvin, H. M., 25, 27, 53, 210, 239
Colyton, 142
Colum, Walter, **1** 83
Colynson, Edward, Canon of Welbeck, 43, 69

Combe (Ideford), 269-71
Combe, Richard de, **238** 221; William, Abbot of Dunkeswell, **189/90** 194, 36
Combe Holeridge (Ideford), 269/71
Combe Mill, 269/70
Compton, Philip de, men. 1285, **279** 258, **305** 272; William, men. 1293, **32** 110, **265** 250, **305** 272; Robert, mid 13th C., **267/8** 250, 217, **305** 272
Compton Giffard, 95, 99
Corbridge, Thomas, Archbishop of York, **196** 204
Corbyn's Head (Corvenasse), **264** 249, 27, 82, 89, 93
Cornwall, Earls of:—Reginald, **247** 242, 49; his s., Henry, **18** 108, **247** 242; Richard, **248** 242
Coryngton, Richard, circator and cantor of Torre Abbey, 67/8
Cotelforde, Richard de, Prior of Torre, 26, 38, 53-56
Court Barton, Coffinswell, 264-6
Courtenay, Edward, Earl of Devon, **209** 206; Gervase, **243** 242; Hugh, men. 1276, **128** 154; Hugh, d. 1341, 37; Hugh men. 1395, **209** 206; Robert, **19** 108, **124** 153, 12; his w. (?), Matilda, **20** 108; Sir Thomas, **222** 215; William Archbishop of Canterbury, **196** 40,
Cowick, Convent Chapel of, 37
Crispin (Cryspin), Guy, **199/201-3** 204/5
Cumbe, see Index II for charter given at,
Curiford, Ralph, **37** 110; see also his p.'s, William and Avelina de Boterau

D.

Dabridgecourt, Sir John, 210
Daccombe (Daccumbe, Daucombe), 87, 257-67; chapel of, 266/7; courthouse of, 44, 266/7; manor of, **284** 260; Domesday mention of, (Wille), 257; lords of the fee, 258/9, 263; Robert de, **288** 272; his s.(?), Michael de, **288** 272/4; Jordan de, **283-7** 260, **290** 272, **291** 260, **294/5** 261, 12, 32, 57, 212/4; his w., Cecilia, **283** 260, **285** 272, 57, 262; their s., Thomas de, **287** 260, **290** 272/4; his s.(?), Alan de, **279** 258
Damascus, pseudo Bishop of; see Hugh
Damyot, William, Mayor of Dartmouth, **209** 206
Danne, Sir John, **222** 214
Dart, River, **81/2** 130, 127, 131
Dartmoor, **1** 82, **240** 235
Dartmouth, **194** 203, **201** 205; Clifton Dartmouth, **196** 204, **209** 206; see also Norton and Townstall
Date (?), Sir Robert, **233** 221; Eustace, **298** 261

INDEX I PLACES AND PEOPLE

Dealdone, Hamelin de, **278** 258
Decoy (Wolborough), 104/5
Deghere, John, sub-Prior of Torre, 56
Deneforde, William de, **257** 244
Deneis, Sir Robert le, **168** 173/5, **206** 205, **265** 250, 57, 182
Denscombe, see Dunnyngestone
Devon, Earl of, as Patron of Torre Abbey, 66; see also Courtenay
Diptford (Dupeforde) church of, 278
Doddenmanneslond (Buckland-in-the-Moor), **84** 130
Doddescombe, Robert de, **265** 250
Dogmael, Abbey of St. Mary and St. (Pembs.), 247-9, **259-62** 247/8, **270** 247, **316-9** 218, 25, 42, Abbots of, see A., Roger, Philip Saundere
Donne, William, 277
Dover, ffubert de, **1** 83
Dreyton (Teritone), Blackawton, **232** 220/9
Dryburgh, Abbey of St. Mary, Berwicks., 14, 18
Dunestal, see Townstall
Dunkeswell, Abbey of St. Mary, Devon, 29, 36, 47, 49/50, 58, 77, 96; William Combe, Abbot of, q.v.; Lord William Brewer's coffin at, 49/50
Dunnyngestone (Clayhanger), 147/50, **114-21** 148/9, 36, 57; chapel of, **120** 149; manor of, **114** 148; Domesday mention of, 147; mill of (Denscombe), 147
Dunster (Dunstorr), Nicholas de, **149** 165
Dupeforde, see Diptford
Durford, Abbey of, Sussex, 7, 42, 66, 69
Dyare, Thomas, Abbot of Torre, 25, 27, 42/3, 78/9, 86, 176, 184

E.

E., father Abbot of the Premonstratensians, 31
E., Bishop of Exeter (Edmund Stafford q.v.)
Eale's (Greendale), 141
Easby, Abbey of St. Agatha, Yorks., 14, 18
Edward I, King of England, **132** 154/5, **302** 272, 73, 207, 269; II, **301** 262, 37; III, **258** 244, 53, 64, 240/1, 267; *the Hound*, **279** 258/9; *the fisherman*, 33
Efrideswelle, (Torre), **1** 82, 251
Egg Buckland, 95, 99
Egglestone, Abbey of St. Mary and St. John the Baptist, Yorks., 14, 18
Eliot, son of William forestarius, **24** 109
Ellacome (Wolborough), **32** 110, 102-3
Ellis, A., 4, 27, 56, 87
Elys, John, **32** 110
Engeram, see Ingelramus
Ernulpho, Henry de Campo, **1** 83
Esse, Adam de, **164** 173; Robert de, 33
Estecumbe, (Bradworthy), **152** 171

Estre (del Estre, Lestre), Geoffrey de, **1** 83, **240** 235/7; William de, **240** 235
Eufemia (w. of Angerus de Hunteba q.v.)
Exeter, Bishops of:—see John, Henry Marshall, Simon of Apulia, William Brewer, Richard Blondy, Walter Bronescombe, Peter Quivel, Thomas Bytton, John Grandisson, Thomas Brantyngham, Edmund Stafford, Edmund Lacy, Richard Redmayne, John Veysey; castle chapel of, **125** 153, 34; cathedral church of, **123** 152, **158** 172; chapter of, **134** 154, **158** 172; Deans of:—see Serlo, Andrew de Kilkenny; Hospital of St. John, 75; houses of Abbot of Torre in, 33; Priory of St. Nicholas, **250** 243
Exminster, 239/40, **249** 242
Eya, Philip de, clerk, **248** 242

F.

Falese, see N., Abbot of,
Fanuel, Ralph, **245** 242
Farms of Torre Abbey, see chapters on Ashclyst, Blackawton, Bradworthy, Buckland-in-the-Moor, Daccombe and Coffinswell, Hennock, Holrigge, Glascombe, Greendale, Kingswear, Sheepwash, Northshillingford, Wolborough
Faukes, John, **200**/7 205
Fawy, Gilbert de, **208** 205
Ferendone (Ferndone, Ferenduna), Henry de, **114**/5/7 148, 57; his s.(?), Nicholas, **118** 148; Sir Ralph de, **113** 145; his s., (?) William, **113** 145
Ferers (Ferars), Fulk de, **276**/8/9 258; his w., Lucia, **276** 258; John de, 37; Martin de, **209** 206
Fewthe, see Fuge
Finamore (Fynamore), William, **216**/7 214/5; his sis., Alice, see Rotomago; his s. Thomas, **206**/7 205
Fishacre (Fisacre, Fissakre, Fysthacre), Henry de, **226** 220; Martin de, men. 1254, 67 120, **214** 214, **278** 258, **293** 261, 217; Peter de, **205**/8 205/6, **233** 221, **298** 261, 33; his w., Beatrice, **205** 205, 213; Warin de, 217; Sir William de, men. 1270, **72**/4 120/1, **233** 221, **297** 261, **305**/7 272; Ives de, **222** 214; Sir William (2) de, mid 14th C., **267** 250
FitzHerbert, Matthew, **191** 203
FitzMartin, Robert, lord of Cockington (mid. 12th C.), **259** 247, **270** 247; Andrew (late 13th C. **234** 221; Nicholas, men. 1271, **235**/6 221
FitzMatthew, Peter, **223**/5 220, **228**/9 220; his b., Roger, **223**/230 220; his b., John, **224**/5/30 220, 33; his n., Matthew, s. of John, **225** 220; Herbert, Matthew's s., **231** 220

FitzStephen, William, **191/2** 203, 12, 74, 209; his w., Isabella de Languire, **191** 203; his s., Richard, **192** 203; Gilbert, Richard's s., **199** 204, **206** 205, 74, Henry, **208** 205; Richard, men. 1285, **200/8** 205
FitzThomas, Sir John, **248** 242
FitzWilliam, Walter, 33
Flandrene, Richard, **226** 220
Fleet Mill (Torre), 90
Fleming, Richard, **191** 203
Fluda (la Flode), **50-3** 118, **59/60** 119, **62-70** 119/20, 121-3; Walter de la, **54** 119, **58** 119, **68** 120; his s., Richard, **50-3-4-5-7-9** 118/19, 122; his sis., Alice, **54**, **58** 119; his w., Odelina, **59** 119, 122; their children: Richard, **65** 120, 123; Robert, **62** 119; Maria (Mariota), **56/7** 119, **65** 120
Foliot, Sampson, **274/8** 258, 57; his s., Richard, **275/7/8** 258
Folour (Fullo), William le, **308/9** 272/3, **313-5** 273/4
Fonte, Walter de, **280** 259
Forde, William de la, **101** 142
Forde House (Wolborough), 60, 104; Grange, 104
Forest, William, **222** 215
Forestarius, William, **24** 109
Fortibus, Isabella de (Countess of Albermarle), **229** 220
Foxley (ffoxleghe, ffoxleye), wood of (Greendale), **96/7** 139/41, 145
Frauncys (Franciscus), Osbert le, **215/20** 214/5/6; his w., Dionysia, **220** 214
Frelard, Robert 33, **40** 110/11
Frinille, Sir Roger de, **248** 242
Fuge (Fewthe), Blackawton, **231** 231
Fulleforde Bridge (near Torre Abbey), **267** 250/1; Brook, 89 **264/5** 249/50/51, **281** 252; mill **265/7** 249/50
Fullo, see Folour
Futerel, William, **216** 214

G.

Galier, Richard, **308** 273
Galle, Philip, **148** 164/5
Gambon, John de Torre, **239** 221; William, **239** 221, 41, 65
Gara, River, 219
Gasquet, Abbé F.A., 27, 35, 65
Gatepathe (Gappah), Richard de, men. 1278, **51** 118, **72** 120, **75** 121, **303-14** 272-4; Thomas de, mid. 13th C., **233** 221
Gaverock, John, 60; his w., Joan, 60
Gayer (Gayr), Richard, **303/10/12** 272/3
Geoffrey, *carpentarius*, **95** 139

Germyn, Robert, **1** 83
Gervase, Abbot of Prémontré, **155** 172; s., of Odo, 25, 30, **34** 110
Giffard, Sir Alexander, **248** 242; Geoffrey, **25-6-8** 109
Gilbert, father Abbot of the Premonstratensians, 35; Brother, 16; Geoffrey, **222** 215; Otto, **239** 221, **281** 252
Giles (de cancellaria), **248** 242
Gilotta, d. of John of Keyberry (q.v.), **41** 110
Giron (Giroun, Geroldi, Mungeron, Mongiron), Drogo (Drew) de Monte, **242/5/6** 242, **251/6** 243, 81, 240
Glazebrook, East and West, 235/6; wood of Glascombe, **240** 235; Glazemeet 235/6
Gloucester, Thomas, Duke of, **196** 204
Gobet, John, **85** 130/1; his s., Bricius **85** 130
Godrik, Robert, **149** 165
Goldmoors (Wolborough), 104
Gonnyldesone, Walter, **84** 130
Gortley, Richard, 78
Grandisson, John, Bishop of Exeter, 27, 35, 37, 38, 53, 55/6
Granger, Walter le, **96** 139
Gras (Cras),Edmund le, parson of Teignbruer, 63; Geoffrey, 54/5; John, Abbot of Torre, 26, 27, 38, 53-56, 64, **241** 235; Thomas le, **310** 273
Gratecleve, wood of, **189/90** 194/9
Greendale (Grendel, Grendull, Gryndell), Woodbury, 132-46, **91-5** 138/9, **99** 139, **109** 145, 34, 82; barton of, 133-6; boundaries of, 140; brook, 134/7; courthouse of, 135; dependents' houses, 135/6; manor of, 146; mediaeval names, surviving, 140/1; mill of, **113** 145, 34, 137; Robert de, **113** 145, **303** 272
Gregory IX, Pope, 11, 60, 97
Grosseteste, Robert, Bishop of Lincoln, **148** 165
Grungnium (Cockington), **264** 249, 253
Guril (Guryll), John, men. 1257, **39** 110, **43** 111, 31; his b. (?) Robert, **40** 110
Grymestone, George, Canon of Torre, 39
Gylbard, see Gilbert
Gylle, Thomas, **239** 221

H.

Haccombe (Haccumbe, Hakkumbe), Sir Jordan de, men. 1282, **267** 250, **298** 261, **306** 273, 217; his son (?) Stephen de, **67** 120; Sir Stephen de, men. 1309, **299** 261
Haggelegh, (Haclega, Haggeleya), Milverton, Som., 151-2 **122/3** 152
Haket, Roland, **138/9** 163/4
Halchewille, Andrew de, **315** 274
Hallond, **40** 110

INDEX I   PLACES AND PEOPLE

Halshanger (Halshangre), William de, **75** 121
Hamptisforde, Richard de, Cellarer of Torre Abbey, 56
Harecombe, Alfred de, **306** 273
Harolesdene (Horaldesdone), **163/7** 173
Harreys, John, Canon of Torre, 277/8
Hartley, West (Hurtelegh), Blackawton, **226/32/39** 220/1/3/9
Havene, Robert de la, **149** 165
Haverford, Priory of, **270** 247
Hawley, John, 40
Haystynges, Symon, Canon of Torre, 277
Haytor (Haitorra), Hundred of, **18** 108
Hele, la, 93
Helena, William de Sancta, **257** 244
Hemingford, Thomas, 74
Hempsham, Walter de, Archbishop of Canterbury, **196** 204
Hennaborough (Wolborough), 103; wood of, 103, 113
Hennock (Hanoc), 115-26; church of, **44/8** 118, 116; advowson of, **48** 118; description of, 116/7; Rectory of, 44, 117; vicars of, 125; manor of, **50** 118; Domesday mention of, 116; ecclesiastical manor of Fluda, 121/2; mediaeval holdings of, 121-5; Roger de, **45** 118, 116; his s., William, **45** 118, 116; Wm.'s d., Beatrice (w. of Philip de Salmonavilla q.v.), **44/5/7** 118, 116; Girard de, **49/52** 118, **59/60** 119
Henry I, King of England, 248; II, 82, **6** 85, 7, 47, 82/5, 232; III, **30** 109, **121** 149, **148** 165, **228** 220, 47/9, 111; VI, 11; VIII, 43, 75, 179; s. of Reginald, Earl of Cornwall (q.v.), **247** 242; s. of Count Richard of Flanders, **1** 83; Bishop of Exeter, see Marshall; the priest, **188** 194; s. of William, **292** 144
Heriet, Richard, **191** 203
Hervey, the priest, **141** 164
Hethe, la (Ingsdon), **240** 235
Heym, Peter, **206** 205
Hidesburga (Bradworthy), 82, **152** 171, 177-9
Hille (Hulle), Adam de la, **300/1** 262; his s., Roger, **300/1** 262/3; his w., Roysa Coffyn, **300** 262/11
Hircy le (de Hyerti), William, **309/12** 273
Hockbere, Edward de la, **54** 119; see also Huxbear
Hocrigge (Sheepwash), **175-8** 187/8
Hoggesbrok (Hoggesbroc, Hokesbroc), 137; Geoffrey, **98** 139/40; Robert, **95/6** 139
Hokemore, wood of (Buckland-in-the-Moor), **76/7** 127, **81** 130/1
Holebeme, John, 78
Holecombe, Osbert de, **75** 121; his w., Mariota, **75** 121
Holland, Lord John, of Huntingdon, **209** 206

Holrigge (Ideford), 32, 269-75; David de, **284/5** 260, **290** 272, **306** 273, 262, 274; his d., Petronilla, w. of Richard de Plymtree (q.v.), **302-5-6-9** 272/3, **313** 273; Okelina de, **308** 273; Richard de, **308** 273; Susanna de, n. of Richard, the parson of Alphington (q.v.), **303** 272, **308/9** 273; Richard de (?), **308** 273; Agatha de, w. of William Chamberlayne (q.v.), **289** 272; William de, men. 1286/7, **302/7/13** 272/3; fulling mill at, 270
Holloway (Holeweislonde), Colaton Raleigh, **104-5-6-8** 144, 143, **292** 144
Homans, Alward, **51** 118
Honewille, **202** 205
Honorius, III, Pope, 60, 278
Hoo (la ho), **9** 95 99
Hope Farm, Ilsham, 95
Hope, W. St. J., 15
Horaldesdone (Bradworthy), **163/7** 173, 183
Horestone (Kingswear), **213** 214/6
Horridge (Ilsington), 269
Horscumbe (Wolborough), 111
Horton, Abbot of, 101; Henry le, **188** 194; Sir Gervase de, men. 1249, **165** 173/5; Thomas de, men. 1311, **164** 173
Houbotone, manor of, **91/2** 138, 133
Hubert, head Premonstratensian Abbot in British Isles, 66
Huddersfeld, William, **239** 221
Hugh, pseudo, Bishop of Damascus, 38, 207; Bishop of Lincoln, **141/3** 164; Hugh (II), Bishop of Lincoln, **142** 164; vicar of Townstall, **198** 204
Huish (Hywys), **51** 118, **67** 120/1
Hulle, William de la, **253** 243
Humaz (Humax?), Richard, **75** 121
Hunteba, Angerus (Ingerus) de, **101/2** 142, 141; his s., Alexander, **102** 142, 141
Huntisbere, **101/2** 142, 141
Hurdestoke (Stokenham), manor of, **224/9** 220
Hurtelegh, West (Blackawton), **232** 220; G. de, **227** 220
Huxbear (Hennock), 122, 125
Hyerti, see Hircy

I.

Ideford, see Holrigge
Ilsham, chapel of, 96/7; grange of, 95-7; manor of, **8** 95, 47, 96; Domesday mention of, 95
Ingelramus (Engeram), s. of Odo, **16** 107, **37** 110, 25, 26; his b., Gervase, q.v.; his sis., Avelina de Boterau, q.v.
Innocent III, Pope, 60, 278
Isabella de Languire, w. of William FitzStephen, q.v. **191** 203; de Waddeton, q.v.

Iscanus, Bartholomew, Bishop of Exeter, **259** 247, **262** 248

J.

J., Archdeacon, of Barnstaple, see John de Bridport
J., Bishop of Exeter, see John Grandisson
J., Treasurer of York and Salisbury, **196** 204
Jakeford (Chagford), see William *tabernarius* of Jerusalem, **282** 260/2; hospital of (Totnes), **211** 213
Johelisforde (Buckland-in-the-Moor), **77** 129
John, Abbot of Torre, 25-27, 38; see also John le Rous, John Gras, John Lacy; the chaplain, 116; Bishop of Exeter, **185** 194; de curia de Bradworthy, **164** 173; David, **317** 248; Duke of Aquitaine and Lancaster, **196** 204; of Holeweyeslonde, **108** 144; his s., Philip, **108** 144; of Keyberry, **41** 110; his d., Gilotta, **41** 110; King of England, 4/5 84, **170/4** 187/8, 47, 51, 74, 84; vicar of Brixham, **221** 214/6
Jordan, the clerk, **268** 250; kinsman of Walter Budeyn (q.v.), **105** 144

K.

Kalixtus, St., Fair of, **103** 142
Karra, Richard, **38** 110
Karswille, **1** 83, **10** 95, 257; Nicholas de, **42** 111
Kelly, William de, **1** 83
Kemys (Cammeis), see St. Dogmael's Abbey
Kermerdine, Thomas, Prior of Caldey, **317** 248
Keyberry (Cavebiri, Kavebiry), **33** 110, **41-3** 110/11, 104; mill of, **101/2** 104/5,; John of, **41** 110/11
Kings of England, see Edward, Henry, John, Richard
Kingsdon (Kyngesdon), **1** 83, **10** 95, 99
Kingswear (Kyngeswere), 213-6, **211/14** 213/4, **220** 214, 32/3; court of, **205** 205; mill of, see Levricestone: Alan de, **215** 214
Kington (Kynkitone, Kynton), Wilts., Priory of, **185-7** 194, 31; Maria, Prioress of q.v.
Kirkham, Sir Richard de, men. 1293, **265** 250; Nicholas de, men. 1531, 44
Kittery (Kitetorra), **212/5** 213/4/5; courthouse at, 215
Kokyntone, see Cockington
Kyne, John le, **113** 145
Kyngdon, Nicholas de, **85** 130

Kypping, Robert, 66

L.

Lacy, Edmund, Bishop of Exeter, **209** 206, 27; John, Abbot of Torre, 27, 41, 65
Laket, (Sheepwash), **177** 188
Lancelyn (Lanceyn), William, **51** 118, **67** 120/1
Lane, Rev. Richard, of Cofflete, 59
Langeforde, Sir Richard de, **159** 172, **166** 173, 32, 174
Langeforde Lestre, manor of, 231/2/5
Langeham, (Greendale), **96** 139
Langescore, **82** 130/2
Langton, Stephen, Archbishop of Canterbury, 48/9
Languire, Isabella de, **191** 203, 209; see also her h., William FitzStephen
Laon, Premonstratensian Abbey of, 7; diocese of, 7
Lapumei, Henry de, **191** 203
Laurence, Abbot of Torre, **126** 153, **166** 173, **284** 260, **295** 261, 26, 31/2
Leger, John St., 2
Leland, John, 22, 87
Lemon, River, 101
Lestre, see Estre
Levricestone (Lethewiston, Liewichestona, Ludewychetona, Ludwigintone), in Brixham; manor of, **205** 205, **216/222** 214, 213-6; Domesday mention of, 213; mill of, 215/6
Leye (Leia, Upley), manor of 241/2; Domesday mention of, 241/2; Adam de la, **310** 273; his b. (?), John de la, **310** 273; Richard de la, men. 1336, **257** 244, 240
Leyland (Leye), Bradworthy, **151** 171, 179
Licques, Premonstratensian Abbey of, 7
Lincoln, Bishops of, see Hugh, Hugh (2), Robert Grosseteste, Dean and Chapter of, **143** 164; Bishop's Official, see Bradewelle, Richard de
Lindhayne (Greendale), 140
Livermead (Cockington), **264** 249, **269** 252/3
London, **248** 242; Benedict de, **233** 221
Lucy, Sir G. de, **248** 242; Godfrey de, Bishop of Winchester, **191** 203, **243** 242, **251** 243
Luke (son of John), **26** 109, 111
Lumena, Sir Richard de, **267/8** 250
Luskes, W. de, a Premonstratensian Abbot, **155** 172
Lydford (Lideford), Michael de, 33
Lyfton, Miles de, 36
Lynham, Ralph de (Seneschal), **200/7** 205
Lynicombe (Hennock), **73/5** 121, 124/5
Lynihuse, see Lynicombe; William de, **75** 121
Lysons, D. and S., 148, 203

INDEX I PLACES AND PEOPLE

M.

MacEnery, Rev. John, 23
Mahimorhilhend (Buckland-in-the-Moor), **80** 130/2
Maloysel, Robert, vicar of St. Marychurch, 36
Man, William, **200**/7/8 205/6
Manor Farm, Coffinswell, 263
Mara, Sir Peter de, **248** 242
Marchasio, Adam de, (a Premonstratensian Abbot), **155** 172
Mare, John, **300** 262; his s., Luke, **300** 262
Margaret of Anjou, q.v.; d. of Seward (q.v.), **271**/2/5 257/8
Maria, Prioress of Kington, **185-7** 194, 31
Markeros, Robert, **175-8** 187/8
Marshall, Henry, Bishop of Exeter, **1** 83, **14** 85, **22** 109, **153** 171, 74, 81, 249
Martin: the chaplain, **191** 203; Rev. Keble, 264/7; IV, Pope, **131**/133 154/5; the priest, **199** 204
Martyn, Robert, **286** 260; Sir William, **299** 261
Mary, the lady, **177** 188
Matthew, s. of Robert, the parson of Torrington, **180** 188
Maynbow (Maynbogh, Maynbough), in manor of Wolborough, **25-8** 109, 111
Meavy (Mewy), Richard de, **297** 261
Melford (Malford?), Richard, 60
Menevia (diocese of St. David's), **319** 248
Meryfeld, John, **239** 221
Michael *carpentarius* **208** 206; Fraternity of St., 196
Middletone, Adam de, **297** 261
Mile, Robert, **188** 194
Mileforde, **188** 194
Milesteken (Greendale), **96** 139
Mills, see Blackawton, Bradworthy, Coffinswell, Dunnyngestone, Fleete, Fulleforde, Greendale, Kingswear, Keyberry, Moreton; fulling mills, see Blackawton, Holrigge
Millebrok (Buckland-in-the-Moor), **77** 129, 80/1 130-2
Milverton (Som.), 151-2
Modworthy, Walter de, **208** 206
Mohun (Moyun), Reginald (1) de, 51, 63; his w., Alice, d. of Lord William Brewer, 51, 63, 231; their s., Reginald (2) de, 21, 32, 63, **12/13** 85, **119** 148, **278** 258; his s., John (1) de, 21; his g.s., John (3) de, 21; John (4) de, men. 1346, 21, 22, 231; Sir John (5) de, s. of John (4), 39 58, 63/4, 87; his w., Johanna, 39, 58, 63/4
Monksmoor (Ugborough), 217, 231-33
Morcelle (Morcales, Mortell), Sir Herbert, 72/4 120/1, 267/8 250, 217; J., Count of, **185** 194; Robert de, **167** 120

More, John, **239** 221; Ralph de, **191** 203
Morland, William, clerk, 34
Moreton (Morton), church of, 278; mill of (Bradworthy), 174
Mottisfont, (Hants.), Abbey of, 47, 49
Mount Boone (Dartmouth), 202
Moynge, William le, **257** 244
Muchelbrook (Michelbrook), Sheepwash, **177** 188
Muchele, William le, **127** 153
Mule, Roger de, 111
Mungiron, see Giron, Monte,
Mychel, William, Abbot of Torre, 27, 40
Myltone, Robert, 71

N.

N., Abbot of Falese, 172
Nelson, Lord Horatio, 3
Nethway (Kingswear), 216
Newenham (Berks.), **5** 84, 30, **187** 194; Symon de, **222** 215
Newhouse, Abbey of St. Mary and St. Martial, Lincs., 7, 25, 30, 66-8; John Swyfte, Abbot of, q.v.
Newton Abbot (Nova Villa), see Wolborough,
Neyvin, Sibilla, **201** 205
Nicholas, the clerk of Kerswille, **42** 111; Pope Nicholas IV, see Taxation of (Index II); Prior of St., Exeter, **250** 243; de Torre, 116; vicar of Chudleigh, 49/50 118, 52/3 118, 61-3 119, 116, 123; his d., Johanna de Babbecombe, q.v.
Nimet (Nymeth, Nymet), Sir Walter de, 266/7 250, 34
Nonant (Novant), Henry de, **9** 95, 49, 99; his b., Roger, **9** 95
Norbert, St., 7
Noreys, Richard, **88** 131
Northlane, Thomas, **28** 109
North Shillingford, see Shillingford Abbot
Northwille (Torre), **1** 82, **6** 85, 30, 82/3, 250
Norton (Nortona), courthouse of, **200**/8 205, 201/2; chantry chapel of, **199** 204,; manor of, 201, **200**/7 205; Domesday mention of, 201; William, Abbot of Torre, **209** 206, 25, 27, 40, 77/8, 176, 184
Norton Park, 201/3
Nowell, William, Prior of Torre, 65/6
Nutcombe Manor (Clayhanger), 147/8
Nywapitte (Glascombe), **240** 235
Nywenham, Berks., **187** 194; Symon de, **222** 214/5
Nywetone, William de, **299** 261

O.

Odelina, d. of Seward (q.v.), **273/5** 258
Ogwell (Wogewyll), East, **29** 109, **31** 109, 112; its church, 77/79; grave coverstones, 25, 40, 42/3, 77/9; 6th C. inscribed stone, 77, 90; manorhouse, 112; Robert de, **67** 120
Olchard (Ideford), 270/1
Oldstone (Olweston), Blackawton, **232** 220, 224-7
Oldman, Edward, **84** 130
Oliver, G., 27, 30, 59, 65, 79
Osbert, the clerk, (Holrigge), **313** 274; (Skidbrook), **141** 163/4
Osmund, Abbot of Rupe, **1** 83
Otterton (Otteritune), **98** 139
Owley (Glascombe), 232
Oxtone, Sir James de, **299** 261; John de, **137** 161/2

P.

P., a Premonstratensian Canon, 35
P., chaplain of Shebbear, **171** 187
P., vicar of Milverton, **123** 152
Pancrasweek (Pankradiswike, Week St. Pancras), 34, 43, 182-6; chapel of, **1** 82, **150/2** 171, 26, 57, 82/3, **168/9** 173; cemetery at, 186; chantry at, **168** 173, 185; church path to, 184; glebe land of, 183/4; mediaeval holdings at, 185; vill of, **100/2/7** 172/3
Paniel, (Panyel), Fulk, **135** 161
Parco, Richard de, **138-40** 163/4, 12; his w., Beatrice (d. of Roland Haket, q.v.), **138/40** 163/4; their s., Walter de, **140** 164; Roger de, men. 1244, **167** 172; Henry de, **162/3** 172/3
Parmentarius, William, **54/5** 119; his w., Alice, **55** 119; their s., Walter, **55** 119; Walter's w., Alice, **55** 119
Passet, Thomas (f. of Johanna de Valletorta, q.v.), **103** 142
Paz, John, **42** 111, **74** 121
Pembroke, Priory of, **270** 247; Walter de, rector of Rattery, **260/1** 247/8, 25; William, Earl of, 112
Pengelly's (Shillingford Abbot), 241
Pentelowe, Robert de, vicar of Stoke Fleming, 36
Penuer (Penver), Jordan, **164** 173
Penylls, William de, **200/7** 205
Percy, Thomas de, **196** 204
Perteheye, Roger **96** 139
Peter, Prior of Plympton, **297** 261
Petre, Sir William, 44, 75
Petroc, spring and well of St., Torre, **11** 85/6/7, 90, 250/1
Petton (Petetone), **116** 148/9; Gervase de, **119** 148
Peverel, Hugh de Sampforde, **298** 261, 32; Thomas, **209** 206
Peysim, Robert, **202/3** 205
Peytevin (*Pictavensis*), Osbert, **29** 109, 112; his s. (?), Thomas, **31** 109, 112
Pictoris, William, **24** 109
Pil, Thomas le, **24** 109
Pilmuir, 93
Pirro, Lettice de, **177/8** 188
Pistor Richard, **208** 205
Place (Dartmouth), 202
Plymtree (Plymtrii), Richard de, **313** 273/4
Plympton; barony of, **229** 220; castle of, 223; Priory of St. Peter & S. Paul, 153, 219, 232; Simon de, Abbot of Torre, **222** 214, **268** 250, 26/7, 37/8, 53; Thomas de, 36
Pole (Pola), Nicholas de, **288** 272/4; see also the de Daccombe family
Pomeroy (Pomeray, de la Pomerio), Gellanus de, late 12th C., **245** 242; Sir Henry de, mid 13th C., **152** 171, 49, 180, 217; Sir Henry de, men. 1331, **222** 215, 63; Sir John de, men. 1395, **209** 206
Ponte, William de, **95/9** 139, **111** 145
Poore, Herbert, Bishop of Salisbury, **4** 84
Pope, Gervase le, **111** 145; Ralph **95** 139
Popes, see Calixtus III, Innocent III, Honorius III, Martin IV, Nicholas IV
Porta, Susanna de, **303/4** 272
Prémontré, Abbey of St. Norbert (diocese of Laon), 7, 10; Abbots of, see E., Gervase, Gilbert, W. For Abbeys of this Order see Index II
Prescote, John, **209** 206
Presteforde (Bradworthy), **151** 171, 179
Preston (Prestatone), Blackawton, **237** 221/9; William de, **237** 221
Prilla, Matilda, **136/7** 161/2
Prise (Apprys), John, **317/9** 248, 42
Pultemore, Sir Richard de, **298/9** 261
Punchardone, William de, late 12th C., **1** 83; Roger (1) de, **74** 121; Roger (2) de, mid 14th C., **267/8** 250, **278** 258
Putford, East, chapel of, 43, 197/8
Pyl, Robert le, parson of Crewkerne, 63
Pynde, Henry, **254/5** 243, 34, 240/1
Pynkenay, Henry, **299** 261
Pyra, Robert, 229
Pyria, John, 229

Q.

Queryngdon (Querndon), Roger de, friar of Beverley, 54/55; purveyor, 55

INDEX I   PLACES AND PEOPLE

Quintin, Walter de St., Archdeacon of Taunton, **123** 152
Quivel, Peter, Bishop of Exeter, **130** 154, 30, 65; master Peter, 33

R.

R., Abbot of St. Dogmael's, **260/70** 247; R(alph de Werewell), Archdeacon of Barnstaple, **173** 187
Radeclyve, see Ruddycleave
Radegund, Abbey of St., Kent, 41/2; John, Abbot of, 65/6
Radeweye (Greendale), **95** 139/40
Radford, Dr. C. A. Ralegh, 78
Ralph, a Premonstratensian Abbot, **155** 172; s. of Richard, **1** 83; de Nova Villa, **73/4** 121; his w., Edith, **73/4** 121
Ralegh, William de (Sheriff of Devon), **21** 109
Ram, John le, **84** 130, **86** 131
Rattery (Rattrew), church of St. Mary, 25, 247-9, **260/70** 247; see also Walter de Pembroke, rector of
Rauleise, Lady Beatrice de, 116
Red, William, **85** 130
Rede, Simon, Abbot of Torre, 27, 43-45, 75/6
Redmayne (Redman), Richard, Abbot of Shap, Bishop of St. Asaph's, Exeter and Ely, 10, 42, 65/71
Reginald, Earl of Cornwall, see Cornwall
Restercumbe, Michael de, **213** 214/6; his b., W., **213** 214/6; his s., (?) Guy, **214** 214/6, **265** 250
Rhodes, A. J., 105
Richard, Abbot of Torre, **32** 110, **113** 145, **127** 153, **200/7/8** 205, **234/7/8** 221, **254/5** 243, **265** 249, **297** 261, 26/9, 34/5; Abbot of Torre, see Cade; Abbot of Welbeck, **1** 83; the baker (pistor), **208** 205; Blondy, Bishop of Exeter, q.v.; a Canon of Torre, **147** 164/5; de camera, **201** 205; the carpenter, **32** 110, **100** 140; Earl of Cornwall, see Cornwall; Richard I, King of England, **1** 82, 7, 47; II, **196** 201, 82, 85, 207; parson of Alphington, **308/9** 273, **310/12** 273, see also his n., Susanna; Priest of Skidbrook, **141** 164; parson of Torre, see Brewer; s. of Richard Carre, 37; s. of Walter, **1** 83
Ridgeway, John, 99/100, 267
Rihille, Richard de, **164** 173
Risdon, 196, 231, 262
Robert, Abbot of Tavistock, **297** 261; Abbot of Torre, **37** 110, **146** 164, **187** 194, **253** 243, 25, 26, 30; lord of Ailenewode, q.v.; chaplain of Bampton, **135/6** 161/2; le Bastard, q.v.; Bishop of Lincoln, see Grosseteste; parson of Torrington, **180** 188; s. of Walter, **101** 142; his w., Eufemia, **101** 142; their d., Cicely, **101** 142

Roche, John atte, 37
Rocheforde, Thomas de, **1** 83
Roger, Abbot of St. Dogmael's, **262** 248; Abbot of Torre, **35/6** 110, **160** 172, **259** 247, 25, 26, 30; Dean of Lincoln, **143** 164; physician of Axmouth, **315** 274; vicar of Skidbrook, **144/5** 163/4
Rotomago, Maurice de, **280** 259; his w., Avicia, **216** 214/5, **280** 259 (see also Cirencester); William de, **1** 83, 116
Rous, John le, Abbot of Torre, **189** 194, **281** 252, **299** 261, 26, 35-7, 263
Rowedone, 30, 81/2, 85, 251
Ruddycleave (Radeclyve), Buckland-in-the-Moor, **77** 128-30; Domesday manor of Radecliva, 129
Rufford Abbey, Notts.: William, Abbot of, **1** 83
Rupe Abbey: Osmond, Abbot of, **1** 83
Russel (de la Gata, de la Porta, de la Yete), William, **203/4/9** 272/3, **311/12/14/15** 273/4
Russel, Percy, 4, 19, 210
Rydon (Wolborough), 105; Davyd de, **32** 110, 105, 113; Luke de, 105, 113

S.

S., Abbot of Torre, see Simon
S., Bishop of Exeter, see Simon of Apulia
Saint Marychurch (Seyntmarichurch), Torquay; manors at, 259; parish of, 95, 98; Avicia, the lady of, **280** 259; see also Rotomago; William de, **279** 258
Salisbury; Bishops of, see Herbert Poore, Robert de Bingham, William; Precentor of, **133** 154/5; William (1), Earl of, **170** 187; William (2), Earl of, **196** 204
Salmonavilla (Sarmunville), Philip de, **44/5** 118, 12, 74, 116; his w., Beatrice, **44/5** 118, 116; see also de Hennock
Saltfleetby (Lincs.), 166/8
Samercy (?), Roger, **51** 118
Sampford Peverel, see Peverel
Saundere, Philip, Abbot of St. Dogmael's, **317/8** 248
Saunzever (Seinzaver), William, **1** 83, 116
Schireborne Nyweton, see Wolborough
Schirewelle, see Sherwell
Scobehille (Scobehulle), Thomas, **299/300** 216/2; his s., Robert, **300/1** 261/2/3
Scobitor (Widecombe-in-the-Moor), **76/8/9** 127/8
Scorche's (Greendale), 141
Scott, Rev. J. G. M., 21, 102, 168,
Scudimore, Peter de, 116
Sedgewell (Ideford), 270/1
Serlo, Dean of Exeter, 30, 74
Seward, **275** 258/9; his d., Margaret, **272/5**

258/9, and Odelina, 273/5 258/9
Seymour, Sir Edward, 2
Shap, Abbey of, Westmorland, 14, 18; see also Richard Redmayne, Abbot of, and Robert Bedall, Prior of
Shearstone (Shinrestone), Blackawton, 232 220
Shebbear (Schefbere), 187-192; church of St. Michael, 170-4 187, 30, 43; advowson of, 173/4 187, 26; sanctuary land of, 172 187/9; description of, 190; vicars of, 191; mediaeval holdings at, 192
Sheepwash (Schepwassch, Schepwaissch, Schepwaysch), 187-92; chapel of St. Laurence, 177 188, 43; mill at Uppcott, q.v.; wood of, 177 188
Sherwell Brook (Schirewelle), Cockington, 265-8 249/50, 281 253, 58, 93, 251
Shillingford Abbot (Selingforda, Lower Shillingford, North Shillingford), 239-46; manor of, 251 243, 81-3; Domesday mention of, 242; barton of, 244/5; courthouse at, 34, 245; former chapel at, 245; cross at, 245; mediaeval holdings at, 31/3, 240-2
    Osmund de, 244/5 242, 256 243; his d., Odelina, 256 243; her h., William de, 256 243; Philip de, men. 1336, 257 244; see also manor of Leye
Shinerston (Blackawton), 232 220/9
Shiphay Collaton (Coletone), Torquay, 98-100, 1 83, 8-10 95; Domesday manor of, 49, 63, 95/8; former chapel at, 98; monastic barn at, 98; demesnes boundaries, 99; old field names at 100; vill of, 1 83, 8 95
Sicta Villa, Ralph de, 1 83
Siete (Fiete?), Adam de la, 293 261
Silverhills (Wolborough), 104
Simcoe, Mrs., 50
Simon (Symon), Abbot of Torre, 13 85, 111 145, 147 265, 230 220, 293 261; (2) Abbot of Torre, see Simon de Plympton; Bishop of Exeter, see Simon of Apulia; s. of Robert, 226 220
Skidbrook (Skidbrok, Skitebroc), Lincs., 163-70; church of St. Botolph, 138-42 164; advowson of, 142 164, 30; description of, 167/8; sanctuary lands of, 148 165; tithe of, 148 165; vicars of, 168/9; Domesday manor of, 166; court of, 148 165; fishery of, 148 165; William de, men. 1223, 146 164; Ralph, s. of William de, men. 1253, 147 164/5, 33
Somerford, see Werplisdone
Sorel, Ralph de Monte, 175/6 187/8, 178 188
Southbinheie (Shillingford Abbot), 33
Southbrook (Buckland-in-the-Moor), 84/5 130/1
Southtown (Dartmouth), manor of, 203
Spek (Speke), Richard le, 282 259/60/2; his s., William, 232/3 220, 295/6 261/2
Speyer, Walter, 66-8

Spichewik, Michael de, 82 130
Spineto, Girard de, 79 127
Stafford, Edmund, Bishop of Exeter, 209/10 206, 27, 40, 186; Edmund de, 196 204
Stanburgh (Blackawton), 234 221, 219
Stanfere, William de, 154
Stantor, Roger de, 268 250
Stauford, see Stowford,
Stephen, Prior of Worksop, 1 83
Stevyn, John, infirmarius and refector of Torre Abbey, 67
Stoddone, Hugh de, 1 83
Stoil, Stephen, 297 261
Stoke Fleming, 44, 203, 223
Stokenham (Stoke, Hurdstoke), 223/4/9 220, 30
Stoke-in-Teignhead, 266; manor of, 132
Stone (Langstone in Blackawton), 239 221/4
Stontorre, William de, 42 111
Storrington, Priory of Our Lady of England, Sussex, 16
Stowell, Sir John, 3
Stowford (Stauford), John de, 104 144
Straypark (Blackawton), 224/7
Strete (Blackawton), 231 220, 219; William de, 299 261
Sudelegh (Bradworthy), 162 172, 183
Suestone, see Sweetstone
Suretone, manor of, 160 172
Susanna, niece of Richard the parson of Alphington, 308/9 273
Sutor, Edward, 135/7 161
Suttone, James, 71
Sweetstone (Suestone), Blackawton, 232 220/9
Swyfte, John, Abbot of Newhouse, 67
Sylk, Dr. William, advocate, 70
Syward, vicar of Shebbear, 33

T.

Tabernarius (taberum), William, 41 110/11
Talebot, William, 160/2 172
Talley, Abbey of, Carmarthenshire, 16
Taunton, Archdeacon of, see Walter de St. Quinton
Tavistock, Abbey of St. Mary and St. Rumon, 257/8/63; Abbots of, see Alan, Robert
Teign, River (Teynge), 16 108,; Teignbridge, hundred of, 70 120; Teign Brewer, 55; Teignwike, manor of, 26 109
Teign Aller (Wolborough), 34
Teritone, see Dreyton
Tetteburne, Luke de, 1 83
Thomas, Prebendary of Ashclyst, 125 153; Bishop of Exeter, see Brantyngham; Duke of Gloucester, q.v., Archdeacon of Totnes, 250 243, 30; s. of vicar of Skidbrook, 149 165;

INDEX I PLACES AND PEOPLE

Earl of Warwick, q.v.; Archbishop of York, see Corbridge
Thompson, A. Hamilton, 15
Thorngrave (Sheepwash), **177** 188
Tirel, Henry, **158** 172/4, 181; W., **185** 194
Tilye (Tylya), Elius, **239** 221
Titchfield, Abbey of St. Mary, Hants., 11, 18, 277
Tongerloo, Premonstratensian Abbey of, Belgium, 98
Torr, J. V., 77
Torre (Thorr, Thorre); Abbey of St. Saviour and the Holy Trinity, Torquay, Devon; Abbots of see Adam, Roger, "W"., Robert, Laurence, Simon, Brian, Richard, John le Rous, Simon de Plympton, John Gras, John, John de Berkadone, William Norton, Matthew Yerde, William Mychell, John Lacy, Richard Cade, Thomas Dyare, Simon Rede; Patron, the Earl of Devon; see also Index II. Parish church of, **1** 82, **13-15** 85/6, **261** 248, 81/2, 90; advowson of, **1** 82, **14/15** 85; church-house of, 43, 86/7; courthouse of, **13** 85, 86/7; oratory at, 85; description of church, 90/1; manor of (also Torre Brewer, Torre Mohun, Torre Prior, Torre Ridgeway), 63/4; sanctuary land of, 93; vill of, **1** 82, 81/5; see also Upton in Tormohun; Ives de la, **75** 121, **309/15** 273/4; John de la, **75** 121; Martin de la **313** 274; Nicholas de, 116
Torr's, 217, 232; Torr's Barn, 232; Torr's Wood, 217
Torwood, grange of, 87; monastic barn at, 87
Torrington (Toritone), chapel of St. James, **180** 188/9; Henry de, **1** 83; John de, **1** 83, **4** 84, **122** 152; his s., William de, **122** 152, **191** 203
Totnes, Archdeacon of, see Thomas; Guild of merchants of, 33; hospital of Jerusalem at, **211** 213; lord of, see Cantelupe; market of, 32/33; Prior and Convent of, **211/5** 213, **220** 214, 32, 33, 35, 125, 215
Townstall (Dunestal), Dartmouth 201-11; parish church of St Clement, **191-5-7-9** 203/4, **210** 206,; advowson of, **193-5-7** 203/4; description of, 208/9; vicars of, 209; chapel of St. Clarus at, 37; chapel of the Holy Trinity (later St. Saviour's church), **194** 203/4, **209** 206, 39; building of, 207; description of, 210; Domesday manor of Dunestal, 201
Tracy, William de, **242/3** 242, **252** 243, 81/2, 239/40
Tregonwell, John, 73
Tregotz, Ralph, **222** 215
Tregrut, church of, **270** 247
Tremeneth (Tremenet, Treymenet, Tribus Minetis), Richard, **61** 119, **66/7/9** 120, 123, **310** 273; his s., John, men. 1294, **51** 118; William, 259
Trendelho, church of, 278
Treverbyn, Andrew, 36; Hugh de, **231** 220
Tudde, Robert, **309/12** 273
Turnerius (*Turnerard*), Baldwin, **162** 172
Twynbrook (Cockington), **265** 249, 93, 251
Tylya, see Tilye
Tynaldclive (Cockington), **264** 249
Tywardreath, John, Prior of, 41

U.

Ugborough (Domesday manor of Ulgeberge), 82, 85, **1** 82
Umfray, Thomas, 69
Underhaye (Ideford), 157, 270/1
Upcott (Uppecote) Barton, Sheepwash, 189; mill of, **179** 188/9; Robert de, **113** 145/6
Uppehom, (Opham), William de, **51** 118, 121, 146
Uppeleghe (Shillingford Abbot), Richard de, **258** 244; Roger de, **253** 243; see also Leye
Upton (Uppetone, Huppetone), Torquay, mediaeval village of, 63, 87/8; Robert de, **271** 257/8; see also his w., Margaret, d., of Seward
Upton (Brixham), **215/20/21** 214/6
Usseburne, T. de, Justice, **191** 203, **243** 242, **251** 243

V.

Valencia, William de, Brother of King Henry III, 30 109, 111
Valle, Abbey of St. Mary de, Bayeux, Normandy, 153/5 171/2/4; Abbots of, Bartholomew, W., q.v.; Beatrice de, w. of Lord William Brewer and Foundress of Torre Abbey, **6** 85, **8/9** 95, 49, 99, 173
Valletorta (Valletort), Sir John de, men. 1282, **298** 261; Reginald de, **103** 142; his w., Johanna, 103 142
Vasci (Vesci), William de, 11, **212** 213/5; his w., Juliana, **212** 213/5; their s., Walter de, **4** 84, **211/2** 213/5
Venn (la Fenne), Ugborough, **241** 235; William atte, **241** 235
Venur (*Vemir*?), Richard le, **164** 173/5, 180; his w., Alice, 164 173/5, 180
Ver, David, le, **311/14** 273/4
Veysey, John, Bishop of Exeter, 27, 43, 44

W.

W., Abbot of Torre, **174** 187/8, 26, 30/31, 56; Abbot of St. Mary de Valle, **156** 172; Archbishop of Canterbury, see Walter de Hempsham; Earl of Arundell, **170** 187; Earl of Salisbury, **170** 187

Waddeton, (Stoke Gabriel), 217/8; ferling (extent of), 218; piers at, 217; quarry at, 217; Isabella de, 57, 217
Wadstray (Blackawton), 227
Wake, (Wike), see Pancrasweek
Walker, Hilda, 4, 99, 259
Walter, Archdeacon of Taunton, see Quintin; chaplain of Bampton, **136** 161; Hubert, Archbishop of Canterbury, **196** 204; s. of Juonis, 116; priest of Skidbrook, **141** 163/4; s. of Yves, **1** 83, 31, 194
Wambe (Wobe), Thomas the chaplain, **201/4** 205
Warin, s. of Johel, **284** 260/2
Warloke, Thomas, vicar of Hennock, 40
Warkdoneswaye (Greendale), **95/6** 139/40
Warth (Worden), Stoke Fleming, **232** 220/3/9
Warwick, Thomas, Earl of Warwick, **196** 204
Washwalk Mill (Blackawton), **223/30** 220
Watersippe (Kingswear), **213/4** 214/6
Watkin, Hugh, 4, 14, 16, 19, 22/3, 32, 40, 50/1, 55/6, 59, 64, 78, 87, 179, 255
Way, Robert at, **88** 131
Wayer, Richard, **309** 273
Week St. Pancras, see Pancrasweek
Welbeck, Abbey of St. James, Notts., 7, 12, 14, 15, 21, 29, 38, 41, 43, 53, 65/6, 69; Foundation charter of, 15
Welle (Wille), Ideford, **314** 274, 270; Walter de la, **308/9** 273
Welles and Welles Coffyn, see Coffinswell
Wemmeworthi, manor of, **233** 221; see also William le Spek, lord of
Were, Ives de la, **72** 120, **308/10** 273; his s., (?), Ralph, **306/13** 273
Werplisdone, William de, alias Somerforde, **130** 154, 34, 154/5
Weryng, Thomas, **32** 110
Werewell, Ralph de, Archdeacon of Barnstaple, **173** 187
Westfoxley (Greendale), **95** 139
Westminster, Abbot of, **133** 154/5; court of, see Courts in Index II
Westwood (Wolborough), 141
White, J. T., 4, 27
White's (Greendale), 141
Whiting, (Whytyng), Nicholas, **88** 131
Whiteway (Whytewaye, Witewey), John, men. 1277, **303-12** 272/3; his s., (?), Richard, men. 1291, **51** 118
Wike, see Pancrasweek
Wike, Baldwin de, **160** 172, 26, 175/83; his w., Isabel, d. of Lord William Brewer, q.v.; his s., Edith, **161** 172, 26
Wille, manor of, see Daccombe,
William, Abbot of Buckfast, **1** 83; Abbot of Rufford, **1** 83; Abbot of Torre, see Norton, Mychel; Bishop of Exeter, see Brewer; Bishop of Salisbury, **248** 242; *carpentarius*, **180** 188; chaplain of Exminster, **256** 244; clerk of Eysselegh, **1** 83; clerk of Skidbrook, **141** 163/4; *faber*, **95** 139; the fuller of Holrigge, **302-8-14/15** 270-4; Earl of Arundell q.v.; Earl of Salisbury, q.v.; s. of Roger, see de Hennock; of Holrigge, **302** 272, **313** 274; de York, Bishop of Winchester, q.v.
Wilton, 81
Willeyurd, 241, **258** 244; Thomas de, **248** 244, 241
Winchester, Bishops of:—see, Geoffrey de Lucy, William de York
Wobe, Thomas, see Wambe
Wodegrene, Thomas, **199** 204
Wogewyll, see Ogwell
Wodetone (Greendale), **99** 140, **100** 140, **111** 145
Wolborough (Wolleburgh, Wulleburgh, Wlveburga etc.), 25, 34, 101-13; church of St. Mary **22** 101/2; advowson of, **16/17** 108, **22** 109; description of, 101/2; path to, 101; chapel of St. Leonard, 40, 105; Domesday manor of, 101/2, 132; demesne boundaries of, 104; mediaeval holdings at, 102-5; vill of, **16/17** 108, 82, 101; wood of 113; Newton Abbot, 101; burgesses of, 40; courts of 104/5; manor house of, 105; market of, **30** 40, 101, 111; Schireborne Nyweton, **30** 109
Wonford, hundred of
Wooda (Pancrasweek), oratory at, 34, **169** 173, 181
Woodbury, 32, **133**/46; castle (Chasteiller), **98** 139/40; Domesday manor of, 133
Wood (Blackawton), **238** 221/3
Woodhuish (Wodehiwis), Brixham, **216/7** 214
Woodland (Wodelond), Sir Walter de, 63
Worksop, see Stephen, Prior of
Worthe (Werthe), William, 269, 275
Wottons (Wolborough), 102/3
Wrangaton, manor of, 232/3
Wydecombe (Wydegombe), Richard, vicar of Townstall, 35
Wyndsore, William de, **279** 258/9
Wyndgate la (Wyngate, Windiete), Cockington, **1** 83, **10** 95, **263** 252, 83, 93, 99
Wynkelegh, Michael de, **113** 145, 34, 137
Wythe, Nicholas de la, 146

Y.

Yameton, Richard de, 73
Yanston (Yeovinestone, Yongestone), in manor of Blackawton, 219 **234** 221; Laurence de, 223
Ybro (Ybrus?), Ibert, **282** 260/2; his b., Michael, **282** 260/2; their b., William, **282** 260/2
Yerd, Gilbert, **239** 221, **281** 252

Yerde, Matthew, Abbot of Torre, 27, 41
Ylsham, see Ilsham
York, Archbishop of:—see Thomas Corbridge; Edward, Duke of, **196** 204; J., Chancellor of, **196** 204; William de, Bishop of Winchester, **248** 242

Index II
Subjects

A.

Abbeys and Abbots of The Premonstratensian Order, see Index I under Bayham, Beeleigh, Dryburgh, Durford, Easby, Egglestone, Newhouse, Shap, Talley, Titchfield, Torre, St. Radegund's, Rufford, On the Continent:—Laon, Licques, Prémontré, Rupe, Tongerloo, St. Mary de Valle, For Abbots, see also **155**; Other Orders, see Buckfast, St. Dogmael's, Dunkeswell, Mottisfont, Tavistock, Westminster etc.
Advowson, **16/17** 107/8, **126** 153, **132** 154, **187** 194, **193** 203
Agreement, **144** 164, **254/5** 243, **265** 249
Altarage, **172** 187, **198** 204
Anathema, 154, 188
Animals:—cattle, 4 84, **87** 131, **98** 139, **190** 194, **264** 249; horses, 23 109, **89** 138, **175/6** 187/8; packhorses, 116, 124; hunter, **89** 138; white horse, **175** 188; pigs, **98** 139, **177** 188, **264** 249, 253; sheep, **1** 82, **98** 139, **249** 242, 82, 240
Aqueducts, see Topographical features—watercourses
Archbishops, see Index I under Canterbury, York
Archdeacons, see Index I under Barnstaple, Taunton, Totnes etc.
Assessment (taxacio), **157** 172
Attorney, 319 248
Augmentation Office, Particulars for Grants (quotations from), 98, 100, 113, 126, 132, 146, 150, 157, 182, 216, 246, 267

B.

Banks, boundary, see Topographical features
Baronies:—Okehampton, 153; Plympton, **229** 220; Tavistock, **295** 261
Beauchief Obituary, 11, 25
Bells (of monastic period surviving), 102, 116, 177, **185**, 191, 209
Benefactors, prayers for, 11, **147** 164/5, **274** 258, 58; masses for, see Masses
Bishops, see Index I under surnames

Body, gift of dead, to Torre Abbey, **11** 85, **29** 109, **76/9** 127, **223** 220, **267/8** 250, 112
Boots, 32
Bradninch, honour of, 269
Burgage tenure, **135/6** 161/2
Burgesses, **196** 204

C.

Calcetum, see Topographical features
Camera, 121
Canons Regular of Prémontré, 7-12
Cartulary, see Torre Abbey,
Carucate, **117** 148, 163
Cattle drift, 134
Cemetery, **157** 172, **194** 203, 186
Chancellery, 248 242
Chantry (grant of), **115** 148, **168** 173, **199** 204, **267/8** 250, 57/8, 64; see also Torre Abbey
Chapels, mediaeval:—(extant), Alfarsworthy, Bulkworthy, Cockington (now p. church), Ilsham, Pancrasweek (now p. church), Petton, East Putford, Sheepwash (now p. church). (non extant), Daccombe, Dunnyngestone, Dartmouth, (St. Clarus), Shiphay, Shillingford Barton, Wooda (Pancrasweek), St. Leonard's (Wolborough), Norton, Torre courthouse
Chapter:—see Exeter, Torre Abbey etc.
Charters:—incomplete, 15 85, **186** 194; misplaced, 270, 292, 285-90; missing, 128, 149, 152; given at Torre, 42 111, **51** 118, **194** 204, **222** 214, **293** 261; royal, 4, 5 84, 30 109, **132** 154, **148** 165, **196** 204, **228** 220, **301/2** 262
Chirograph, **13** 85, **50** 118, **208** 205, **279** 258, **297** 261
Chudleigh, charters given at, 22 109, **197** 204
Churches:—consecration of, **194** 203; dedications of, 105, 195; lights in, **199** 204/5, **274** 258; lands of, see Sanctuary lands; repairs of, **194** 40
Church-house, 86
Clergy, convocation of 37, 41, 43
"Collectanea Anglo-Premonstratensia", 65/71
Confraters, 11, 58, **147** 165, **274** 258/9

299

Conversi, 10
Court, suit of, 33, 84, **223**/9 220, **241** 235/7; hundred, 4 84, **18** 108, **248** 242; shire, 4 84
Courts: King's, **206** 205; St. Bride's, London, **284** 260/2; Exeter, **43** 111, **117** 118, 148, **167** 173, **253** 243, **279** 258, **299** 261; Westminster, **126** 153, **147**/8 165, **166** 173, **230** 220, 30, 32; Wilton, **187** 194, **251**/2 243; Ecclesiastical courts of Torre Abbey, see Index I under Ashclyst, Blackawton, Court Barton, Greendale Barton, Hennock, Kingswear, Shillingford Barton, Underhaye, Wolborough
Courthouses, **84** 130, **99** 140
Crosses, **98** 139/40, 245
Crusade, 7, 105
Cumbe, charter given at, **120** 149
Cummin (as rent), see Rents
Custody, see Wardship
Custom (lastagium), 4 84

D.

Deans, see Index I under Exeter, Wells etc.
Dartmouth, charter given at, **194** 204
Demesne, **95** 139, **123** 152, **168** 173, **177** 188, **190** 194, **253** 243
Devon Lay Subsidy, 1332, quotations from, 113, 146/9, 157, 181, 192, 203, 211, 223/9, 267, 275
Divine Office, suspension of, **194**/99 204, **209** 206
Dogmael, Abbey of St., charter given at, **319** 248
Dowry, **50**/3/4/8 118/9, **61**/2/3 119, **90** 138, **307** 273

E.

Easement, 182, **240** 235
Enclosures (parca), **238** 221, **299** 261/3
Entry, egress and exit, rights of, 1 83, **11** 85, **81** 30, **264**/5/7 249/50
Esquire (armiger), **199** 204
Exeter, Bishops of, see under surnames, Index I; cathedral of, **155** 172; charters given at, **123** 152, **158** 172; Dean of, **76** 127, **123** 152; Dean and Chapter of, **134** 154, **158** 172, 30, 74; Library, original charter in, 59; County Court of, see Courts

F.

Fair, **30** 109; St. Kalixtus's, **103** 142
Fee, **199** 204, **229** 220, **295** 261; knight's **9** 95, **16** 107, **19**/20 108, **32** 110, **89** 138, **222** 214,

234 221, **242** 242, **246** 242, **288** 272, **282** 260, **296**/7 261; lords of, **19** 103, **102** 142, **150** 171, **160**/2 172/5, **245** 242, 231, 240, 274
Ferendon, charter given at, **153** 172
Ferling, extent of, 3, 179, 218, 223, 232, 263
Feudal dues, see Court-suit of, homage, relief, scutage etc.
Field names: Buckland Brewer:— Reigheye; Buckland-in-the-Moor:— Dodenmanneslond, Nywehay, Wlueslond; Cockington:—meadow of Chilleston, meadow of Cockington, Twynbrok; Daccombe and Coffinswell:—la ffunteyne; Greendale:—Baghemore, Morsplot, la Segge, Vudelhister, Withemore; at Blackberry, Holesweislonde; Hennock:—Coldeswillesmore; Ilsham:—Asshynden parke, Calfen parke, Forendene parke, Litelberie, Long acre, Stanberehill, Stowlles, Warbury parke; Kingswear:—Little and Lower Orestone; North Shillingford:—la Suburgehaye, Ulvescroft, Widehay; Monksmoor:—Ash park, Cross park, Torr's Meadow; Shiphay Collaton —Branhay, Brodeparke, Brodepark meade, Colaton parke, Culver parke, Hod, Lang parke, Swardon parke, Este Wetherhill, West Wetherhill, Whiden parke; Skidbrook:—Brothercroft, Coketrigges, Cotestede, ffolsig, Genwordegne, Houdales, Outgangrig, Petpole, Somercoteswra, Skitebrokwra, Wolbyncroft, Wolfow; Waddeton:—Tor's; Wolborough:—Benorharigge, Ellacome, Holland, Laigahaie, Laxin (an orchard), Slade, Stamford.
Fishing rights, 1 82, **6** 85, **16** 108, **144**/9 164/6, **269** 252; drying of nets, **269** 252; trawling, 1 82
Fishponds, 1 82/3, **6** 85
Fluda, charter given at, **68** 120
Forfeit: a vat of wine, **110** 145; half a sester, 195
Freemen, **84** 130, **199** 204, **231** 220
Fynetone, charter given at, **125** 153
French, charter in, **269** 252; soubriquet-le franceys, fransiscus etc., **215**/20 214
Fullers, see occupations

G.

Gagbulagium, **274** 258
Gardens, **60** 119, **87** 131, **136** 161, **164** 173, **168** 173, **180** 188, **199** 204, **204** 205, **249** 242, **289** 272, **305** 272, **314** 274
Gelde, 4 84
Grazing rights, 1 82, **6** 85, **76** 127, **84** 130, **98** 139, **100** 140, **105**/7 144, **110** 145, **189**/90 194, **216** 214, **237** 221, **240** 235, **277**/80 258, 231
Greendale, charter given at, **109** 145

H.

Heathfield, 237
Heraldry:—coats of arms of Beeleigh Abbey, 18; de Brewer, 21; de Mohun, 21; Tongerloo Abbey, 18; Torre Abbey, 21
Heriot, **159** 172
Hideage **4** 84
Highway, see Topographical Features
Homage, **111** 145, **257** 244
Horses, see animals
Holrigge, charter given at, **311** 273
Hundred:—Bradninch (Bradneys), **247/8** 242; Haytor (Haitorra), **18** 108; Teignbridge, **75** 101, 269; Winkleigh, 36; suit of, see Court, suit of
Hundredpenny, **4** 84
Husbote and haibote, **76** 127, **78** 127, **189/90** 194
Hutiban (hutibannus), **262** 248

I.

Indenture, **222** 214, **317** 248
Infangene thef, **4** 84
Inspeximus, **51** 118, **109** 145, **121** 149, **134** 154, **143** 164, 40
Interdict, 48, 116
Irrigation of land, **255** 243, 240

J.

Jury, service on, **4** 84
Judges, **251** 243

K.

Kings of England, see titles in Index I
Kitchens, **11** 85, **255** 243, 240, 250
Knight's fee, see Fee; service, see Scutage

L.

Langleye, charter given at, **302** 272
Lateran Council, **249** 242
Leases given by Abbots, 43/4
Leats, see Water-courses (Topographical features)
Letters, papal, **185** 194; patent, **196** 204, 44; of testimony, 26, 27, 38, **21** 109, **250** 243, **260** 247, 55
Librate, **90** 138, **228** 220

Lincoln, for Bishops etc. of, see Index I; charter given at Cathedral of, **143** 164; gifts of land to, 163
London, charter given at, **248** 242

M.

Malborough, charter given at, **170** 187
Manors, see Index I under, Bradworthy, Buckland Brewer, Buckland-in-the-Moor, Cockington; the ecclesiastical manors and sub manors of Torre Abbey:—Ashclyst, Blackawton, Coffinswell, Daccombe, Fluda, Greendale, Holrigge, Kingswear, Shillingford Abbot, Wolborough; q.v.; court, see Court; lords of, **112** 145, **136** 161, **168** 173, **189/90** 194, **203** 205, **233** 221, **267** 250, **271** 257, **299** 261; ladies of, **177** 188, **280** 259; service to, **284** 260
Markets, 30 109; toll from, **103** 142
Masses for deceased benefactors, **115** 148, **168** 173, **267/8** 250, **283** 260, 57/8
Mass pennies or halfpennies, **194** 204
Menevia (St. David's), diocese of, **319** 248
Mills, see Index I; molture from, **1** 82, **152** 171, **179** 188; suit of, **223/30** 220, **237/8** 221, 33; timber for repairs of, **179** 188; fulling, **223/30** 220
Millstones, **23** 109, **264** 249
Millponds, **1** 82, **152** 171
Millrace, **265** 249
Monks' burial ground (Sheepwash), 189; paths, 91, 184
Mortmain, licences in, **121** 149, **132** 154/6, **258** 244, **301** 262, **302** 272/5; statute of, 73/5

N.

Napoleonic Wars, 3
Nicknames:—le bastard, **212** 213; le hound, **279** 258; le moynge, **257** 244; le pil, **24** 109; red, **85** 130; le rous, **189** 194; le spek (?), **282** 260, **295/6** 261
Norton, charters given at, **200** 205, **208** 206

O.

Oath, sacramental, **73** 121, **159** 172/5
Occupations:—archer, **42** 111; baker, **208** 205/6; barber, **24** 109; carpenter, **32** 110, **95** 139, **180** 188, **208** 206; carter, **137** 161; cobbler, **135/7** 161; fisherman, 33; forester, **24** 109; fuller, **302** 272; granger, **96** 139; hunter, **164** 173; painter, **24** 109; perrymaker, 229; tailor, **55** 119; taverner, **41** 110

P.

Packhorse, see Animals
Paignton, charters given at, **14** 85, **198** 204, 73/4, 188
Papal charters and letters, 152, **131/3** 154, 215, 236
Parliaments, see Bury St. Edmunds, Carlisle, Lincoln, Northampton, Westminster, 35/36
Patronage, **48** 118, **124/5** 153, **131-3** 154, **173** 187, **183** 193, **187** 194
Park (parca), see Enclosure
Permission: to crenelate, 22; to embank, **80** 130, **97** 139, **112** 145; to make water-courses, **1** 82, **6** 85, **11** 85, **265** 249, **267** 250; to enter and clean same, **11** 85, **264** 249; to take materials for repairs, **179** 188, **264** 249
Peat, see Turbary
Pensions, 75/6
Perry-making, **94** 139, 145, 149, 229
Piers, 217
Pigs, see Animals
Plympton, honour of, 269
Ponds, see Topographical features; see also Fishponds, Millponds
Powderham Records, 43, 86, 102, 116, **51** 118, **67** 120/1
Premonstratensian Order: 7-11, 48; dress, 7, 67, 71; Founder, 7; hospitality, 10/11; titles of Abbeys, see Abbeys; Virgin Mary, devotion to, 7
Prémontré, charters given at, **155/6** 172
Priories and Priors:—See Index I under Bodmin, Caldey, Cardigan, Exeter (St. Nicholas), Haverford, Kington, Pembroke, Plympton, Totnes, Tywardreath, Worksop
Prioress, see Kington
Protection, King's, 55

Q.

Quarry, **264** 249, 253

R.

Recognition (gifts made in return for grants or privileges):—horses, **89** 138, 135; hunter, **89** 138, 133; gold piece, **212** 213; gold ring, **89** 138, **286** 260; silver ring, **212** 213; two golden talents, **135** 161; silken whimple, **212** 213
Rectors, **249** 242, **260/1** 247
Relief, **295** 261, 175, **300** 261
Remission, **239** 221
Rent:—1lb or ½lb of cummin, **59** 119, **177** 188, **199** 204, **204** 205, **216** 214, **292** 144; hogshead of water, 86; gloves, **56** 119; white gloves at Easter, **40** 110, **49** 118, **136** 166, **175** 187, **286** 260; a third part of a pair of spurs worth 3d., **71** 120; gilded spurs, **114** 148; white rose at Midsummer, **308** 273; 1lb or ½lb of wax, **54** 119, **212** 213, 270, **314** 274
Rushes **1** 83

S.

Sach, see Soch
Salisbury, Bishops of, see Index I; Precentor of, **133** 154
Sanctuary land, **149** 165, **172** 187, **184** 194, **263** 252, 37, 93
Scutage, **121** 149, **226** 220
Serfs, **87** 131, **216** 214, **280** 259; household of (sequela), **87** 131, **216** 214/7, **280** 259
Servant (domestic), **199** 204
Service:—customary, **222** 214, **231** 220; hutiban, **262** 248; knight's, see Scutage; royal, **279** 258
Sheepfold, 23/4
Shrievalty, **4** 54, **121** 149
Soch and Sach, **4** 84
Spanish prisoners of war, 23
Springs, see Topographical features
Stannary, 235
Suicide, 35

T.

Taxation of Pope Nicholas IV, see mention under Bradworthy, Blackawton, Buckland Brewer, Daccombe, Dunnyngestone, Haggelegh, Hennock, Holrigge, Ilsham, Greendale, Shebbear, Shillingford Abbot, Shiphay Collaton, Townstall, Wolborough
Tenants, in chief, **79** 127, **246** 242, **257** 244; servile, **87** 131, **216** 214, **280** 257, **295** 261
Terrier (Buckland Brewer), 198
Testimony, see Letters of
Thol and Theam, **4** 84
Tin, see Stannary
Tithe, **109** 145, **123** 152, **194** 204, **249** 242, **316/7** 248; small, see altarage
Toll, **4** 84, **103** 142
Topographical features:—bank (fossatum) 125, 168/9, 182, 191, 200, 209; canal, **267** 250; causeway (calcetum), 81, **1** 82/9, 93/5; cliff, **264** 249, **269** 252; close, **84/5** 130; copse, 104; firebeacon, 131/2, **98** 139/40; highway, **240** 235; King's, 86; moor, **54** 119, **121** 149, **240** 235; ponds, **113** 145, 82, 141; the three rocks, **80** 130/2; rivers, see Batherm, Dart, Gara, Lemon, Teign; springs, **11** 85, **96** 139, **199**

INDEX II SUBJECTS

204/5; streams, see Aller burn, Blakewille, Efrideswille, Estecumb, Fulleford, Glazebrook, Gryndell, Laket, Muchelbrook, Sherwell; watercourses, 30, 137, 245/9; wells, see Blyndewille, Honnewille, St. Petroc; Willows, 122; woods, see Cockington, Glascombe, Foxley, Grateclyve, Hennaborough, Hokemore, Sheepwash, Torr's (Monksmoor), Torwood, Westwood, William de Baldrygtone's, Wolborough

Tormohun, parish of, 86-9

Torre, Premonstratensian Abbey of St. Saviour and the Holy Trinity:—Abbots of, see Index I; altars in church of: (a) St. John the Baptist, **267/8** 250, 58; (b) Holy Cross, 57, 217; (c) chapel of the Cary family, 20; attack on, 54; barn (description of), 23; benefactors of, 12; boundaries of, **1** 82; building of, 12, 30; buildings, description of, 13-23; burials at, see Body, gift of; Canons of, 67-71; cartularies of, 1, 59/61; chantries at, 37, 57/8; charters given at, see Charters; churches attached to, see Index I under Bradworthy, Buckland Brewer, Hennock, Shebbear, Torre, Townstall, Wolborough; Chapels of Cockington, Pancrasweek, Sheepwash; churches, title to, 30, 35, 73/4; corrodies at, 122/3; crenelation of, 22, 38; dedication of, 13, 30; Demesne of, 82; discipline at, 66-71; excavation of, 4; execution (alleged) of Canon, 277; foundation of, 7-12; foundation charter of, 30, 81/3, 133, 231, 239/40, 250; witnesses of, 83; engraving of 1662, 14,; granges of, 88, 95-8; history (post dissolution) of, 2/3; hospitality at, 30, **183** 193/4; income of, 12; library of, 277; manors of, see Manors; mills attached to, see Index I; names of Community (1455-1500), 67-71; Patron of, 66; possessions of, 12; Prior's duties, 67/8; Suppression of, 75/6; visitations of, 65-71; water supply of, 19, 23, 249-53; walls of, **281** 252/3

Torr's—survival of possessive title, see Index I

Totnes, charters given at, **199** 205

Townstall, charter given at, **206** 205

Transit, rights of, **23** 109

Trawling rights, see Fishing,

Turbary, 87 131, 102

Tyronesian Order, 247

U.

Utgangene Thef, **4** 84

V.

"Valor Ecclesiasticus"—quotations from, 12, 100, 106, 146, 150, 152, 157, 211, 216, 229, 245

Vicars, lists of, 125, 168/9, 182, 191, 200, 209

Villein tenure, **94** 139

Villeins, **94** 139, **230** 220, **279** 258, **298** 261

Virgate, **89** 138, 101, 104

Visitations, 25, 29, 42

W.

Wagons, **23** 109

Wardship (custodia), **50/3/61** 118/19, 175

Warships, **196** 204/7

Wax, for lights, **199** 205, **274** 258

Wells, 86

Westminster, charters given at, **196** 204, **301** 262

Wilton, charters given at, **243** 242, **251/2** 243

Will (of Simon Rede, the last Abbot), 45

Winchester, Bishops of, see Index I

Writs (Parliamentary), 35, 36